the inside *hustle*

a mystical misfit's travel adventure into the ~~un~~known

Joanna Walden

This is a memoir of a certain time in my life. These are my memories, recollections and perceptions personal to me and heartfully intended to entertain, inspire and enlighten others.

First published in 2020 by JLW PUBLISHING
Copyright © Joanna Walden

Edited by Brooke Anne Olive
Cover Design by Lukas Kelly
Author Photo by Russ Flatt

ISBN: 978-0-473-51244-6

This is a work of creative nonfiction. The events are portrayed to the best of the author's memory. Parts of this book have been fictionalised to varying degrees with some names, details, places and identifying factors changed to protect the privacy of the individuals involved and avoid unnecessary hurt. References are provided for informational purposes only and do not constitute endorsement of any other websites or other sources. Readers should be aware that the views expressed in this work are solely those of the author. The author of this book does not dispense any medical advice or prescribe the use of any technique described in this book as a form of treatment for physical, emotional or medical problems without the advice of a physician, either directly or indirectly. The intent of the author is only to offer information of a general nature. In the event that you use any information within this book, the author assumes no responsibility for your actions.

JLW PUBLISHING
WWW.JOANNAWALDEN.COM

This book is dedicated to all those who have the courage to sing their own song, do things differently, shake up the status quo, believe in that which cannot be seen, change the rules, wear sequins in the most unlikely places and dream beyond anything known on this planet.

To Devo, my heart.
My inspiration, motivation, elevation and celebration.
Standby! Hold All Tickets!

Although I would be somewhat mortified for you to read this,
I desperately wish you were still here
with me to read it anyway.

♥

To Annie, my light.
My catalyst, expansion, strength, determination and courage.
You put the P in Powerful.

Without you, none of this would have
happened, nor been possible.

At the time of going to print the world is gripped in the Covid-19 global health and financial crisis. Now more than ever, we are being asked to re-evaluate all that has gone before to remember what is truly important. To find new ways of living, being and working with each other, and the planet moving forward. This situation is asking us to dive deep into who we truly are, to face our fears, find the gold buried in the darkness, keep calm in the chaos and feel love and gratitude for everything and everyone above all else. My experiences in this memoir have given me the tools and wisdom to navigate these challenging times of uncertainty, and I know you will find inspiration and comfort in them too.

Contents

Wisdom From Chaos

The building was on fire, smoke billowing upwards. I felt detached. As more people arrived at the office they came streaming upstairs. I saw disbelief and then horror, which slowly turned to panic, as the second plane hit. There is nothing ordered about fear. When it starts to creep in, emotions lose control. I saw people carried away by tears and hysteria. Inconsolable husbands and wives with friends and family who worked in the building. The emotion went up another notch in a matter of seconds. To breaking point. I felt the change, a palpable shift. I could choose to get taken away with it, and see where it was going, but that wasn't me. I sent love and understanding silently with my energy field. I projected calm thoughts and went downstairs to my computer.

"This is not a fucking accident," I said to my colleague. "767s don't just fly into buildings."

Half an hour later, I had confirmation when a plane hit the Pentagon. A small chill raced around my body. There were two more hijacked planes in the air. Then there were four. I looked at the buildings flaming on the TV screen.

"They look like they could fall over," I said.

"No, they're built to sway, they can't fall over," my colleague answered.

Twenty minutes later one of the Twin Towers crumbled. Little did I know they would come down, both of them, the tallest buildings in the world. They would melt and the floors would collapse like dominoes and we'd see bodies jumping from the buildings. As I watched, it didn't seem real.

The next installment came in the form of another plane crash. This time into the Pentagon. On the TV they were talking about Camp David being targeted next, yet another emblem of American symbolism.

Given the escalation of events, and only having lived in New York for a few months, I called home and woke up Devo and Annie for a second time.

"No, you don't understand, we are under terrorist attack here, watch the footage, watch the footage."

I'd called earlier. The third call woke them up. I'd gotten a husky "Hello?" and told Devo what had happened and that I was alright. "Oh, really darling?" he said groggily. "Okay, well have a cup of tea and a lie-down and you'll be fine."

I heard him wake Annie. "This is Jo darling, something about bombing buildings? Here, speak to your mother."

I heard the sounds of the phone being bumped as I'm handballed to Annie. She was half asleep, "Uh darling. What's happening? Are you being bombed darling?"

"Yes Annie, the US is under attack," I said frustrated. "Watch the footage."

"We don't have TV darling. We're in the boat shed for the renovations remember?"

"Oh right, how could I forget," I muttered. "Get Devo to fill you in. I have to go."

I looked outside at the sea of people filling the sidewalk on Madison Avenue. There were floods of people coming up the street from downtown. The subways had shut down. I saw people freaking out, panicking, running, desperately trying their cellphones. I needed a smoke. I spotted Megan in the hall and I read similar stress on her face. "Let's go for a ciggie?" Absofuckinglutely.

Out on the street it was a mess. I looked downtown to see smoke on the horizon. I felt mayhem in every direction enveloping me. For a fleeting moment, I felt a whisper of rising panic. Not only could I see the chaos, I was living the chaos. There was a disorientated man beside us. He didn't know what to do. How would he get home to Brooklyn? We checked he was okay, offered him assistance and headed back upstairs. It felt safer in the office.

I saw people with bags. They were going home. The Rockefeller Centre was over the road, St. Patrick's Cathedral next door and the UN building a few blocks away. Potential hot spots. Were we evacuating? It seemed surreal. I called Devo and Annie again and managed to get through the jammed phone lines after a few tries. They were having a cuppa and finally seemed to have grasped some semblance of the gravity of the situation. They couldn't sleep now. I heard the radio on in the background.

"Okay, I'm leaving the office. The phone lines are pretty much down and it's all a bit crazy, so I'll talk to you in a few hours. Love you lots, bye."

My new bestie colleague Liza and I walked uptown with my boss Paige in a daze. It was safer on the Upper East Side. We made a beeline for the nearest pub. As did every other person looking for some sanity. We finally found a seat in an Irish pub and sat glued to CNN sipping pint after pint in disbelief. Both towers had crumbled, and another large building had collapsed when Liza's cellphone suddenly started ringing. It was Triple Z, a radio station from New Zealand wanting me for a live report from the ground. Suddenly after a fair few pints I was outside on the eerily empty streets doing a live radio interview to New Zealand. Luckily I had more than enough Dutch courage on board, and managed to get through it relatively smoothly after we finally got a secure line.

The streets of Manhattan were deserted apart from numerous fire engines, ambulance, NYPD and emergency workers. It was beyond ominous. I wasn't sure I could go back to my apartment, so I stayed uptown at Liza's, ate pizza and watched some light-hearted relief on HBO. The next morning, we got up and walked to work to better understand the protocol in this kind of situation. We walked empty streets taking comfort in the routineness of it all, knowing deep down it was far, far, from normal. The few people we did see looked like they were sleepwalking, making their way in a daze to some unimportant destination. Being at the office was ridiculous. Those that were there were definitely not working, minds were nowhere near the job. I had a huge amount of email from all over the world.

It was amazing to find that so many people cared about me, and were showing their love and support in its entirety from around the globe. Liza and I left the office after a few hours and went to lunch to lift our spirits. What else does one do at a time like this? We boycotted the subway and walked downtown toward my apartment, taking in all the American flags flying at half-mast, and the large number of emergency vehicles and police along the way.

Around forty blocks later we arrived in Chelsea and my apartment on 15th Street and 8th Avenue. 14th Street West had been evacuated and was a secure zone now. A couple of blocks down on Chelsea Piers, the ice-skating rink had been turned into a temporary morgue. There were bodies with sheets over them amongst an array of debris. I was lucky to be able to get into my apartment at all.

The smoke was hanging down low overhead despite the beautiful bright blue day. After some lunch and a few vinos in quiet contemplation, we headed back uptown for the only safe haven I could think of, Central Park. We reached Central Park South, armed with newspapers as a camouflaged Hummer casually rolled by, army generals at attention inside. Another F-15 fighter plane flew overhead and I realised that this was really fucking serious. The numbness was wearing off and the reality of the situation was setting in.

Central Park was like a small urban sanctuary amidst the disaster. Although the bars, restaurants and cafes were empty throughout Manhattan, the calm comforts of the park's eight hundred and fifty acres were brimming with people. Everyone just wanted to be together. The main field was filled with groups of people hanging out, playing frisbee, eating a picnic lunch, reading the paper. It almost felt normal. It was reminiscent of a horde of kids in a gigantic playground. Just as children play with toys to work through their emotions at school or with a therapist, it seemed that the actions of adults in that park that day echoed these primal instincts.

Later that evening, with the 'trigger-happy Bush' screwing up yet another vengeful speech on national television, CBS cut to the mother of all battleships sitting out in the harbour. People were talking World War III. Fuck. Throughout the night, the Empire State Building and Penn Station had bomb scares with more evacuations. Another building had turned to dust and there were two more structures that were incredibly precarious and worrying. I saw the trillionth hysterical wife on TV with pictures of her missing husband, and this was just day two of the national disaster in the 'Attack on America'.

At the agency the mood was somber. People's friends were still missing, someone's brother was going to 'Ground Zero' as a search and rescue helper on the front line and there were colleagues' friends and family who were dead. Grand Central was evacuated after bomb scare threats, as were a few other areas in the near vicinity throughout the morning at work. Every five minutes someone was talking about another evacuation near the office. No chance of writing my creative brief on a rather unimportant billboard sponsorship and print ad. I checked in with my boss and left.

The A train was jammed to the hilt after the evacuations at Grand Central. There were a hell of a lot of people on the train. It felt strange being sandwiched so closely to people at a time like this. Back down on 15th Street, there were more sirens and vehicles whizzing by on the empty streets. Tired doctors, nurses and officers were stopped along 8th Avenue for a bite and a small break. I sat at home for the rest of the afternoon watching CNN, writing and catching friends for a comforting chat in New Zealand. My flatmate arrived home a few hours later and we hung out in the apartment, discussing the possibilities of Bush taking us straight into World War III. The F-15s were thundering through the sky constantly. Army tanks, troops and battleships were a dime a dozen, littered around Manhattan. All of it was starting to really freak me out.

After some dinner and more coverage on the box we decided to get a drink from the deli across the road. The wind had picked up and there was a sinister burning smell outside. My eyes were dry from all the ash flying around in the air as we walked around the block taking it all in. I kept my mouth tightly closed. We passed posters of missing people, on cars, walls, lamp posts. Sirens blared everywhere and the reverberating blast of the fighter planes continued overhead. People in the streets were wearing dental masks for risk of asbestos poisoning. We rounded the corner past the police blockades and for some reason, chose a different deli from the norm to stop by.

After getting our drinks we crossed back over the road. Half a block from our apartment we were met at our usual local deli by five NYPD pulling up, a couple of ambulances and firefighters too. They were carrying out a young Middle Eastern guy who had just been stabbed multiple times in a hate crime. Our safe little gay neighbourhood didn't seem so safe anymore.

As the officers were cordoning half of the block off with yellow tape, I dragged my room-mate across the road and back up to our apartment. I could feel the weight of aggression in the air around me. It was unmistakable. I shivered. Damn, I was out of cigarettes. I'd just witnessed the scene of a stabbing across the road and I was out of cigarettes. Twenty minutes later, I figured things must have cooled down over the road, so I stepped out to get a pack of Camel Lights. I scoped out the officers putting up more tape around the blood from the crime scene. The yellow tape seemed to make it more real. I ran over the road to yet another different local deli, and waited patiently while two security guys ran through a lengthy order for themselves and their colleagues.

In the meantime, another gentleman was standing at the counter aggressively yelling. "Are you gonna take my money or what? Are these fucking free tonight?" The first guy in the line looked less than impressed. "He's taking my order." In the seconds that follow a full-scale altercation erupts. I had nowhere to go. The door was blocked off and I stepped back, shaking in my boots while keeping all the universal love preaching going on in my head, to myself. The world was going mad. After buying cigarettes, I resolved to stay indoors at night over the coming days. Being moments away from getting caught in the midst of two aggressive incidents in the space of one hour signaled that I should not tempt fate.

As I curled up in my bed an incoming storm hit Manhattan. The growling cracks of thunder made me reach for my blankets in comfort, and the lightning toyed with my imagination behind my closed eyes. Not able to sleep, I looked out at the glistening raindrops as they pounded onto the ground. A torrential thunderstorm seemed threatening in current circumstances, especially to the rescue operation happening around the clock downtown. I turned it over in my mind and decided that the rain might seep through to dehydrated survivors buried below the rubble, and the lightning was far more powerful than the rescuers' searchlights. I said a small prayer and went to sleep.

Upon opening my eyes on Friday morning, I felt different than I had for the last two mornings. Maybe that's because I couldn't feel anything. I didn't know what to feel or how to be. It was a strange feeling. I felt disorientated and slightly lost. Like the rug had been pulled from under me. I didn't feel emotional. I didn't feel distraught. I guess you could call it shock.

More F-15s and sirens, more police, more people in the haze of bereavement. At Union Square and Washington Square Park there were masses of people and shrines there for their loved ones. It dawned on me that I was witness to a nation in mourning. One of the biggest and greatest nations of our time. Grief and sorrow were written all over the streets. I couldn't get away from it. It was everywhere I turned. I sent another message to the Universe to look after all those in need, whichever realm they may be in, physical or non-physical. I headed home around 1pm to prepare for Annie's group worldwide peace meditation that she was holding at a friend's home. I lit some Sai Baba incense, a candle and put on some music. I had a picture of the Twin Towers, taken only a week before laid in front of me. I started meditating around 1.45pm. After a while I saw various shapes and faces combined with feelings. Halfway through, the top half of my back started burning. The heat was incredible. I imagined myself in a circle of sapphire blue light, turning around me at different angles as I moved to the music.

The many angles created many circles of blue, so I was enclosed in a moving, revolving sphere of blue light. After I had been doing this for some time, I moved the healing sphere to wrap around the WTC site, next moving it out around Manhattan Island. I lay down at some point after finding myself rocking from side to side. When I hit the bed, I realised the intensity of heat on my back. The heat continued as I lay meditating on my bed. I opened my eyes almost two hours later, hoping that I had overlapped with Annie's session at home and made a connection that could help. I grabbed a cup of tea and stepped out onto the fire escape for a cigarette. The trees applauded as they dropped all the raindrops from their leaves in unison.

President Bush was visiting Ground Zero later that day. I walked past hundreds of people at the memorial sites in Union Square, large American flags and photo-encrusted shrines littered with candles. The F-15s patrolled Manhattan airspace the entire afternoon. Every now and then I would look up amidst the noise of the raging jets to see four F-15s flying in a quad up and down the length of the island. High security measures all round. Like they needed any more fuck ups. We lit a candle outside the apartment at 7pm for the candlelit vigil to all those lost in the terrorist attack.

That night I dreamt I was hiding under the table. It had a long tablecloth to cover me. I heard the sound of Darth Vader. That evil wheezing. He was hunting me, walking around the table. I was trying to be as quiet as possible, while sweating with fear. Devo and Annie were suddenly there, and they fought him. Fighting against the dark side.

Monday back at work feels strange. At our agency meeting mid-morning, our CEO read out all of the emails received from the network around the world. People are crying, everyone emotionally drained from the previous six days and we end in silence. Although we were slowly moving back into our routine, it felt anything but. Most of us were still in shock and no one could really keep their mind on the job. We kept up for appearance sake, waiting for the feeling of normalcy to return. As the weeks went by it came, slowly but surely. It felt peculiar, almost guilty, to be getting on with things, but what else could we do?

I was still searching the depths of my soul for meaning in the madness. About six weeks later, I had a realisation. I knew why I found myself in New York at this time. I understood why I felt the way I felt, during the incident. I understood why I couldn't feel the world's pain. I understood why I couldn't feel the world's anger. I was here to observe it and hold space and to work out *why* I felt indifferent. Because what I was really doing was remembering. I was remembering God. I knew there was no evil, that's why I couldn't be angry. I knew there was no pain, therefore I couldn't intrinsically feel something that I knew did not really exist. Because everything is an act of God. Goddess. Nature. The Universe. The divine intelligence in all things. It was divine will. The reactions of others were based on their perceptions and beliefs, and the paradigm Universe that they had chosen to surround themselves by. At the time I did not know why this was not a reality for me, but I knew it didn't feel right to buy into the hysteria of it all. I was here to experience these feelings so that I would remember who I was. It was a gift from God, a raising of my consciousness. This incident was to remind us that the current state of mass consciousness had created this event. It was not Osama Bin Laden. It was all of us. This is where the sadness came from. The sadness comes from here.

I had put it all together. The pieces came towards each other, meeting in a fleeting moment of awareness. Of distilled clarity and inherent knowing of the ultimate perfection of it all, of the divine intelligence that pervades all things. I had a deep understanding of the importance of energy consciousness. I could see how it all made perfect sense. I could see it all through a different lens. If I could only keep that moment, or moments, and be in that level of understanding, every hour of every day... but then I guess I wouldn't be here.

Off To Get Zapped

My eyelashes, despite their enviable length, were no match for the rapid-fire raindrops which were now assaulting my eyeballs. I squinted, raising my head up slightly. I couldn't see two metres in front of me. Heavy rain, now turning to sleet, was whipping my body from all angles. I kept walking despite my growing anxiety, head down with the full force of my body and backpack positioned against the raging elements. This wasn't exactly what I had in mind when I announced that I was abandoning my rapidly advancing advertising career on Madison Avenue for a spiritual pilgrimage in Spain. Minutes later, I noted that the track I was walking seemed to be much smaller than before.

My head snapped up as I screwed up my eyes into the wind-whipped rain, spinning to look behind me. I seemed to be on a smaller goat track. For three hundred and sixty degrees all I could see was blanketed white. No pilgrims, no wide main gravel track, no signposts, no nothing. Just thick white fog in all directions. Last night's revelation of the deaths in the Pyrenees due to bad weather three weeks prior was replaying in my mind. Fuck! On one level this was slightly terrifying. On another it was completely unsurprising.

The entire journey to this point had been bumpy at best. First up I missed my flight from London to Biarritz. Not because I was late mind you, but because I was supposed to fly out the day before. Being a bank holiday weekend, I had to pay an exorbitant fare to the airline, which I sucked up under a smile covering gritted teeth. It certainly wasn't the synchronistic start to the journey I had been hoping for. I needed to ensure I immediately got back into my uninhibited universal flow that was my vision for this trip. So, I boarded the new flight with a refreshed sense of hope and renewal along with fifteen guys wearing colourful sombreros and fake moustaches, unfazed and ready for take two of the kick-off to my very first spiritual adventure.

Gazing out onto the tarmac, I revelled in the excitement of my impending spiritual awakening. However, my dreamy inner peace soon came to a crashing halt, as a loud altercation between the flight hostess and a passenger took centre stage. I assumed it was one of the leery 'Mexicans', but as the shouting grew louder, I peered back over the seats to see it was a very well dressed, middle-aged man. Suited and booted, he was ironically devoid of any form of gentlemanly behaviour and absolutely going for it at the hostess. It became clear this expensive suit was merely a disguise for being a ginormous asshole unleashing his inner psycho, not only on the poor hostess, but the entire plane. After forty-five minutes of delay, airport security finally boarded the plane and he was forcibly removed, leaving his wife and kids on the aircraft. Clearly no father of the year award there. I was back to square one again, trying to reclaim my tranquillity, centre myself and cultivate positivity for the beginning of my Camino.

I arrived in drizzly Biarritz, albeit late, full of fake confidence and joie de vivre. Attempting to get my bearings outside the airport, I noticed another girl loitering with a backpack. Correctly guessing she might be on a similar journey I immediately made her acquaintance. She was an Aussie who was also setting off for Saint-Jean-Pied-de-Port, so together we made our way to the train station. Upon arrival, we were informed there was no train because of a crash that had occurred the week before. Lucky for us I guess. The bus station was an easy switch and we were soon booked onto the next service with twelve other, soon to be pilgrims.

As I surveyed the scene, I noted every single person was kitted out in well branded, very expensive, technical-looking hiking attire. I was certainly the unorthodox splash of colour in my bright pink skirt and diamond dangly earrings to complement my hiking boots. Driving through the centre of Biarritz, past a muddy-looking river and various alfresco restaurants lined alongside, the Aussie unleashed a barrage of questions in her ever so soft voice.

"How much training have you done? What does your pack weigh? Did you bring snow gear?"

"What?" I kept asking after each question. She was incredibly hard to hear. She was a social worker so maybe her tone was helpful when she had to talk to a wide spectrum from problematic social circumstances. She shared her numerous concerns, despite a very regimented six-month training scheme, and from what I could understand, packed for every possible weather scenario. I glossed over the gear and prep talk with sweeping generalities, attempting to resist the rising panic of my unpreparedness.

"So how did you hear about the Camino?" she asked, finally moving away from discussing the contents of her pack.

"Well, ultimately I'm doing this to be zapped," I said casually. "I read *The Camino* by Shirley MacLaine, who said that this ancient pilgrim path follows the ley lines of the Milky Way and you get zapped and realigned with all the energy from corresponding star systems, which can provide shifts and changes in consciousness."

Blank face. She had no idea what to make of that. It shut her up perfectly. I was certainly not wanting to focus any further on what was becoming omnisciently clear; my distinct lack of preparation. On all levels.

It's not to say I hadn't done anything. There were a few key things I researched and evaluated as more important than the rigorous scripted training and expensive gear lists I saw online. I had a flashback to the meeting I had arranged with a Camino-conquering older couple in Auckland. I had arrived full of naive enthusiasm regarding my upcoming transformational travel adventure. I was going to attain the ultimate pilgrim body and re-emerge into the world twenty times hotter and more spiritually on point than when I went in. These guys looked like super outdoorsy types given their khaki pants and merino wearing, on what was an average Tuesday in the city. As it turned out, they were hiking professionals and had completed all ten of the Great Walks of New Zealand. And, they were members of an actual tramping club! Suffice to say it was a giant reality check and I thankfully noted down some key intel from these keen experts, which meant I felt I could pretty much disregard everything else.

I sourced the lightest pack possible, custom designed and made in New Zealand by a couple in Remuera who had personal experience of the Camino. I spray-painted a gold scallop shell, the symbol of the Way of Saint James, on the front of my pack to distinguish it from others. However, it could not have been more different from the other packs around me. Mine had a distinct lack of pockets, frame and sections. On the same advice, I'd gone to the podiatrist to get my feet scraped of rough skin and purchased recommended hiking boots from Germany, which I had worn in walking the hour-long commute to work and back each day. In the high heat of summer, this was no mean feat, not to mention how ridiculous the work blazer and hiking boot combo looked. Such was the self-sacrificing pilgrim-to-be I was.

The bus was buzzing with pilgrim chat. While shouting yet another "What?" to the Aussie, I overheard a couple of pilgrims in the seats beside us voicing grave concerns about the Pyrenees crossing the following day.

"Those two seem to be ridiculously worried about the Pyrenees tomorrow," I said quietly, leaning toward the Aussie.

"Yes, I just overheard there have been a couple of fatalities on the mountain crossing a week or so ago in bad weather," she replied in hushed tones.

Fatalities?! Bloody hell! My approach to packing now seemed more than questionable. I had mostly skirts, sparkly earrings and colourful tops. I did purchase a hiking jacket and the brightest merino base layer I could find from a proper hiking shop, but I was suddenly feeling a distinct lack of technical equipment. Not to mention my 'training' which had been a lot more focused on long distance wine drinking, rather than any lengthy hikes. I could feel the fear in more ways than one. I pushed it from my mind and concentrated on my ace card, which was a yellow-stapled guidebook, the official guide from the Confraternity of Saint James. It had about eighty pages detailing listings of refugios, or places to stay, in each town and the number of kilometres between them. Looking around I didn't see any fellow pilgrims with this gem, so I patted myself on the back for that.

After a couple of hours of driving through lush green French countryside under stormy skies, we arrived in Saint Jean in the late afternoon. The narrow, cobbled streets were lined with white buildings, terracotta roofs and red window shutters. Matching colourful flowerpots were scattered outside the arched doorways, the occasional one decorated with dangling hiking boots above. Seeing a wooden staff and backpacks leaning against one doorway, I felt the joy of enthusiastic pilgrimage all around. Alarmingly, it was much colder and foggier up in the mountains than I had anticipated. I pushed the lack of prep anxiety again from my mind as my new friend and I hurriedly made our way through the rain to the official pilgrim office. We needed to register and get our pilgrim passports before it closed.

The French chap in the office took our details slowly. He then showed us the recommended Napoleon Route through the Pyrenees on the map on the wall while we waited for our documents. Highly concerned after the revelations of the bus journey, the Aussie interrogated the French chap in a surprisingly loud voice about the weather and safety of taking this recommended route considering the previous week's events.

"I have never heard of it," he said curtly in a thick French accent. "It is totally safe. Two hundred people went yesterday. All fine," he confirmed, nodding.

"But what about the weather?" said the Aussie, agitated and unconvinced. "It's rainy and foggy outside."

I noted that he had only mentioned 'yesterday' but decided to nod along anyway so as not to add fuel to the fire. My memory of French sportsmanship against the All Blacks questioned whether I could really trust the Frenchies at all, but again, I kept that to myself. We received an A4 sheet of recommended daily distances and elevations split into thirty-four small sections to Santiago, plus our Carnet de Pèlerin de Saint-Jacques 'Credential del Peregrino.' The passports were a rectangle bi-fold card with an upside down scallop shell on the front, stating, 'Les Amis de Chemin de Saint-Jacques Pyrénées-Atlantiques', Friends of the path of St. James Pyrenees-Atlantic and the St. Jean office details. Inside was space for name, address, passport number, start date, signature, pilgrim number and space for an 'end date' and stamp at Santiago below it. The next page had a French quote, which roughly translated to:

I throw you from St. Jacques, Old Europe, a cry full of love, find yourself, be yourself, discover your origins, revive your roots, revisit in these authentic values that made your glorious history and your presence in the other beneficial continents. Rebuild your spiritual unity in a climate of total respect for other religions and true freedom.

Pope Jean Paul II

I was officially a bona fide pilgrim.

Of course, the Aussie had already booked the relatively basic M'aison Esponda albergue, a couple of doors down. As luck would have it, they had room for me also. I hadn't bothered to book anything. I was more about leaving things to chance and seeing what the Universe delivered. We had a simple meal of bread and soup and went to bed early in preparation for the following day.

The next morning, we arose early with the first 27.1km of hiking ahead of us through the French Pyrenees to Roncesvalles. It was still misty and grey at 6am, but off we set, rain jackets on under our packs and excited at the prospect of day one of the Camino Frances, Camino de Santiago. This is one of the oldest routes of the pilgrimage from France to Santiago, since 812AD, although there are many others that make their way to Santiago from all over Europe. There were a handful of older male pilgrims in their fifties loitering out on the street as we exited. They looked extremely fit, healthy and unsmilingly serious about what lay ahead.

In the first light of day, St. Jean was a gorgeous medieval city overlooking the surrounding countryside. We made our way through the tiny streets crossing the River Nive via a quaint, arched stone bridge, finally coming to the brick wall with the Gate of St. Jacques, a UNESCO World Heritage site from the fifteenth century. This signified the official entranceway to the Camino. There were small statues encased within the wall either side of the arched doorway, one a gold-painted Virgin Mary and the other John the Baptist, both blessing all those who moved through the gate. Shortly after we came upon a Fromagerie that was open for business, complete with a beret-wearing chap carving up massive wheels of cheesy goodness. I ordered the brebis, or sheep's milk cheese, and a couple of bread rolls, all by way of pointing but feeling oh so very French, nonetheless.

As we headed out of town, we passed the Route de Napoléon sign with its coats of arms, and we were officially on our way. The lush green paddocks with hungry white cows were brilliantly set against the grey skies. It was rolling farmland as far as the eye could see, with the occasional house covered with rambling red roses. In stark contrast to the lush scenery, the first two hours of the walk were about as vertical as you could get. Hmmm, I thought to myself as I was puffing up the never-ending hill and cursing the fact that I hadn't given up smoking, lucky I did that Five Volcano Walk back in Auckland. This was literally the only training I had accomplished in preparation for 750km plus through the north of Spain. The term 'volcano' admittedly made it sound far more rugged and challenging than the reality, which was a few small hills on an easy three-hour stroll through the largest city in New Zealand. Clearly not quite the intensity of training needed, but better than nothing I surmised.

About a quarter of the way up the weather really set in on us, and amid torrential rain, thick fog and bone-chilling cold we sheltered in the last possible rest stop for a warming coffee. This was the last of civilisation before heading into the thick of the mountains. Lord knows I needed the break. The cafe had dark wooden beams with matching tables and chairs and a roaring fire. I sat there with my steaming mug of coffee reading my guidebook for the first time, curious to know what lay ahead. *The route is dangerous in the months of short daylight hours. Even in summer.* It was May so between winter and summer in this northern hemisphere, yes that applied to me. *DO NOT attempt it in low cloud, high winds or bad weather.* I looked outside at the intense fog, pelting rain and bitter cold. Yes, check. *If you leave St. Jean early there will be no bars open so buy provisions the day before.* Thank God for the small roll and few slices of cheese we just picked up but if there is nothing else for another five hours and 15-20km then clearly, I was going to starve. *Water is scarce so carry some with you.* It's not so bloody scarce outside I thought, as torrential rain thundered on the roof, before promptly dashing to the bathroom to fill up all my water bottles. It seemed the Aussie wasn't being so dramatic last night after all. Oh well, too late to go back now.

We continued in the treacherous weather. After a quick consultation of my topographical map while in the cafe, it was slowly sinking in that 21km of the 27km total for the day were on a stupidly steep incline. I guess it was the Pyrenees after all. My fresh pilgrim arse was doing its best to cope, but I was most certainly out of shape. I was now rapidly discovering this was going to be a massive challenge. I'm not quite sure what I thought Pyrenees mountains were, but it was apparent I hadn't taken the key word, mountain, too seriously. I stopped just off the main road to take a video of the conditions, complete with sarcastic VO of the guidebook warnings. A few pilgrims stopped, asking me in French and then English if they were going the right way as we were now in non signposted territory. "Oh yeah, sure we are," I said confidently. Honestly, it was the blind leading the blind.

The rain eased off a touch and I looked up between the leafless tree skeletons to see other pilgrims up ahead on the winding road in the mist. I noticed a horse in the paddock beside us with her gorgeous foal. The foal bucked its front feet into the air, jumping for joy while the mother plodded along behind. It renewed my sense of excitement for the adventure I was now officially undertaking. Against all odds and lady lush behaviour, I was on the road. I was walking an ancient pilgrim path; I was an actual proper pilgrim. And not only that, I was in France and hiking the Pyrenees. Don't mind if I do!

We trekked higher and higher, through the vibrant greenery, with the occasional purple wildflowers peeping through. Continuing ever higher, we passed a stone marking the way with a yellow spray-painted scallop shell. It looked like rays of light. It was in amongst a pile of stones from previous pilgrims, one with a red-painted cross with a heart-shaped bottom. There was an eerie looking skeleton of an animal slightly in front. The fog grew suddenly thicker giving a three hundred and sixty degree view of grey mist. I could see a large fenced cross on the hill. "Hopefully that's not 'cause somebody died," I said to the Aussie dramatically. Up close, the cross had Celtic designs with *Ne naiz bidea,* and *Je suis le chemin* engraved at the bottom. Translated it means, *I am the way.* It was surrounded by offerings of red roses, crystals, stones, written messages, rosary beads and feathers. Phew, no tombstone here. The Aussie and I stopped and sat on a nearby rock for a cheese roll, our bright blue plastic ponchos flapping in the wind. There was a long way to go in the mountains so might as well fuel up.

We set off again into the thickening mist amidst the jingle-jangle of bells from a herd of rams. Their small black faces and feet were engulfed by long woolly carpets down to their knees. They were scattered amongst large stones now breaking up the green landscape. We seemed to be right at the top, although it was hard to tell given the claustrophobic fog surrounding us. The rain pelted down even harder. The icy raindrops were now solidifying and looking back I noticed that the Aussie was nowhere to be seen. Her pace was consistently slower than mine and as the weather grew worse, I couldn't wait around in the freezing cold. I had no snow gear whatsoever. My pathetic quick-dry pants were sodden, but I cracked on, head down into the wind. It was at this point that I got lost. In the middle of the Pyrenees Pass. On a tiny goat track in the middle of bumblefuck nowhere.

How the hell did I get here? I thought desperately as the snow and wind beat against my face with increasing velocity. I stood there looking around at a blanket of white surrounding me. I couldn't see two feet in front. "Hello?" I yelled into the raging rain and wind. "Hello?" Nothing. Not even a jangling sheep. My fear was rising. I must be more off track than I thought. Was this going to be the first and last spiritual pilgrimage I would ever undertake? Panic began to set in. What was I thinking? I was aware of the importance of not losing my nerve. I made an instant decision to go with my gut feeling and made my way assertively across the terrain, going off any semblance of a track and into the unknown completely. I just headed in the direction I thought might be the main path with fear-fuelled determination. A few minutes went by. No path. More thick fog and sleet. Five minutes gone and I was trying to manage the barrage of worrying thoughts in my mind. The fog became less dense for a split second revealing more of the same terrain. Who knew where I was, but I was here now and there was nothing I could do about it. I was going to need to carry on. Another five minutes went by, walking in pure white-out. As another nervous terror was furiously rising in my chest I suddenly bumped into a broad proper pathway. It seemed to be the right track. Oh, thank fuck for that! I thought, finally breathing out. I seemed to have been holding my breath for minutes. "I'm okay. I'm okay. I'm OKAY!" I said chattering away to myself. I marveled in my extraordinarily fluky powers of navigation, while simultaneously acknowledging the harrowing thought of how easy it was for people to get lost and die in these conditions.

A large concrete sign stated, *Saint-Jacques de Compostelle – 765km*, above a giant scallop shell. Yes. Back on track, I thought with a sigh of relief. I'm going to be alright. I was surprised to come across an antique-looking fountain tap adorned with scallop shells. There was water freely flowing from a black hose to the side. No mountain drought at all then. There was no need for a refill as I'd been too freezing and terrified to drink anything. I continued, passing lichen-encrusted trees and heading towards what appeared to be another cross up ahead. Nearing closer I saw a name, dates and *Peregrine Brasil* written on the stone. I stood there and shivered as someone walked over my grave, thanking my lucky stars and whoever was looking after me in this mountain peak, guiding me back to the right path. I gave my respects and then persevered along the track finally heading downwards through endless silvery beech trees in the fog.

I felt like I was now starring in a cliché scene of an eerie horror flick. It was only 3.6km to Roncesvalles but the spookiness of the gravestone and my potentially fatal close call only exacerbated my already wild imagination of getting abducted by a chainsaw masochist, or zombies appearing from the woods or some equally, utterly ridiculous scenario. I powered down to Roncesvalles at speed, arriving at 4.15pm, taking me about eight and a half hours. I have never been so pleased to see signs of life, even if it was a large and rather spooky-looking ancient monastery. Once inside, I was immediately entranced by the haunting soundtrack of monks chanting prayers which filled the dimly lit room. It felt eerily atmospheric and very sacred. I checked in, and felt chuffed to get my first real stamp in my pilgrim passport.

The monastery was a huge wide-open space housing a hundred bunk beds with a high ceiling of wooden beams, lit by only a handful of wrought iron medieval chandeliers. These provided minimal atmospheric light amongst the stone walls and medieval arches. After securing a bunk, I grabbed my toiletries and hobbled to the showers to warm my aching body. As I dressed myself, I could feel pain in every minute movement from muscles I never knew I had. I lay on my bunk bed, feeling like I'd been hit by a freight train and listening to the incredibly haunting singing, which according to my guidebook was possibly the "Song of Roland". *A great medieval poem recalling the battle of Roncevaux Pass in August 778 when Charlemagne's rear-guard was ambushed, and Roland blew his horn to summon the Emperor.* That put a rather grisly spin on what I had assumed were some amazingly high vibrational spiritual blessings and prayers. New pilgrims were still pouring in, including the Aussie, finally, and they shuffled around quietly as they organised themselves. We assembled for a communal dinner at 7pm. It was €10 for a three-course pilgrim special of bean soup, grilled trout, frites, yoghurt and wine. It wasn't long before I headed back to the bunk to pass out.

It is of the utmost importance to take this time for you.
Although it feels extraneous, it is in fact a requirement.
It can be easy, or it can be hard, it is up to you. Know that.

You are on perfect target for all you have to deliver.
Realise that this is a process by which you are unaccustomed
and therefore it will take time to perfect.
To get the results you want, and require.
However, this is the beginning of something of divine perfection,
if you will only allow.

The great change is upon us.
And you will navigate this with ease.
As you have done the work and preparations.
Never far from your higher self, the true self, the eternal self,
which led you to this point today.
And for this we are grateful.
For your energy is of vital importance.
Each individual has more power than they know.
And holding and maintaining this light, is a rite of passage.

Miracle Vino

We were awoken at 5.55am to the same eerie musical sounds of monks singing. Despite being in pretty bad shape from the day before, it was still a wonderfully peaceful and spiritual way to start the day. This pilgrim business was certainly a shock to my system. I had experienced a blaring symphony of snoring overnight. The decibels of said snorers were so high that it produced actual reverberations through the metal frame of the bunk bed I was lying in several bunks away. My entire bed was rattling so much I barely slept a wink, despite the physical exhaustion. I noticed in the morning that the culprits were generally French men, fifty-five years or older. I would be avoiding sleeping anywhere near them in future.

I set off with the Aussie again at 7am to Larrasoaña, another brutal walk of 27km on tender limbs that were still recovering from yesterday's beating. I kept the vision of my ultimate pilgrim body in mind as I attempted to speed up my pace. This time we had endless mud to navigate due to the continuing bad weather. Somehow my pre-pilgrimage estimations of a casual 15km a day seemed to be, unsurprisingly, a little off. I was particularly happy to have survived the Pyrenees though, after hearing it officially confirmed at dinner the night before that two people had in fact died up there less than a week ago. Thank God for my decent sense of direction or I quite possibly could have met the same fate.

We followed scallop shell signs and yellow arrows painted on walls and roads and rocks. No need for a map around here. We walked through endless gorgeous green fields and rolling hills peppered with small villages of terracotta houses and the obligatory church, which still looked cute despite the dismal weather. The sun returned later in the day as we ventured further from the mountain area, passing horses, rivers with stone bridges and yellow wildflowers in spades. Beautiful red poppies started appearing the further we went. The Aussie was peppering me with questions about my spiritual interests and why I was walking The Way. I told her how Annie, my South African mother, had her awakening during the Harmonic Convergence in 1987 when a voice told her it was all about 'consciousness'. She was into all things spiritual and energy, so I'd grown up around it really. Although it was more of a closet interest for me after Annie's spiritual beliefs elicited intense controversy and confrontation whilst growing up.

"But still, why on earth would you leave New York?" she asked starry-eyed.

"Let's call it a cosmic kick up the arse from my Saturn Return," I said.

She looked confused.

"Your Saturn Return is an astrological occurrence which happens at age twenty-nine-and-a-half years and is known as a 'cosmic coming of age', which pushes you into adulthood. It's often a time of re-evaluation and change for people. Which is why, here I am at thirty-years-old, following the Milky Way and a bunch of arrows across Spain, looking for clues and direction in my life," I said, laughing. "I actually think even before that living through 9/11 in New York triggered some kind of energy remembrance within me. I had a flash of being some kind of broader consciousness that took me out of my humanness. It was always there, it just became quieted by my everyday life. Ever since, it reawakened my deep knowing that there is more to life than the status quo. And I have been determined to find out more and find my place and purpose in this world. That's more important to me than a fancy job on Madison Avenue."

The Aussie raised her eyebrows. "Wow, that's quite courageous," she said, eyes wide. "A successful career in New York must have been hard to give up. Especially as it's so hard for us to get there. So how did you manage to end up there anyway?" And so, I told her more of my story.

"There's a new guy who's taken over the helm in the New York office. I've heard he wants to hire lots of young, shit hot people from all over the world. I've organised an interview for you," said Devo down the phone, real name David, otherwise known as my father. I hadn't called my parents mum or dad since I was eleven when Annie insisted on them being referred to by their names, as we had done before we started school. It was far more civilised apparently. I was in Melbourne interning at a global advertising agency during my last term of university.

"But I've seen intercompany ads for a role in Dubai," I said excitedly. "I rather like the idea of marrying a sheik and rolling around in a fleet of Mercs!"

"Don't be absurd!" he said in his exaggerated faux hoity-toity delivery. "I am not letting you run off to Dubai to marry a sheik! They don't even drink for Christ's sake."

I had no idea what I was getting into. The naivety of my twenty-two-year-old self didn't even really know the meaning of New York, what it was, what it represented, but I let Devo's plan sweep me away and off to the other side of the world to see what would happen. I figured I may as well give it a shot. At least I would see this famous city of New York that everyone kept going on about. If nothing else.

Before I left for my New York interview I had another interview for a New York position at a rival global network, meeting with the Global CEO while he was in Auckland. Moments after arriving, he quickly informed me that, "It takes a certain person to make it in New York and I'm not sure that you are one of them." He was brusque, and clearly gave me the impression I was wasting his time. I wandered out of there after fifteen minutes, crestfallen with my tail between my legs. Although this dampened my already wobbly youthful confidence, it is possible that the entire embarrassing experience unconsciously gave me a burning desire to prove him wrong. I went to New York and aced my interviews and proceeded to have a very successful career full of groundbreaking and award-winning campaigns for big famous brands.

"Wow!" cooed the Aussie. "That's so cool. I still can't believe you left New York to chase energy lines on this pilgrimage though. That's really quite mad!"

Why did everyone always say that? After all that rabbiting on, before we knew it we had arrived in town. We'd heard on the pilgrim grapevine that there was no space at the number one ranked albergue, the ayuntamiento, also known as the town hall. We decided to go to the ayuntamiento anyway and get our passports stamped en route to finding alternate accommodation. To our surprise, we were ushered in and given two beds upon arrival. Not only that, but we had two beds in a private room, away from the snorers! Although I'd only experienced one night of snore-deprived sleeplessness, it was more than enough for me. Thank you, angels! We showered, did our washing and then shared a lovely pilgrim dinner with a French couple before turning in for a restful sleep.

Larrasoaña to Pamplona was a much more palatable 20km. We left at 6.30am strolling through beautiful forest along the river towards Pamplona. These last couple of days were hard, but not quite as horrific as the first day which gave a huge shudder to my supremely unfit system. The Aussie continued asking in-depth questions about all aspects of my life. She seemed inordinately enamoured with every word. I was feeling a little weary at this point, not only from the pressure of ongoing storytelling, but also from physical exhaustion. An interaction with a chap from Nicaragua was a welcome reprieve. He'd lost all his money for the trip at the casino the night before leaving for France. He had nothing to his name. The Aussie looked horrified. I genuinely felt sorry for him and wished him luck. What a cock-up! A proper genuine pilgrim experience for him then.

Against all out-of-shape odds, I had now made it to Pamplona, about 65km in. From Lady Lush, to Lady Look-Where-She-Is-Now, conquering the perils of the Camino de Santiago day by day. I had a distinct sense of surprised accomplishment in myself. I was not the only one. The announcement of my Camino intentions at home was met with a myriad of wide-eyed responses. I even tried to convince my brother to set up a black-market betting scheme on my success rate, given the odds stacked against me.

So far so good though and my odds were looking surprisingly better by the day. Especially since I had now discovered a foolproof recipe to ensure a good solid sleep no matter what kind of earth-moving snorer was in the vicinity. It was a three-part recipe. 1.Walk more than 20km a day. 2.Take a double dose of magnesium. 3.Drink an entire bottle of wine. This I had ascertained was the perfect combo to knock you out good and proper. A bottle of wine a night, oh how traumatic for me! Easily done when a free bottle of wine was provided for each pilgrim with their Pilgrim Menu on the road.

Pamplona was the first proper city, nestled in a valley at the side of the Basque Mountains. With less walking that day we had the afternoon to explore the fortress city wandering the old town, to the main plaza and beautifully adorned town hall building. Thankfully there was no running of the bulls, which happens later in July, for which I was quite glad. We visited the Catedral de Santa Maria, a gothic building built in the late fourteenth century. It was full of ethereal music to soothe the soul, glorious gold detail and magnificent cloisters.

Being the first city on the Way of Saint James also meant our first amazing tapas bars. We chose a classic-looking, dark, wooden establishment full of patrons sitting at the bar under dozens of ham legs hanging from their hooves above. The counter was filled with all sorts of different, delectable looking tapas dishes. Although pescatarian for many years up until this journey, I indulged in some freshly shaved Iberian ham, tortilla española, and garlic prawns which went superbly with their house vino tinto. I ordered what I thought was eggplant, which turned out to be blood sausage. Eww. My flexitarian rules didn't stretch that far. I had heard prior to the pilgrimage, that Spain was not particularly vegetarian friendly hence my new expanded palate. I'd been reintroducing a bit of meat here and there in anticipation of being stuck for a month in the Spanish countryside with nothing to eat. Sure enough, so far, the standard vegetarian pilgrim menu option was potatoes with giant runner beans that had been boiled to death and doused in tomato sauce. That was the dinner option in every single restaurant menu I'd seen so far. It was textureless and flavourless and blindingly obvious that the Spanish had no clue how to cook vegetables. One night of this was enough to convert my refined foodie taste buds back on the road to meat.

Upon leaving Pamplona, I ditched the Aussie. She had developed a needy sense of co-dependency, but even more concerning was that I was starting to get a hint of another agenda. First there was the intense interest in everything about me. There was a growing tactile affection, and after the third time she sat gazing deeply into my eyes over lunch, I knew I had to make a break for it. Legend has it that everyone has a great lover on the pilgrimage, but quite frankly, there was no way in hell I was letting her get in between me and my pilgrim stallion to come. Seriously. So, the next day I left at the crack of dawn, strategising to hustle myself a giant 32km over an entire recommended section of the topographical map to Cirauqui. I bypassed the tiny Cizur Menor, then Zariquiegui before heading up through the mountain ridge of Alto Del Perdon. There was an interesting modern iron sculpture of different pilgrimage silhouettes at the top, people walking, or hunched over, some on donkeys and horses with flags and staffs. The sculpture was overlooking dozens of wind turbines littered along the hills. With some time to myself, I'd been enjoying my own company and welcoming the space for spiritual epiphanies throughout the day, but all I could seem to think about was rosé. Down to the town of Uterga and through acres of grass ornamented by the occasional wild poppies, with no time for a siesta, I powered through Puente la Reina and up again to the small hill town of Cirauqui.

Cirauqui was a picturesque little town overlooking wine country, in the Navarra region. My back was killing me after carrying my weighty pack up the hill in the beating sun. Last I checked it was weighing in at around 14kg, but it was about to get a hell of a lot lighter. Another ruthless cull was required. I checked my guidebook and dragged my weary body through the streets, admiring the gorgeous stone buildings, whose windows and terraces were filled with colour from terracotta flowerpots.

Albergue Maralotx was not far, and when I arrived it was super cute with three big arched windows framing a balcony overlooking the street. Inside everything was nicely decorated and appeared new. How fabulous. I freshened up, tossing my beautifully picturesque, but rather weighty Spanish guidebook plus an extra journal in the lounge room for the next lucky pilgrim. I was dying for a vino rosado, but siesta meant that absolutely everything was closed. Drat. I wandered around the town stopping to take pictures of a delightful old farmer who was relaxing in the sun under a fig tree overlooking the valley. He sweetly took a couple of snaps of me, my bright pink singlet and beige patterned floaty skirt a stark contrast to the evergreen vista. We had a lovely interaction, not mattering that I did not speak nor understand much Spanish. Sometimes language is no barrier at all. I ventured back into the centre of the village to find some possible sustenance (read: wine), surprisingly finding myself at what looked like the local RSA. The bar was full of little old ladies with pink and purple hair. It appeared to be one of the old birds' birthdays and they gave me a delicious chocolate, bless them. I ploughed through five vino rosados whiling away the afternoon, relaxing, writing and taking it all in. Well deserved after eight hours of hiking and a 100m climb in the heat of the day.

Back at the albergue, I joined a couple of Spaniards for a dinner of meatballs and spaghetti. I had met these guys en route, and they were travelling with an Alsatian dog wearing its very own pilgrim pack coat carrying his doggie essentials. The vino and meatballs combined with the excessive daily kilometres and heat were a definitive recipe for pass-out central. I hit the hay at the very RSA friendly time of 9pm. I'm sure the old birds were up longer than me.

The next day I was on a mission to Villamayor de Monjardín approximately 25km away, a hefty task in the unforgiving Spanish heat. I got up at 5am and ventured out onto a road blanketed by darkness. The moon was still up with a few twinkling stars on the horizon. The early start was all good in theory, aside from the fact that my pathetic head torch barely lit up the road in front of me, let alone any yellow arrows or signs along the way. After one false start with a wrong turn leaving town I seemed to be back on track, on a stony old Roman road heading towards Lorca. The thick black over the hills was lightening to deep indigo blue before grading to burnt sienna as the sky filled with light. It was liberating walking alone at that hour of the morning witnessing the changing colours in silence before everything came to life. I watched the sun rise over the vines and trees. The birds eventually started chirping, the colours faded, and the sky lightened even further as the sun rose. I reached Lorca an hour-and-a-half later, noting the pilgrim and scallop shell decorated houses, denoting this pilgrim thoroughfare. Not needing a break, I continued to Villatuerta another 5km away. The path became muddy after the Roman stones came to an end and I carefully made my way through so as not to slip over. After crossing a large gothic bridge on my way into town, the path became unclear with no signs. I carried on through, thanking my lucky stars for my ace card guidebook that helped me find my way out of town.

I hit Estella an hour later, taking time to peruse the famous north doorway of the Church of San Miguel. I was just over halfway through the day's scheduled kilometres when I discovered a pilgrim perk beyond my wildest dreams. In fact, it is one of the best things I have ever discovered in my entire life. The beautiful Fuente de Irache at the Monastery de Irache. It was a dual fountain, with modern stainless steel tap fittings set into scallop shells between the pilgrimage cross. The name and coat of arms was pictured above in the steel, and the entire unit was set into stone in the wall. One tap was *Agua* and the other tap was, wait for it, *Vino*. Yes, vino. Vino tinto flowing for free, in the middle of nowhere, in Spain, on the Camino de Santiago. It was truly a miracle. Now this is the kind of spiritual gratification I was looking for. Hallelujah. I always knew I liked those monks. Given it was soon to be siesta time, which literally correlates to a complete shutdown of every shop, bar and restaurant in every town in all of Spain for a minimum of two to three hours, I thought it best to fill thy water bottle with a few swigs for the remainder of the trip. According to the legend if you drink the wine from the fountain then you will arrive in Santiago in good health. Well, you could be damn sure I was going to be all sorts of fine when I arrived given how much of that vino I was downing. I loved the guidebook; *A little discretion is advised on hot afternoons.* Brilliant. I refilled my bottle again. By this point I was already plotting to go back with a small tanker, fill up with the wonderful blessed wine and transport it back to London.

Maybe this was my calling. Bringing blessed wine to the party scene in London. I was definitely qualified. I had six years of expert navigation of the party scene in New York. I'd made friends with bouncers, shagged waiters, been romanced by DJs, had dalliances with bartenders and used my 'exotic' Kiwi accent to talk my way into some of the best parties in town. All the while leading a double life, running off to the latest philosophy talk, doing un-cooking lessons with David Wolfe and the fledgling raw food movement or heading upstate for a weekend course on angels and power animals. I was a true walking contradiction. Maybe this could combine two of my greatest passions in one? I felt a strong potential market for blessed vino tinto from the Camino.

The rest of the day's walking was, as you could imagine, entirely different from the first half. The beginning bit, post wine fountain buzz, lulled me into a false sense of security with deceptively flat lush green fields full of vibrant red poppies. The hills loomed in the foreground with their steep climb of at least a few hundred metres. The heat was growing more intense by the minute. A few hours of sleepy, boozy, meandering later, my feet were burning as I climbed up the hill to Villamayor de Monjardín under the beating hot sun. I was wrecked. Slightly delusional, I actually thought my eyes were playing tricks when I saw the Villamayor sign. It seemed far too early for me to have reached there, given the amount of kilometres and wine. I arrived with Jay, yet another Aussie, with a big build and larger than life character. It was 1.30pm, and the albergue didn't open until 4pm so we headed to the nearest bar for a few refreshing claras (a mix of lemonade and beer). We talked shit for an hour or so, with typical Australia versus New Zealand rivalry. Although I'd spent my primary years growing up in Melbourne, I was very much a New Zealander.

I took my leave after the second drink, heading to the only place I knew would be cool, the church. The Church of Santa Maria was charmingly small with gothic cloisters and a thirteenth century statue of the Virgin. I was alone in the church, finally taking the opportunity to have a moment to myself. I had just lit a candle and was settling in when someone else entered the church. As I was serenely dropping into meditation, the silence was broken by a series of incredibly loud tumultuous gurgling sounds. What the hell was that? It soon became clear that this person's stomach was firing off all manner of disagreements which were now echoing around the church. I turned around suggestively, seeing a German woman with her eyes closed, hoping she may get the hint and be on her way out. No such luck as she continued to sit there, unfazed. She wasn't going anywhere. The gastro noises continued, getting louder and louder to the point where I was suffocating the giggles. It was impossible to concentrate, let alone have any kind of spiritually enlightening meditation or sacred moment. So much for being spiritual for two seconds.

It is time.
It is time to surrender to the true purpose of your journey.
Your visit to this place called earth.
I have seen through eons, the different energies.
Of different lands in space and time.
The light is all there is, and all there ever was.
Your unique way of working with the light is a gift to the planet.
By not being your light, you are doing a disservice to yourself. And All.
As I said to you then and I say to you now – you are pure love and light.
Speak your truth, know your light, be your oneness.
For the benefit of All.

From Pilgrimage To Party Time

I checked into a refugio run by the Dutch God squad, purely due to the fact that the guidebook said their food was seriously good. Religion and I were not friends. Our high school reverend once told me I was a 'devil's child' because I had dressed up in veiled attire, and danced into class yelling and wailing with the occasional Kum-ba-ya thrown in. I stopped my dramatic performance just long enough to inform him I would no longer be attending religious education class as I had changed religions. Suffice to say, I was branded the D word by the furious reverend which, now that I think about it, could have scarred me for life. I'm sure if this had happened in America I could have sued.

Despite my loathing of organised religion and all its rules I figured there wouldn't be much opportunity for similar sermons at the refugio. The idea of yummy Dutch food was too much to pass up. The accommodation was clean and there were hot showers which was a blessing after my 24km stint. Ranged along our table of twelve were myself, two strapping German blokes in their thirties, a French couple in their fifties, a fifty-nine-year-old German woman, a middle-aged Swedish lass, an older German guy and a Spanish chap around my age. The ceramic jugs disappointingly contained water. Why could they not take a leaf out of the book of the monks up the road? Unsurprisingly, we had to say a prayer before the meal. I never minded a bit of thanks and appreciation so did my own version to the Universe minus Jesus and all that jazz.

We enjoyed a satisfying stew with the usual pilgrim banter. I chatted to Victor who sat opposite me. He was Spanish, with dark features and glasses, and a particularly dry sense of humour. Just before dessert was served my naive sense that I might narrowly escape a brow-bashing was shattered. A series of speeches brimming with religious fervour were pitched at us. Some pilgrims crossed their arms in front of their chest. Others sat there awkwardly. I spent my time eyeballing Victor across the table trying to make him laugh. Finally, twenty minutes later it was over and we were all handed a small present of the Book of John, which we were informed had a reference to the Camino in it. Of course, they wouldn't tell us where it was, we had to read the book to find out. Really? An invite to sing with the squad came shortly after. I politely declined, making a break for it outside to have a fag. As I was puffing away the wailing sounds of *Kum-ba-ya My Lord*, ironically came wafting outside. Time to hit the hay.

I set off alone the next day, against the beautiful burnt skies and a few clouds. Through the darkness I could just make out the words Castillo de Monjardín on the building to my right. A winery! Damn. If only I had known. I continued on as the sky turned to watercolours and finally the light of the sun caressed the clouds to reveal a sandy-coloured stone road to a small village way up ahead in the distance on the hill. This was Los Arcos, 12km away. I passed some grapevines as I got further up the hill. I was just starting to get into proper wine country. Now we're talking. Rioja, here I come!

I followed the painted yellow arrows juxtaposed against graphic stencil street art through the village, laughing at the phone number of a taxi sprayed onto the road. I continued on for another 6km to Sansol where I stopped for a break. I took my boots and socks off, lying down with my feet up in the air against the blue backdrop. Sansol was looking particularly tiny with one measly albergue offering, so I decided to try my luck on the other side of the river at Torres del Río which had three options. It was still early enough in the day that I continued on further to Viana which sounded much cooler than both previous options due to the Baroque and Renaissance architecture. Not to mention, even closer to Rioja.

After six days, and many kilometres on the road I was getting the hang of this fly by the seat of your pants pilgrimage set-up.

However, Viana was another 11km away, making my daily total a whopping 33km. I had spent hours upon hours hiking through the countryside while perving at strapping young lads working out in the fields. What was a few more in the big scheme of things? My imagination by this point was running wild with fantasies of being bent over a hay bale by a hot young Spanish farmer. It certainly made the time whizz by. I hadn't had any action in months. I'd spent the last few years searching for a boyfriend in New York, which resulted in a stack of drunken hook-ups and dates that went nowhere. Unless one counts the lengthy fling with a self-destructive, incredibly moody actor slash bartender from Los Angeles. Then again, it was more of a series of one night stands over eighteen months that had the illusory effect of some kind of casual relationship, which in fact did not exist outside the hours of 4am to 8am. Eventually I found out he had a long-term girlfriend in Europe. No wonder he was unavailable. By this point I think we were both addicted to the epically satisfying sex. This may have been due to the fact that I outed his foot fetish and then took it to a whole new level with a discovery of foot fetish porn. Deep down I just wanted to be wanted, although I wasn't particularly clear about what it was that I wanted. Relationships with men certainly weren't one of my strong points so far.

Viana put me at 156km and about a fifth of the way there. Not a distance to be sneezed at, which was abundantly clear from the shape I was in. Currently dying. Although I was doing so gracefully with four glasses of rosé upon arrival at 2pm. This pilgrim thing was pretty hard going I reasoned. My body was now exhibiting signs of what I liked to refer to as 'pilgrimage rejection syndrome'. All of my muscles were sore. In fact, everything was aching. My feet were super tender and I was walking like a cripple. Not to mention I was just so incredibly tired. Sometimes it felt like my body was almost tricking me into wrong turns, just to see if it could get me furious or in pain enough to quit. I was becoming wise to the challenge, no matter what state I was in. It was comforting to see that everyone, bar the locals, looked like some kind of ninety-five-year-old geriatric whether they were twenty or fifty-years-old. Thank goodness I wasn't the only one.

I'd been walking a fair bit with Benzion, a twenty-six-year-old Jewish chap from Manhattan. He was a burlesque artist which apparently wasn't particularly lucrative, because he was also a pastry chef, a waiter, a tutor, a baklava chef, and a bartender on the side.

"God, my orgy has pretty much worn off," he lamented. Did I mention he was camper than a feather duster?

"Orgy!" I exclaimed. "Do tell!" It was time to spice up this pilgrimage.

"Well," he said in his New York Jewish twang, "I totally had sex with five men in two hours at the gay sauna in Barcelona just before I started," he said rapidly, leaning in to me. "Ya know, to fill the tank?"

"Oh yes," I agreed heartily. "I feel you. It's been drier than the heart of a haystack for me, so I actually resorted to taking care of business the other afternoon in the dorm room," I said.

"No!" he said with a dramatic shocked-but-not-shocked face.

"Well, yes it was a rather sensational roll of the dice where I banked on hopefully no one walking into the fifteen-bed dorm room, but I think the added excitement of an impending pilgrim bursting in on me made it quicker and better," I confessed.

"Oh, you are so naughty, I love it," he gushed.

I love the gay boys. They love every last dirty detail and nothing fazes them. Benzion was suitably impressed as I gave him the highlights of my New York dating career. The marauding Moroccan who threw me around my apartment so much I was bruised from head to toe, requiring a scarf for two weeks. D1, D2, D3 and D4, the four Davids I dated simultaneously which caused for much confusion. Eric Benet Guy 1 and 2, both the spitting image of Halle Berry's incredibly hot husband, who Benzion also fancied the pants off. And the inevitable Hot Bartender of course.

As I came to the end of the Navarro region, I reflected on the spectacular scenery I had been witnessing every day, although my body did not have the same appreciation for the constantly changing countryside. I rarely got a few hours of unbridled peace before it spat the dummy these days overpowering any attempt at spiritual connection. Or was that the point? I wasn't really a fan of this old school idea of suffering for enlightenment. Sore feet, sore hips, sore calves, sore neck, sore back, sore shoulders. My body seemed so royally pissed off it could literally say 'FU' in a hostile tone. Barely a week in and I was starting to feel the tiniest bit sorry for myself. Enter Mrs Midlife Crisis, an Aussie in her early forties, who had escaped her family and white picket fence down in the South Pacific to come to Spain and re-evaluate her life. She had been having a terrible run of pilgrim luck so far, ranging from the flu to food poisoning to some severe skin rashes. After hearing about all of this in great detail, I had no doubt there was more to come. There was something about her that told me this might well continue until Santiago. That is if she ever made it. It yanked me straight back into having a better perspective. I had a lot to be thankful for, given at this point I was still relatively unscathed. The trail had so far been full of stories of lethal blisters, ill health, deaths and injury. There had even been cases of people falling off top bunks in the middle of the night. Now we were in a new territory that came with three-tier bunk beds, the danger was even more real. This pilgrimage caper was not for the faint-hearted.

I walked 9.5km from Viana to Logroño next, my mouth watering when I saw a giant Comunidad de la Rioja sign. Yes, Rioja. I had officially crossed an entire region of Spain. Logroño was a big bustling city, unsurprising being the capital. I passed loads of peregrine pilgrim graffiti art wishing *Buen Camino* as I wound my way through the outer city streets, following the shell symbols and yellow arrows. I thought my Spanish was coming along nicely, until another incident at lunch where I ordered what I thought was a vegetable tapas. It turned out to be something I can only imagine coming from somewhere I didn't want to eat. I surreptitiously snuck it into my backpack for a stray dog, feigning satisfying deliciousness and that I had wolfed it down in record speed to the lovely man behind the counter. This was followed by lots of hunger-related miming as I ordered my standard tortilla española afterwards. There was only a certain amount of frittata one could eat, but it was my go-to in emergencies such as these. I demolished it rather quickly before heading off again towards Navarrete.

After an unremarkable stay in Navarrete, I cracked on through another stunning sunrise and the quaint little town of Ventosa. I passed an area full of hundreds of piles of small stone stacks, which I had seen here and there in a much smaller scale along The Way. These were what the Spanish call *milladoiros*, to show the way for others, originally a pagan custom to invoke spirits to protect travellers. I placed my rock on top of one of the many small towers, saying a small prayer of thanks for being guided and protected thus far. Oh, and if I could get a spiritual awakening or past life experience à la Shirley MacLaine, that'd be great too I added at the end. Something, anything! When I reached Nájera I had done plenty of kilometres for the day and was contemplating the various albergues over a midday vino with Mrs Midlife Crisis. She was filling me in on her latest development - constipation. A few pilgrims came by the table including Spanish Victor. He explained that they were on their way to a fiesta in Santo Domingo that night, one of the most famous villages on the Camino. My ears pricked up immediately. Did someone say fiesta? It was another 21km away but with an injection of vino rosado I had renewed vigour to make the journey. Mrs Midlife Crisis was less enthused considering the extra weight she was carrying in her bowels and elected to stay put to try and find some prunes.

The scenery through Rioja had changed dramatically from the previous lushness to something akin to the Arizona of Spain. It was dry country, with giant red rocks, endless grapevines and eternal sunshine. When I arrived in Cirueña, it was thirty-five degrees Celsius and 32km later. I must have been mad to undertake such a massive daily quota, but the lure of a fiesta and potential FOMO, (fear of missing out) was too much to dismiss. I fuelled up on a salad and two cervezas to make the last 6km into Santo Domingo de la Calzada a breeze. I met Simone and Bridgette from Germany, Victor the Spaniard and Marcus the Italian along the way engaging in standard pilgrim banter about the state of our feet, the weather and the previous day's kilometres until we entered into town. Again, I talked with fervour about my Milky Way zapping, but sadly I had nothing new to add to my spiritual experiences thus far. Quite disappointing, given by this point Shirley had had a tonne.

When we arrived, there were no beds available in any albergue. Just what we needed after eight hours of hiking in what was essentially the Spanish desert. I was beside myself and ready to collapse on the side of the road somewhere when there was a ray of hope. Thank goodness I was with the Europeans who could work out what was going on and get directions. We were dispatched down the road to the local school. Before long we arrived at the school gymnasium a short walk away, where we had the entire floor space at our disposal, the size of two basketball courts. The guys dragged down some thick gymnastics mats to sleep on, which were actually more comfy than some of the beds I'd slept on so far. We set up our beds for the night all together on the side of the giant gymnasium by the stadium seating. It was kind of like school camp. Not so bad after all. There were showers and toilets and everything we needed and the added benefit of no albergue curfew. Perfect.

The fiesta that night was a visual feast. There was a fair set up down the main street with neon lit carousels, games, balloons, candyfloss, the works. The street was decorated with banners of two chickens facing Saint Dominic hanging above. The town was named after the Benedictine monk who had devoted his life to pilgrims in the eleventh century. It seemed the entire town was out on the streets in their Sunday best, apart from a group of about twenty guys. They had red bandanas tied around their necks and were all wearing identical t-shirts. The t-shirts depicted a chimpanzee with its arms around the neck of some guy, obviously their mate, and likely the guy in the monkey suit they were wheeling around town in a giant locked cage. They would occasionally stop to make a spectacle and hurl peanuts at him.

However, the sight that made the strongest impression on me that night was Gabriel. He was a pilgrim I had seen along the trail in various towns. Whenever I saw him I lost all notion of time and space I was so transfixed by his good looks. Tan, muscly but not too built, come to bed eyes, glistening stubble and a killer smile. Totes Euro vibe. He was absolutely dreamy. I had never officially met him until this evening. Oh mi dios, I thought to myself as I attempted to act cool and aloof instead of a desperate pilgrim stalker. It was hard not to gawk at him obsessively as we toured the sights and bars of the town. We were all out, pilgrims en masse. After substantial imbibing, we stopped by the cathedral for their famous Mass. The church was packed.

"Church is like aerobics for old people," whispered Spanish Victor in my ear as the service started. I stuffed an attack of the giggles deep down in my chest taking in the scenery as a distraction. Directly across from the tomb of Saint Domingo was an ornately decorated green and gold altar structure with the town symbols of a painted hen and cock above it. A real cage with the live version of these animals inside, sat underneath. They proceeded to cock-a-doodle-doo throughout the entire service. Legend of the cock and hen allegedly dates back to an ancient incident involving a teenage German pilgrim travelling with his parents on a sacred pilgrimage to Santiago. The daughter of the innkeeper where they stayed for a few days fell passionately in love with him, propositioning him the night before they were due to leave. Being on a religious excursion, the young German declined her advances, at which point she vindictively planted a silver bowl in his bag. The next morning, she cried thief, and despite his innocent protests, he was arrested, found guilty and then hung. His body was left on show for a week as an example. His parents went back to the gallows after dark to say their final goodbyes to their son's dead body before they continued their pilgrimage. They were amazed to find that their son was still alive. He said, "Fear not, my dear father and mother. Blessed Saint Domingo holds me in his arms now as I speak. Run, run with all your might and tell the honourable judge that I am alive. Saint Domingo will perform a miracle!"

When the parents rushed to the judge's home they were turned away by the servant as the judge was eating his dinner. They barged their way through to the judge who was just about to plough into his dinner of two roast chickens. He did not believe their story saying, "My dear pilgrims, your boy can be no more alive than these two chickens." At which point the chickens came squawking to life, jumping off the table and crowing as they ran away.

Given the cautionary tale, I was on my best behaviour for the rest of the fiesta, despite the alluring Gabriel.

I heard later in the evening that if the rooster crows while a pilgrim is in the Cathedral of Santo Domingo, those who hear it are considered to have special favour in the eyes of Saint Domingo. I felt truly blessed. I stumbled home in the wee hours to a host of other pilgrim bodies littering the floor of the gymnasium.

Be and experience as you wish.
This planet is about the experience.
The entirety of experience.

Be in joy and fulfil your destiny.
To be the light you truly are at this time on the planet.
In simplicity. The simplicity of your daily life.

There are no extraordinary circumstances required here.
There are no longer any places to be or things to do.
Just be.

As when you are conscious in your light,
no matter where or what or who, you are you.
The you, you came here to be.
Your version of the light in physical form.

This is completing your mission on the planet.
This is remembrance.
This is unity.
This is love.

The Universe Has An Interesting
Sense Of Humour

When I departed at 6.30am the next morning, there were a few pilgrims still partying in the corner after being up all night. That morning I was reminded again that nasty hangovers and pilgrimage treks should not mix. This may be obvious to some but my terrible FOMO, combined with questionable willpower, meant socialising and boozing to excess, often so far. This was not a new thing for me. I was no stranger to a good time, no matter what situation I might have to deal with the next day. I blame genetics as I most definitely got this stamina and enthusiasm for good times from Devo. I was feeling it for sure, but not as much as the party-all-night-pilgrims who were lit up like Christmas trees as I passed them on my way out. Perhaps I wasn't so bad after all.

As I slowly got into the rhythm of the day, I spotted snow on the mountains in the distance, exactly in the direction I was heading. I felt my stomach flip. I realised afresh I had no snow gear whatsoever. Although given I'd pretty much experienced the full gamut of weather so far and made it through okay, I convinced myself I would manage. It was not too far to Grañón, a tiny little town of one street and some decrepit buildings, where I spied a familiar Alsatian and packs sitting outside a bar. Hallelujah, an excuse for a break. I was just in time to order with the Spaniards, requesting whatever they were having plus a tortilla. I noticed the bartender making three coffees, each with a generous nip of booze in it. I had observed that the Spaniards generally seemed to start with a carajillo, or a shot of straight liquor in coffee at 7am, and then continue on with several drinks throughout the day until the evening. Surprisingly, they were never drunk but instead moved through the day in a constant state of semi-saucedness. No one blinks an eye at ordering a rather strong kick in the pants in the early hours of the morning. I'd come on this pilgrimage with expectations of a puritanically spiritual experience. In fact, I needed it after being a vehement booze hound for years. Apparently, that wasn't very Spanish in the slightest. I took it as a sign from the Universe that perhaps detox wasn't on the agenda after all.

After finishing our coffee, the three of us and the Alsatian set on our way. I was suddenly feeling absolutely magnificent. Not only was my hangover easing, but I couldn't feel the dull pain in my muscles anymore. I had finally figured out how to meld the painful existence of a pilgrim with authentic Spanish life, which was a marked improvement all round. I must be a complete muppet to have not realised this earlier. Especially given the fact that most booze is cheaper than water. I was now a pilgrim in much less pain. Thank you Spain, for being such an excellent teacher. I made a mental note to be more Spanish at all times from now on.

I said farewell to the boys who were taking it slow due to the tender paws of their pooch, and powered on ahead. Despite the snow-capped peaks looming in the distance, I wasn't worried. I'd survived the Pyrenees in torrential weather. How bad could it be? I gazed up at the vivid sky blue, filling my lungs with the beauty of it all. I passed through Redecilla del Camino, a couple of kilometres later, Castildelegado, then Viloria de la Rioja. I was aiming to stay at Villafranca that night 18km away.

An hour later, out of nowhere, I was hit with a howling gale. I stretched out my right leg with all my strength and it lingered in mid-air. It was slow motion at best. I stomped my boot down firmly to get it to the ground and then started to pull up my left. The force of the wind was holding me stationary. Was this some kind of cosmic joke? Had Mother Nature heard me talking about the fact that I had experienced the full range of weather and just wanted to point out that I had missed gale force winds? It's not often you are power walking and making little to no progress.

It was a rather depressing irony to think of the hundreds of kilometres to go, while simultaneously going nowhere. All my energy was taken with trying to stay vertical and move forward. I had never felt anything like the force of this. I suddenly felt stinging on my legs. I was now being pelted by stones as the wind ramped up even further. In fact, as the intensity increased it felt like they were being fired from a machine gun. I never read anything about needing bloody body armour for this damn pilgrimage. My pack straps were lashing at my sides and the back of my legs leaving red welts as I struggled forward. I hadn't eaten lunch and was rolling the back end of my hangover. The wheat fields were swaying wildly beside me in a mesmerising pattern. As I was sucked in by the rolling waves, I realised I was hallucinating. Was it some kind of acid flashback from my experimental youth? I shook my head out of the lure of my trippy surroundings to concentrate on the task at hand.

After struggling on for another two hours without much progress, the conditions finally got the better of me and I pulled an emergency stop at the closest refugio I could find in Tosantos. There were no two ways about it. I was benched.

I was ushered through a low-ceilinged doorway by a monk. He didn't say much, nor make eye contact and directed me down the hall under low exposed wooden beams. Making my way upstairs, I found myself in what appeared to be an attic. The long, sloping roof was uneven, and exposed wooden tree branches jutted from a very rough plastering job. It looked rather ramshackle. I raised my eyebrows at the other couple of pilgrims in the room. "Is this it then?" I said, pointing to the paper-thin, woven mat on the floor. The pilgrims nodded. They didn't seem particularly friendly either. The whole place had a very strange air to it. Although it would have been even scarier if I was alone, so I was thankful for the company.

We went downstairs at 7pm for dinner and prior to digging in, the monk announced he was going to lead a singing prayer. I was excited to experience this after the exquisitely haunting sounds of the monks singing in Roncesvalles. I hadn't heard anything as beautiful since. The monk started making some rather guttural sounds from the back of his throat, which I thought was initial throat clearing, however it progressed into a multi-tonal wailing, which was not much better. It was more strangled cat than singing. I could feel the laughter rising, which I pushed down, by holding a stoic smile. My body shuddered as I held it deep within, eyes tightly shut waiting for him to finish. He breathed out heavily and I relaxed thinking he was done, only for him to start up again in the next breath. It was a sort of freestyle feline strangulation symphony. He continued wailing over and over again as the entire table somewhat poorly followed along to join in. I looked at the table, not a vino in sight. Lord have mercy. The dinner, if you could call it that, was a bowl of insipid mush and I was glad for my snack stash upstairs. I raided my first aid kit and doubled up on anti-inflammatories for the night on the floor, but they didn't help much. After a shocking sleep, I got up stiff as a board early the next morning. I couldn't get out of there fast enough.

I bumped into some old chaps I affectionately referred to as The Muppets in the next town and stopped for a coffee with them. They were both sixty-seven-years-old. One was Italian by birth, living in Germany and tall and skinny, while the other was a more traditional type German, short and stout with a handlebar moustache. They were dead ringers for Statler and Waldorf, the two old men puppets who shared the balcony box in the Muppet theatre. Tall Muppet was always arriving first and making plans. Short Muppet plodded along slowly and surely on their impressive daily 30-40km. Short Muppet spoke no English but had a roaring chuckle. I had been bumping into them on and off almost daily. Their hilarious *Odd Couple versus Fawlty Towers in an episode of The Muppets* act was an absolute crack-up. After I told them of my previous night's dismal proceedings, Tall Muppet laid it on thick about their amazingly delicious three-course dinner and abundant vino while Short Muppet roared with laughter. Way to rub it in.

I was excited to arrive in Atapuerca, an archaeological site where the oldest human remains were discovered. Devastatingly, it was closed, but I met up with the Italian boys and the American couple for lunch instead. What I hadn't realised was that the young American couple were highly religious. I sat there, trying not to prickle at their religiously ingrained comments as they seemed genuinely very nice people. Of course, the conversation circled back to our feet, as it always did. Bill was off back to the refugio to tend to his, as he was now experiencing severe blistering of his little toe. "Well there is a correlation ya see," said the American guy. "Those blisters on your feet are like the material and the spiritual. We don't want those two forces to fight against each other." Now that I could agree with.

On the hill coming out of Atapuerca, the darkness was lifting to reveal a grey, moody cloud cover. I passed a giant cross set into a huge pile of stones and threw a rock of my own on, as I passed. I then noticed an armchair through the lifting darkness, randomly sitting on the hill in the wide-open space. As I continued to the very top of the hill, a giant spiral created out of thousands of tiny stones was laid in front of me. I looked down over the plains to see the twinkling lights of Burgos in the distance below. I reached Burgos a couple of hours later, after an easy 23km day. I had some chores to do in the big city including checking in at the post office. I had sent a small extra backpack from St. Jean to meet me in Santiago with my non-pilgrim clothes. It was advised to check in the main cities to ensure the package was tracked and en route. There was the small issue of the language barrier, but they seemed to be telling me that my bag was lost entirely. It totally threw me off. I felt the tears come. I was upset that my clothes, the few pairs of earrings and precious things I had sent myself could be gone for good. As I left the post office, I headed to the cathedral seeking solace and fell on the front steps. More tears. I was not having a good day. After bumping into the sympathetic Simone, Marcus and the American couple, we headed inside as a group.

The breathtaking architecture of the absolutely stunning Cathedral of Saint Mary of Burgos was a welcome distraction. Built in the gothic style, its cream-coloured multi-story facade had the most incredible ornate detailing, sporting many spires, figures with shields, suns, crosses, saints, angels, and winged beasts adorning every section of the exterior. The building was constructed with an abundance of sacred geometry, inside and out. The front showcased an intricate display of three pointed arches of the 'Portal of Saint Mary'. The 'Seal of Solomon' was a pentacle star above the main doorway and was again depicted in another consecrated circular piece above. Inside, it had an intricate eight-pointed star shaped dome roof with natural light pouring through the stained glass. It felt incredibly special to experience this magical place, its ceilings full of more sacred geometry and renaissance artwork. I stood there absorbing it all into every part of my being. The rest of the interior was full of richly sculpted wood, gold, paintings, art and sculptures. A divine visual symphony.

The following day over 31km through endless green fields and rolling landscapes under grey tinged, cloudy skies I bumped into The Muppets midway in Hontanas. I stopped to join them at the Hostal Restaurante Fuentestrella, immediately taking off my boots to get my swollen feet into the air. Although swollen, I was still miraculously blister free. My foot scraping, combined with the morning and evening routine to look after my feet, seemed to be paying off. We enjoyed some wine and lunch, sitting outside on the street in the now brilliant sunshine. The town consisted of a few buildings and a couple of bars with outdoor seating. Inevitably, pilgrims flocked there to while away the afternoon. Sure enough, Mrs Midlife Crisis appeared, hobbling towards us.

"Is there a Farmacia in this town? We're not even halfway there and this hobbilitis is killing me," she said, coughing. Her hip and leg were obviously still playing up, not to mention she was still coping with the end of her never-ending flu.

"And now look at this!" She thrust her legs in my direction. The rash had progressed to alligator skin that spread from her arms to her legs. "It's on my feet too."

I probably shouldn't ask about the constipation.

"Oh my gosh. No pharmacy here I'm afraid. There are only seventy residents in this town. Oh well, you are obviously getting rid of old stuff," I said, trying to make her feel better about all of her ailments. "I believe there's always a rhyme or reason for these kinds of things. If it's any consolation, I have crippling joint and muscle pain, pretty much daily now too," I said slugging back the rest of my rosé. "That's why I need another one of these," I said getting up with my glass. "Anyone?"

Just after Hontanas I officially started walking the Meseta Central, or central plateau which would last for the next eight days. The pilgrim grapevine had warned me that there was little to no shade and to take plenty of water. I purchased a cheesy grey 'Camino de Santiago' hiking hat in preparation. As expected, I woke to a clear blue day, the sun glistening across the various shades of green of the mostly flat terrain. After passing through two small towns, the now off-white dirt road could be seen winding and weaving through fields and paddocks, punctuated by large pieces of metal farming equipment scattered around. I could see the odd pilgrim up ahead as I passed more scallop shell signs guiding me to Boadilla del Camino, where a herd of sheep blocked the road for some time as I headed into town for lunch.

Upon arriving in the village, I was met by a delightful little old Spanish gentleman. Despite the heat, he was wearing a shirt, tie and dress pants. Layered over the top was a trout fishing vest adorned with various pins from around the globe. His black dress hat, also studded with decorative pins, was worn on a slant framing his kind sparkling eyes, dimples and cute smile. He was wearing a Parisian lanyard around his neck and many bracelets, which looked to have been gifted to him from various peregrines. He must have been in his seventies, was very chatty and utterly charming. My two-week-old Spanish skills picked up from the road were sadly not up to scratch enough to extract the full potential of the conversation, but it was a heart-warming chat with this pilgrim cheerleader nonetheless. He wanted to take a picture with me but was struggling with his camera, which looked like one of the first digital cameras ever made. An English pilgrim woman arrived and took over the photographic duties, capturing us as he cuddled up against me, barely reaching my shoulder.

It was only another 6km to Frómista where I dumped my things at the albergue and freshened up. I spent the afternoon exploring some of the beautiful Romanesque churches, supposedly some of the most perfect in all of Spain. The following day looked to be another scorcher. Awakening quite stiff, I took a slower pace as I meandered through Población de Campos and Villalcázar de Sirga and then on to Carrión de los Condes. This was a vital stop as the guidebook warned,

IMPORTANT: Before leaving Carrión, buy some food and plenty of water. Between Carrión and the next town Sahagún (43km) is an arid plain with little accommodation except the hostal (15km) and a few bars and shops in Calzadilla de la Cueza.

I was contemplating staying in Carrión when I bumped into Mrs Midlife Crisis. She convinced me to crack on with her, so off we went planning to stay in Calzadilla, 17.5km away according to my guidebook. We caught up to The Muppets shortly after leaving town, who were walking with an Italian lass.

We walked in unison along the long winding dirt road in the afternoon sun. It was a glorious day, with vibrant greens emanating from the landscape ahead and wildflowers winking different colours at us from the side of the road. It was astonishing to think of the hundreds of thousands of pilgrims who had walked this path ahead of us since ancient times. Shirley said famous heavy-weight peeps, some with max spiritual cred had been down this road like St. Francis of Assisi, Charlemagne, Ferdinand, Chaucer. I mean that was probably just the tip of the super spiritual iceberg. My mother Annie was convinced that I was walking this healing path for all of us, for all of our ancestors and all those who have gone before. As we are all made of energy, we are in fact all connected, and so by one of us undertaking healing, adventure or expansion in any way, it ricochets into the collective field of energy for the benefit of all. I wondered what famous feet had walked ahead of me in times gone past paving the way for all of us.

Mrs Midlife Crisis was racing ahead as usual and we soon lapped The Muppets powering forward. We were about 25km into our day and battling the oppressive heat rising from the plains. By then the laundry hanging from my pack was crispy dry and when we came to a small tree with a teensy amount of shade, Mrs Midlife Crisis decided to have an impromptu siesta. She collapsed into the wildflowers on the side of the road right there and then. I'd never stopped for a siesta before, but it sure was hot enough to start now. I ditched my boots in favour of my trainers which were far less hot, and much more comfortable. We had a twenty-minute break before gingerly getting up again to attack our last 12km. My tender feet and aching hips were feeling every single step, and my shoulders were burning. Despite ridding myself of most extraneous materials, I was still carrying 12kg in my pack. My hips were in such severe pain, I let Mrs Midlife Crisis race off. My pelvic pain had gotten progressively worse over the last five days and was now starting to become unbearable. A few kilometres later I saw a big red 'Taxi 9299556' scrawled on the road in paint. Exceptionally good placement and extremely tempting, however, I pushed through the pain barrier and the debilitating Spanish sun, arriving in Calzadilla in the late afternoon for some medicinal vino.

The eternal truth that you are is the creator,
is the light, is the peace, is the joy.
For only momentarily clouded in the imbalance.
The imbalance of your being, through emotion, body, mind.
The knowing of all aspects of your beingness,
to bring you back in to balance, is the key.

Be here now. Be here in your body, fully and completely.
Be here in your mind, present and conscious.
Be in alignment with the all that is.
For this is where the magic lies.

Pilgrim Crisis Mode

The next morning, I departed early, taking the pilgrim path alongside the road. About 12km later, at the entrance to Moratinos, two blackboard signs took my attention. They were standing against a stone wall, behind an old tin watering can and two small potted plants. One read, 'Hola Peregrinos! Hay cafe y agua caliente para te y sopa. Buen Camino! James y Marianne xx.' The other, 'Please help yourselves to some tea or coffee or cold drinks in the ice box. I hope there is still some fruit and muesli bars left for you. Love James & Marianne xx.' Set back beneath a grove of young oak trees was a big old concrete water tank with a sign stating 'agua no potable'. The iron lid had been turned into a table top which was laid out with decorative mats, carved wooden boxes containing tea and for donativo, (a donation), a square tin containing muesli bars, candles, teacups, a plate of oranges, an old metal orange juice press and a couple of teapots. There were two large thermoses and a small plastic rubbish bin. My heart swelled. What a lovely thought and service. I'd just had breakfast, so I didn't stop, although the thought was very much appreciated. If only we'd come across that yesterday as we battled across the Meseta in the heat.

I walked another 12km or so passing other pilgrims on foot and bikes. My hip pain was critical now and I was enduring searing pain with every step. As soon as I reached the next village, I limped my way to the nearest farmacia. I was absolutely beside myself and on the verge of tears when the male pharmacist started asking me questions in Spanish. I pointed to my hips and burst into a flood of emotion. He smiled compassionately and went off into the back to get some pills. I hoped they were super strength to alleviate this excruciating pain. I sat outside and had them with something to eat, waiting for them to kick in so I could continue. The pilgrimage had officially brought me to my knees. And all I could do was surrender. Please God, angels, guides, anyone out there, please help me with this pain. Although not in my awareness at the time, the hips metaphysically and spiritually are all about making decisions and moving forward in life. My direction and purpose in life was something I was struggling with, and the answers were not as forthcoming as I had hoped.

After some rest, food and the horse-sized pills I was given, I was ready to continue. I was still experiencing dull pain, but not nearly as bad as before. I cracked on in quiet contemplation. An hour later I was surprised when Mrs Midlife Crisis came up behind me. She'd stopped for some lunch and a rest as she too was experiencing physical challenges. We passed a concrete sign with a yellow-painted arrow pointing to Santiago 315km away. I hoped my hips were going to last another 315km. Below the sign was the word 'Ultreia' which I thought was the next town, but Mrs Midlife Crisis informed me that it actually comes from Latin and literally means beyond. It's another salutation of the Camino. Instead of wishing people *Buen Camino,* it implies encouragement to keep going, to reach beyond. A pair of mangled abandoned boots sat next to it, both beaten and broken, an icon of the pilgrim path. It was the little push we needed to finally reach our 26km for the day to Sahagún. We were both in serious pain and were grateful to limp our weary selves into the nearest refugio.

Mrs Midlife Crisis and I agreed the next day that our new mantra would be not to exceed 25km a day. Anything more generally created some major form of crippledness for at least a day after, which was now to be avoided at all costs. Considering the poor state of her body, Mrs Midlife Crisis agreed, muttering something about being two weeks into the Camino and still not knowing how to estimate time and distance accurately. The weather had clouded over, and the uncharacteristic rain drizzled down our bright blue ponchos all morning through the endless boring landscape of the plains. These were sporadically dotted with tiny, run-down decrepit concrete towns. Despite the rain, every time we reached a new deserted town I almost expected Antonio Banderas to appear with the strum of a Spanish guitar. It was very Wild West. As we wandered, I mulled over the fact that when undertaking such ventures as a pilgrim you are supposed to have time to clear your mind and reflect on your life, not to mention experience *blow-your-mind spiritually enlightening occurrences* just like Shirley. Yet as I had made my way over the Meseta these past few days, this was very much not the case for me.

My head was filled on a day-to-day basis with some predominant thoughts. God, this hurts! What can I ditch from my 12kg pack on the side of the road right now? When are we going to get there? Is the zapping happening? And Christ, I need a vino rosado. I think the thought of the vino was the only thing that kept me going really, particularly given the €0.70 price and the fact that it was proven authentic Spanish life by having it at all hours of the day. The pilgrim figure was also proving difficult. There seemed to be a distinct lack of anything remotely healthy in Spain. The vegetarian option on every menú del día was still, hundreds of kilometres later, the dreaded beans and spuds cooked to within an inch of their life. And bread, bread, and more bread. The à la carte menu options were too expensive for this meagre pilgrim and so despite walking 30km a day, I didn't seem to be seeing any drastic changes to my body. There was still hope for me yet with more than 300km to go. Perhaps a liquid diet, less food and more wine.

The weather worsened progressively throughout the day until we were caught in a heavy thunderstorm mid-afternoon. So much for the oppressive sun of the Meseta. There were cracks of thunder echoing around and fiery streaks of lightning piercing distant grey skies. Ironically, despite the completely barren surrounds, we still managed to lose the markers. We assumed this was the usual missing signage, which is always disconcerting but a very common occurrence on the Camino. We had both been tripped up by this issue several times already. We ploughed on for some time, finally accepting our error over an hour later. We had not seen a yellow arrow or scallop shell in quite some time and were getting more sodden as time went on. It would be annoying to backtrack. Mrs Midlife Crisis saw a car passing by, heading from where we had come. She started waving her blue poncho like mad until they pulled over. Her pidgin Spanish was unsuccessful in determining where we were or being able to hitch us a lift back and they drove off, leaving us drenched and weather-beaten on the side of the road. We spent the next ten minutes not knowing where to go, sitting tight and waiting for a moment of clarity.

I proposed a detour through a paddock to attempt to get us directionally back on track. Mrs Midlife Crisis was sceptical at best, but she didn't have any better ideas. I was determined not to add another 5km to the already long and gruelling day, so I leapt the fence into a paddock, making a diagonal beeline into the never-ending green distance. It was bumpy and wet in the paddock, our boots sinking into the now mushy clay from an entire day of rain. We battled on, heads down against the elements, for a good half an hour until we saw the fence on the other side. After climbing over, we appeared to be on a road. There were no markers in sight, but I saw a tiny figure in the distance making its way towards us. As it got closer, I could see his giant pack. Another pilgrim! Hurrah! We had done it. By some miracle we had bumped straight into a Dutch pilgrim on the gravel track on the other side. Which was great news until we realised he didn't seem particularly confident on the direction either. At this point we were mentally and physically exhausted, and soaking wet so we sat down to rest on the road in the rain asking the Dutchie to give us a sign if there was actually a town up ahead. Sure enough, fifteen minutes later we saw frenetic waving in the distance, so we continued on eventually making it to Reliegos as it got dark. It was still raining. We had completely blown our 25km maximum, finishing at 31km and aching and sore all over again. We were sodden, cold and knackered. It was warm showers and a quick meal before passing out.

The following day was thankfully our last on the Meseta before reaching León. It was abnormally pissing with rain for the second day straight. The weather had caved in completely on what was supposed to be the hottest part of the Camino. Word in a local pueblo was that this was apparently the worst weather they'd seen in years. Oh, that Universe had a funny sense of humour didn't it. My gear was barely dry from the day before, but I put my damp jacket and bright blue poncho back on and set off. Mrs Midlife Crisis had raced off early, wanting to reach León in time to get to the farmacia before siesta close. Her alligator skin had progressed to Elephantitis and she was in terrible need of a consultation that wasn't so Wild West.

I was now seventeen days and 473km in. I had moved past the pilgrim pain and crisis mode and had finally entered surrender mode. All I could do was go with the flow and meet each challenge as it happened. I was getting there. I'd never been particularly sporty or attempted any kind of physical challenge, let alone one of this proportion, so I was rather pleased with my performance so far. I felt like the Jo Walden action figure taking Spain by storm. Granted, I might need an upgrade or potentially a whole new body after all this, but so far I miraculously didn't have half the problems of some of the other pilgrims. I'd met and passed younger and newer models whose feet were so bad they had to abort the mission entirely. I'd passed far fitter older people who were medically ordered home. I really had to thank my lucky stars I was still here, fit and reasonably able.

I walked for a few hours on my own marinating on all this and how proud I should be to have made it thus far before coming across Pierre-Louis. He was a young chap from Belgium with a very curly full beard and light moustache. He had long wisps of dark brown hair peeking out from his grey Trilby hat, which was adorned with a bright orange flower. He didn't seem bothered by the constant drizzle of rain, which was glistening on his beard before trickling off it onto the ground. He was generally very reserved, although every now and then I saw a wide smile and friendly eyes with a flicker of something behind them. He reminded me of some kind of nature spirit or leprechaun as he plodded along with his stick and the tiniest rucksack I had ever seen. His bag was essentially half the size of your average day pack, about a tenth of the size of my pack.

I had no idea how the hell he was surviving on so little, but the strong stench of sweat told me that he needed a bigger bag. He was the first pilgrim that didn't look at me cross-eyed when I told him about following the ley lines of the Milky Way and the energy-zapping we were receiving by walking this path. Okay, so we were halfway and I hadn't really felt any of this energy so far, but I reasoned that even if I wasn't feeling it on a physical level, it didn't mean that it wasn't happening. We can't see energy physically after all and with the number of drugs I was taking to get through, it wouldn't have surprised me that I might be numb to any sort of energetic upgrade.

As we walked through the boring paddocks of the Meseta, we became so preoccupied in our discussion about the greater questions of the Universe and why we were all here that we lost the track. Not again! We hadn't seen another pilgrim, nor a way marker since a fork in the road maybe an hour or so ago. Damn it, arrow negligence had claimed me as a victim once again. That was now twice in a row. That'll teach me. We were in the middle of nowhere. Trusting my directional intuition once again, I started climbing the fence into a field of crops just as the rain became a thunderous downpour. Pierre-Louis, The Leprechaun, didn't need much convincing on my suggested shortcut. As we made a concentrated dash through the crops in the torrential rain, I got the impression that he was no stranger to madness. On a positive note, at least in such driving rain we were in no danger of being chased by a mad Spanish farmer, which I had heard on good authority was also another very real danger in this area. Sure enough, twenty minutes later we popped out onto a road.

We headed towards the adjoining streets and a few blocks later saw another couple of pilgrims in the distance. Pierre-Louis was beyond impressed when we got ourselves back to the main path. My intuition had saved the day once again, yet I blew it off as luck. I made a note to pay closer attention when walking with other pilgrims. It certainly seemed like every time I became too engrossed in pilgrim chitchat things went awry, although these added detours seemed to spice things up a notch on the adventure side.

I finally reached the city of León after two days of trekking through torrential rain and I did what any pansy pilgrim would do. I got myself my own room in a hostal. Yes, my own room. León was 472km in and was over the halfway mark. It was time for a bit of well-deserved R&R and celebration. I happily ensconced myself in my room in Hostal Boccalino spending two nights in the biggest city on the pilgrimage so far, and the fourth largest in Spain. I indulged myself with delicious tapas, fabulous wine and perusing the beautiful sights of medieval pilgrimage in the cathedral, churches and basilica at my leisure. I even found a bag of spinach in a supermarket and some ingredients to make a *never heard of in Spain* salad when back on the road!

Mrs Midlife Crisis escorted me to the post office where we established that my bag wasn't lost and should actually be in Santiago when I got there. What a relief! It was like all my Christmases had come at once. Not to mention the cherry on top which was sleeping on a proper bed, without disturbance, and the ability to do whatever I liked, whenever I liked. Burlesque Benzion would be quite jealous.

I gave myself a complete overhaul. I dried out my gear, freshly washed everything and repacked my bag. I was almost starting to feel like a semblance of a normal person again. The odds of me actually finishing this thing seemed to be looking much better now. One other motivating factor was that the men were generally getting hotter as we got to the bigger cities. This was very exciting as my daydream fantasies of a dashing young Spanish farmer whisking me off to some farmhouse every time a tractor rolled by had gotten progressively more frequent. The build-up was reaching crucial point. Where was my pilgrim stallion when I needed him? It was quite obvious that a young, naive Spanish farmer would probably have a heart attack if he met me. Time for a new fantasy.

After León, I hiked my way to Villadangos del Páramo through heavy rain. From there I stopped in Astorga with slightly less miserable weather and the super cute Albergue de Peregrinos San Javier, an ambient new age refugio. I arrived with plenty of time to see the Palacio Episcopal, at least from the outside anyway before the afternoon thunderstorms set in. It was built by Antoni Gaudí, the famous Spanish architect. It looked more Disney castle than cutting edge architecture, but it did have a gorgeous garden with three beautiful angel statues carrying processional items that had a wonderful mystical air to them. I had dinner at the Gaudi Hotel with Mrs Midlife Crisis and Simone.

"You're looking rather tanned from the looks of your pilgrim tan lines there," said Mrs Midlife Crisis. "Another thing to add to our pilgrim pros and cons list!" she quipped.

"Why thank you! The Meseta, before the crazy unseasonable weather was at least good for something!" I laughed. "My pilgrim tan seems to be taking a downward turn though since the weather caved in. Annie seems to think we tan up nicely because we have Spanish blood in us. Or Portuguese. She's not entirely sure. Her evidence of this heritage is purely because she thinks Grandpa looked Spanish. Considering we thought we had Māori blood in us until a few years ago it's anyone's guess really." I said, casually. I'll never forget that hysterical phone call in New York from Annie. My mind leapt to the fact that someone might have died, so panicked was her voice; meanwhile it was because Devo was apparently having a full-blown melt-down. "Your father's having an identity crisis," she sobbed. "We're not Māori, we're Irish!" she shrieked into the phone dramatically.

Simone and Mrs Midlife Crisis burst out laughing. "What?! Wait, hold on a minute!" laughed Mrs Midlife Crisis incredulously. "Māori?! You're hardly Māori!" she exclaimed.

"Well, long story short, we got invited to this family reunion where everyone was Māori and the family tree showed how I descended from a Māori princess, so I was stoked, and, you know my cousin had a legit afro, so I thought anything was possible," I replied.

We made our way back to the albergue still in fits of laughter at the absurdity of it all, looking forward to our bed and a good night's rest in the dorm room. Midway through the night however, I was awoken by a stonking snorer. I was alarmed by the fact that he seemed to be making pained noises and sounding like he was actually having trouble breathing. Oh no, I thought, jolting upright. It sounded like he was having a heart attack. I listened again, getting ready to leap out and perform some kind of makeshift CPR. The noises seemed to be getting worse and worse. Was he actually about to die right there in front of me? I attempted to see more in the dark, shining my headlight just to give enough light to make out the man. I could see his face quivering as he lay in his bunk. His body was juddering and jolting as he made various disturbing noises. I was just getting out of bed when he suddenly turned over and the noises and movements subsided completely. Jesus, Mary and Joseph! He had given me the fright of my life. It was two in the morning and my adrenaline was pumping. This pilgrimage never ceased to amaze me. I took another magnesium and closed my eyes, hoping to reclaim my slumber as my heart raced.

The next day I groggily walked into the mountains, thankfully noting the bolded guidebook warnings for preparations and supplies *for the long hard 50km across the mountains of León from Astorga to Ponferrada. It is uphill virtually all the way for 30km and steeply downhill thereafter.* Surely it can't be worse than the Pyrenees, I thought, trying to quell my fears. The good news was that the scenery was finally devoid of any semblance of the repetitively boring Meseta. I walked through the Maragatería region, spotting a heart painted on a tree; it felt like a good omen. The Maragatos still live there, a proud and honest mountain people whose ethnic origins were apparently unknown, but according to the guidebook they were potentially Phoenicians or the Berbers from the ninth century. For centuries, these people were actually the muleteers carting huge amounts of cargo.

I saw a figure carrying some kind of wheeling trolley up ahead, but as I got closer I realised it was a fellow pilgrim, not a muleteer. As I grew near I realised this grey-bearded man had two walking sticks, a traditional pilgrim hat with a scallop shell attached to the rolled-up brim at the front and wore an elaborate vest. From his trolley swung the symbolic dried butternut squash pumpkin. The pumpkins were used to carry water and although not in use today, they were still a strong symbol of The Way. This was quite possibly the most kitted out, traditional pilgrim I had seen the entire journey. After a cordial greeting, I realised he was French.

The villages were high up in the mountains and black and tan goats roamed through the bumpy dirt and stone streets. I passed a big wooden cross through one village with shingle cottages left and right. I read later that night that the cross commemorates a Swiss pilgrim who collapsed and died there in September 1998. I saw nobody, except one little old lady. She was covered from head to toe in various brown shades of winter woollies, including her wooden cane which she was fiercely leaning her weight on to get up a particularly steep part of the stony overgrown road. A grubby looking stray cat followed at a distance. Most of the stone cottages were in various states of ruin and I wondered exactly how people lived up here in these decrepit, albeit unconventionally beautiful surrounds. A cow, heavy with bursting udders, mooed as I passed a church set prettily against a backdrop of blue-grey skies. It seemed to be clouding over rather rapidly. After the villages I kept climbing upwards and met a thick mist slowly creeping in, softening the bright pink mountain wildflowers on the bushes that flanked both sides of the road. I kept going past the remains of an original pilgrim church and hospice and continued upward.

I could barely see through the fog at this point. Was I potentially gearing up for Death Defying Pyrenees Round Two? No, all was well, and I finally reached the Cruz de Ferro, the cross on the Camino at 1504m. A tall pole with a small cross mounted on the very top of a cairn, it was traditionally constructed from stones from the hometown of each pilgrim who passed by. Pilgrim flags, ribbons, notes, flowers, scarves, stickers and all sorts of tokens had been tied to the pole, which was originally to help pilgrims find their way across the mountains. Not long after me the Frenchie with his trolley arrived. He was worried about the weather. He was right as it was noticeably colder and the fog was getting ever thicker. I cracked on, passing the obligatory myriad signs showing the distance to Mexico 9376km,

Jerusalem 5000km, Machu Picchu 9453km, Rome 2475km and finally something useful, Santiago 222km. I descended down misty sage green hills with cattle grazing quietly. The scenery was spectacular despite the haze. Yellow and purple wildflowers were peeking through the wild grasses as I went down the stony road, looking down on the roofs of the village a short way ahead. This was Foncebaddon and after 26km of incline, I was glad to find a new private refugio and claim my bed for the night.

Walk. Journey. Take your time.
There is a whole world open to you.
A world beyond that which you see in front of you.
There is nothing you need to do or be or think.
Just be in the knowingness of all that is
For you are processing the old to make way for the new.
A new chapter.
A new way of being and living.
A new mode of apparatus.

Everything is happening as it should.
The doors are opening and there is much prized information,
for those who come in purity of love and peace.
All the information already beats within you.

The Highs And Lows Of Tippy-Toe Jo

The next day I passed the abandoned village of Manjarín and not long after reached the highest point of the Camino Frances; 1517 metres. *Don't be fooled, it's not all downhill to Santiago – far from it!* warned the guidebook. Way to rain on my parade. It was 7km to El Acebo, 4km to Riego de Ambrós, 4.5km to Molinaseca and 8km to Ponferrada. Each village was cuter than the last. Gorgeous historical stone houses with tiny balconies tumbling with red flowers; Romanesque bridges and gorgeous, colourful wild poppies. It was romantic and medieval and dreamy all at the same time.

When I arrived in Ponferrada I was certainly ready to put down my pack after a punchy 27.5km day. Unfortunately, the way marking to the refugio left a lot to be desired which provided a frustrating end to the day. Had I consulted my trusty guidebook more closely, I would have been advised of this, not that it would have helped, as it didn't contain directions either. Once I finally got to the refugio I headed straight for the showers. Feeling clean and refreshed, I was making my way outside when I noticed a young South African chap tending to his very raw blistered feet on the balcony. I winced as I passed.

"Shit. Are you okay bro?"

"Yeah," he said slowly, "they're infected. The doctor told me my Camino is over. I have to go home yah. He told me not to walk for the rest of the year."

I was shocked. He looked fit and healthy and far more likely to make it to the end of the Camino than a veritable lush like moi. Shaking my head in disbelief, I made my way to the plaza, passing four delightful old ladies sitting together on a park bench. With their hand fans and newspapers, they were enjoying a good old gossip. There was something inspiring and delightful about this up close and personal view of real Spanish life; it was miles away from how we lived in Auckland. After a photo, I spied Mrs Midlife Crisis and Burlesque Benzion having a beer on the other side of the square.

"How's your Camino body going?" asked Benzion immediately, before updating me that he'd had to have another two masturbations en route, and that he'd already lost twenty-one pounds. He was clearly a front-runner in this competition.

"Oh, and get a load of this," he said excitedly in typically camp fashion. "I heard through the pilgrim grapevine that some French bird got locked out of her albergue because she was getting a pilgrim 'seeing to' on her birthday. Not only that but it's her *third* guy in a row on the trail."

Mrs Midlife Crisis raised her eyebrows. "Good on her," she said.

"Well, she shits all over my performance," I said, "which at well over the halfway mark, is a big fat zero pilgrim stallions. In other news, there's a Saffa in my albergue with feet so infected he's being sent home by the doctor and can't walk for the next seven months!" Cue horrified gasps from my audience.

It was grey, drizzly and cold the next day, so I was back under my bright blue poncho to combat the miserable weather. Finding some trees en route laden with deliciously sweet cherries brightened my day immensely. Looking out over the lush green scenery set against the grey skies, I could see the mountains of Galicia. They were not so far away now at all. I wandered through Camponaraya and then stopped in a bar in Cacabelos for a warming drink and tortilla. I was excited to get to Villafranca de Bierzo. It was supposed to be the most attractive place to visit along the Camino and apparently had the added benefit of excellent wines hardly known outside of Spain. The only spanner in these 'wine-excited' works of mine was that it was the final stop prior to the long steep climb up the mountains of Galicia.

True to its reputation, Villafranca's coloured houses and ancient stone structures were gorgeous despite the moody grey atmosphere and I enjoyed some of the delicious wine with other pilgrims at the albergue. Moon, a Korean pilgrim, known for her very short-stepped pilgrim shuffle finally arrived and everybody cheered. She was always the last to arrive, but never without a big smile. She really was the sweetest thing. She had even given me an amazing full-body massage one night where she used her whole body, including her feet, in miraculous ways to ease my tight muscles. Sometime later we all went out for dinner, where I found myself resigned to the standard pilgrim fare and destined to never achieve that ever-elusive pilgrim bod.

After a few more sumptuous red wines I wisely cut myself off and went to bed, knowing the task of the morning would be horrific, or perhaps impossible if I was suffering a hangover. By morning, I was glad to start walking and warm up after having to shower outside in the cold.

From Villafranca there was the choice of three routes, one via the road, and two up through the mountains with extra kilometres and steeper climbs. My friend Stephen had recommended the second route via Pradela. It was still steep but only two extra kilometres. I left town early in the misty chill of the morning. I enjoyed more lush brilliant green scenery as I wove my way into the mountains. The trail seemed really busy this morning as everyone was up and at 'em, determined to get a head start on conquering the mountain. As we crept higher and higher, I overtook the Frenchies, and many other familiar pilgrim faces. I thrust my lips to the free flowing agua of a stone water fountain en route and stopped briefly in Herrerías, one of the last towns before the steep climb up O Cebreiro. Although it was only 8km, the guidebook advised it would take three hours due to the intensely vertical incline.

It was a stunning walk to the little hamlet of La Faba. Wonderfully ancient churches made of stone and enormous trees all set against bright green surrounds. There was something very Robin Hood about the entire scenery. It felt magical. I was deep in thought considering all the possibilities that lay ahead in life for me as I wound my way up a muddy path covered in overgrown emerald-coloured vines and brush. I soon overtook Hot Gabriel and rowdy Australian bushranger Katie to continue ploughing upwards, higher and higher. There were a few hard grafts, but I generally found the 29km climb up to O Cebreiro not as difficult as I was expecting. I guess despite not seeing the dramatic weight loss I was envisioning, there was something to be said about the progress of the strength of this pilgrim bod after all.

O Cebreiro was situated at the top of the last lot of mountains on the whole of the Camino. Thank effing God. On reaching the top, the fruits of my efforts were obscured by heavy, frosty mist. I quickly cracked on with finding somewhere warm to stay instead. It was a tiny town of twenty or so stone houses, some with typically Galician thatched roofs. The village was purpose-built for the Camino and appeared to be somewhat of a tourist trap. I was informed the albergue was 'under repair,' so I was given a spot in a temporary albergue, which was eight bunk beds shoved in a trailer. It was absolutely freezing, and the bathroom was in a separate trailer altogether with no hot water. It was almost too cold even for a birdbath, so I did a quick wipe, changed clothes and set off to find a snack.

I found a cute little kitchen with a stable door and ordered some queso con miel, a local specialty of fresh cheese drizzled in yummy local honey atop fresh bread. It was absolutely divine. Later, I enjoyed yet another menú del día at a place which supposedly had a view overlooking the mountain, although given the weather I couldn't see much at all. I bumped into various pilgrim friends from the road and we sat together. They were commenting at how fast and strong I was which completely took me by surprise. I tried to contain my laughter and smiled on the inside given I was the most unlikely candidate for this kind of compliment. In the same breath though they were oddly very concerned about my feet. I looked at them quizzically.

"You walk on your tippy-toes the whole time. Each time we see you, you are always walking on your tiptoes. We are wondering as to the terribly bad shape of your feet if you can't put your heels on the ground?"

They were genuinely distressed. I knew I'd always walked on tippy-toes as a child but had no idea I was still doing it now.

"Haha, no, my feet are fine. I've only had three teeny blisters the entire way. A miracle really."

How fascinating. Unbeknownst to me I had been tiptoeing across the north of Spain. Surely there was some kind of Guinness Book of Records award for something like this?

"We will call you Tippy-toe Jo," they said.

The next morning, I had an early start hoping to see some of this acclaimed view but was met with a complete white-out. There were a few more valleys, hills and villages to go before heading 13km downhill to Triacastela. As I wandered, I reflected back on the surprising number of compliments I had received about my pilgrim performance. Now, as I was bounding down the mountain like Bambi in the springtime, I had a revelation. It was possible that I might accidentally be good at hiking. No training, minimal prep, barely a blister the entire journey. Maybe this all added up to be my undiscovered gift, my calling?! Who knew I would discover a hidden talent on this pilgrim path? I had instant visions of taking hiking championships all over the world by storm. Well, mostly of me busting open the fizzing bottles of champagne with my trophy really. Probably more motorsport than hiking. Maybe it was my destiny to change the face of hiking championships forever! Perhaps this was my ticket to fame and living the life of my dreams!

Triacastela was a welcome reprieve from the mountains and Mrs Midlife Crisis was already at the albergue when I arrived. Burlesque Benzion rolled in soon after, followed by Stephen and the French Couple. Against all odds this wee lush of a Kiwi lass had made it 646km. I only had approximately 150km to Santiago to go. I was almost in disbelief. I should have agreed to my brother setting up that betting scheme now that I was veritably beating the odds. Although the triumph of meeting the physical goals was great, I was still nowhere near my spiritual goals, of some kind of supernatural experience. I was, however, in good time to shop for some much-needed vegetables to cook dinner at the albergue. I cooked up a huge plate of zucchini with onions, garlic and topped with fresh avocado. The Frenchies' noses lit up with the smell of my meal, and they came over to have a good ol' look at what I was eating. Hallelujah for vegetables. It was almost a spiritual experience after all.

I was now twenty-four days in, and it was again pissing with rain. I had a 31.5km hike ahead of me to Ferreiros. It was more mystical Sherwood Forest style with perfectly lush, vibrant scenery, possibly due to all the rain that we had been experiencing. Apparently, I had chosen to trek cross country in the rainiest season they had seen in Spain for a very long time. Figures. The sun finally came out in the afternoon while walking from Sarria to Ferreiros, shining on charming countryside filled with enormous amounts of delicate pale coloured wildflowers, stone walls and mossy trees. This part of the Camino through Galicia was so far my absolute favourite; its beauty could not even be dampened by the rain. It certainly rewarded those who made it through this mountainous region which could only be seen by foot.

It was still hard to tell whether my zapping from the Milky Way was making any progress as I'd not seen the stars any night since I'd begun. I hadn't noticed any particular spiritual changes and, disappointingly, I had not had any past life flashes or spirit visitors or visions or been taken to the very origin of the Universe, let alone Atlantis or Lemuria; *clears throat, thanks Shirley. I felt underwhelmed. I had spent a lot of contemplative walking time alone, appreciated some sacred sites and yet still, nothing. Still time left though spirits, masters, energies, anyone! I'm waiting. However, waiting for me in Ferreiros was Ingrid, a delightful middle-aged strawberry haired Austrian woman who I had met a few days prior. We shared some traditional Galician gastronomic delights including pulpo gallego, or octopus boiled in giant vats of red wine. It was remarkably tender and served sliced with a drizzle of olive oil and a sprinkle of smoked paprika. The delicious Albarino white wine was the perfect accompaniment. That was one thing I had to love about this pilgrimage, literally everybody enthusiastically drinks the wine at every opportunity, and for some reason it never seemed to make one drunk. Both of us were terribly excited that it looked like we were going to make it to Santiago in about four or five days. We had less than 100km to go. I was still somewhat in shock at myself, truth be known.

It was a beautiful sunrise as I set off the next morning and the rain seemed to have finally eased. I walked on to Portomarín which was a pleasant but unremarkable stretch of the Camino. Portomarín itself was disappointingly modern after being rebuilt when the old version was submerged in the reservoir waters. It was still pretty though, so I stopped at a local bar for a refreshment where I made the acquaintance of Ben, a rather fit and good-looking Englishman with a delightfully posh accent. He was enjoying the remainder of a carajillo which was apparently excellent.

"Coffee without alcohol in Galicia is like a woman without tits," he said.

I laughed. "I guess I'll have what you're having," I said. "Uno mas," I yelled to the bartender.

English Ben made his leave, grabbing his giant pack like it weighed nothing with a swoop of his wonderfully bronze, taut biceps. The entire swift ever-so-manly manoeuvre made me want to reach out and touch them.

After fuelling up, I cracked on through the next few unremarkable towns until 34.1km later when I reached Palais de Rei. Although my pilgrim body seemed to be finally toeing the line in regards to the fitness and pain thresholds, I was spent after such a punchy amount of kilometres. I immediately rocked up to the closest refugio hoping for a bed and was glad to bump into my Spanish friends with their Alsatian. Later that afternoon at the pub, I made the mistake of asking the Spanish boys to teach me how to play cards. My beginner's luck faded quickly and then went from bad to worse. With every hand, there seemed to be a shot of the local Orujo de Hierbas, a digestive, and we burned through the bottle quicker than you could say Galicia. That was until I realised we were doing shots just for the sake of it and there was not much legitimate playing going on at all. Orujo is essentially Spanish rocket fuel and about fifty percent proof. This ensured we were all completely bombed by early evening. Thankfully I recall shovelling some pulpo and delicious goat cheese drizzled in honey down my throat at one stage before we got kicked out of the bar. Not due to me mind you, but those crazy Spaniards were so drunk by this point that they hilariously started a bit of biffo with each other. One came out of it with a mean looking shiner on the right cheek. And that was my cue to leave.

I weaved my way to bed and left them to it, only to be woken up what seemed moments later by the two of them teetering next to my bed and slurring at me for cigarettes. I awoke the next morning in a haze and saw that the two of them had never made it back to their beds in the albergue. By some stroke of luck, I had fallen into my bunk before curfew, thank goodness, and was relieved to find my camera, wallet, and passport close by. I winced with every move of my head as I stuffed my things into my pack and headed out the door, albeit much later than my usual sunrise exit routine. I nearly tripped on their two lifeless bodies, sleeping outside the front door of the refugio when I left. Ouch.

I had a roaring hangover, the extent of which was reflected in my pace as I crawled through San Xulián and Ponte Campaña, before stopping for a clara at the incredibly appropriate time of 9am. When in Spain… From then it was slow progress to Casanova, Leboreiro, Furelos, Melide, Boente, Castañeda and Ribadiso do Baixo before getting to Arzúa. A small town famous for its cheese and the second to last stop in my Camino. It had been 29.5km of absolute hangover hell. Hangovers and pilgrimages just do not complement each other in any way, shape or form. Why I continued to ignore these facts and torture myself I will never know. I put the pilgrim figure on hold and ordered some of the delicious Arzúa-Ulloa cow's milk cheese and bread. It was so delectably moreish I then decided to get some Cebreiro con miel. They also had San Simon da Costa which I hadn't tried and Burgos Queso, so I figured I better try them too whilst I was in the neighbourhood. Of course, with more delicious Spanish wine, my 'hair of the dog' saviour.

About half an hour later I felt my stomach starting to churn. This was quickly followed by sharp shooting pains. Turning a lighter shade of pale, my gut was wrenching and gurgling like it contained a creature from another planet. What transpired next was reminiscent of the scene with Meg Ryan on the train through the French countryside in *French Kiss*. Although I am not lactose intolerant, I was pretty sure this was what it feels like. I raced to the bathroom, only just making it in the nick of time as the squirts started. I moaned through a painful, explosive release. After considerable time on the toilet, I was still feeling horrible, so I made my way back to the refugio, sphincter and butt cheeks clenched tighter than a nun's you know what.

Just keep going.
Surpass the doubts and lap them as they fade into
the background of your expectations.
For in trusting all that you are, you move forward
in the weight of understanding,
that everything you innately know to do is true and
right and connected to all that you are.

Trust in yourself so implicitly that there is no other option,
no asking opinions, no looking for answers.
For the trust opens the door to the genius buried within.
There is treasure there for you,
if you trust enough,
it unlocks the door.

My Pilgrim Stallion Prize

Arzúa to Monte de Gozo, also known as Mount Joy, was the final full day's walk of the Camino. That would leave 5km tomorrow, Sunday. The perfect holy day to arrive in Santiago. Unbelievably I had only 40km to go. I was literally gobsmacked. I had completed almost 800km in twenty-nine days. Well and truly under the thirty-four days mapped out in the official guide. I was astounded. Still no sign of any kind of dramatic spiritual awakening, so it'd better hurry up as time was running out. Shirley had had a dozen breakthroughs by now! Meanwhile I was already envisioning an expensive hotel room with a fancy bubble bath and some champers. I could not wait.

As I reached St. Irene, I realised that the official concrete markers showing the kilometres left till Santiago did not match up with my guidebook. I thought I had 32km to go, but really it was 37km. This was slightly irritating. At that point, I just wanted to get the bloody thing over with. Then I caught myself. This was a once in a lifetime experience and had I been rushing it? Did that mean I was too focused on the end to be in the moment to experience the mystical experiences I was craving? Was I hustling to keep up with the rest of the crew rather than give myself the time and space I needed for the true purpose of my journey? I was annoyed at myself. There was a niggling feeling in the background that I had inadvertently deprived myself of the experience I so very much wanted.

"These pilgrimages are overrated," I muttered to myself as I plodded along, both feet and patience starting to wane.

The walk itself was pretty tough going, with lots of ups and downs and dismal scenery contributing to my mood. Screw dorm rooms and carrying your life around on your back and snoring old men. And not even one spiritual revelation to make it worth it! Damn it Shirley! I decided my backpacking days were over. Physical exhaustion, dorm rooms and rucksacks were a thing of the past. I began to make future plans in my head for a proper job in London so I could get back to the life to which I was accustomed. Back to excessively drinking for pleasure and not pain, dining alfresco on any menu you want, back to planes, trains and fancy hotel rooms. Back to being the lady of lushness that I knew so well.

I arrived at Monte de Gozo with such sore, raw feet that I had to get my boots off immediately. My romantic vision of beautiful Mount Joy and the last night of the Camino was quickly dashed by the reality of a stark concrete complex of abandoned stores, looking like some kind of weird deserted theme park. Originally one would have been able to see the towers of the cathedral in Santiago from here and therefore it was a place of great celebration for the pilgrims, but not anymore. The trees had since grown in the middle distance, blocking the view. The accommodation itself was outrageously overpriced too, just to top it off.

Slowly most of the mongrel pack of pilgrims I had met along the way started hobbling in. Burlesque Benzion, Mrs Midlife Crisis, Moon Shuffle, The Muppets, Austrian Ingrid, The Spanish Duo and their dog, Spanish Victor, Gabriel the Italian Stallion, The Frenchies, Bushwalker Katie, Posh English Ben and Aussie Jay. Not forgetting Denmark Dennis, Anty the Fin and Pierre-Louis The Leprechaun. I really had met a crazy set of characters. Maybe that was enough. Santiago was going to be a good ol' celebration with this crew if nothing else.

Cue music: Chariots of Fire.

In slow motion Pilgrim Jo hobbled into Santiago de Compostela amidst the fog and cool morning air on June 3rd, 2007. She headed for the cathedral in keeping with tradition, placed her hand on Saint James, and gave him a hug from behind whilst basking in full pilgrim glory as the priests gave a standing ovation and she saw an apparition of Saint James himself who gave her a personal blessing.

Take that Shirley.

Well actually, that didn't quite happen. In actual fact, Austrian Ingrid and I could barely keep our eyes open after a broken sleep in the rip-off albergue, so after downing a few cafe cortados in order to keep conscious, we dragged ourselves to the cathedral. I looked up at it in front of me.

"Finally. Thank fuck for that," I said to Ingrid.

I hugged the little old ugly chap in the cathedral and said, "Show me the quickest way to pilgrim rehab." Luckily he didn't understand English.

This pilgrimage had far exceeded even my primed, lady lush drinking, liver limitations. As it had with just about every other pilgrim I talked to. Instead of a spiritually enlightening experience, it was a booze cruise on legs. There, I said it. Shirley would be horrified. I tottered off to the Peregrino Office in a semi-delusional state to get my pilgrim diploma and be done with it. There was a huge queue of scruffy and dishevelled looking pilgrims waiting to get to the tiny window. I looked back at my pilgrim passport and the dozens of stamps from the past eight hundred kilometres. Coats of arms, famous pilgrim icons, an array of elaborately designed scallop shells, churches, crosses and emblems. It perfectly brought the colourful journey to life on paper. Minus the hangovers.

I put in a call to Devo and Annie to share the good news of my arrival and achievement of my final pilgrim stamp.

"Darling!" Devo answered convivially. "Congratulations. What an amazing achievement. We are very proud of you." He seemed elated. "Your mother and I have been celebrating your achievements all day in fact, over a lovely long lunch."

Brilliant. The folks were drunker than I was, and I was the one who bloody completed this ridiculous journey.

"Here talk to your mother."

There was a kerfuffle as the phone was handed over to Annie who by the sounds of it, was in a worse state than Devo.

"Hey darl. Oh, I just think it is so a-maaazing what you've done," she said slowly with a considerable slur.

"Yes great, thanks Annie," I said.

"Un-believable," she said again lost for words and sounding like she was welling up. Whether this was from genuine emotion or the long lunch I wasn't sure.

"Okay, well I'll let you get back to finishing the rest of your night. I have to get off to pilgrim Mass," I said, trying to draw the conversation to a quick close.

"Okay darling, well we love you lots, and we are just so proud of you and we… Waa, wa, wa, wa."

Her voice had turned into Charlie Brown's teacher and I didn't have the patience to continue. They were as pissed as chooks.

"Okay, gotta run, love you. Bye!" I said hanging up.

I made it back to the cathedral by 12pm to have my *moment* during famous pilgrim Mass, but not before I'd spent some quality time exploring the excellent range of mini champagne bottles at the famous Parador, a fancy Spanish hotel across the plaza. It may have been the champers, but I found the Mass to be heart-warmingly gorgeous. A nun led the singing with a spectacular voice, and the words spoken seemed filled with feeling, despite me not understanding most of it. I even had a wee tear in my eye at one point as my emotion bubbled to the surface. Thank God I'd had a few beforehand because it was a rather lengthy service. These religious types, they do go on don't they! After the fleeting moment of emotion and sacred awe, all I could seem to think of as the service plodded on, was sex. Pilgrim Stallion sex. It had been far too long and with the limited opportunity for self-gratification over the last month I was gagging for it. Prayers. Sex. Singing. Sex. I want it. I need it. Where was that legendary pilgrim love of mine? More prayers. I really needed to get laid. I was distracted by various free-form fantasies as the service continued on at snail's pace in the cathedral. Finally, amidst endless flashes of naked flesh, sweat and the release of a final pilgrim-shagging celebration with my imaginary Pilgrim Stallion, the service finally came to an end. Then, I was off for a refresher quite quickly.

That evening our pilgrim gang met in our best dress, at a gorgeous tapas bar with an array of amazing pinchos. Being Sunday, I wasn't able to pick up my parcel from the post office which was a shame. I had found nothing to wear so was in the same thrashed pilgrim garb which I attempted to dress up with my flowery sarong. I could not wait to burn these clothes. We ate gorgeous food and drank a plentitude of cava to celebrate. Pilgrims around me were having dramatic tearful reunions like lifetime long lost friends, which I couldn't help but feel was a little much. It was camaraderie overkill in my mind, but then again, I had often carved my own path and spent a lot of time solo chasing my elusive spiritual enlightenment. This pilgrimage had certainly been a sizeable challenge. It was the hardest thing I had ever done in my life. I had surprised not only everyone at home, but especially myself, by making it through. There was a saying that people get what they need from the Camino, not necessarily what they want. They also said that although you may not understand the meaning at the time, it doesn't mean that you won't understand the deeper meaning in the future. I was just glad it was over, and I was excited for what might come next.

It was rather ironic that two days later, I found myself back with my pack and making my way slowly to Finisterre. The thought of adding another hundred kilometres to my mileage was too tempting, mainly because there was no way in hell I was ever, ever, ever walking this far again. And so, the last and final chapter to my pilgrim story is the leg to Finisterre.

After a couple of nights catching up with the crew in Santiago, I was in particularly bad shape when I started walking. I was supposed to be leaving at 6.30am, but after getting back to my room a couple of hours beforehand, this clearly did not happen. Why, oh, why did I drink that God awful Orujo stuff again? With the hangover from hell, it should have been an easy decision to delay my Finisterre mission by a day. But no, my fear of missing out on good times with the gang meant a painless solution was not on the menu.

It was like I was on autopilot. I reached the first bar after 7km and ordered a rather large clara. I bumped into some of the crew, who I noted were in exactly the same boat I was. The next 15km or so were pretty brutal. It was two hours climbing up through massive hills of eucalyptus forest, not even the potent menthol of which was enough to clear my pounding fuzzy head. The intense afternoon sun was an absolute killer combined with two nights of solid dehydration, so when our slow, sorry hungover arses finally reached the albergue it was late, and of course, full. No big deal though, as with a belly full of yummy rigatoni with cream, tomatoes and bacon, cooked by our highly skilled Italian friends, I crashed out on a few mats we scraped together. The rest slept in the garden.

The next leg to Olveiroa was a whopping 37km. There was fiery heat, no shade and zero cover for the last 20km. This experience was further intensified by the superabundance of snakes. It was an arduous journey, but I was more than thankful that this time there was no hangover. I even managed to get one of the last beds at the albergue on arrival.

We arrived in Finisterre the following day, the true finale of this journey after the final 32km. Seeing the ocean again for the first time in over a month was something to be relished for this island pilgrim from the South Pacific. Some of the crew from the Santiago reunion had caught the bus to greet us and we stocked up on some booze before walking the final 3km out to the lighthouse. The lighthouse was the most western point possible in Europe, or what the pilgrims in medieval times thought was the end of the world. We found a remote position out on the rocks and got stuck into our old friend the Orujo de Hierbas whilst watching the sunset and belting out a few songs.

We built a fire and set alight everyone's pilgrim wear to keep with tradition, although of course I forgot to bring my mangled clothes with me. A good crew we were, most of the people I had met along the way and also a handful of new faces, creating a global pilgrim party. Not surprisingly we got carried away, and I neglected to muster any kind of forward thinking to contemplate the difficulty of getting out of this secluded spot after three hours of over-celebrating post sundown. I encountered some difficulty in the dark, navigating the very narrow track full of rocks and spiky gorse bushes whilst absolutely trolleyed. I was genuinely surprised that I didn't take a dive down into the depths of the rocks and bush below. Then again, I had grown accustomed to these small miracles of the Camino.

All twenty or so of us stumbled back to town and took ourselves off to the local discotheque, bleeding gorse scratches and all. Unfortunately, upon my wobbly 6am return I was locked out of my hostel room, which I had forked out extra euros for, to share with Katie. I ended up following some of the others and staying on a mat illegally in their albergue, so I didn't have to be on the streets. I was awoken around 8am to an array of loud Spanish expletives by a very angry lady yelling and prodding me with her stick. I was dazed and confused and took some time to register what was happening. The prodding repeated numerous times, getting faster and more exaggerated, digging into my side before I could coordinate my pained body up off the mat. The albergue was completely empty. I was promptly kicked out and the door slammed shut behind me.

I managed to gingerly navigate my way back to my actual accommodation and find some snacks in an attempt to sober up. I passed out again and woke up slightly more refreshed in the late morning. I showered and set out to find the others and get my last official pilgrim stamp. Unfortunately, the only albergue in Finisterre where I could get my certificate and stamp for the last leg of the journey was the albergue I'd been kicked out of hours before. What were the chances? It was even the same nasty lady behind the desk which was far from ideal. After waiting in the queue and trying to vaguely disguise myself as someone else, I got abuse hurled at me again and she refused to give me my certificate. So much for potentially not recognising me. She even threatened to rip up my pilgrim passport full of a month's worth of stamps. Bitch! I pleaded my innocence trying to explain about being locked out with nowhere to go, and therefore the mistake of sleeping over without registering was my only option. I tried to throw money at the problem, but she was having none of it, looking at me with ferocious anger. I sat in the chair in a standoff, adamant I was not going to move until I got what I came for. With a growing queue of people behind me starting to shuffle and complain, she launched into yet another lecture in Spanish mentioning the policía a number of times before finally handing over my documents. It certainly wasn't the romantic nor spiritually triumphant end to the journey I had envisaged. I was shaking not only from the hangover when I left, but I got my goddamn certificate in the end anyway.

Upon checking my phone, I had received some bizarre and urgent texts from Devo and Annie. The last one from Devo read, *For God's sake get in touch. Your mother is having kittens because you are MIA. Send us a text asap! x D.* Cripes, I'd just walked over 900km across Spain for the last month totally fine, and now you have a panic attack when I am at the end?! They really were mad. I sent Annie a text to say all was A-OK and got one back about an hour later. *F*ck! Thank God! Thort u assailed by some stray bull or mad gypsies! Sorry! Only ANGSTY ANNIE WHO has just krapt her pants! Those lentils last nite + mad images of du CAP Finisterre! Peace + love 2 u! X A.*

Never a dull moment in my family.

I spent a couple of days in Finisterre in the afterglow of achievement relaxing by the seaside and avoiding the blacklisted albergue. I took particular enjoyment in the fact that I didn't have to walk back. In fact, I never had to walk again with this backpack!

On my last night in Santiago, I went out for dinner and drinks with Posh English Ben and Bushwalker Katie. Katie left as she was flying out early the next day, so I got to know Posh Ben a bit better. Turns out he was an ex-SAS agent. He had been working undercover in Colombia for the last four years fighting dastardly drug lords. No wonder his Spanish was so fluent. Mental note to self, do not get drunk and share any of my familiarity with the Colombian goods nor party girl history. He had since retired to travel and figure out what was next. I excitedly told him how I'd officially been in breach of the National American Security when I boarded the wrong plane to the wrong airport once, but he failed to be impressed. I was mesmerised. A real-life secret agent; how dashingly brave and thrilling. We continued chatting for some hours as the drinking escalated.

Before I knew it, I found myself down a back alley where he pashed me on the way home. Following my exhilaration at being in the arms of a secret agent, I decided it would seem only fitting to sneak him back to my room in my pensión which had a strict no visitors' policy. He was staying in a dorm room so that was definitely not an option. He was my Maxwell Smart. I was his Ninety-Nine. So, taking my new role of secret agent sidekick in my stride, I navigated us back to my pensión with numerous stops to lock lips. I unlocked the gate and ran up the marble stairs to check if all was clear. I opened my door while I was at it and ushered him upstairs, in as secret agent sidekick style as I could get. And then, finally, after almost a full month, I had my hot sweaty pilgrim stallion sex. What a body. Go the SAS!

In the morning we exchanged information, as he was going to be back in London around the same time as I. Thank you God. My dream of marrying a secret agent might come to fruition after all. Later that morning as I checked out, the little old lady who ran the pensión was talking to me in very rapid Spanish and saying something about a chico. She seemed to be demanding money for the extra person staying. Oops. I gave my best confused expression and said a quick, "No entiendo. Gracias, ciao!" as I urgently squeezed myself and my backpack down the spiral staircase. I did not want a reprise of the threat of the policía in Finisterre. It was definitely time to leave town.

Be at one with the ALL of you now.
Shake off any seriousness, for the energies are present for you to play.
In light and love and laughter.
Be at one and allow.
Allow the lightness of your personality self,
as the lightness of your being, to take over.
These earthly parts of yourself are not to be
destroyed or dislodged from your system.
For they provide the tools you need on the earth at this time.
To carry forth your light for the benefit of all.
Be not of the illusion conveyed by many
as to what is light and what is not,
what is 'right' and what is not.
For this is not the game to play any longer.

Oversharing Is For Amateurs

After partying for a few weeks in Mallorca undoing any semblance of good I might have done on the Camino, I arrived back in London, dossing with friends while I looked for a job and some new digs. After a month of networking, recruiter interviews, chasing leads and saying no to bottom of the barrel online poker advertising contracts, I picked up a temporary role at a small agency, that focused on business to business clients. At least it would keep me afloat.

My creative team were the coolest of the very reserved bunch and we got on like a house on fire. I distinctly remember the moment when our friendship solidified a couple of weeks in. I was terribly excited that Posh Ben, my pilgrim stallion had gotten in touch and was in town for the week before heading off travelling again. I was also somewhat terrified, as what semblance I had of a pilgrim body had pretty much gone out the window. My body conscious demons were back and in full force. To detract from the frightfully boring meeting we were supposed to be having, I was oversharing with my creatives, Andy and James, about my potential date that week.

"Well, I met him on the pilgrimage," I said, casually assuming the secretly chuffed attitude of a bona fide pilgrim with nine hundred plus kilometres under their belt. "He had this *amazing* body. Now I'm talking hard as a rock. I mean, he was a member of the SAS after all."

"Jesus, the SAS?" asked Andy with raised eyebrows.

"Yes!" I shrieked. "I know unbelievable right? It's totally been one of my dream fantasies to marry a secret agent. I'd prefer a more James Bond type man really, but do I not look like the perfect Ninety-Nine?" I cooed, striking a few poses with a stupid smile.

Andy was looking at me quizzically. James scrunched up his forehead and gave me an intensely scrutinising gaze.

"You do know what the SAS is right?" said Andy slowly. "… and what they do?"

"Yeah, yeah," I nodded excitedly, "… they go on secret missions getting posted around the world, and they work undercover and…"

"Oh my God James, show her," said Andy, shaking his head and motioning to his big screen.

Moments later I was looking at the fluorescent green hue of a night vision film. It was a SWAT team of SAS agents raiding a house. They seized the room and blew away a handful of people with submachine guns in hardcore military style. I didn't particularly like or enjoy the violence, I was a lover, not a fighter, and so I watched through semi-covered eyes, trying to avoid as much as I could.

"SAS agents kill people," Andy said matter of factly.

"And not just the bad guys either," said James. "That was just the scene of them dealing to a group of innocent civilians," he finished, looking at me with the most serious face he could muster, as Andy pressed play on what appeared to be another killing spree.

I looked at the YouTube title. It definitely said SAS on it. In fact, there was an endless list of SAS videos with keywords like 'brutal' and 'mercenary'. There was no way they were pulling my leg on this one. I looked at each of them wide-eyed. There was dead air. Crickets.

"Oh my God, are you saying I slept with a murderer?!" I yelped in piercing decibels with horrified theatrics. Andy and James were looking at me in laughable disbelief.

"I can't believe it," I said in shock as my secret agent husband fantasy dissipated into thin air.

"They're not Maxwell Smart. Nor secret agents. And not technically murderers given it's in the line of duty, but they are cold hard killers," said James dramatically, attempting to keep it together while suffocating his laughter.

"But I've got a date on Thursday night," I said, my head spinning with the weight of this intel.

"Well how are you going to look him in the eyes wondering if he's a so-called 'murderous mercenary?'" asked Andy, now pissing himself with laughter.

I gathered up the scripts we had been reviewing and took my leave. Whatever was I going to do? My head was overwhelmed with these revelations for days afterward and combined with the daily taunting from James and Andy on the status of my date I worked myself into a tizzy. Turns out I needn't have worried as D-Day arrived and I spontaneously started throwing up at the office mid-morning. It seemed I had some kind of food poisoning and I was sent home. I spent the rest of the day with my head in the toilet bowl until it wore off twenty-four hours later. The prospect of having to stare into the face of my killer shag, no pun intended, was gone. Date cancelled.

Some months later an opportunity to work on a multimedia project requiring account handling and production skills came across my path, which was exactly what I was hoping to expand in to. The Universe was finally aligning itself for me. Yay! I resigned from the agency to take the role.

It soon became clear that the new exciting project I was working on wasn't going to be as hands-on as I had thought. Without the challenge of a complex job, I became comfortably bored. This translated into the usual retox-detox cycle that I was famously known for in New York. It was fun getting stuck right into London life and building my new social circles, but as per the norm, I had a habit of going overboard. My lack of feeling fulfilled in my job, combined with my hectic social life, meant that I spent more and more periods between retox and detox getting sick. My hormones were all over the place, and I was continually stacking on weight as I fed my emotions and lack of self-worth. I had intended to make this year more about balance. So rather than resorting to the extreme anorexia-style weight loss of the past, I decided to take action. I quit smoking, and, to up the ante, booked in for some professional help at a naturopath centre.

Arriving at the apartment in Hampstead, I was greeted at the door by one of the therapists who sported a slightly bohemian look. Dressed in a long flowing skirt, she had straight brown hair and wore feather earrings. She ushered me into the office area where I met the second woman, who was shorter and dressed in conservative plain coloured clothes. I was given a form to fill out and a glass of water. The form was very long and very detailed. It was pages and pages of not only my health history but family history too. I usually filled these things out with generalised truths, skipping over anything controversial, but this time I thought, in commitment to myself and finding balance, I was going to just lay it all out there. Fifteen minutes later, the two of them were sitting in front of me with their clipboards. I felt an uncomfortable sense of apprehension mixed with awkwardness, as I sat in the spotlight in front of this consultation panel. Hippy 1 started reading out my form, skipping over the basics and getting straight into the issues. Getting sick constantly, hormonal imbalance, overweight. As she got down into my health history, I elaborated on my glandular fever at fifteen-years-old where these cyclical patterns seemed to have started. They went through my diet, nodding and looking at each other, affirming this didn't seem terrible.

"Fifteen glasses of alcohol a week," she said reading further down, eyebrows raised and looking at me over the top of her glasses.

"Oh yeah about that, maybe a few more, depending on the week I guess," I said with casual deflection, knowing full well it was probably more like twenty to twenty-five.

She looked at her counterpart and then scribbled something down on her notes. I was starting to get a distinct feeling that perhaps being so honest wasn't the best idea after all.

"LSD, marijuana, ecstasy," she said eyes widening to the outer extremes of their sockets as she glanced quickly to her partner. "Speed, cocaine, magic mushrooms... " she continued reading, her face twinging and starting to flush as she struggled to keep her bulging eyes in her head.

She looked up at me, attempting to hide the judgement and shock that was consuming her. She looked at Hippy 2 next to her, and they held each other's gaze for an uncomfortably long moment. Then both scribbled furiously on their notes again.

"Well yes, it was my experimental youth," I said quietly, again trying to play it down and move things along.

"So, you had your first cigarette at twelve?" she said taking the tone of a stern school teacher.

"Or thirteen, somewhere around there," I said casually trying to buffer the blow. "You know, with everyone at school."

"And first E at nineteen?"

Oh, dear God. It was slowly dawning on me that I had undoubtedly revealed too much. I sounded like an absolute train wreck on paper. Interestingly I didn't really feel like one, yet here I was sitting in some hippy office in north-west London confessing to the many sins of my youth, and feeling like a troubled Hollywood child star from the eighties.

"Well, it was with my parents," I said attempting to play it down whilst inadvertently throwing fuel on the fire. I had grown up in a very unconventionally liberal environment, mostly because of Devo's advertising lifestyle, full of glamorous creative types. I was always treated like an adult who could make my own decisions, and was at the time dating a young man from his office which meant our worlds collided more than ever. It just happened to be when Auckland was having a resurgence of hedonism at the height of the designer drugs trend in the late nineties. Annie generally did not partake as one toke on a spliff sent her orbiting into the cosmos, igniting an unspoken rule that no one was to offer any drugs to Annie. On this particular occasion, she had been slipped a pill which meant I was high for the first time with my parents.

The Hippies didn't know what to do with that and quickly skipped along.

"And so, you have also done cocaine recently?" she said, taking a deep concerned breath as she looked up at me clutching her clipboard in front of her like a shield.

Oh crikey, I had really done it this time. I could feel myself slowly sinking into my chair feeling smaller and smaller. Did they not know that working in advertising this was merely par for the course? And that even in broader social circles in London it was more common than a G&T? Then again it looked like the last time they went for a night out was circa 1967.

"Oh yeah, a wee while ago I guess now…" I said my voice trailing off, trying to make it seem a far cry from last weekend.

They looked at each other again, raising their eyebrows, pausing, and then scribbling more notes. All I wanted to do was get out of there. I was grasping the sides of my chair wishing it to be over as I ran through answers to period questions and PMS with flushed cheeks. Finally, the Spanish Inquisition was complete, and I hopped on the bed for some kinesiology. After a series of muscle tests, I was prescribed some immune remedies and a detox program which basically cut out anything fun for the foreseeable future. When it was done I made a beeline for the front door, wanting to shed the uncomfortable feeling of naked vulnerability and breathe in the expanse of the non-judgemental outdoors. I gave a limp wave and awkwardly backed out the door leaving the hippy duo to huddle over my case notes.

The power in the present moment gifts you with an awareness
for your highest evolution, expansion and joy.
For change is constant, which energetically syncs
you in every moment to the new.
Yes, our humanness holds on to the static, to the old,
to the status quo, in its resistance to change.
But change is to be embraced.
Feel comfort in the dynamic movement of change.
With this dynamism comes excitement and
the thrill of being on the edge.
On the edge of energetic leaps and bounds into the future.
It can be as fast or as slow as you wish.

Houston, Do You Read Me?

Not one to do anything by halves, I decided to embrace celibacy with my anti-rinse cycle. Whether or not this was an actual conscious choice as opposed to a by-product of complete sobriety was unclear. It was rather unfortunate timing given my Susan Miller, legend amongst astro legends, January Horoscope, which described the planets being aligned for grand loving epicness. Alas, sobering cultural events were on the menu instead.

I started back at the gym with a *12 Week Get Results* programme. To be at the top end of the healthy weight range for my height, I allegedly had to lose thirty-bloody-kilograms. That's basically half a person. Regardless of how unrealistic it seemed, I gave it my all and committed with new bridled, focused enthusiasm to turning over a new leaf. I was now a wagon riding, law-abiding, upstanding citizen. A detox loving dream. As Devo used to say, albeit sarcastically, "Captain Fantastic says yes to health and no to drugs!"

Three weeks in I was already feeling mentally clearer, and updating my gay boyfriends in New York with promises to show off my new-found goddess-like self that summer. "Let me spare you all the pathies and ologies, it's the booze!" said Big Gay Andy in his cutting yet comedic manner. Arv was a hair more cheerleader-like. "I like it. Detox, celibacy, don't overdo it though. However, I am here to support you. A line a day keeps you from falling off the detox wagon. Relatively speaking of course." Typical, given Arv and his navigation were the cause of a missed flight after an all-night bender in LA despite leaving with hours to spare. "Anyway, I like it," he continued, "… all this hippy-dippy shit… even if it's crap it makes me feel good and clean. Sometimes scotch makes me feel that way too. Hmmm. Anyway, keep the peace pipe going; it's the best remedy." Go figure.

On the one hand, while I was taking great action to sort out one area of my life, I was still unhappy in others. The job had not gotten any more challenging, and each day dragged on. I was desperately over this advertising game and wishing for pastures new. I had moved from New York to London for the freedom to open new doors and expand without visa constraints, or better yet, change my career in line with my purpose or whatever it was I was meant to be doing on this planet. However, I still had no direction as to what this might be. No broader opportunities arrived. It was turning out to be much harder than anticipated.

I'd been back and forth via email with Annie for some advice.

I know how you must be feeling regarding the job. It is very much like that now. People don't want to work in areas where hypocrisy, lies and only profit are paramount. This, I think, is proof that the consciousness is beginning to shift. It is more noticeable now more than before as it has sped up. Maybe just go with it, see how you feel. Try to spend some time with yourself and work out what it is you truly want. Ask to be guided to what would suit you.

I spent months and months asking angels and spirit guides, and whoever else would bloody listen, for some direction and guidance. I needed some non-physical support here. My mind continued to whir on the hamster wheel of my perceived limitations, abilities and potential, and I felt the weight of dead air as I was unable to identify any guidance. Nothing came to the surface. I wished for some fab opportunity to fall into my lap or someone amazingly talented to come across my path to take a punt on me. Alternatively, some form of divine intervention where the Universe propelled me into something else that was more aligned with my soul would be just perfect. I'd heard about these incredibly synchronistic occurrences of fate happening to others. When was it going to happen to me? So far none of these options had arisen, and I was muddling along in the status quo with more confusion than before. It was about time those angels came to the party. Were they on holiday or something?

I was equally as unhappy on the celibacy front. Celibacy kept me focused on the stamina to stay away from males, and again avoid looking at the root of the problem. My relationship history encompassed a string of one-night stands, unsuitable boyfriends and unavailable men. After swapping sob stories with a friend, talking about energy and the law of attraction, she recommended *The Secret*, a book that had just come out in the last year. I decided that I was immediately going to focus on manifesting my man. I got the book, read it in a couple of hours flat and promptly told everyone to standby for Mr Foxy AF boyfriend to enter my life. I followed the vague instructions in the book, attempting some dreaming, visualisation and writing lists of the qualities for this perfect man I was manifesting. After a few weeks, despite what I was doing energetically, my reality stayed the same without any entrance of Prince Charming. Despite doing what the book said things did not change one iota, and my initial enthusiasm waned with no results. So far, the planetary alignments for love had delivered well under par. Until a notification popped up on Skype from Twin Hamza Ali. "I'm looking by Skype about my future-wife very seriously. I believe that Skype is a great introducer among people, as I met with my friends and with my twin brother." Really Universe? That's the best you got? Is this some kind of cosmic joke? Big Gay Andy, on the other hand, thought it was priceless. "Go for it – twin Hamza, hubba hubba!"

Months later I was still no closer to dating my dream man. At the prodding of my parents, I had contacted a long-lost friend in London. I grew up with him during my childhood in Melbourne and hadn't seen him since I was about eight. He had his own magazine, lived out east and was pretty cool apparently. Of course, after we got in touch via email, I spent the week fantasising that this might be my long-lost soulmate who would sweep me off my feet. I could see our wedding in the English countryside, full of cool artist types, and a honeymoon in the Maldives. I was set to meet him that weekend at the Lock Tavern in Camden, which was affirmatively hopeful as it was a cool hipster pub, usually full of a myriad of gorgeous young men. I arrived with butterflies in my stomach and waited outside with bated breath. Mr Potential Right stepped outside the pub to greet me, and my hopes were dashed in the blink of an eye. He was gayer than a feather duster. And not only was he gay, but he was also rockabilly gay. Affronted by the polar opposite of my delusional fantasy, I hid my devastation behind a quick squeeze and double-cheeked kiss before being rushed inside.

After some overexcited gay hugs and claps, I met the rest of the party, about fifteen new camp boyfriends. Post retelling the long-lost childhood friends reunited story at least four times to a symphony of gushing gayness, I was promptly invited along to Gay Bingo at the local RSA. As much as they were all genuinely adorable, I mean who doesn't love bingo and gay boys, I politely declined to take my sorry, romantically deluded arse back to north-west London. And, more importantly, towards somewhere with an abundance of red-blooded males.

The summer proved a glorious mix of travel and fun with friends, which was a welcome distraction from my incessant Virgo-like self-reflection about not living up to my own expectations. Berlin proved to be all it was cracked up to be with a whirlwind weekend of fantastic art, bars, clubs and little sleep. One bar played music solely from before 1969 featuring wild-west classics, another was a Russian disco complete with original Oompa band where I danced side by side with legit Ruskies, another was in an old war bunker disguised as a Chinese takeaway joint featuring effortlessly cool clientele. One of whom used to be Mick Jagger apparently. Of course, the weekend would not have been complete without the threat of potentially getting arrested at the airport flying out. No surprises since we had just come straight from a club. Although my close call was marginally better than my friend, who got strip-searched.

The highlight of my trip to Marrakesh was escaping an attempted mugging in an alleyway with rugby-tackle skills

I never knew I had and outmanoeuvring some seriously professional scammers. As usual, never far from an inadvertent debacle. Ibiza lived up to its reputation. A huge pimping villa with a private chef, ten friends, fantastic restaurants, bars and amazing music. It was the perfect balance of poolside lounging and partying, with a little bit of clubbing thrown in for good measure. It was Ibiza after all. Mid-session lounging by the infinity pool one afternoon, my phone rang with a New Zealand number. It was a friend calling to offer me a great job in Sydney as an account director for some large well-known clients. Of course, she happened to be sitting with Devo and Annie, who were talking over the top of each other in the background saying I should seriously consider it. I told her I'd have to talk to her when I wasn't under the influence. You know, standard Ibizan behaviour. My mind started whirring at a million miles an hour. Sure, I wanted out of the current contract, but it felt like I was only just getting started in London. I had big dreams of getting out of shallow advertising, and into a career of passion and purpose but I had no idea how or into what. So far it was a hard road with nothing quite working out as miraculously or synchronistically as I'd hoped.

Perhaps I should reconsider something that was a bit more of the usual route, making decent money and back down with the family in the South Pacific? Or was that my material ego trying to pull me back into the very advertising world I was trying to get out of? The swirling thoughts meant a world of confusion within me. The doubt escalated into an arsenal of self-judgement and criticism from inside my head. I was thirty years old, had no idea what I was doing, no man in sight and no plan. I was hardly excelling at life by common standards. Maybe when opportunity knocks, you should answer and see where it takes you? Would I be bored and miserable back in standard agency client service, or would it be a different ball game down there? The hamster wheel kept running.

I arrived back to London with a thud. I was feeling all sorts of frisky. Perhaps it was all the naked bodies in Ibiza, but bitch on heat was an understatement at this point. My inner wild child had enjoyed the taster that was the crystal isle of Ibiza and was now looking to continue the party. This on the wagon, working my arse off for bare minimum results was growing tiresome I thought to myself. It's so much easier to get skinnier on a diet of cocaine, cocktails, and clubbing. Maybe I'm not cut out for this moderation stuff. It just doesn't seem to be working for me. I blame Devo. And Annie. And the advertising eighties excess childhood. Perhaps I just need to work with what I am good at and what's in the genes. Life is too short. I could feel the rebel rise within me. My self-sabotaging mind was not helpful.

True to the rustlings of the naughty alter ego inside of me, the Universe aligned me with opportunities to continue the party for the next few weeks. On arrival in London, my flatmates were on a bender. Then it was the last of the blazing London summer with everyone out on the streets drinking every evening of the week. I squeezed in one last festival, dancing my arse off at Lovebox in East London. Then it was an end of summer adventure to Champagne to peruse the Champagne houses. So far this year between work and play, I'd been jet-setting to New York twice, Prague, Stockholm, Berlin, Morocco, Finland, Paris, Tenerife, Amsterdam and Ibiza. If there was one thing I was achieving, it was my travel goals. In fact, perhaps someone could offer me a job as a professional traveller. I certainly was well qualified.

Of course, all good things must come to an end and as my drinking binges continued my healthy lifestyle went from pitiful to non-existent. These things have a habit of creeping up on you only for you to realise after it's too late. I starkly woke up to this fact one week in October as I was having a fatter-than-Chunk-from-The-Goonies day. I may as well have stood on my desk to do the *Truffle Shuffle* there was so much jiggle in my jangle. As my weight crept on my insecurities sprang forward. Cue emergency juice and salad cleanse for the weekend. I even signed up to a kinesiology course to shift my focus. I was motivated to try new things to get my life back on track and ditch this fatty pants feeling. I made deliriously dull plans of gym, study, veggie juices and a face mask.

Despite being determined I would sparkle by Monday, my good intentions were thwarted at the first pass. My new flatmates had a huge house party for no apparent reason which made it virtually impossible not to join in. It concluded with me getting to bed at 10am. I even pashed an ex Calvin Klein model from Israel, but he was more complicated than a Facebook status. He had barely split from his psycho girlfriend when a woman popped up who was about to give birth to his baby. He was so bad on paper that my logical mind told me to take a wide berth. Yet, he was so incredibly hot that my body didn't listen. We ended up having a cheeky kiss at the party. I even offered to make him a guinea pig patient for my kinesiology to help him through the emotions and stress of his current circumstance, which was a thinly veiled attempt at getting to know him better and inadvertently woo him.

"Isn't that against doctor-patient rules?" he said grinning as he held me on his lap.

"Details, schmetails," I whispered back.

The weekend was a fantastically fun write-off. By Sunday I was, of course, at the Westbourne pub with a bunch of other glamorous young professional almost-alcoholics to get over the unexpectedly debauchery filled weekend. I 'accidentally' pulled a hot African bartender. Being one of my local pubs that I frequented, this was a horrifying disaster. It wasn't my fault though. I was in a major drought. I was pushed to the edge. In fact, I was in the middle of the goddamn Sahara. I beat myself up to no end for the indiscretion, replaying visions of my drunken flirting on repeat as my insides recoiled in pain. I mean, who pulls on a Sunday night? Really?

"Getting some action is perfectly normal," said my friend Georgie. "And you have been in a significant dry patch," she said supportively.

Of course, he didn't call, although I wasn't sure I wanted him to anyway. And so, my usual disastrous career with men continued ever enduringly, despite the manifesting and energy work I was inconsistently performing. There was hope on the horizon though as Venus turned direct into my house of True Love. Times would be a-changin'.

In Soho one night, after more than enough Jäger shots to toast a friend's last hurrah before journeying into matrimony, I made a run for the last train home. I belted down to Piccadilly Circus with all my semi-drunken might, determined not to have to front a twenty-two quid taxi fare back to my north-west hood. I got down to the platform to find a bunch of people waiting. It was hot and sticky, and I was feeling the grime of the low rent karaoke room where I had spent the last two hours being showered in other people's beverages. After some serious huffing and puffing and inevitable British moaning from my fellow commuters I decided to take the only vacant seat close by, certain that London Underground was having one of its daily 'We provide an exceptionally good service on all London underground' fails. The loudspeaker was bleating on, but it blended into the background. The guy sitting to my right had earpieces like some tribesman from the depths of Africa and was chatting to an older Swedish looking woman who appeared equally confused. I cracked some joke about the fiercely reliable London transport system and light banter ensued when I realised he was a visiting Kiwi.

They finally cancelled the trains altogether. I asked the guy where he was headed given there was no other trains to mine and we might be going to the same place. He said he was going to Hackney.

"Well you were on the completely wrong platform to get to Hackney in the first place, dude, it's the opposite direction."

"But my iPhone said so," he said, like it was the gospel.

"Well I live here and take this train every day and I'm telling you it goes in the opposite direction to Hackney," I said amused.

We tried the Piccadilly line in a last-ditch effort, but we'd missed the last train. On the way up the escalator he said casually, "Well, I'm coming home with you obviously."

"Oh right, is this the bit where you tell me you have nowhere to stay and are a poor traveller?" I said. "Gee couldn't see that coming a mile away…"

Him, "Well kind of, yeah."

Me, "Right."

"It'd be nice to maybe sleep with you too," he said blatantly. I just laughed.

"No really. Come on, I'm waiting for your answer," he said with his best puppy dog eyes. This wasn't working due to the incredible amounts of tribal jewellery he was adorned with, which wasn't really up my alley at all.

"So, you seriously have nowhere to stay?" I said sarcastically. "Do you think I was born yesterday?" I was trying to think if I even remotely fancied him and came up with a blank.

"Well, not really no. I can't get hold of my friend," he said.

"Okay, well we're splitting the taxi and you're sleeping on the couch," I said, giving in. Surely there's Universal brownie points in that.

"I'd much rather sleep with you," he said, trying it on again.

"It's not gonna happen. I'm doing a nice thing for a fellow Kiwi. Be happy with that," I said finitely. We grabbed a cab and headed north.

"You do know you're in a cab with a complete stranger, right?" he said trying to feel me out further.

"Yup. I'm no stranger to randomness, for some reason it seems to follow me everywhere," I replied. If only he knew. All sorts of polite chit-chat ensued. He lived in Melbourne, was on his big OE trip and was a vegetarian.

"At first I really wanted to have sex with you but now I'm not sure if I hate you. I hate people who are vegetarian and then take up meat again," he said, somewhat disgusted after I disclosed my fair weather flexitarianism. He leaned in to grab my face. "I just really want to kiss you right now."

I pulled away. "Umm no. Next time, I wouldn't announce it if you want more luck."

"Hmmm. Okay," he said, seriously taking on board this feedback.

We bought mixers at the local twenty-four hour store, making jokes with the store guys and leaving in fits of laughter.

We walked home and made drinks. He plugged in his iPod and asked if I liked the tunes.

"They're alright," I said.

"They're mine – I'm a DJ," he said with a sense of pride.

"Oh nice," I replied, suitably unimpressed. Thinking, everyone's a fucking DJ.

He pulled out a wrap of some dodgy shit he bought on the street. I took one dab and it tasted like chalk. "Sorry buddy. Ain't no gear in that."

"Oh, so you don't want this line then?" he said somewhat incredulously.

"No. All yours. Chalk it up to experience. No pun intended," I said, trying not to giggle.

We were drinking vodka. He was smoking out the window, telling me I make a good drink. By this point it was 2.30am and I made a move to prepare the couch bed. I came back with pillows and a duvet and put them on the couch. I said goodnight and as I was on my way out the door he said, "Remind me again why we're not having sex?"

Me, "Umm I don't know you. Sorry," with surprising definitiveness. If Venus was going to come to the party in my House of True Love, then I expected more.

"Don't say sorry. I've just never been denied before. I mean no one has said no."

"Ah well. First time for everything ay. Nighty-night then," I said, blowing him a kiss before turning towards the door.

"Oh, and I sleep really deep, so you have to wake me up quite hard," he said.

"Roger that," I said heading to my room.

In the morning I put on the washing, made breakfast and was in and out of the lounge but he barely roused. I took another look at him and decided he was way cuter than I initially thought, and maybe I should have tapped that arse. He had amazing tattoos covering a rather fit body. I finally woke him up and found the best way for him to get to Hackney. I also gave him his phone which I had charged for him.

"Wow man, well thanks. You were awesome! Your hospitality

is amazing. Great couch. Gimme a hug," he said and pulled me towards him with a kiss on the cheek.

I smiled, "No worries. Take care ay."

"Guess I'll never see you again," he said, somewhat forlornly.

"Guess not," I said smiling.

"Well thanks again," he replied.

"Cheers. Have a good day."

My kinesiology training was going well, which reined in my overzealous socialising somewhat. Systematic Kinesiology is a holistic health therapy based on muscle testing to ascertain flow of energy and I found it fascinating to learn about the different circuits in the body and the links to eastern medicine. I'd always believed in energy and energy healing, and this was proving it to me in action, how our thoughts, feelings, emotions and external factors had an effect on our energy and our body in the flesh. As I practiced on different fellow classmates every week, I also got the opportunity to do a lot of work on my own healing with the weekend-long classes each month. I addressed my immune system, hormones and did a lot of emotional release work on experiences buried in the depths of my being and subconscious. The results were remarkable. I was feeling better, looking better and was more internally satisfied than I had been in ages. I had a glut of guinea pigs on the go to get through my fifty case studies required to pass my practitioner's course. My friends were generally supportive, and the visible results were always well received.

However, this was not the case with my mother. I enthusiastically offered my new-found knowledge up to her two great nemeses, quitting smoking and psoriasis as I was excited to share this helpful information. I got a curt response, devoid of all pleasantries.

"I am on treatment already from the psoriasis clinic. And it is working. I would not take your recommendation as it has berries in it which are acid. I have to keep to alkaline as much as possible. The cream I looked up too, has tea tree oil, and I react to that."

I felt my usual prickling from what felt like a dismissive reaction. Would it hurt to be supportive? Or a bit more tactful about it? I couldn't help but fire back.

"Okay well, I guess the twenty-two years' experience of my teacher with psoriasis cases won't work for you, despite working for everyone else. Bummer for you!" I finished in childish retort. If there was one person who knew how to push my buttons, it was my mother.

"Now who is in a huff?" Annie replied. "I don't want someone else's experience! I know people's intent is always good! But the energy is different now, and each individual must be responsible for his or her healing! The healing is of the way we THINK! The body has no intelligence of its own as we are taught! I am on a completely different level of thinking NOW and it changes with every NOW moment! I am quite entitled to do what I feel is appropriate for me right now! I don't have to be under anyone else's influence or control – particularly YOURS miss JEHOVA JO!"

I was infuriated. And it wasn't just the ridiculous use of capital letters in her text messages. I didn't agree; I believed the body does have its own intelligence. However, this was typical Annie behaviour, partially culturally driven by her South African heritage and an upbringing with strict parents lacking in emotion and communication skills. We were often at loggerheads over something or other.

My contract finally finished up on the tiresome work project and six weeks later I picked up a role at a newish small agency that seemed like it was going places. They didn't pay very well, but I figured there was potential to advance quickly and I could negotiate another pay review in six months or so. I started on the standard three-month trial back in client service and was put on the biggest account, which had a huge project launching in a few months. The project snowballed and after only a few weeks I was working late, consistently pulling fifteen-hour days which turned into weekends and bank holidays. Little did I know this client was known to be the most notorious to work with in the UK. No one had a good word to say about their experience working with them. Of course, I only found this out after experiencing it first-hand.

Soon enough I was back to square one, overextending myself and being a client arse-wipe doing a thankless job that frustrated and exhausted the hell out of me. This was an exact repeat of what I was trying to move out of in New York. I had let paying the bills and the comfort of something I knew well dictate me into my status quo which wasn't the point of coming to London at all. What was I doing? I was tempted to bail to the Himalayas for six months on the hunt for Ascended Masters and secret temples I had read about, or move to Byron Bay and descend into hippydom. Maybe Australia wasn't such a bad idea after all. As much as I dreamed of various fantastical escape scenarios, I was far too busy and up to my ears in this project. I was in too deep, so due to my work ethic I ended up staying the course.

Almost three months into the project the entire team was rinsed out, and the clients were unreasonable, rude and unappreciative. It was a tough time. One snowy night during the Christmas holidays we were waiting for client feedback for hours late into the night. It never arrived, and the frustration of the team was palpable. In the heat of the moment the executive creative director and owner of the agency told me to send them a very curt note about respecting our time during the holidays. So, I wrote to the client, in a firm but slightly more palatable way. I was tired and at my wit's end, so I was more than happy to oblige in politely putting them in their place.

The client reacted badly, and a few weeks later at my three-month probation review, I bore the brunt of it. They said my performance was faultless, I had gone over and above in dedication to the company and job, I was clearly very well trained and an expert in managing tough projects, but I had not made the right judgement call on the client communication. The ECD had never had to do this before, but they were not going to make me a full-time employee. I sat there gobsmacked. I literally had no words. I had given up my life for the last three months for this project, and he wasn't going to have my back for something that he actually instigated with the client in the first place? Here

I was, the sacrificial lamb, literally lambasted. Although given they were the key account and keeping the place afloat, I could see why, but I felt it was incredibly spineless. I was in shock and reeling as I went back to my desk to gather myself. This turned into pure mortification as the stern-faced office manager stood by my desk. I felt like a criminal as I packed up my things. She then escorted me out of the building. It was awful. Nothing like this had ever happened to me before.

My mind was working in overdrive as to exactly what had happened for this to transpire. I was replaying the months of dedicated work going over and above, the ECD's comments in my head that night, the email, the meeting and wondering if I was going mad. I had made a lot of friends at the agency in my short three months there who were equally in shock. Every person I spoke to genuinely could not understand how they could have come to this decision given my performance.

Despite the emotional turbulence I was feeling on the surface, I had a deep understanding that on an energetic level I had somehow created this myself. In theory I knew we were in charge of our energy, we use it to create our reality, and everything we experience is in direct effect of this. I didn't know exactly how I had done it, but I knew I had inadvertently and probably unconsciously had a hand in it somehow. Cue severe self-judgement. I beat myself up good and proper as the weight of this notion came crashing down upon my severely bruised and ashamed ego. Although I was deeply wounded, I took solace in the fact that there must be a bigger plan at play. For some reason, I had attracted this experience. Although traumatic, I was determined to see it as a gift from the Universe. When one door closes, another one opens and all that. This was an opportunity to try something new.

Be in the moment.
Do not analyse how you will be in the future
or past because of these moments.
Too often we see the dissecting of the minutia of the human experience,
trying to define one thing or another.
However, this is not the way.

There is freedom in the moment.
The now moment in which you operate, has the greatest power.
Do not police yourself. Do not suffer through the
'what ifs' and the 'could bes' and the worry,
for this is not of your vibration any longer.
So do not hang on to it here.

Let it go, let it go, let it go.
Feel your body relax and the tension dissipate as we say this to you.
For your body does not want to hold this tension.
It must if you insist but this is not the space
your body would like to prepare from.

Relax, relax, relax.
This process is one of relaxing and letting go of everything
that is now outside of your vibration.
Shed those layers, shed that which used to be.
And open to the light of all that is.
The only way. The only peace, between worlds,
that matters here for you at this time.

Where Will The Current Take Me?

Instead of drowning my sorrows predictably in a lake of wine, I got a fringe. For the first time since I was five. This put incredible strain on my next to zero ability at girly grooming. I barely knew how to work a hairdryer, let alone deal with the expertise required for maintenance of a lengthy fringe in my extremely curly hair. A questionably rash decision at best. A better decision was booking a weekend away at a country retreat in the South Downs. I signed up for a detox package of healthy food and juices, plus a reflexology session, massage and an emotional balancing session. This was how I attempted to change my behaviour with self-love. The emotional balancing session turned out to be an intuitive channelling session. Being in such a vulnerable place, I was interested in what spiritual guidance might come through for me from my guides and the non-physical world.

Vivien, the Intuitive and owner of the retreat, first mentioned my descent from an Irish lineage of females who struggled to be respected, heard and successful. Although I now knew of my Irish roots after that whole identity crisis caper, I had little or no connection to it. Now Vivien was telling me all about it and how it was affecting my current incarnation as it was handed down the family line.

"You haven't found a way to express who you are yet. Your interest in the spiritual side is getting stronger, but you must change the aspects of self that are not working and find the unconditional side of self. Stop people pleasing. You have some blocks from not honouring self. You need to honour where you are. You are a deep-thinking soul. Learn to create your own tribe, not tag on to other tribes."

I asked, as always how to connect to be able to hear my own guidance which I never seemed to be able to crack. My homework was to sit for ten minutes each day, in the same place, at the same time and concentrate on a purple flame, or a purple flower.

"This will connect you with your inner voice."

The reading resonated on many levels, and it provided a feeling of strength, clarity and support to my self-judging mind. After returning to London, I continued the purification with a diet of no dairy, wheat, meat or booze. A new Bikram yoga studio down the road was doing a thirty-day introductory special, so I signed up, heading to the inferno yoga every two to three days to sweat out all the toxins and self-loathing. I knew I needed to keep physically and mentally aligned at this time when I was feeling so vulnerable. Putting strategies in place to keep me there was critical.

As I slowly started contacting recruiters, I was soon connected with a friend of a friend who was training to be a life coach and needed case studies for her qualification. It was free and she was also an advertising recruiter, a perfect match. We did a deep dive into my passions, values, strengths and weaknesses. It was a fascinating journey of discovery, but at the end of the day although I knew I was passionate about philosophy, spirituality and energy, I was stumped as to how to translate this into anything tangible or meaningful, let alone a new career.

My friend Georgie inspired me to investigate marketing jobs in non-profits for something more soul satisfying, so I started widening my search and applying for a few positions slightly outside of my normal skillset. I met with more recruiters whilst managing the waves of emotion that were still surfacing as I processed the shock of what had happened. Most recruiters were surprisingly supportive and sympathetic. I did my best to release and forgive the agency and the ECD for what happened, per instructions from Annie but I still couldn't help but feel used and discarded. I wasn't quite ready to accept one hundred percent responsibility for what I had created for myself. However, being in the last couple of months of my kinesiology practitioner's course meant lots of opportunities to work through it on all energetic layers; physical, mental, emotional and spiritual.

I gave myself a two-month deadline to find a new job. If I was meant to stay in London, then a job would come to me before the end of June. If not, then I might take that as a cue to leave and head to Sydney. A boatload of interviews ensued, and although there was only positive feedback, I didn't manage to secure a position. Either the brief had changed, they decided to fill the position internally or I wasn't quite one hundred percent right for the job. The UK economy was in complete recession and at its worst for thirty years. The media was filled with doom and gloom on a daily basis. Ad agencies themselves were feeling the pinch. With the proliferation of digital media and the downturn of traditional forms of advertising, they were very much struggling for relevance and new business. Then I received a £7K tax bill in the mail. Thankfully it was half of what I was concerned it might be. I observed everything that was happening in my reality closely.

Despite all the positive actions I was taking, it was clearly telling me that I was not energetically aligned. I knew I was passionate about spirit and energy and the mystical side of life. I knew I was creative and an excellent communicator and deep thinker. I was analytical and strategic and could also produce. I just didn't know how to make a job out of it, and the life coaching nor anyone else seemed to be able to give me the solution. I defaulted to the path of least resistance interviewing back in client service jobs while finishing my kinesiology course, healing and doing the life coaching sessions.

Follow your passions, I was told from everything I read or heard in the spiritual community. That will lead you there. So, in the meantime, I dove into my passion project recreating a journey of eleven scientists who travelled to the Far East in the 1890s. It was written about in six book series called *The Life and Teaching of the Masters of the Far East* by Baird T Spalding that had fascinated me endlessly since I was a teenager. I was poring over ancient maps of India and measuring mountain heights while cross-referencing descriptions of the terrain in the books. Given it was so long ago, it was tough research but I eventually worked out that a lot of the journey was in Old India through what is now the south-west Himalayas and the border of Pakistan and Afghanistan. I was excited about the prospect of this renaissance mission.

"The border…" repeated my brother slowly, "… of Pakistan…" he continued, "and Afghanistan? Are you mad?" he said. "You can't go to bloody Afghanistan. It's a fricking war zone right now, you muppet. Devo and Annie will go spare."

"Oh Mike. It wouldn't be an adventure without a little danger," I said enthusiastically. "And I always wanted to be in *The Goonies*," I finished dreamily.

"You are not going to Afghanistan! End of story." My brother, although generally amused by my antics, wasn't having a bar of it and hung up the phone.

Despite remaining positive, life coaching, and putting work into my dream project, the unemployment ticked on. A month in I started to feel more and more anxious. As the anxiety set in, I felt my confidence slipping. Before I knew what was happening, I was on a major downer, a slump I just couldn't seem to escape that had me questioning everything. I was seriously wondering what I was going to do since things weren't coming together for me.

Just as I was starting to panic, I received a call for an interview at a new small agency. A ray of hope, which helped pull me out of my self-created hole. The company were repositioning themselves as a forward-thinking, progressive agency who got shit done and made brands famous. They seemed to have the right mentality and were working in a very agile structure with 'an idea can come from anywhere' philosophy. I had a candid interview with the founders, and as luck would have it, a few weeks before my self-imposed deadline, I got the job!

I was soon back into the swing of things, naturally working on the agency's toughest client yet again. The months disappeared, and before I knew it, I was comfortable, content and I'd forgotten all about the bump in my road, let alone changing direction. It was a great crew to be working with in a personable small shop. I was now part of the furniture with a whole new set of fun playmates to work hard and play hard with as life ticked along back to the safety and security of 'normal'. However, my blundering mishaps continued to plague me when I accidentally CC'd my client James instead of my gay colleague James on a note to my work chums about a new hotel down the road. The hotel miraculously offered 'The Broom Cupboard' for ninety quid, perfect for an 'Afternoon Delight' I quipped. "How delightful," my client replied. "Will it be all four of us?"

The bright shiny glow of a new job and agency wore off at the usual seven-month mark, and I was back to the exact same undercurrent of problems, only in yet another different scenery. Things on the home front had gone equally downhill when my soul sister rescue dog Stella passed away. Annie was beside herself.

"Pinot Grief has been in full flow in the Walden house following Stella's dear departure to doggie heaven. I am quite distraught as to the loss of my darling Stella."

A few days later, Annie had a massive fall and ended up knocked unconscious by the garage door. Devo was upstairs in bed and never heard her crying out in pain. She was there most of the night until she managed to drag herself up the stairs and into bed around 6am. Devo took her to the hospital in the morning, and she had severely fractured her ankle in multiple places. She went into surgery shortly after. I felt the guilt and pain of being over the other side of the world when these kinds of things happened. I understood we were all non-physical, including Stella so we never really left each other, but it didn't make it any easier for the human part of me to be unable to physically say goodbye. Not being able to be there to help Annie after such a tricky operation was also hard. I had to make do with Skype calls and updates from Devo. I wondered if they were telling me the true extent of it or not. Which turned out to be correct, as the surgeons had in fact screwed up the surgery on her foot, making Annie's recovery that much more difficult.

Being neglectful of my family responsibility weighed on me from over the other side of the world.

Soon enough it was my birthday and my spirits lifted in the morning when I received a voicemail from home with Devo bursting into song with great enthusiasm.

"Happy birthday to you, happy birthday to you, happy birthday to Jo. Happy birthday to you! Hello darling, it's your mother and father calling. Your mother's just saying she's feeling weary because she thinks she's channelling going into labour with you thirty-three years ago! I mean, hello!? Anyway, it's the evening here, and we're just toasting your good health. I hope you're well darling and I hope you have a lovely birthday. I mean you're very difficult to buy for so I didn't know quite what to do, so what we have is a very special gift for you which I will send over to you, and… no, I'm not going to tell her," he said talking over Annie in the background. "Although your mother can if she wishes. So, I'll just pass the phone over, and anyway – happy birthday darling, and I hope you're having a lovely, lovely day. Hold on…"

I heard the phone drop and then Annie pick it back up again. They had possibly had more than one toast.

"Hi darling, happy birthday, I've gotta be quick because this is a message, but I do have something special here for you. And I want to tell you what it is personally actually. But… um… ugh… sorry, I'm a bit tearful at the moment. I've been achieving all sorts of things and, ah (sighs), you know when you're in a wheelchair," she said starting to cry. "It's a little bit um… and then it's your birthday – and you're not here and wah, wah, wah and I wanna be with you… wah, wah wahh. Anyway, lots of love darling I'm okay really, you know… just um the tears are happening and ah doodle ladalaye. Okay, darling bye, bye. I hope the sun's shining where you, um, are, it was kind of today here. Bye, bye. See you. Lots of love."

As life ticked along and the change of seasons came, the chill set in again. The London weather was typically dismal with rain and cold and a string of never-ending grey. I didn't mind much as it was quite nice to cosy up. On the surface I was more relaxed and satisfied than I had been in a long while, although deep within me there was something else brewing.

I continued on with my usual work hard, play hard ways with plenty of other thirty-somethings until one fateful dreary Sunday, when I arrived at a friend's baby shower forty minutes late with my tray of crudités. I had, by this point recently quit smoking, for which I was quite proud, I just hadn't managed the same restraint in regard to alcohol. The afternoon descended into a flood of drinking to get over the previous night's hangover. Which worked perhaps a little too much.

I bumped into Eamon the local crazy Irishman at the pub hours later, who three bottles in was swearing to a friend that he knew Colin Farrell. More wine and two stumbles in heels later, my friends had departed and I'd almost gotten into a fight on the dance floor with some uptight shape-cutters about my exuberant dancing. Eamon was quite quickly ordering a bump to sober me up. It worked for about five seconds when I called my flatmates to find recruits to continue the party at home.

We arrived home with another two bottles of wine, which we promptly polished off with Liso and James, along with a bag of fun. Although technically they were drinking beer, so I guess I polished off the wine. I recall nothing, but allegedly stumbled around the flat erratically hiccuping, stomping and wall crashing. I weaved my way to my bed leaving my handbag in the lounge like an amateur, which held my iPhone, my only alarm. I awoke to the sounds of school kids at play in the yard across the road. A normal Monday, except in my case I was seriously incapacitated, still drunk and naked at 10.20am, making me very, very, very late for work.

In a fit of panic, I called in sick. I mean technically that much was true at least. It dawned on me that I had forgotten a vital piece of information, that when I quit smoking my drinking is amplified tenfold by needing something to do with my hands. If only I had the brilliance to remember this before I drank a small lake of rosé. The good news was I got so drunk that I forgot I wanted a cigarette. A small silver lining at least. Still feeling the effects of the night before, I called my brother in New Zealand telling him of my escapades and the woeful situation I found myself in, cursing my shenanigans. I heard my other line go mid-rant and saw that it was my client. I pressed the ignore button and continued my slurring expletives to finish the story of the weekend's escapades.

Suddenly I heard a female Scottish accent going, "Jo, Jo. Are you 'right Jo?"

Oh fuck. Fuckety fuck, fuck, fuck.

I had done what only a hungover, bumbling, trouble magnet muppet of my calibre could do, and that was answer the other line by accident. What a fucking idiot.

I quickly exaggerated my sick sounding low-toned voice. Luckily I'd had more than enough late nights to add a good amount of raspy authenticity. I explained I was off sick.

"Oh no, that's awful," she said. "Sorry to bother you."

After a few hours of dissecting the wheels coming off and wallowing in a bottomless pit of self-loathing and guilt, topped off with some additional mental abuse, I crawled into my flatmate's room and decided to snap out of it quite quickly. I mean the bottom line was that I wasn't being paid for sick days being a freelancer so it wasn't like I was ripping anyone off. In fact, it was obviously a form of self-sabotage above everything else.

"Let's go get some tacos," I said. "I may as well do something to make the most of this surprise day off... and I fancy a margarita."

"I'm broke," he replied.

"Oh, bugger it. I'll pay," I said.

I realised at that point I could barely walk. I looked down at my ankles and saw I had gained some form of swollen cankles overnight. I had flashbacks of rolling my left ankle en route to the bathroom at the pub. At the time, I thought I did a great job of recovering myself without anyone noticing but then proceeded to do it again thirty minutes later to the right ankle. I guess I was balanced in some respects.

We grabbed a taxi and headed to Taqueria. Mmm, Mexican. I down a few classic margaritas, a couple of agua frescas and enough tacos to soak up a third of the booze. Math was never my strong point. We felt like playing pool, so we wandered to Portobello Road. Mau Mau was full, so we hit The Castle for a pint. At this point I'm drinking Leffe Blonde, one of my favourite beers, although little did I know it is also one of the strongest. I was tipsy already so we headed back to Mau Mau for take two; some hilarious banter and a few games of pool alongside a few more bottles of 'I wish I knew they were so strong' beers. I was three sheets to the wind. Again. On a Monday. And I had accidentally wagged work. We left after a few games, and I managed to kick Liso's arse in at least one so I'm happy.

We took a bus towards home, a little drunk, but more than capable of a bus ride. We hopped off at another local pub, The Chamberlayne on the way home, so of course headed in for another beer. Again, I ordered another Leffe and proceeded to solidify the pending drunkenness. We wandered back to Queens Park to walk off some of the booze. By this stage it was early evening and we bumped into the colourful regulars at our local. I thankfully switched to red wine. Ah, the Malbec. One of my favourite drops. Thankfully, I had the where-with-all to order a small pasta in order to remain semi-sober. Okay, that's a lie. Maybe it was really so I could stay sober enough for long enough to socialise some more and pack in some more booze. Just. Maybe. The queen of FOMO continues.

I moved outside to sit with some of the artsy locals. An interesting bunch at the best of times. Before you know it I was chatting up a hot architect and DJ called Scott and having intelligent conversation about branding. For some reason the crew expanded and the wines, without my going to the bar kept coming. Who doesn't need magic wine on a Monday night? Me. That's who. More chats, more wine, more moving into the wrong territory with Scott who is demanding that Peter calls his dealer to get a load of coke. At this point, given my previous three days of partying I decided to leave knowing that if I didn't, I was going to truly hate myself. Or potentially I was more scared at what I might do to myself. Scott demanded I have another wine and I caved at the speed of a well-trained boozer with a good disregard for reality and its various responsibilities. Thankfully after that, Scott disappeared inside on the phone and I made a run for it, getting home before last orders and in time for a decent sleep, albeit considerably drunk.

I arose the next morning at 7am for work, feeling the full effects of days of partying and a little worried that the boss might catch me smelling of booze. I decided it would be more plausible to have another day off sick anyway. The sign of a true wagging professional alcoholic-in-training. Technically, I had been grappling with a barrage of emotions for weeks since we put Stella down, not to mention the worry about Annie and her leg. So, a couple of unpaid mental health days to recover from emotional trauma actually seemed justifiable. Although it didn't escape me that this was about as self-destructive as you could get. I brushed it off as yet another 'It would only happen to you Jo' story, which was my brand after all. My stupid fucking brand.

I was aware I was going through one of my phases where I was living with reckless abandon, rolling the dice and letting the naughty gene win, yet now I didn't have my twenties as an excuse. The 'fuck it' mentality was overriding almost everything I did. If our whole time on the planet was supposed to be enjoyable and a good time then I didn't see how this shouldn't work out for me. However, it seemed that occasionally I got a right slap in the face from the Universe when I seemed to screw up royally, or something would go horribly awry. Where – I asked the Universe – is the fairness in that? Had I run out of luck? Was it the by-product of getting too cocky? Although Devo always got away with it, so surely not. Or was it a rerouting from the Universe in some way? Why, oh why, spirit guides? Tell me that?

My thoughts were transported back to my life in New York. At the end, despite a successful career I'd been in the depths of despair, not knowing who I was, what I was doing on this planet and what I was truly meant for. For years, I'd been living behind a mask of the party girl who always had a fun night out leading to a multitude of unbelievable occurrences that seemed more appropriate in a movie script. I was always the girl with a story. The problem was, when I stripped all that away, who was I? Would people care if I didn't have some dramatically hilarious trouble inducing antics to report? Was I in fact unconsciously in the very same place I was then, now? Right now, I was feeling distracted and irresponsible. Like I wanted to run away. Life was too short to be in a career that didn't ignite my inner passions and dreams, which is why I had left New York in the first place. To find my purpose and create a different life. To feel a deep sense of connection to what I was doing and the reason for it. To contribute to the bigger picture on this planet and why we are all here. Not working to live, building a nest egg and a family like every responsible adult 'should'. Was it irresponsible or was it, in fact, responsible to hear the callings of the heart and go against the current? I had a feeling it would make life so much easier if I found my partner, my person, so we could at least build something and work it out together. It seemed to have worked like that for most of my friends anyway to help them find their way. Yet I was further away from any semblance of an intimate relationship than ever. I knew I couldn't rely on anyone else to figure this out for me. But that knowledge didn't stop me yearning for the easy way out.

The time is now.
There is no time for getting in your own way.
Step aside and allow us to reside
within the oneness that is your true divine self.

Release the reins.
As the reins will constrict you in all you have to offer.
This new way of being requires that you let go.
Let go of the doubt. Let go of the fear. Let go of your unconsciousness.

We are with you at this time, waiting for you to grasp
the grandeur of the being you truly are and step into it.
Step into it without fear. There is no fear in your own power.
Only more comfort than you have ever known.

Allow yourself to sink into the unknown of what is.
You know deep down inside you what you have come to share.
It is time for you to recognise this now.

Recognition is ownership, and ownership is
claiming it, and all of this, is knowing it.
Knowing it so you can be it for yourself.

Pastures New

My position at the agency continued years past the freelance cover date. I had managed to morph into a more expanded and creative production role, but although I was doing what I thought would deeply satisfy me, I now realised this was not the case. I had the same feelings as every agency I'd worked at. It was nigh on impossible to find one without difficult client personalities, politics, ego and slave labour. Such is agency life. The problems were just with slightly different parties and in slightly different guises. Essentially it was all the same. Despite the step up in my job and achieving some of my career goals, here I was newly thirty-three and again mulling over what the hell to do with my life to placate this profoundly unfulfilling feeling that was constantly residing in the background of my being.

Again, I was smacked in the face by my inner knowing that there had to be more to life than this. This surviving, this getting by. Having an okay career, but not an extraordinary life. I wanted the full package; I wanted the dream. I wanted to be doing something with purpose that utilised my natural talents. I wanted to be paid to be me and be in service not only to myself, but others, the planet and the wider Universe while doing it.

I took a punt and wrote into Jenny, the Angel Lady at *Soul & Spirit* magazine. Which was pretty much the *Heat Magazine* of the spiritual world, and yes, as trashy as you could get but desperate times call for desperate measures.

Hi Jenny, I have been for a long time trying to re-evaluate my path to be more in line with my soul purpose and find a career that I am really passionate about. It feels even harder during a recession when one feels grateful to have any job. I've been finding

Who would have thought, but my question got answered with a channelled picture of my very colourful angel in yellows, pinks and corals and was published in the next issue. I was encouraged to not give up and keep pursuing my dreams. My heart would get me there.

I was desperate to solve the problem of myself, and I just knew deep down it was an inside job. It could not be solved by traditional means of career counselling, life coaching or just knuckling down and getting on with it. I carried a continual feeling from a young age that I was here to do something purposeful. This weight in the background was propelling me forward and yet fuelling dissatisfaction within me at the same time. I needed to get into alignment with my soul and what I was here to do.

Despite exploring many avenues through books, courses and events, I didn't seem to be any closer to cracking it, which translated into me feeling anxiously oversensitive and self-conscious. I'd cancel plans and stay home, unless I was feeling really on form, as I took some time out hibernating from the social scene. I was also having very visceral energy experiences where I suddenly felt like I was rolling in the sea. It was as if big waves were washing over me, which was dizzying to say the least. It had started on a trip months before. Although not as big and intense as the strong jolt I got then, it certainly felt like something was energetically happening to me.

In response I started a series of weekly healing sessions with Camilla, an energy healer Annie had been going to in New Zealand. Camilla's healing sessions began working in different areas. I needed time for self, in particular, time for my soul as I was going through a massive initiation. I was a soul who needed a lot of light and energy to feel balanced. This initiation was a transformational process where my consciousness was being pushed to move up, but part of me did not want to go, causing this push-pull feeling. Supposedly in ancient times, we all used to understand the process of initiation, which is not the case now. Now it is given a new name, depression. We cleared the unconscious emotional clutter that was depleting my energy. Some sadness related to a past life with Devo, and self-destructive patterns to help keep me on my own path, to stay in my truth not others' ideas. She programmed in harmony, love and joy into different areas of my being with the assistance of non-physical beings and energies. I could feel sensations of pricking, prodding and buzzing in different parts of my body while it was happening, remotely via Skype from New Zealand. I was advised to write. Write through the pain. Write my feelings. I was taught breathing techniques combined with visualisation to project these feelings out in the distance, plus advised to do Reiki healing on myself every morning. I needed to bring in the energy from the divine mother and angels to support this. Although I wasn't immediately cured, I certainly felt relief of some of the emotion I was holding after each session and I slowly started to feel more energetically on an even keel.

My love life continued in fits and starts, unsurprising given where I was at. Instead of taking time out for myself and creating the space needed to work through it and heal, a charming colleague from work kissed me on a boozy night out but I soon got the 'not a good idea with work people' speech. I was rejected once again. To make myself feel better, I lined up a rendezvous with Stunt Cock, a dalliance from a stint in New Zealand a few years back, which unfortunately ended when his larger than life stunt penis refused to work. This only amplified my feelings of inadequacy. I masked the embarrassing sequence of disastrous male interactions with a series of nights out to medicate my discomfort in my own skin. All perfectly executed, except now in my thirties they came with next day anxiety, which was license for my internal dialogue to hold me ransom in my head. I sure liked to put the boot into myself when I was down.

I booked a long weekend getaway to Cinque Terre in Northern Italy with my friend Ange as a distraction. Italian women in six-inch heels hiking between the cliff-hugging villages proved to me that perhaps I didn't have the silliest foot forward after all. The weekend was full of delicious food and

Italian wine, which we gave a good nudge when we ended up in a late-night lock-in at our local cappuccino bar in the sleepiest of Italian villages.

I arrived back to the real world with a terrible sore throat to pay for my sins of the weekend and a twenty-one-year-old Israeli student who had been moved into the flat without consultation. He seemed nice enough but certainly wasn't a flatmate we would have chosen. It was the straw that broke the camel's back with a problematic landlord. I woke up the next day to "If it's not working – move out. If you're not happy – just move out. Get a move on – just move out," playing on my iPod shuffle. I took it as a sign from the Universe and made my decision right then and there. There was a certain amount of liberation that came with making a decision based on messages from the non-physical. I was of the belief that nothing in actual fact was random, because we don't live in a random Universe at all. Everything was far too perfectly formulated in nature to be anything otherwise. Why would we be any different?

It was the perfect decision for a change to get me out of old patterns. I moved to a new gorgeous flat overlooking the leafy green of Queens Park with one of my best old school friends. It was a newly renovated two bedroom flat just a few doors down from Sienna Miller, and Thandie Newton lived on the opposite side of the park. Although only a few blocks away, a major step up indeed. Despite the injection of fresh energy from the move, my healing sessions and my own work I had been doing on myself, I still felt like an emotional basket case. My very dear old friend soon cottoned on, gently asking me one summer's day whether I was depressed and perhaps needed to see someone about it. The thing was, technically I didn't feel depressed. My job was going fine, I was in a fab new flat, I had a surplus of friends and travel adventures. I didn't really feel sad about anything despite being highly emotional. I wasn't in my dream career, but I didn't feel like it was a lost cause. It was a work in progress.

What I was feeling felt more to me like a chemical imbalance in my body, versus a mental issue. My persistent hormonal problems had worsened to PMS for three weeks out of every four, no doubt a major contributing factor. My gut feeling was that I needed to go on the pill to balance it all out, so despite being very resistant to doctors and medications, I made an appointment the following week.

"Sometimes as much as you hate modern medicine, it can be a solution," Camilla said in my next healing session.

It worked, and as the weeks passed, I started to feel better. I knew, however, that underlying all of it was that I had been ignoring my spirit and needed some time on my own to recalibrate. Instead of going to my flatmate's birthday party, I booked a weekend away in Glastonbury to peruse the sacred sites of the Tor and Chalice Wells. Some time and space for my soul exploring as prescribed. I always felt better when I was in nature. It felt immediately healing for me as I was more connected, grounded and nourished.

It did not last though, so as soon as I got back to the city, I immediately broke up with alcohol again and jumped into another absolvent attempt. I got back into my tennis, started kickboxing lessons and continued my social shenanigans sober. Despite the lack of social lubricant, my natural energy had me dancing on tables in a Corona cowboy hat at Guanabara bar at 2am, although karaoke was more of a stretch for my sober wings. I had proved to myself that I could do it though and have fun either way.

I continued my search into other avenues to further my learning and interest of all things holistic, trying to find the right path. I sent Annie an email with some trepidation, asking her thoughts on a potential Cellular Awakening, six-month-long course. She had run the gamut of most spiritual modalities, courses and learnings over the years, so naturally tended to brush off anything in a been there done that kind of way.

Jo, I was always keen for you to do whatever you wanted. After all, at some point in all our lives, we are curious and wish to explore what this world offers. However, it may have been that when I myself realised that 'all is not as it seems' here in relation to bodies and minds and the physicality of everything, that I became cynical which is a tendency of mine without a doubt! It is the cynical part that needed to be stimulated beyond itself and that started after Disappearance of the Universe by Gary R. Renard which led me back to a Course in Miracles for the past three years. Then my accident led me down other corridors in my mind – and these are very difficult to find my way around! What I am saying is that YOU have found something that excites me beyond measure! All we ever did or got involved with prior to now, is simply stepping stones or way-showers to prepare us for the next part of our journey! I am horrified that I made you nervous! I do apologise! It was never my intention to do so! Of late I have been strangely aware that I do need to go beyond cynicism for my own self! It may well be that what you have found could be it! As Don Miguel Ruiz says in *The 4 Agreements*, 'Do not take things personally!' It may take a while to get that for some! A key factor is to desire more than anything in oneself to be rid of fear! Fear is basically a big con. This world runs on it and makes mega bucks out of it! Naturally 'they' don't want you to discover that it is simply an 'implant' and can be removed! XXX A

I wasn't convinced the course was the one for me, so I passed on it but managed to make it to forty-one days with no booze and no cigs. Not so good on the chocolate, naturally substituting one thing for another. With everyone commenting about how glowing and healthy I looked, I tried not to take offence that I looked like shit generally. Despite over two months of puritanical behaviour, however, I was still feeling well below average. Toxins fleeing or not I was starting to wonder if it were more than that. It was like some kind of reverse breakdown. Suddenly I was thinking about volunteering in Africa. Or joining a cult. All this behaving like a Brethren made me feel like I needed something to spice my life up a bit. A cult could be just the ticket. It's fine to be crazy, you get to grow your own veggies, and they all have sex with each other, which is more than I was getting in my hideously sad excuse for a sex life. Annie had her own take, as usual.

> What the egotistical little runts of our society do is blame everything on our addictions/inability to detox, and all those amazing made up things! I do apologise here – this is not a go at you – but NZ IS GOING CRAZY – NUTS! It is in all the papers! At the moment we are even being told to have a certain drug to take – a body to have etc. The media is going MAD! Peace is about not buying into the rantings and ravings going on in our world but by tuning in to the energy that makes it function!

My inner boxing match continued like a broken record. What do you do if you don't know who you are, who you want to be and what all of this means? I constantly felt that there must be more to life than this but each search came up empty. Not only that, but I was disappointed that I was not making more of myself, of doing things differently, of being creative and having the guts to put it out into the public domain. I was spiritually aware, tuned in to my surroundings, open to the possibilities and signs. Why was life not throwing me in the direction I needed to make more of myself? To fulfil my role on the planet? Why was I not meeting the right people to propel me into other territories and experiences? I didn't question this from a victim mentality, because I had done some amazing things in my life but my endless curiosity for cracking the code of my reality meant I couldn't help but ask why. And want more. If life came along with opportunities to jump ship into another career or another world, I would leap at the chance. I just couldn't work out why these opportunities weren't showing up for me no matter who I talked to, what I did or how I put myself out there.

I loved to write, but my experience was very limited in this field. I was working on an idea for a book but the story hadn't even happened yet. I didn't know what to write about. I felt like I was sleepwalking through life, generally unsatisfied and looking for some kind of escape. Who the hell was I now? I was not sure I ever knew actually. I had just experimented with different personalities and fronts to see what fit. Here I was in my mid-thirties, with a good chunk of my life gone and nothing seemed to fit. What was the point?

I realised I was angry with this life. Angry and frustrated because things weren't going my way. I knew it was a choice. A choice in my perception of how I wanted to be and feel, but wasn't that just faking it? I'd been faking it and not feeling it for twenty years. I think it was safe to say that it didn't really work. I felt conflicted and unsettled. I'd had enough.

An email from Annie arrived at the appropriate time to guide me to trust.

'Oh, my dear Jo ~ What a week! Goet Allah! Today has been amazing for me – my whole body seems to have accelerated 'back to mine' – I know no other way to put it! I am revelling in some kind of 'peace state' that I remember from some distant past – but with a new twist perhaps...hmm...I find it fascinating...Devo is OK ...HA! I got so worried earlier – he seemed to skid down into some type of oblivion. Thank you for your wise words – to not get inveigled! Mostly I have not let that happen – or so I thought! It all passes ... All the crap stuff that is ... I mostly notice that it is not ALL ME! I get affected momentarily by another person's meltdown which I realised was not my own...Then it all kind of dissipates... And goes... Wherever it does go to!!!!!!!! I have never felt so down, and then UP so fast in all my life! Not that I go for the down bits, I am always on the alert to some degree! My hairdresser was telling me he was having major night sweats and thinking he was having a stroke or heart attack! Well, 'Annie White Witch of Herne Bay' could not resist to say: Oh, don't worry about those – I've been having them too! It is just the planet stepping up on the light frequencies! Ha! The woman next to me just did a double take and her newly applied dye just about melted. There is more going on behind the scenes than we know! I trust it all for the good of all! XXX A.'

Be at one with who you truly are,
for you have much to offer, much to give.
Your wisdom is infinite and your embrace of light everlasting.
You are light. You are the light where there is none.
You are a being from beyond space and time,
who carries this light with you to light the way for others.

Be who you can be. Do not be afraid to let this show.
For there is much wisdom within you. Access this now.
Delve deep into the ocean of your being to find
the treasures you have stored there.

Take the time to sit with the knowing
of the transcendent being that you are.
For the way your consciousness works is unknown to many.
And it will be of surprise to you that this is where your gift lies.
But you must work out how to bring it forth.
As only when you do you will realise, this is your light, your truth.

This is who you are.
Not who you think you are.
But who you truly are.

When In Doubt, Cactus Will Work It Out

I soon tired of trying to resolve my unsolvable issues and reverted back to my usual social escapades. Despite not being able to magnetise my perfect career opportunity, I could easily attract any form of random trouble on a night out. Looking back, I see that this was more impatience and distraction from the lurking dissatisfaction of my life, as nothing I was doing seemed to solve it. Although this time I was keeping up my healthy behaviours and good intentions to balance out my natural inclination to the opposite. Or, as somewhat of a mature progression, a mash-up between the two.

On one particular instance, I got home at 2am after too much imbibing but was up at 7am to attempt one of the *Timeout 30 Country Walks* near London. Solo. It was all going surprisingly swimmingly until I got off the train to start the walk. No sooner than ten minutes into it and I was already going off-piste and having to backtrack. Good start Jo. After figuring out the missed turn I headed into the country walking up a storm, feeling all healthy, spiritual and holier than thou. Getting in touch with nature for some connection and some alone time was just what I needed. No sooner was I ensconced in my new-found virtuosity than it came tumbling down. Lost. Again. Wrong turn. Again. Clearly not paying enough attention at this point. One hundred and twenty-two degree turns here and then a north-west turn after five hundred yards there. The Timeout guide was proving far too complicated.

After a couple more wrong turns, through not following my intuition, I decided to follow this over the book instructions entirely. To try and hear that voice that should be navigating me through the roads of life without bother. My spidey sense had been previously correct for the last two 'lost' incidences. I was obviously more equipped than I gave myself credit for. This philosophy was all fine until I ended up lost again. In the middle of nowhere, completely and utterly disorientated without directions matching the book in any way, shape, or form. After traipsing through some paddocks in a best guess scenario, I found myself communing with some horses. I was channelling my inner Dr Doolittle, given I had always found these creatures slightly unnerving after almost falling off one. I liked horses, I just didn't like being on them. After some successful horse-whispering, just when I thought I was making progress, I heard some stomping and neighing from a distant horse that sounded far from friendly. I upped my walk to a run as I was narrowly chased out of the paddock at speed by said horse. Horses 1. Jo 0.

Some time later, I arrived in a tiny village, still lost and had to ask directions. Somehow, moments later I stumbled past the landmark Oast houses, denoted in the guide book. Clinging to the compass on my iPhone and the last of its twenty percent battery for dear life, I was by this point thirsty and starving. I finally made it to the scheduled lunch spot in the guidebook, albeit at 3.30pm instead of 12.30pm, a veritable triumph nonetheless. I staggered into the bar and ordered a pint, which I proceeded to skull in about three gulps. I ordered a bottle of rosé, water and a salad. One might note the significantly unbalanced alcohol to food ratio, again. After eight hours of no sustenance, clearly this was going to have a significant impact on one's ability to continue with the second half of the walk. However, it was a beautiful afternoon as I sat bathing in the sun with my rosé. Before I knew it I was joking with the locals, as you do, chatting up a storm and getting the local lay of the land. They were incredulous when my ex-flatmate Joanne called, or Jo 2, who was also my namesake. Her dad and Devo were best friends and she was named after me when they didn't know what to call her. Allegedly, Devo insisted on her being called Joanna, so they went with Joanne to be different or so the story goes. I blatantly blagged her into making the train journey out with the promise of a tantalising social scene including ten amazing pubs, and some hot locals for a pub crawl.

My new friends were in fits. "Jo, you're mistaken," one said in a thick English accent, "it's one-and-a-half hours to get here not forty-five minutes, there are no taxis at the train station and there are all of four pubs in the village!" Of course, I vaguely knew this. Tricking unsuspecting campaigners into adventurous journeys was one of my highly skilled credentials, but they were right in predicting that Joanne would likely be fuming by the time she arrived. They helped me order her a taxi to meet her train, which was the key to pulling off this caper for my impromptu country party. An hour and forty-five minutes later, I was surrounded by handfuls of new country BFFs and holding court when Jo 2 pulled up in the taxi. She gave me the look of death as soon as she alighted from said cab. No sooner had she arrived at the table I had a glass of rosé at the ready saying, "The vista Joanne, look at the vista!" before distracting her with introductions to my new country crew.

A bottle of wine later, she was well adjusted and genuinely excited at the randomness that had become her afternoon. We headed to the next pub where Jo 2 was in fits at my impressive local status, knowing pretty much everyone in town in a matter of hours. We proceeded to pub crawl through the four delightful pubs in the area, creating quite the scene. I was on form, holding court with Devo's gift of the gab, personably commanding presence coming out of me in spades.

Sure enough by 10.30pm, after an afternoon and eve regaling the locals with stories and drinking our weight in rosé, we were well on our way. We were now at one of the four pubs for the second time that evening. It was only then that we discovered the untapped supply of young hot country lads. Suddenly there were plentiful offers of places to stay, as we were leaving for the last train home. "You're amazing, you can't leave, you're the best thing that's happened to Mayfield all year!" they yelled.

I had to drag Jo 2 away who was quite besotted with said men, but we made the train just in time. "This is one of the best nights I've had in ages!" said Jo 2 cheerily as we sat on the train, her head drunkenly lolling on my shoulder. "I've got to hand it to you, you are quite something. Who would have thought we'd be the celebrities of Mayfield in the space of an afternoon."

Jo Walden. Famous in Mayfield. I never did finish the last half of that walk.

Being a self-confessed walking contradiction, my wholesome debauchery meant I was still very much on the hunt for a miracle. Or, some sort of holistic practice that would give me all the answers I was looking for to find my purpose and guarantee me a new fulfilling life. I attended various lectures all over London learning about healing and energy work, this philosophy or that technique but nothing seemed to click. I usually went alone, and never discussed much with my friends. I was basically hiding out in the spiritual closet. In semi-delusional desperation to find answers, I spontaneously decided to partake in plant medicine. A San Pedro cactus journey was being hosted just outside of London by an Australian shaman who had apparently spent time in Peru since the late nineties. She had trained in apprenticeship with a shaman and spiritual teachers there, which meant her work with plant medicine was highly regarded and respected. If you can't go to Peru, then let Peru come to you.

I was running late due to work and after confessing I was going to a Peruvian shaman ceremony, minus the bit about the crazy cactus juice, the taxi driver spent the entire journey from the train station telling me about all of his spiritual experiences and the medium he regularly saw to chat to his deceased mother. Naturally. As the taxi rolled up, I saw firstly a weather-beaten picket fence that hadn't seen a new paint job in years, accented with a yellow sarong decorated with suns and moons tied to the front gate. The fence encased a house and garden which were equally as ramshackle-looking, and littering the lawn were tents, blankets and various makeshift structures. In amongst it all were a couple of people wearing tie-dyed tops and Thai fisherman pants. Hmmm. Not exactly what I was expecting. I contemplated getting the cab straight back to the station. I gave myself an immediate talking to. Don't judge a book by its cover Jo! I grabbed my bag and opened the gate, heading towards an open door which led into a kitchen. I asked the small group of girls where Julie the organiser was, and they said she was around somewhere. Their eyes were as big as saucers and no one was wearing a bra. Clearly. Suddenly a blonde girl talking about "how at one with nature we are," took off her clothes and streaked out into the garden. I was gripped by an incredibly strong urge to flee. I turned back to the street. No taxi in sight.

Julie finally found me and directed me to the lounge where I waited until I was introduced to 'Shamanista Sheryl,' the shaman imported straight from the Peruvian hillside. She was an older woman, probably in her sixties with long, straight white hair that fell to her waist and aged spotted skin, conjuring up visions of some kind of witch. Her pupils were so dilated, you could barely see the blue of her striking coloured eyes. She took me outside to the back garden where mounds of bodies wrapped in coloured blankets lay all over the lawn. I felt like I was in a scene from the apocalyptic movie *28 Days Later*. I followed her into a tent where she pulled out a jar of brownish powder which she made into a drink. She told me to drink it. No chit-chat, no ceremony, no shamanic advice, no spiel about what I was doing there, or what I could expect.

She said it would take forty minutes or so to kick in and I should lie on the lawn while it took full effect. Depending on how I went with this dose, if I felt I needed more, I should see her. This was more like a drug deal and hardly the sacred spiritual experience I was hoping for. I'd clearly missed any form of explanation, ritual, not to mention ceremony, and my shaman seemed kind of high herself. Brilliant.

Best make the most of a bad situation then, and off I went to attempt to carve out some sort of space on the lawn. Gazing at the sky, the sun felt good on my skin. I could hear hippy music wafting from the house, "Mother I feel you under my feet, mother I hear your… heartbeat." Cringe. This was almost my worst nightmare. There was a reason why I didn't take myself off to all these spiritual group experiences; it had just been so long I'd forgotten why. After a while of lying there, I snuck a few looks around to see who else was around me and what was going on. One girl was crying. Another was convulsing. One other was being sick into a bucket. A couple walked by who looked like they were walking on the moon. It seemed ludicrous, but my late arrival seemed to have thrown me into an anxious and disconnected space, which was completely out of sync with the utter lunacy of what was going on around me. Where were the zombies when you needed them? At least they could have put me out of my misery of weird outsider awkwardness. I decide to just grin and bear it. I was not wasting three hundred and fifty quid on nothing. After the kick-in period, I noticed a heightened sense of nature. Nothing heavy hitting. Just a subtle nudge up to high definition colour, sound and connection. Come on San Pedro, whatcha got?

I felt uneasy. I laid on the lawn not knowing what to do with myself. I went to the bathroom just to give myself an opportunity to check what else was going on. Stopping by the kitchen for some water, the streaker girl was in the middle of some highly dramatic gesturing about feeling the universal love being like nothing she had ever known. Her eyes looked wild, and she was flailing her body around like a half-naked drunk. I leant against the bench while I drank my water and then left. No opening in the conversation there. Probably best since my cynicism was out in full force, and it was only adding to the feeling I had of being incredibly separate from the group. This in turn fed my anxiety, which only seemed to escalate matters. I bumped into the shaman witch outside who asked how I was doing. I said I thought I potentially needed a little more. In fact I knew I did. At this point getting high was far more appealing given what I was confronted with. After a second dose of cactus juice, I lay down again for a while trying to sort my head out. I started laughing. What do you expect if you run off on some cactus journey in greater London with a bunch of people you've never met? I saw a couple of people heading out the back gate towards trees and a field. I sat tight for ten minutes to give them a head start before following.

I walked down the drive, past some chickens and a few goats. It was semi-rural living. Once I was through the back gate, it opened up into a walkway lined with trees. Here, I wandered aimlessly and finally decided that the field adjacent looked like an excellent spot to park up. I fell backwards into the waist high long grass. Sitting up I could barely even see out into the rest of the world. It was a great hideout. The grass was whispering in the wind around me. The clouds were beaming me messages from the sky. I contemplated the experience thus far. Definitely not hallucinogenic. A very chilled out tickling of the senses. A far cry from my experimental acid tripping youth. At this point, some of those experiences felt more impactful. What the hell was I doing here again?

After forty-five minutes or so of quiet meditation with nature, I went back to the house. I met a couple of guys outside and immediately warmed to them, thankfully having some meaningful conversation and sharing of ideas of a spiritual nature. Then we lent a hand to making the 'love soup', which we were to eat that evening. Over dinner, I was asked to regale the group with the same *28 Days Later* story of my arrival, which I did with some embellished dramatics. The entire room was roaring with laughter. It was good to feel part of the group, finally. After dinner, sitting around with cups of tea I finally felt like I was getting the spiritual nourishment and connection I came for. Later one of the men pulled me aside saying he had totally shifted due to the conversation we had, and he was very grateful. I was chuffed. Maybe it wasn't about me at all. Maybe that was all I came for. To be the key piece in someone else's puzzle.

We finally went to bed, which was a couple of cushions in the lounge. Certainly not my idea of the kind of sleepover one should be having with new acquaintances, but it topped off the bizarrely disorganised experience I had been having.

With the cactus journey being devoid of any real insight, and my health an ongoing bugbear including a string of stomach bugs, fevers and flus; I couldn't drink alcohol without vomiting, London life continued in a far more lacklustre manner and as it did I continued to contemplate the meaning of life and why mine wasn't more amazing. I didn't know what to do, so I did what any desperate, slightly-bananas, mid-thirties single woman would do. I decided to climb a mountain.

Be not that which you see around you.
Be your own version of the truth.
For it is who you are, and you can never avoid this.
This is you!

The spirit of truth you are working with at this time.
Call on truth in any situation.
Truth for yourself and others.
Although you may not viscerally be able to feel it
this place holds great resonance for you, and all humanity.
For there are keys here, keys to unlock that which you are looking for.

We beckon you with the freedom you deserve.
For love is all there is and more.
Distinguish between the souls you wish to progress with.
Use your discernment for you spent much time gaining this.

Stop trying, forcing, pushing and just relax into your being.
For that is more than enough.
Just close your eyes and be.
Relaxation is key for you.
For this journey is yours alone.

A Killer Climb

I was invited to Cape Town for a wedding, so since I was in the neighbourhood, I figured I'd climb Mount Kilimanjaro en route. Nothing like a ridiculous physical challenge to provide focus with the dangling carrot of self-accomplishment, and the possibility to potentially heal your self-worth. If I could in fact, pull it off.

I immediately bought some new boots and started hiking all over London to wear them in. In the weekends I went on country rambles, enjoying delicious pub stops in between the endless miles of delicately pretty English countryside. I was covering a lot of terrain, but not a lot of hills. You can't really count the South Downs. England wasn't exactly filled with challenging mountain ranges. However, this didn't faze me. I managed the Pyrenees with little to no training. This was a seven-day slow climb up a mountain. Surely, I'd be fine.

I convinced my old boss from New York to accompany me on the climb. I was genuinely surprised she was interested, given she was more Punjabi Princess than Intrepid Hiker. Ritu fired over a series of typically American yet genuine concerns, regarding the seriousness of the challenge. These were met with my very Kiwi *'She'll be right,'* sweeping generalisations and an array of positive stories of successful climbers far older than ourselves. The Machame route was basically one of the easiest anyway, I told her assuredly. Once she was finally all signed up, I received an email, *Martina Navratilova Forced to Give Up Climb of Mount Kilimanjaro.* I guess she still had doubts. I decided not to dwell on the fact that even a great sports star couldn't do it and cracked on in my usual blind naivety.

My attempted training was going well, although despite all the healthy behaviour and staying in on weekends, I was still regularly afflicted by sore throats and fevers. It was now absolutely clear that this did not correspond to my extensive social life or drinking habits or diet. Something else was going on entirely. A decade later a prominent medium asked if I was plagued by illness in my thirties. She said I was a planetary healer who had at some point in my soul journey signed up to process a certain amount of healing for Mama Earth, which is why it was relentless and didn't necessarily make any logical sense. This was certainly food for thought. There is so much we can't remember in the amnesia of our dense consciousness when we incarnate on earth that can contribute to illness. Emotions, thoughts, environmental factors, blocked energy, soul contracts. No matter how much research we do in the medical and science fields, they are still not accounting for all contributing factors. I truly believe nothing is as it seems and we will continue to evolve our understanding as we give more credence to the unseen, as much as the seen.

Leaving for Kilimanjaro, I was in a mad panic. Between trying to find a new roommate, training and packing for the trek, fundraising for an African orphanage and covering not only my client service job but the TV production role at the office, life was incredibly hectic. I kept the faith, and everything finally fell into place. Right at the last minute I signed a new roommate and got to the airport by the skin of my teeth. I was madly firing off emails right until the plane took off but as soon as those wheels left the tarmac, I let the frenzy of it all fade away as I made my way to Africa.

Not long from landing in Tanzania I opened the blind next to my seat, gasping as I saw beautiful Mount Kilimanjaro bathed in early morning sun. I could see the top of the mountain right up here in the clouds just below plane height. Holy guacamole, it really was rather tall, wasn't it.

The Kilimanjaro climb was like nothing I had ever attempted. After we made our way through the Machame Gate and into the rainforest on the first day, it was a steep climb upwards on a muddy path. The steamy jungle temperatures had me dripping profusely in sweat, while porters loaded up with vast amounts of heavy gear sped past us like lithe mountain goats. Rather embarrassing.

Team Kilimanjaro encompassed Bob, a sixty-year-old vet from Boulder, Colorado, John of similar age from the same place, Patty, a fifty-one-year-old chef from Oregon and her teenage son Adrian, Gill a fifty-three-year-old Canadian artist, two German women, Catherine from Berlin and Julie from Munich, a couple of Irish guys and Ritu and myself. Our guide John was a Maasai as was his brother Jakobe. Both came from a large family as their father was a typical Maasai elder with a wealth of wives.

The terrain changed a few hours later to more lush sub-alpine shrubbery filled with beautiful African wildflowers. At a rest point, we looked back to see a never-ending trail of people behind us. The altering mountain terrain was breathtakingly beautiful. It was like being in Fred Flintstone's back garden. There were all sorts of fascinating prehistoric looking plants and rocks that I'd never seen before. The plan for each day was to hike to a particular high point and then sleep lower, as a method for acclimatisation. The first day was spent hiking uphill for seven hours and we camped that night, pitching our tents on a rocky, barren slope. I wasn't a massive fan of camping in general, let alone camping on the side of a mountain but when we were presented with an absolute feast that night I wondered what I was worried about.

The second day was slower and more methodical, as we climbed through the rocky lower alpine terrain. We were only going 5km, yet it took us five hours. It was ten times steeper than the day before with some scrambling over rocks thrown in for good measure. The peak of Kilimanjaro, Uhuru, was in the background, seen in glimpses through the clouds. The dawning realisation that I was actually climbing a mountain set in. It certainly looked very far away and alarmingly, rather snowy. How on earth was I going to get up there? "Polay, polay," the porters and guides kept telling us. Meaning 'pole by pole' or 'slowly' in Kiswahili. One foot after the other will get you there. Shiva camp was a few hours of steep rock climbing, which was a million miles away from the gradual saunter up a mountain I was envisioning. It was already more challenging than anticipated. Perhaps Martina was right after all.

The following day was a big day of 11km and six to seven hours. We hiked up to the Lava Tower and Shark's Tooth rock formation at 4,600m, and then back down to sleep at the Barranco Camp at 3,900m. The camp was famous for being the last stop before the treacherous Barranco Wall. As the team set up camp and our new latrine, we had hours to contemplate the humongous crazy wall looming ominously in the distance. This instilled a palpable amount of fear amongst the troops. Ritu, who had done far more research on the terrain than I, was particularly concerned, "Are they doing this to strategically do reverse psychology on us or what?!" she exclaimed in between panicked breaths. Bob was busy going over the notes and exercises from his therapist, which kept him on the straight and narrow after some post-war addiction problems. American John was imparting an array of fascinating geographical information about the terrain to Patty who had proved herself far mightier than her tiny pint-sized frame and Adrian was brooding around not talking to anyone as every seventeen-year-old does. The German Girls and Gill were having an in-depth discussion about their volunteering experiences in Tanzania, including strategies to stop getting married off to a Tanzanian man in the process, all of whom want a white wife! This was all an excellent distraction from the hideously terrifying height of the Barranco Wall not far away.

I had no idea exactly how dangerous it was until the following morning when I was up close and personal with said wall. It was a 297m steep rock face with a sheer drop on the other side. There were no safety ropes, nor much to hold onto. It was rocky and wet and an almost vertical climb, so we were scrambling our way up, hands and feet gripping where we could. The height made my knees go to jelly and my heart skip a beat if I glanced downward. This did not stop the porters going at top speed, overtaking us on tiny ledges, which meant hazardous situations occurring minute by minute. I clung on for dear life with porters crawling around me as I saw packages come loose and tumble way down into the ravine below. I shivered at the unthinkable. It felt like I held my breath for the entire climb. This Barranco Wall was no fricking joke. One wrong move and you could be a goner. When we stopped for lunch some hours later we were informed by our lead guide John that a porter had plummeted to his death that very morning. This information hung in the air as no one knew what to say.

As we moved into high alpine zone later in the day, it was very misty at higher altitude with lots of yellow-brown grasses and lichen plants in the other-worldly desert like terrain. There were also beautiful mountain daisies peeking through every now and then. Thankfully, this part of the trek had a few larger rocks which meant we ladies could take a pee. The crowded trail and desolate, barren landscape had meant relieving ourselves was often a challenge. Oh, to be a boy and just point and shoot anywhere standing up.

That night in the mess tent over dinner when our guide John was briefing us on what was to come, he said that although the Machame route was more challenging and adventurous than others, the scenery like we had today made it worth it. Ritu glared at me across the table. "It's pretty much the same as the Marangu route though, right John?" I said trying to downplay the situation. "Well, if the Machame route is known as the Whisky route and Marangu route is known as the Coca Cola route, what do you think Jo?" he said sarcastically. Ritu was fuming.

Overnight we were hit with a freak snowstorm, which was unheard of in this low-level area of the mountain. This meant that the trek was harder work as we trudged through snow all the next day. The weather descended into blizzard conditions by the afternoon. I was wrapped up in multiple layers, polar fleece and a heavy-duty poncho over my hot pink weatherproof jacket. My sunglasses kept the snow out of my eyes as we continued on, pole by pole. I had noticed I was feeling a little nauseous on and off. Being the au natural hippy, I hadn't bothered with any medication for altitude. There was no guarantee it would work, and it would also have other side effects, so I was taking ginkgo biloba to help any symptoms. So far, I wasn't sure if it was working. In fact, I was deeply suspicious it was not working at all by the constant headaches and slight queasy feeling in my stomach, which tended to come and go more frequently as the day went on. I was praying I'd be able to make it up the summit the following night, a full blue moon. At this point the freak weather was more of a concern. What were the chances of me climbing a mountain in the worst weather it had seen in ten years?

The following day after some serious trudging in blizzard conditions for hours on end, we reached the Barafu camp at 4,680m. It was freezing, and we were all beyond exhausted. The tents were set up on a slope of rocky terrain in full snow. There was not usually snow this low down on the mountain. We could see the clouds down below us. I was almost sure there was no life up here at all until I saw a tiny cute gerbil looking creature run around the back of my tent. We stretched and kicked back for a couple of hours as we waited for our amazing local chefs to prepare our meal. As we hung about on the snowy ledge, we were passed by an older European couple in their sixties who were strolling around the campsite with their sticks and thick accents. I felt a digging of Ritu's elbow in my side. She was furiously nodding towards the couple.

"Did you see the capes they were wearing? And full faces of makeup? What the hell!" she whispered to me. By this point Ritu and I were a little on the ripe side and most definitely feeling the effects of camping three-quarters of the way up a mountain.

"They look like they are taking a casual stroll through Kensington Gardens!" she shrieked.

By the end of this crazy weather day everything we had was wet, including Ritu's gloves which she relied on heavily for her princess fingers.

"How on earth are they going to get dry?" Ritu said forlornly as she shivered in the cold.

"Sleep with 'em on. That's what we did in 'Nam," said Bob the veteran. Ritu nodded along obediently.

It had become abundantly clear that Bob had way more experience in pretty much everything, not to mention he was the head of the pack each day by miles. He was, at this point, our hero. As I was chatting to the Irish lads on our team, we saw a commotion to our left as a handful of porters struggled with a stretcher containing a body above their head. They were yelling while trying to make their way down the mountain with extreme urgency. We found out later it was one of the porters from another company. They had lost him in the end. I felt a pit in the centre of my stomach. This was the daily danger for these Tanzanians, who worked on this mountain to care for their families. None of them had proper footwear or gear for the conditions, and there were fatalities, which was a constant reminder to me of how fortunate I was. This event did nothing for my already shaky confidence.

I'd chosen Focus in Africa to climb with instead of a commercial company. It was a non-profit organisation that used the funds to help local communities at a grassroots' level with volunteering programmes, orphanages, women's aid and HIV awareness among others. I'd fundraised a couple of thousand pounds to help build a new orphanage but when I saw our team and their lack of proper equipment for such dangerous conditions, it seemed they needed it as much as anyone else. Despite the tragedy all we could do was refocus on what was ahead of us for our own safety and everyone else's.

A few hours later we were served an early dinner, as we were to hit the hay for three to four hours before starting our midnight summit. "So, the summit later tonight is going to be a lovely hike in the moonlight with this full moon. Right, John? Surely it can't be worse than what we just did?" I said innocently after our particularly gruelling day. John gave me another incredulous look which had become a regular nightly occurrence since we started, as I wound him up with my naively upbeat questions and comments. Ritu was not only cursing me at this point, but was also feeling the effects of the altitude, despite taking the medication, and decided not to summit. Julie also decided not to go. I was feeling pretty sick myself, but there was no way I was hiking all this way and then not going to give it a go. Stubborn determination meant not attempting the summit was never an option in my mind, despite having clear symptoms of altitude sickness. I figured I could take an anti-nausea pill and give it a crack. Our guide told us that the percentage of people who don't summit was much higher than one would think, at around eighty percent for the Machame route, which was terrifying. Although later I found that was from the official National Park figures, which were very out-dated. It's about sixty percent of people who actually do reach the summit now. Which still isn't that high! Some make it to Stella Point at 5,739m and then never make it to the true Uhuru peak. However, I wasn't deterred. The freezing conditions combined with the constant feeling of nausea meant I hadn't got a wink of sleep when the bell went at 11pm. As much as I wanted to throw in the towel and stay in bed, I got up and prepared, ready to leave after a cup of tea and biscuit in the mess tent. Just think about the inevitable effects on tightening up your arse Jo, I thought.

When we started the ascent, the snow had turned to ice and it was very, very slippery. It was difficult to see the terrain in front of me properly with my tiny headlamp but I could see hundreds of lights shining and moving up ahead. Hordes of people were summiting. Many were far, far up ahead. It was super steep and in the dark the climb was very hard. It was precarious and quite scary on the slippery ice. The terrain was supposed to be rocky until two hours from the top, but the freak weather conditions brought snow and ice from the very beginning, and cloud to cover the moonlight, which made visibility especially challenging. I kept plodding away but it was very, very slow going. I passed others having rests along the way who also seemed to be finding it as tough as I was. I had fallen well behind the group but just continued on at my own pace with one guide alongside me. I was so nauseous I kept throwing up on the side along the way. I couldn't keep any food or water down and with little sleep at altitude in the days preceding, there wasn't much juice in the tank. I tried to muffle my desperate crying. Every step felt so heavy and difficult trudging through the snow in pitch black darkness and I wondered why I was doing this to myself. I saw many people who had given up and were on their way down. It was just too tough. One of them was a marathon runner. They wished me luck.

The clouds cleared a bit to shed the light of the full blue moon, which helped a little. At sunrise I was more than halfway, but nowhere near the summit, where I was supposed to be at that time of the morning. The guide who had stayed with me was far from sympathetic. In fact, he seemed genuinely annoyed at my incredibly slow pace. Every time I stopped, he would tell me to get up and keep going. Even when I was doubled over vomiting. I collapsed on the snow to watch the sunrise over Kili's third peak and take a breather. Mr Guide sat there frowning and looking like he hated me. I turned on the waterworks and he suddenly seemed a bit more sympathetic and put a supportive arm around me. Although I just wanted to give up, something inside me wouldn't allow me to. It was a perfectly clear morning with a golden horizon line. The beautiful golden light reflected on the snow was quite something and filled me with the determination to keep going. I still had two hours to go but at least I could properly see where I was going now. It was incredibly steep. Steep to the point where you are unbalanced and might fall and roll down the mountain. There were a few other slowpokes like me, which made me feel a little better as I trudged my way up the snow in what had quickly turned to piercing sunshine. I finally reached Stella Point and collapsed. There were crowds of people who were lining up to head to the preeminent peak a short distance away. No one was there from my team that I could see. On the way to the peak the glacier was visible off to my left, seen just before the highest point of the mountain. I reached the official summit point a little before 9am. There were three wooden signs tacked to a couple of poles with bright yellow writing.

Congratulations you are now at Uhuru Peak Tanzania, 5895m. Africa's highest point and the world's highest free-standing mountain.

They were decorated with flags and ribbons and writing and stickers. At this point I couldn't give a toss about the sign and just wanted to be done with the entire thing. The guide was insistent that I shouldn't leave without a picture. I felt sick, delirious, emotionally, mentally and physically spent. My guide looked at me nervously as we stood in the queue, "We need to get you down immediately," he said. "You are not a good colour."

Others next to me in the line nodded in agreement. "You don't look so good… you are actually quite blue. You should really go now."

I waited in line a few more minutes for my guide to take some pictures of me. I posed with my fingers like a gun to my head. This was literally the hardest thing I had ever done. I was exhausted beyond belief. Afterwards, I curled up on the ground and told my guide to leave me there. I was quite serious. All I wanted to do was sleep. He dragged me to my feet.

"We need to leave now Miss Joanna," he said.

The thought of having to make it all the way back down was too much. Couldn't they just send a helicopter? The hike down was almost as hard. There was so much snow, which had now turned slightly slushy and I was utterly drained after being unable to keep down food or water for hours. Let alone the lack of sleep. The sun was blazing and I kept having to strip off more layers. I was delirious and wobbling back and forth as I slid down trudging through the snow with ski-like steps. I was still feeling like I was about to vomit at any moment. My guide held me under the arm to help keep me upright while gaining momentum as we slid downwards. It took around four long painful hours. I wish I could say it sped by on the descent from the motivating forces of accomplishment, but it felt like forever. All I could do was keep going. Bob was, of course, the first person back to our camp and was absolutely dead on his feet. When Ritu looked at the state of him she was terrified, given he was the fittest of us all by far. American John, Gill, Adrian and Catherine trickled in some time after that. When I finally got back, I unzipped my tent, looked at Ritu and burst into tears.

"Aww honey, come inside and lie down," she said, helping manoeuvre things out of the way.

I stumbled in, falling onto my mat and sleeping bag. My

eyes were now burning and stinging like crazy. My sunglasses were obviously not polarised as I thought and after the blinding mountain summit much later in the day than anticipated, I was now suffering immensely. My body felt like it had been hit by a freight train. Ritu undid my boots and took them off. All I wanted was to sleep and make it all go away.

"Do you need me to get you anything? I can try and find some leftovers from lunch?" she said.

"No, I can't eat, I've been vomiting since I left," I said in a choked up, crunchy voice.

"OK, well let me go and see if I can get you a hot tea. We have to pack up our stuff. We are leaving in half an hour to head down the mountain."

"What?!" I sobbed, the information slowly sinking in. "You've got to be kidding me? I haven't slept in over thirty hours and I can't even have a nap?"

My oxygen deprived brain couldn't comprehend what I was hearing. I didn't even have the energy to feel hysterical. "Can you talk to them or something?"

"I'll see what I can do," she said quietly.

A few minutes later Ritu came back, not with the tea but with John. "We gotta get going," she said. "Let me know if you need me to help you pack your things." They started breaking everything down around me as I lay there lifeless.

"You need to get up and go. Now," said guide John without a smidge of humour.

I had descended from the peak so late, I only had time for a fifteen-minute rest before I had to get up and start packing my things. I was beside myself but I had to do it. I had no choice. Ritu tried to help as much as she could, bless her, but I mostly had to do it myself. The joys of living out of a cramped and tiny backpack where everything had its place. I took some painkillers, put some eyedrops in and skulled an Emergen-C vitamin electrolyte drink. I gave myself a pep talk, rebooted and stepped outside the tent. My eyes were bleeding they were so sore, and I was still delirious as anything, but I put one foot in front of the other. Pole, pole.

It may well have been the delirium or the fact that it was

almost over, but the walk down was much, much easier. In fact, it seemed like a walk in the park compared to the last five days. I was no longer vomiting so that was a game-changer, and the nausea was easing off the lower we got. Of course, heading down, not up, was certainly more pleasant and easy on the body. At 5pm we reached one of the lower base camps. It was getting pitch dark but I had heard through the grapevine that they had cans of Kilimanjaro branded beer for sale, and I wasn't disappointed. My old flatmate was an accomplished marathon runner, and her doctor said that beer was more hydrating than water after such physical exertion, because it contained carbs. I wasn't going to argue with that. Despite having nothing in my system and a couple of hours to go, I went and bought one immediately. It tasted like the most delicious beer I had ever had. Suddenly I was far more chatty and back to my normal self.

Given it was now dark and we were the last to come down the mountain, we were being ushered out by the guides pretty quickly. The last couple of hours sailed by as Ritu, Gill and I walked down the mountain together. After a couple of Kilimanjaro beers it was a tad easier, despite us falling over ourselves with exhaustion and barely able to see with our head torches. Gill's legs were absolute jelly and I was so delirious I could barely feel mine. We made it to the Mweka camp where we would spend our last night on the mountain before the final three hours out to the gate the next morning. I was feeling elated with not only the accomplishment of having climbed a mountain against all odds, but the fact that I was almost off said mountain with a hot shower and decent food in my not too distant future. I finally got to sleep at 9pm that night, three hours shy of being up for a straight forty-eight hours and climbing the world's highest free-standing mountain peak during that time.

Be still and feel the power of this moment.
Be still and feel the joy
with the power of your heart
as you connect to the cosmic heart
and the heart of our Mother Earth.
Through all hearts combined we step forward into new territory.
A new age.
And it starts within yourself.
For the self is the all that is.

Your connection here has the same power it ever had.
Power beyond comprehension of your earthly abilities.
Discover this power. Play in this power. Speak this power.
For the vibration of your soul signature is heard
throughout the multiverse and beyond.

Be it. Own it. Claim it.
Claim everything possible for yourselves in this moment.
For this moment is all there is.

Unleashing My Inner Ashanta

I had successfully completed months of detox, health-focused pursuits and training. I'd climbed a mountain in the most challenging of conditions, raised thousands of pounds for African orphans and had a lovely holiday unwinding in exotic Zanzibar and reconnecting with friends at a wedding in Capetown, yet I couldn't help but feel that it was all overrated. Yes, I felt somewhat satisfied and accomplished, but it still hadn't fulfilled the deeper calling of my heart.

I thought perhaps it was more about my potential, finding my true purpose, and what I felt I was destined to do on the planet, as opposed to the 'right' career path. As if on cue, out of the blue, I was given another nudge from energetic forces when I was given a month's notice at work. I'd been freelancing there for over two years at a pretty good rate, secretly knowing they paid poorly for full-timers and therefore I purposely did not pursue a permanent contract. After we lost a couple of big clients including my key account, the agency was more scrutinising, and they knew they couldn't pay me what I was worth. It had been a good run though with a good crew and I was genuinely excited that this next twist of fate may lead to more aligned pastures new.

My never-ending drought on the relationship front meant that I was considering breaking something in my house, "… so the reasonably handsome manager from the building site next door could come over to 'fix' it," I told my energy healer Camilla as we continued our sessions to support my realignment of energy and healing in London. "Well, have you put in your order with the Cosmic Cock Ordering system?" she asked me casually. I had never heard of such a thing. In two shakes of a lamb's tail I was sending out my order to the Universe, and would you believe it, the order miraculously worked. The only problem was, it wasn't quite as on brief as I'd hoped. A drunk Scot threw himself at me in an alleyway after work. A married man tried to jump my bones on the street while his wife was having a glass of wine upstairs in my apartment. Another male friend in a committed relationship tried to get a bit on the side during a walk in the park. The cosmic ordering was working to full effect although it was barely what I was looking for and somewhat out of control. Backfire. Clearly I needed to specify 'bed' next time, amongst other things.

Of course, I was not identifying the real problem, which was me. I wasn't going to find a decent relationship until I was in right relationship with myself, although I still didn't know it at the time. I was asking for the Universe to bring me what I wanted, yet I didn't have my own self-worth cultivated enough to believe deep down that I deserved it. The misalignment was causing a different vibrational match.

Despite holding myself back from undeserving suitors, two weeks later, drunk, with a raging libido and desperate for attention, I got home just after dawn and sent a saucy message to a man who had tried to shag me at a party that night. To be fair he was a nice guy not to mention fit, but far too drunk. Hours later while sitting with my shameful self, I was filled with regret. I felt the sting of dishonouring myself yet again, and beat myself up to the point of outright self-rejection. This inevitably translated into partying to make myself feel good and drown out the voices in my head, which continued to have nothing nice to say for weeks afterward. The pièce de résistance at the end of my dive downwards was when I somehow managed to pick up an Albanian painter one night on the walk home from the Tube, a mere ten minutes away.

When I took a look at his extremely ugly and very cheap looking Cold War country shoes the next morning, I was almost sick in my mouth. He was extremely clingy in a 'I see a free ride and all my Christmases have come at once,' kind of way. Yes, the Balkans was a step too far. Leaving my self-worth with those shoes on the floor, I ushered him out the door as fast as I could.

"Well, at least he's an artist darling," comforted my friend in New Zealand after I confessed my tawdry transgression.

"Yeah, unfortunately he's not that kind of painter," I said quietly.

The beauty of London was the amount of freelance work available, which meant a more lucrative and non-committal working life. In between contracts it was always nerve-wracking however, so I of course took the opportunity while not earning any money to enter into another economical detox regime. I became healthy and vibrant, and was using the latest abundance manifesting techniques with the eclipses and new moon. "I'm not sure if it's working or not, but I'm feeling far more generous," I said to my flatmate one day. "I mean now I keep giving all my money away instead of getting it but I guess it's doing something," I said, jokingly.

Energetically things were definitely moving as it was only six weeks before I picked up a job in account management, although this time it was back in a more traditional permanent suiting role, as a joint global account director. Although I felt relief to be back in stable full-time employment and earning money again, it meant I once again parked any grand plans for a dream life on my own terms. I threw myself into the new role with gusto, albeit falsely manufactured excitement. I had talked myself into pros of the job to justify the big fat con that it was out of alignment to where I wanted to go, which was out of advertising entirely. I genuinely convinced myself this time could possibly be different, but in this instance, just a few months later I found myself back in familial feelings.

I was irritated with the same set of agency/client problems and politics. On the bright side with it being a big agency, I had a decent work-life balance, so I spent as much time as possible outside of work secretly going to spiritual lectures and trying new things in order to uncover an opportunity more aligned with my passions. When I complained to my healer Camilla about the lack of Universal opportunities coming my way, she told me my light was needed in these corporate places, which was why I was consistently ending up back there. However, I just didn't think that the effect on my emotional well-being of a job I didn't love was helping anything. Let alone getting me to where I wanted. I wasn't buying it.

How was I really in greater service by working in advertising when I felt out of alignment with it? Was there anything I could do to increase the quickening of my true path? Supposedly, relationships are the most important tools for growth, so why had I not had a proper serious intimate relationship over the last ten years?

What was standing in the way of me understanding serious unequivocal energetic guidance? How come I felt so disconnected from everyone and everything? Why was I constantly seeing number sequences like 11:11, 12:12 and so forth ad nauseam? How could I make a career and support myself in this material world out of my interest in the spiritual realm? Why did my emotional ups and downs so regularly throw me off so much when I was doing all the 'right' things for balance?

I was teeming with questions that I didn't have answers to. I threw them out there into the Universe, but I didn't seem to hear any response from the non-physical world. So, I booked an Akashic record reading with a lady in the States. The Akashic Records are a record of everything that is, has been and could be throughout the Universe since creation. Essentially, an enormous energetic database. Your Akashic record was supposed to contain answers to everything for your individual soul blueprint, so I figured given my limited success on my own, this would be like going straight to the Source.

The reading talked about my soul lineage being from Mintaka, the third star in Orion's Belt. That my soul name was Ashanta, resonating with the frequency of Mozart's music. And that the energy template I had signed up to work with most in this life was that of love.

"In the context of your soul blueprint, it is the relationship that you have with yourself. It is about self-love. How do you treat yourself? Are you compassionate, kind, caring to yourself?

Or do you judge, criticise and reprimand yourself? The core quality of this energy stream is loving yourself unconditionally. Forgiving your past mistakes and realising that you're a spiritual being having a human experience. You were not taught how to do this before you came. Of course, you'll make mistakes.

The energy stream of God, higher energy, the Universe is divine love. When I enter the Akashic records I tell people that the love that is there for you is beyond mind-blowing. There is nothing that you can do wrong. It is all regarded as a learning experience. If you have this energy stream, your focus is on healing your relationship with yourself. Connecting to your heart energy. The more you do that, the more you will offer others."

Well, that certainly hit the nail on the head. I was positively awful to myself most of the time saying the things I wouldn't say to my worst enemy. She also went on to state that my primary life lesson was truth, and the secondary, joy. The primary life lesson is said to be closely related to your purpose, and the energy you are here to bring onto the planet.

"You stand for truth, speak the truth and know all that is. It is your very nature and energy stream. Yet, it is a hard lesson to learn on this planet as very few are the same. Joy refers to you relaxing into your very being and enjoying all that the Universe has to offer. Being the gift and contribution, you truly are, by just being you. Let joy emanate from your very being as it allows others to do the same. This is how you teach and serve, being your beautiful self."

It was a very thorough report with a wealth of information, much of which made complete sense and resonated with me. I still needed to figure out how I could translate this into my daily life, or '3D world' though.

I sent it to Annie to see what she had to say about it.

Hi, Jo – I was reading that it is the twenty-fifth anniversary of Harmonic Convergence this year and things may become clearer. In my lifetime the Harmonic Convergence was very significant in 1987. I noticed the frequency changes from then on. I think I was one who lost my way this time!

Sunday I had this HUGE kind of meltdown, not outwardly, I just felt really strange. Then on Monday, enormous peace. I still go by Gautama Buddha's saying – not to believe in anything – no matter if it is held in high esteem and to basically find out everything for yourself and conduct yourself thereto. I just continue clearing things up, I feel we all do our work wherever we are at any one time – because it is *what we think* that counts the most – not so much what our job or what we do here. I have always felt that.

Devo – funnily enough, has been an amazing teacher. He has taught me that other people think entirely differently to me! Including him! They don't know how frustrating it is for me sometimes! It was only recently that this young woman came up to me at Devo's work party and thanked me for what I had said to her at a dinner once. I remember scribbling over the paper tablecloth and yakking on about something or other, but she said it changed her whole outlook on things – so much so that she was off on a new venture and was going to work in Sydney! I like working like that – because it never occurs to me at the time – and then they come to thank me! Stay cool Ashanta Star Lady!

I decided to start putting myself out there, doing what I enjoyed a bit more as a first step in fostering more of the joy vibration and qualities spoken about in my reading. I joined the agency softball team, got back into jogging, hired a personal trainer and started working on a business idea. Yet despite the influx of wholesome activities, yet again it was still not translating into any breakthrough results I was hoping for. I wanted to be in alignment and flow with synchronistic events leading me to my purpose, yet nothing seemed to be shifting despite my best efforts.

I oscillated as usual between nun like behaviour and giving wild London life a good nudge, as I threw myself out into the world hoping for something to stick. I'd indulge in a party pants three day bender one week, get a call from some guy I never remembered on my cellphone, contemplate that weirdness in general naivety and then spend the following weekend locked inside my flat. I certainly put the swing in swings and roundabouts. My crew were always on the party scene. We worked hard and played hard. Never getting bored or running out of steam for the copious amounts of calendar opportunities to push the envelope. With my upbringing in a house of excess, my natural in-built specialty was burning the candle at both ends, so I just kept on doing it. I wasn't ready to give any of it up and I had already proved that puritanical behaviour barely made a difference. Not that I believed in that anyway. This was par for the course in London life I rationalised. We were in our prime years in one of the greatest cities in the world after all.

Your resistance is the persistence of the outdated and the old.
Of the been and gone.
You have no ties to what lies ahead.

Stop reaching for what has gone before as where
you are going is beyond the beyond.
There is nothing to hold on to, just your courage
as you step into the unknown.
Step into the potential of your highest expression of the divine.

For you to step into the most expansive nature of who you truly are
you must be willing to let go, to step away from all which you know.
The self-judgement, criticism, belittling and keeping yourself small.

Live joyously in all circumstance without the
conditioning of that which you have been.
For your destiny is to be as big and bright as you can be.
To shine in a way which you have never done before.
To shine with the radiant truth of all that you are.
For in the shining you will find the opening, to that which you wish.

Where You Land 'With The Band'

I began working at my new job just in time for their annual summer event. I was keen to make a good impression and made a mental note to not get too carried away. It was a long bus journey through terrible London traffic, made barely comfortable by the two drinks we were given in our party pack. I quickly downed them in an attempt to gain some Dutch courage en route to a knees-up where I barely knew a soul. Get a few on board and then ease off, I thought to myself.

The party itself was in a convention-style centre which didn't really have the most fantastic ambience, but it did have a lawn out back and a stage set up inside for the bands. There was a dress-up box by a photo booth, and a bar. The cocktails were terrible and with no vodka in sight, it was slim pickings on the drinks front for something clean that wasn't going to send me sideways. I reluctantly went with a glass of average rosé and began to look around for anyone I knew.

The first band started an hour or so later and as it got a bit darker and more atmospheric people started passing around shots. Being the newbie, I of course had to accept as a rite of passage, and just like that we were off like a yacht catching the breeze. I think it was at this point that my out-of-control alter ego started making an appearance. I became so complimentary to my softball coach that I may as well have given him a flat-out proposition. After hours of dancing, being silly in the photo booth and rolling around on the lawn doing a live body sculptural photo shoot, the party was over. At this point I most definitely did not need to continue on, but I had forgotten all about my vow of keeping myself in check and was cajoled along with everyone else to the after-party at the hotel next-door.

By this stage we were all three sheets to the wind and sailing at full force. I jovially struck up a conversation at the bar with two chaps who I discovered were part of the headlining band. The lead singer, Josh, was especially good-looking, and he was sitting with his best friend, who wasn't in the band but 'with the band'. They were both in their mid-twenties. This is the point where it all gets a bit hazy. I do remember the lead singer flirting with me, yet I seemed to be drawn to his mate who invited me out for a cigarette and kissed me. Before you know it, we were ducking around the corner to make out, and then, to avoid the windows into the bar, he took me off into the depths of the hotel grounds, where we proceeded to make out some more. Thirty-five years old and rolling around in the grass with a twenty-six-year-old, on the grounds of a five-star hotel. More arse than class.

A fair while later, at approximately 4.30am, my thirty-five-year-old senses decided to make somewhat of an appearance when I proclaimed that we needed to just bite the bullet and get a room at the hotel. I went to make a move to do up my clothing, but at this point my tights were caught in my shoe buckles and I couldn't get them up. No problem for my dashing twenty-six-year-old, who reached down and ripped them clean off in one fell swoop. My expensive lace G-string was a casualty in the process, but it was such a hot move that I immediately had my profoundly impaired sights set on getting a room quite quickly. I got myself up and made a beeline before realising I had no idea where I was. We were soon bailed up by a security guard shining a torch on us and asking where we had come from and why we were there. I attempted to look confidently respectable and, speaking in a posher than usual accent, explained that we had been hosting a party there and were now trying to find reception to see if we could find some 'accommodation'.

He didn't seem convinced and accompanied us to the reception desk, where we were greeted by the night staff.

"I'd like to know how much a room is for the night, please?" I said, with a fake haughty tone.

"Our basic room is £348 excluding VAT," she said.

Unfazed by the eye-wateringly expensive room, which would be only for a few hours, I reached into my handbag for my purse, felt around and was shocked to find that I could feel nothing there. I pulled the small, cream leather bag off my shoulder to further inspect it in the light of the reception desk. It was empty. No phone, no purse, no lip-gloss. I felt my stomach drop. Thankfully my house keys were intact in the side zip pocket.

I dispatched the security guard and his torch with the twenty-six-year-old Toyboy towards the doorway while I stayed in the warm flash lobby, commando, trying to be very astute with my still drunken fingers incessantly dialling my phone number while they searched outside. It could be anywhere; the convention centre, somewhere between the convention centre and the bar, or out in the bushes. Who knew? Urgh. These are the kinds of inevitable drunken fuck-ups I had come to loathe.

The boys returned. No luck. I couldn't call any car services, let alone pay for anything. I looked to my Toyboy, and he informed me that all he had was an Oyster card. Turned out his lead singer friend paid for everything. I sure knew how to pick 'em. I could have gone with the hot lead singer who was just as flirty with me, but no, I defaulted to the dark and stormy, slightly weird-looking friend who was 'with the band.'

Finally, 'With the Band' Toyboy plucked up the courage to call the band's car service and beg for a cab to my place. They begrudgingly agreed and sent a car for us. It took about forty long minutes, during which time I was draped in a wingback chair facing away from reception with the Toyboy's hands up my skirt.

When we finally got home it was all sex and no sleep, until around 8.30am, when I had to get ready to go to work. Toyboy had other ideas. I came back from the shower; he pulled the towel off me and we were at it again. I showered again. Sex. Showered again and dressed. He ripped my clothes off. More sex. Re-showered and re-dressed. More undressing and sex. Leaving the house was impossible. For the fifth and final time,

I wouldn't let him take my clothes off. I was already two hours late for work.

I would rather have stayed in bed all day, but it wouldn't be a good look if I took a day off after the summer party. I was feeling immensely sorry for myself and my pounding head although impressed to have broken another drought. We walked down the road and he mentioned hooking up the next day after he came back from a festival.

Of course, when I got on the Tube, I remembered I had no phone, and the sickening thought of all the horrifically embarrassing things I possibly did and said at the party the day before came flooding back. I was in a complete state by the time I got to the office, my mind working overtime and beating myself up about every possible wrong move. I felt intense shame, guilt and resentment towards myself about my behaviour.

Arriving at the office I went straight to my desk, attempting to appear in high spirits although slightly hungover, and as if nothing had happened. Telling anyone about my lost wallet and phone debacle would only contribute to my already tarnished reputation. At one point, my boss approached our junior planner and asked how the party went and if there was any gossip. I happened to be walking to the bathroom when I heard it.

"If you want to know about the office gossip, just ask her," she said, laughing and pointing in my direction. Cringe.

I felt myself go beet red and hastened my way out the double doors to the toilet while dying of mortification. I felt sick. I needed to leave the country immediately. Why, oh why, did I do these stupid things?

You fucking idiot, Jo. You've really done it this time. I sat in the toilet for a good five minutes, trying to turn myself invisible. When that failed I tried to find the courage to go back out there, while racking my brains at what could have eventuated and why she would be saying that. Did she see me pashing the Toyboy, or worse – could she and the rest of the office have seen me rolling around on the ground somehow? Dear God. My head was spinning with the possibilities and I felt more and more nauseous as the anxiety ate me up.

It must be the fact that the Toyboy pashed me outside, I reasoned to myself. The other options were too grim to think about. After a few more minutes I pulled myself together, held my head high and went back to my desk as if nothing had happened. I put my headphones in and kept myself busy. I had the most roaring hangover and my mouth felt drier than someone doing the Weet-Bix challenge. However, I just couldn't go to the water cooler twenty metres across the room, through sheer embarrassment that I might encounter the cute softball coach who sat right next to it. Or anyone else.

I emailed a mayday call to my work friend on the second floor. 'We need a hangover lunch date asap. I have had a small nightmare, lost phone and wallet and dignity and can barely function. In dire need of some serious TLC. Please save me. X.'

I watched the hours tick by until 1pm and I was already outside waiting when she joined me, desperate to make myself scarce as soon as I could. I told her the story over a cerveza and burrito while she was in fits of hysterical laughter.

"Don't worry about it darling. I think we all secretly want to marry the softball coach so no harm done there, and you were very jolly but perfectly fine when I was leaving. I haven't heard anything through the grapevine today so I'm sure it's nothing. Diana is so young and geeky, don't worry about her," she said, kindly lending me fifty quid for the weekend.

Back at the office I spent most of my time pretending I wasn't dying and wilfully trying to speed up time so the day would end. My boss was cracking a joke a minute about the possibilities of what had transpired. I gave him a very severe look and he finally gave up, sensing my sensitivity. It was the last thing I needed: my witty boss with a sniff of something mortally embarrassing.

In the late afternoon I remarkably, given my sorry state, remembered that I could try 'find your iPhone' to see if I could track my device. I looked around to ensure no one was watching. I couldn't believe it when it matched a house in the area of the party. There was hope after all, and possibility of redeeming myself. I checked the train times but rather inconveniently couldn't print the satellite image of the house to take with me, so I had to note down some descriptive details about the colour and surroundings so I could find it the next morning.

The following day, I woke up feeling almost as bad, despite a night on the couch with a load of takeaways. My puffy eyes, dark circles and sallow complexion told the tale of my sorry state. The only good news was that I didn't have to go to work, being Saturday. I gathered myself together, rechecked the train times and the price just to ensure I had my ducks in a row. Twelve pounds forty for the journey. Crap. I ran to my room and searched through my drawers for change. Scrounging for shrapnel to get to butt-fuck-nowhere on a Saturday morning on day two of my hangover. "This is the last fucking time you are going to let your stupidly drunk out of control antics put you in this kind of situation Jo," I said to myself furiously. I went down to my flatmate Frida's room, who was at home in Sweden for the weekend, and found a small change dish with just enough for the train ticket. I wiped the sweat from my brow. Phew.

I took a deep breath and left home for the mission across London to Amhurst. I was tired, hungry and felt like I'd been hit by a freight train, but I'd put on a cute shoestring-strapped floral dress and massive gold sparkly sunglasses to lift my spirits, and at least get the most out of the summer sun while I was on this bothersome venture. Thankfully a free granola bar handed out at the station ensured I wasn't entirely destitute. Who knew how long this could take?

With my Olympic power bar and a bunch of naive delusion tucked under my arm I hopped off the train, strolling in the direction of Amhurst Gardens. I noted some interesting characters with very odd fashion sense along the way, a wildly different calibre from the north-west London set. I looked around, surveying the small, shabby, cookie-cutter houses, and although it wasn't a Council estate, there was a certain resemblance that sent off electrical triggers within me. I ignored them and turned down the street busying myself with trying to recollect the satellite picture, counting the number of driveways from the funny overhanging tree I'd seen on the map. I started door knocking when I thought I was close.

I was greeted at the first door by a guy, early twenties maybe, standing in his tighty-whities and no shirt, squinting at me like I had just rudely interrupted his lie-in. I knocked at the next house and the door opened to a huge black Rottweiler launching to attack while another smaller, yappy white thing deafened me. A little old lady was keeping me out of the jaws of the giant dog whilst yabbering in some eastern European dialect with a cig hanging out her gob. She started shaking her fist at me so I departed rapidly. I continued, still relatively unfazed, to the next house up. On the way to door number three I walked towards a large, dodgy-looking Bedford van which resembled a kidnapping vehicle out of a movie. Just as I made my way in, a greasy-haired, middle-aged guy wearing gold chains and a white wifebeater singlet came bursting out a gate, checking his nostrils in the wing mirror and wiping some remnants of white powder away.

"Ah, excuse me, excuse me," I said in my best 'sweet young lady in distress' voice, asking about my lost phone. He brusquely waved his hand at me, gold chains swinging all around the place, and pointed me down the road to the house with the Honda. So that would be the Honda that was jacked up on the driveway with no tyres and wires flailing around under the ignition. A shell of a stolen vehicle. Excellent.

I slowly walked to the house as directed but there was no answer behind door number four. I was almost relieved. It was at this point I decided to write notes with my contact details and stick them on the windshields. An African Mama told me I was crazy and there was no hope. Then a runner wearing a full grey tracksuit, hood up and all in twenty-two-degree heat asked if he could help as I looked suspicious. Me, in my cute sundress and sandals with my Hello Kitty notebook and slightly terrified smile, I looked suspicious? I promptly gave up.

Later that afternoon at home, whilst cancelling my last credit card I was passed a message with a number to call the police about my belongings. I could not believe it. Amazing! I immediately called the officer, who sounded ultra serious on the phone. He asked what my name was, where I lived and what I was doing out there where they found my stuff in the grounds of the hotel.

"Oh, you know, just carousing in the grounds at a work party," I said casually. There was a lengthy pause down the phone. I interrupted to break the uncomfortable silence. "And, so exactly where did you say you were again?" I asked, making the officer hold while I got a paper and pen to write down the address.

After telling my minicab driver a topline, far more PC version of the story en route to the cop shop, she gave me a moral dressing down. I was already beating myself up enough, let alone having to listen to it from a complete stranger. We arrived, and the place looked like Fort Knox with barbed wire and huge gates encasing the complex. I excitedly thought it might be some kind of 'special operation' police centre. An officer greeted me, and we walked inside.

The walls were full of mugshots with categorisations; drugs, burglary, assault and murder. Officer Plod had apparently gone down the road to the local supermarket for dinner and would be back soon to unlock my stuff. In the meantime, I distracted myself with the excitement of being in the 'operation' headquarters and spent the time casually asking for their best crime stories. The two officers were not engaging in the slightest, despite my best efforts, so I zipped up and proceeded to imagine my own version in my head. The officer finally arrived and put down his dinner, heading towards the back of the office. He pulled a big plastic evidence bag, just like on the telly, out of an unlocked cabinet. He brought it over to the table where I was sitting and asked in a very serious manner if it was mine as it was "found at the scene." I could clearly see my tights, and my lace G-string, thankfully not my La Perla. Willing myself not to flush with embarrassment I quite quickly denied they were mine and reiterated that I had lost only my wallet and phone.

"Of course," I continued nonchalantly, "… there were a, err, 'group' of us, so perhaps they were someone else's?"

Not quite sure why at this point I thought it was a good idea to imply that I was having an orgy, instead of assume responsibility but it was already out my mouth before I had time to think it through. The officer was looking at me carefully and again waving the bag, asking if I was sure it was not mine. Just as I thought they were about to bust out a lie detector test, another officer arrived to defuse the tension. He unlocked another cabinet and pulled out yet another large plastic evidence bag, where I identified my wallet, mobile, and the lip-gloss. There was also a large black cable, and a pen in the bag which I quite quickly clarified were not mine. This perfectly corroborated my story that the tights and G-string were nothing to do with me, but also works with the kinky orgy side of it as it looks perfect for asphyxiation! Brilliant!

After more interrogation and feeling like quite the criminal, I was eventually allowed to sign for my belongings and led through the six locking doors and barbed wire fence back out to my waiting taxi. Thank God that was over. I was shaking as I hopped in the cab.

Being in a vulnerable state I needed a vino that night as part of my recovery. As I was staring shamefully into a glass of red at The Salisbury, recounting the full chain of events to my bestie she was nodding along profusely, the corner of her lips jerking as she tried not to laugh at my misfortune. Her long and perfectly curled lashes grew longer and wider as I gave her the blow-by-blow. "Oh, so they thought you had been raped?" she said, nodding emphatically as she was stating the obvious. The veritable penny clunked onto the ground with a high-pitched ting. Shit. They thought I was raped?! Oh my God, they thought I was bloody raped!!! I was supposed to be an unbalanced and emotionally tortured rape victim, which is why I was given the Spanish bloody inquisition. That was why the officer was so strange on the phone and at the station. They were scoping out the victim. Me, the victim. Me, the fucking potential rape victim, who basically confessed to having an orgy on the grounds of a five-star hotel instead. Oh. My. Actual. God. FUCK. My new work buddies thought the culmination of this work party tale was priceless. Me, not so much. The ego satisfaction of always being the girl with a 'good story' had truly worn off.

The heart burns through all the incidental humanness that
gets in the way of alignment. Anchoring in the heart and living
inspired action from this place, will ensure your emotional field is
balanced, there is peace in the body and your mind is at ease.

This delicate balance is the still point, the zero point within,
which requires delicate attention, minute by minute, hour
by hour, as you entrain your being into this place.
The body will adapt, yes it will, and get used to this mode of being.

Balance and alignment and trust of the self
will bring you the great gifts you are due.
Balance from the heart will exponentially grow your frequency,
and call in that which you wish to be and more.

Everything will come to meet you in this new energy,
this new paradigm, which is, all new.
It requires you to flex and change and adapt,
and relearn this way to live as a human.

Changing times, with changing energies,
call for changing frequencies and being open to the new.
The unknown has more gifts than you know,
but your reality will meet you where you are at.
Paradise awaits.

The Congo

The embarrassment wore off slowly but surely, for that instance at least and life continued on as it always did, with a variety of new opportunities to sabotage myself. Despite all the spiritual material I was inspired by in the moment and being on top of my fitness, my spiritual yo-yo dieting practice and cyclical detox-retox system weren't shifting anything deep internally. Reality set in. Here I was, six months into my new job, back in client service in the daily grind, and it was the same as it always was. Wasn't there more for me out there somewhere? I was working my arse off just to make enough money to sustain my, albeit privileged, lifestyle. I was still flopping around trying a gazillion different spiritual modalities, healings, practises to fix myself and find my life purpose.

I realised that my faith and/or reliance on the Universe and the divine to magically bring me my destiny had actually put me in a perpetual state of waiting. Waiting for my soulmate to serendipitously cross my path. Waiting for the Universe to synchronistically guide me into the perfect career. Waiting for brilliant ideas to solve my problems. Waiting for my life to fall into place. Waiting for things to become easy and not hard. With all of my spiritual beliefs, practises and pursuits, I couldn't understand why none of it seemed to be impacting my reality in a breakthrough way. Was I doing it wrong? I was very aware of my downfalls, but I also didn't agree that living life as a perfectionist puritan was the only way to get there. I just inherently knew that more programming and belief systems weren't the answer. I was angrier and more frustrated the more I thought about it. What the fuck Universe?

Although on the outside, people saw a successful, adventurous and independent woman with wide interests, accomplishing a lot around the world, on the inside I was a sad, drooping, wilted salad, having a pity party for one. I had gotten to a point where I was exhausted with myself. It took a lot of energy to be wearing these masks I had created through my own conditioning and fears of stepping into who I truly was. I didn't know if I could be bothered continuing at all. I was overly emotional, crying all the time and falling into self-destructive behaviours like getting drunk to the point of oblivion, with little to no self-control. I was sick to death of feeling like I wasn't getting anywhere in life. Or where I wanted at least.

I felt a sense of hopelessness that I had never felt before, and I wondered what was the point of all this? Was it even worth it? Was it ever going to work out? I was in a downward spiral. I busted out of London, blew off all plans and took off on impulse, solo. An impulse I'd been ignoring for weeks. An impulse which made me feel like I was desperate for nature. Desperate to run away. Dying to pay some kind of tribute to that which rises within. Why did I keep ignoring myself? I had a million thoughts in which I inflicted grievous bodily harm to myself on a daily basis. Was this S&M on the self? It may as well have been because I had beaten myself to a pulp. Did I deserve it? I didn't know. But I couldn't help the obsessive self-judgement and condemnation that had come over me. That was haunting me. Eating away at me.

I fantasised about killing myself. I thought about throwing myself onto the tube track, finding a gun in the countryside somewhere, being assaulted to death by an intruder, overdosing, a colossal accident and I was googling how to stab myself to death in an instant. Anything to stop the pain. The only thing that prevented me was that I would never wish that hurt upon anyone else. I would never make them live my pain forever more through me. It didn't mean I didn't want to though, so I concocted a genius plan. I decided I would go to the Congo. I had just read an article which told me that the Congo had the highest murder rate in the world. I could be easily murdered, and my family would never have the guilt about me giving up on life. I guessed random accidents were somewhat of a comfort, knowing that no one can control fate's roll of the dice. I'd given myself a time limit. End of the year.

After the extreme low point, I peeled myself up off the floor in another attempt to find a solution before implementing my Congo plan. If all the things I was doing in my physical life were still not working, then I needed to look further into the energetic realms to see what I was missing. I booked a session with a psychic medium recommended by a friend. She spoke to my grandmother and to the various guides with whom I was working, to receive messages for me. I was told I was getting tangled in the endless loops of questions of my mind, all coming from a logical place and wanting to create perfection, but this was a concept not a reality. I needed to honour my higher self and pay more attention to this wisdom which was naturally strong, not the left-brain logical side of me. This was where I received all the golden nuggets that I needed to inspire me and propel me forward. In relationships, I had some lessons I needed to learn as a lone wolf. I needed to experience this sadness and loneliness. Ultimately I wouldn't be happy in a relationship if I was not happy in myself.

My father in this lifetime was connected to my struggle with the male species. I needed to be aware of his subtle controlling tendencies and the unconscious programming that I had absorbed from him that said I wouldn't have freedom in a relationship. My patterns of self-doubt and grief needed to be moved on from. I needed to let go, give myself the green light and step into the unknown. "Change can be scary, but it can also be extremely exhilarating. Even though life can have its bulges and tears, everything that happens is a divine expression. God is writing his own story through us." I was given some tools to scan my energy field to ensure it was clean and clear daily, to flow easily. I was incredibly sensitive and empathic, picking up way too much from the world around me, which was confusing to my senses.

The reading did enough to quell my fears, and renew a sense of trust that everything was going to be okay. That I was supported and that I had clarity and the tools to continue on. I got some balance back to my life in London as I started working consistently with even more energy practises daily and started a writing project, but in the same breath I noticed a string of discordant energy emerging in my relationships. Men from the past came back to haunt me, my relationship with my mother hit a rough patch, there were challenges at work and I suddenly fell out with a dear friend. I felt an internal wobble from all these events that caused me to feel unsure of myself yet again.

I found people nit-picking at what I said and did, and taking personal offence to a version of events that was not my experience at all. I tried to explain that perception was everything, and one only reacts to something in someone else, when there is something unresolved within the self that needs to be dealt with. I was told I was 'turning it back on them.' It was an interesting predicament when one is looking at these situations with detachment and conscious awareness. People can only meet you at the level of consciousness they are at.

I analysed the long and the short of it with significant self-inquiry but couldn't pinpoint exactly why all this was confronting me in my reality. My gut told me that I was experiencing these events for a reason, and I could only attract what was being summoned by my own energy field. I was doing the work and changing my vibration now though, so why was I suddenly attracting these lower vibrational experiences? An intuitive friend told me that when embarking on creative projects it was essentially going into the womb of creation, which can often throw up things from the past to clear the energy to move forward. It was clearing and transmuting to make space for the new.

Despite months of self-healing, my own energy work, kinesiology, fitness, nature walks and all manner of good that I was doing, I felt myself despair at the lack of real significant change I was experiencing. I found myself dancing in the depths of my own darkness. Again.

Release yourselves from these shackles.
Do not be bogged down by the energies.
Do not let them nestle in and bury themselves deep
as there is no reason for you to be dragged down.
For this is the old way, and you are carrying new technology within
to be able to process these energies far more
efficiently than ever before.
Let them float through you and back to Source.

This is a process of discovery. Exciting discovery of self.
For everything is changing. You are changing.
And the planet upon which you live is changing.
Via the portal of love and the channel of light,
these are the last few clearings of your physical
incarnation being played out,
to rise into the new.

Accept and embrace where you are at.
And be thankful for these old memories coming to the surface
to be purged back into the light.
Transformed for good.
And moving you along.
For the benefit of all.

Dearest Motherfucking Spirit

Dear Spirit,

I'm not sure how aware you are of this, but I am extremely upset and frustrated. I have spent almost my entire existence on this planet grappling around, trying to figure out how the damn thing works. And by damn thing, I mean creating my own reality, understanding how energy flows and manifests, attracting the things I want into my life and ascertaining where I fit into the wider plan of the Universe and why we are all here.

I have spent extensive time researching spiritual healing, including fascinating spiritual leaders, therapies and crafts. During my thirty-five-and-a-half years I have been living in this body on this earth, I have never been in love. Real love, not lust or made-up love in the movies. Soul evolving love, in partnership, with a bigger purpose. I mean, shit, could be a woman or man, I'm so desperate at this point, but all joking aside, you know I like cock. I know this may not mean much to you, coming at it from a higher spiritual view where none of it really matters, which I find a bit holier than thou to tell you the truth; but it is very important in this physical realm. Isn't that supposed to be one of the perks of this physical experience? It makes life enjoyable, enriches it and can also provide various opportunities. My sexual prime is being thoroughly wasted, and apparently, I have the master-fucking-plan to thank for that which I supposedly signed up to before I came. What kind of bloody crap system is that?!

Given spiritual people keep banging on about how life is not supposed to be hard, nor a struggle – if it's supposed to be fun, easy and magical, then fucking prove it to me. You know it just doesn't make sense to me. If this life is a lesson in self-love for me, surely there are many ways to approach this. Is cutting me off from the kinds of earth experiences that make this earthly life bearable really just a waste of my time here?

Repeatedly I turn inward; I look at myself to see if I can change anything I am doing in my head or heart to try and reverse this. I am positive, I focus on good, I do kind things, I spend a lot of time alone, I help people, I do my best to be open-minded and not to judge, I look to the bigger picture meaning in everything. I make changes to my lifestyle and thoughts, and I try to accept my life for what it is and the cards I have been dealt. But you know what? It hasn't changed a thing. I see ZERO results from any of it. Divine timing, my arse. I've surrendered, numerous times. I have broken down and begged, and you show me no mercy. Not one iota, which exacerbates my feelings even more. Am I doing it wrong? Well, tell me then or provide me with a teacher so I can clearly see how to do it right. Am I barking up the wrong tree? Well, point out to me the right fucking tree in this goddamn forest. I AM SICK OF IT.

Why are things not falling into place for me to fulfil my purpose? I am not just moaning about romantic love; I am talking about career and home, the whole shebang. Not one of these things is working adequately for me right now. Nor has it been for the last ten or more years. Hell, even my body feels like crap no matter what I do, so just speak up and tell me right now, what is working? 'Cause I sure as hell cannot see anything that is. Maybe I came from some utopian planet or something 'cause this one seems shit! Why do I not have any communication from my angels/guides/relatives and friends who have passed over? The Ascended Masters, even? I am talking crystal clear messages that come through, that I understand and can decipher. Why hasn't someone come to speak to me in person during my darkest hour? Or actually, hours, as there have definitely been a few and they just keep on coming.

Do I need to go to the fricking Congo to get the fuck out of here and make some progress? That's beginning to feel like the only option, as I truly do not understand the point of all this. You got me there. What the fuck is up with this madness? Not only am I unhappy, but I feel unsupported and unloved, on the earthly plane and beyond in other dimensions. So, tell me, why the hell should I do this any longer?

I don't understand the point to my being here. I have nothing to contribute or offer this world because I am constantly battling every day just to survive. No other person or being is enlightening me, so what the fuck? I am struggling to see the way, know the way, hear the way, feel the way because I am not being guided clearly enough. I know that I am really talking to myself here, to my own spirit and not anything outside me, as I get that we are the Universe and it is all within. So how do I access it all? Tell me, for God's sake, as I am completely over this bullshit. This whole Earth thing is a bloody joke.

Maybe that's what you want me to do? Go to the fucking Congo. Perhaps I should have done that long ago. It certainly beats anything going on in my life at the moment. Maybe this whole incarnation thing is a complete bunch of bullshit?! A con. And I don't care if I sound like a whinging earthling who doesn't get it. Maybe you should make it a bit fucking easier if you want me to be able to concentrate on anything I am supposed to achieve in this life. You do know we have finite time as humans on the planet, right? Oh no, let's just go and waste another twenty years figuring it out. Cannot wait. It seems there is a serious malfunction in the programme here. Have a think about that. Real hard. 'Cause I have officially hit my limit. Either my life changes drastically, quickly, magically and amazingly, with more than I could ever wish for, or I am fucking outta here. Do you understand?

Thanks. At this stage, I guess I'll see you in the fucking Congo.
Joanna

There is a choice before you every day in how to be.
A choice can make the difference.
Know the perfection in all things.
Know that you are exactly where you are meant to be
and exactly who you are in this moment is divinely perfect.
This divine intelligence pervades the Universe,
and Universes within Universes, in the giant matrix of this experience.

We only go to the lower levels when that is
where we meet our consciousness.
By merely observing and allowing, one is able to transport
themselves up the layers to a different vibrational perspective.

A different way is required for this
new world for which you are wired.
To elevate oneself out of the challenges of the human
existence requires looking at things differently. And not
being afraid to have an alternate point of view.

Nothing is wrong or right, but there is the most expanded thinking
aligned to your true self, and that which is further away.
The gift is there for you to see who and what you truly are.

As you expand into the limitless potential and
live in this way, think in this way,
breathe in this way – you are in divine alignment with nature.
This divine alignment gives birth to beauty and grace.

That which you were chasing in your humanely existence,
only to find that, solely from within can you align to the outer,
which brings you into accordance with the whole,
and the truth of all that ever was.

A Radical Change Of Heart

The anger and frustration were pouring out of me. I felt destabilised and completely unsupported by the Universe. Was it all an utter crock of shit? I was now living a healthy lifestyle, yet my body was far from it. I was applying spiritual practises, yet I was still experiencing a life out of flow with cyclical ups and downs. I was experimenting with all sorts of practices to open up super-conscious abilities, yet I failed to perceive any guidance nor see any angels or beings of light, or any of the other stuff paraded in the spiritual community. The mystical experiences of my youth suddenly came flooding back into my memory. A premonition vision of a police raid that saved our bacon when I was seventeen and up to mischief. Seeing Annie's amazingly beautiful giant aura full of moving and merging liquid colours whilst she was doing Qigong when I was eighteen. A fateful meeting of an undercover spiritual master with messages for me when I was twenty. I knew it was all real. I already had proof of that. I just wanted to fulfil my destiny.

Despite everything, I continued my health regime, persevered with discovering spiritual teachings that might provide answers, and vowed to do everything I could to find my passion and reason to be on the planet at this time.

The more dark periods I went through, the more questions I had. Why couldn't things happen as magically as we were led to believe by the spiritual community? Why wasn't it possible to find the right way to connect and get my own answers? Why were there so many different spiritual teachers all saying slightly different things? Why didn't different modalities work for everyone if we were all essentially the same energy beings? Why, if I hadn't been drinking for ten weeks and was quite healthy, did I feel so absolutely awful, drained, and find it so hard to be positive? How do we stop our subconscious mind from interfering in what we are consciously trying to create? If going back to love and ascending back to light is the point, what was the purpose of putting light beings through a process full of suffering if they already came from a place of light? If this was about soul progression and soul development, what was the end goal? Why have we forgotten that we came from the light if we already are God? And if we are all sparks of Source consciousness then what is the bigger purpose of all this anyway? Some things just didn't make sense nor add up, so I asked Annie for her take on it all.

> If I had my own personal input, this is how it is: This entire human experience is a setup! It was an experiment that we agreed to enter into – for reasons we have yet to find out for certain! I have spoken to what I can only call spirit – ALL my lifetime – this one! I have told them it needs improvement! What you MUST get a drift of is that WE – as humans – MAKE IT UP! It is WHY I say it is all ILLUSION! Unfortunately – AND FORTUNATELY – the NEW AGE gave birth to many modalities that try to explore all the reasons WHY? I have explored MANY of these – INCLUDING kinesiology – which has earned reasonable respect – I may add! To cut a long story short – all these modalities are helpful up to a point .... YES! But they do not CUT it in my HUMBLE opinion! The entire 'trying to find out the reason WHY this happened to you' is FUTILE! You just HAVE to SURRENDER to it all – THERE IS A HIGHER reason MAYBE? MAYBE NOT! People do NOT like what I have to say in this regard! That is MY EXPERIENCE! YOU *have done NOTHING* wrong! (Echoes of religion!) YOU just signed up for the human experience! The PAIN we go through – ALL THROUGHOUT our LIVES – if dealt with matter of fact – without delving into emotions, the psyche, and such things, that bring up the lie, guilt/shame/embarrassment/inadequacy and so on

– are all things human – bless us all, concocted in order to uncover, research, find out, solve our so called insecurities!

ACTUALLY – there is NOTHING WRONG with ANY OF US! We are living in a reality that I call a playground – and until we realise this we will continue to take life seriously and imagine we have problems! 'NO PROBLEM IS SOLVED AT THE LEVEL AT WHICH IT OCCURRED!' So said EINSTEIN! So that excludes EVERYTHING WE EXPERIENCE HERE! WE – as HUMANS – LOVE TO pontificate! In my HUMBLE opinion – this entire reality is basically and DOES boil down to a perfect MIND FUCK! I have said it forever and some get it, and some don't! We are here to enjoy this ride! No matter WHAT! ENJOY THE MIND FUCK – BUT BE AWARE OF IT ......LIFE takes on a new meaning when you start leaving all the human ideas OUT of the equation – and start getting a gist OF THE ALCHEMY of what is truly going on! AND – I speak of the ALCHEMY OF THE THOUGHT PROCESS!

Further......we cannot go backwards to go forward! Our time – our society, our teachers currently tell us to do this! It does not work! So...I say...GET INSIDE OF YOU...YOUR HEART CENTRE – & you are 100% perfect! Open ... be open to what it is in YOU – and you will find this perfect centre! We all put this off – all of us!

You consult who you do, & you believe what they tell you! Time to start believing in YOU – not this other thing! I did that for 30 years! How do you know they are 100% correct – or even that your muscles or body are telling you the truth, according to THEM!? Your body could actually be saying to you: 'Time to go it alone darl'! THAT THIS modality has run its course! Eventually – as I found for myself, Jo ... I am the creator of my world! It may not seem so to you, at a distance, – you tell me all sorts of stuff – over the years ... but I do not see that it helps you ... and I KNOW ... what I dream – it has HELPED ME TO SEE THE LIGHT ....by ignoring it (as others portray it) and creating my own way to create / see/ imagine – not according to others – or a way, or any modality! To dare to dream or imagine rather than go with what OTHERS say!

We go through our lives putting it off – this is fine as there actually is no pressure – from spirit – spirit (the REAL YOU) allows you this lifetime to do exactly as you please! You do not EVER have to CONFORM to human ideals – personally – I think human thinking is so behind the times! Spirit wants YOU to dream / go crazy for your own SAKE – not for the sake of the common herd! Anxiety – in my own personal experience comes from NOT following your OWN HEART!

Your question tonight has made me come OUT a bit and SAY something! I am not an expert – neither am I right or wrong! I do not wish to tell you what to do! That is the worst scenario! We are not talking here about humans – and their ways to go about life – we speak here of a very delicate way – the way that is led by one's HEART! Anxiety is a modern affliction that can be overcome with persistent determination! Personally – my FEELING – is that anxiety is a FALSE situation that is a warning sign from spirit to help you get away from something that is no longer serving you! And I would not say this without personal experience of it myself!

LOL XXX A

I completely missed absorbing some of the deep wisdom and truth in her email because I was so ticked off at receiving yet another novel that I felt made massive assumptions regarding my thinking, where I was at and what my views were. Annie was my greatest trigger and in hindsight I see now that she was also my greatest teacher. However, in that moment all I felt was her broadcasting at me with a giant megaphone from the South Pacific. I felt the whole reason we were spiritual beings was to come here for a human experience. To have a human, emotional experience in the body, not deny it, make it insignificant, wish to be out of our bodies, not believe its innate intelligence nor rationalise everything with spiritual bypassing by saying it's all an illusion and none of it matters. In my opinion she was missing something here massively.

From my perspective, this whole 'the world is an illusion' talk from spirituality had been so twisted from its original meaning that it was well away from the pure intention of it all. It seemed to be used as a manipulation, or justification of not properly taking responsibility for your soul's effort in this particular human experience. It was possible it was maybe missing half of the equation.

I was using systematic kinesiology for the stage I was at, as one way to help understand the various layers we all deal with and how energy works. Kinesiology didn't just deal with the physical, but the emotional, mental and multi layers of our energy field too. Even the subconscious. I didn't feel I was 'believing what someone told me'. This was about what the body as a part of our wider energy field told me. Annie didn't even know any form of detail around what I had learned in kinesiology, and I felt that her trying to throw everything out was unsupportive and challenging. I knew deep down I had chosen her as my mother for a reason on a spiritual level but the wounding from years of volatile behaviour in my upbringing was getting in the way of me seeing the value.

Unsatisfied with Annie's answers, in a last ditch effort I lined up a series of sessions with an expert soul mentor to coach me on my relationship issues and find the answers to all my questions. We examined things that were bringing an emotional charge for me and looked at the patterns. These patterns needed to be released from the cellular memory with energy work. The cellular memory holds all our belief systems, so from this point of view we needed to heal them in order to stop them from interfering in my life.

"You have got awareness that you create your own reality. Now you just need to get rid of your programming at a cellular level, so you can move on. You are consciousness, so the only way you can heal is with consciousness. Through the mind we express what we are. We have to experience shadow aspects to be fully light."

I knew at some level that I had co-created these experiences with those around me for my highest good. Just like I had created everything I had been experiencing in my world via my inner-most workings. Whether I liked it or not, I needed to accept it. The conflict was gifting me the opportunity to heal. We can't change anybody else, but we can change ourselves. If I could let go of the triggers inside me, then I could move on.

"Your higher self always knows what to do," she reminded me. "When the lower self triggers, you acknowledge and then move back to the place of your higher self. Whenever you are feeling low, remind yourself, 'I am love, I am light, I am divine spirit having a human experience.' This will help you move out of the illusion of whatever is going on in your reality, without getting caught up in it. Know who you are and remember who you are. This is your higher path to embark on. This is what you are doing now, starting to walk the path of truth. Walk the path of what your soul has come here to do."

I felt like I already knew this on a deep level, and attempted various ways to approach this in the past, yet things had just not worked out or come together as I'd hoped. However, I was aware that in some circumstances I had perhaps been trying to control things too much and allowing outside authorities, circumstances and perceptions to override me.

"People make the mistake, when it's not falling into place, of pushing it. Hand it over to the Universe. Be in a surrendered place and let the possibilities unfold. There is never one course of action, there are several possibilities out there. If attached to a particular one, we block the others. Just let it unfold. Trust the Universe, and if it's meant to happen, let it happen."

I kept myself focused on weekend hikes in the country, the agency dodgeball team, and a writing course, which I was getting some positive feedback from. I continued to pursue my passion for energy and spirituality with the latest spiritual teachings and meet-up groups.

After some months of strong focus and energy work, I seemed to turn a corner. I went from not knowing what to do, to being inspired and flirting with an abundance of new ideas that could potentially become my purpose and lead to a new career. I was experimenting with automatic writing and learning more about my particular vibrational make-up to better understand more of what my soul had carried into this particular lifetime. When some inheritance from my grandmother became available to me after her house was sold, it was enough for a deposit on a flat, so I started looking for potential options to buy in London. That was the sensible plan of course, to spend my nest egg investing in property. However, after a series of unsuccessful viewings, and a lightning bolt inspiration for a blog I heard my grandmother's words ringing in my ears, "Spend it on your heart's desires my dear."

My heart's desire was not really an investment property in London. Where was the excitement in that? I wasn't sure why I was trying to conform to the norm now. Instead I began planning a sabbatical to South America, where I could find transformational experiences to write about, learn Spanish, and of course, change the direction of my life once and for all. South America had been on my bucket list forever, with its sacred sites, shaman, ancient spiritual practises, amazing music, food and fascinatingly different cultures all on one continent. It was the perfect place to give me what I was looking for.

Nature is perfection in its imperfection.
Not unlike humans. And great beauty none the less.
For in the imperfection of the details is the divinely orchestrated truth.
The truth of matter manifest.

From the seed of creation.
Starting with a speck, in the womb of eternity.
The dark womb from where all light, and all things come.
This is the zero point. The space of neutrality.
The space from which you create.
With passion and poise. I AM created with universal law.
The sacred geometries running through the entirety. As you.

Recognise this.
Recognise the incredible technology of that which you are.
Wake it up inside you, to surpass all previous ways of being.
To transform, evolve and elevate you from that which you were.

Following Fate To The Wild West Of Brazil

My bestie Ange and I checked in separately and only met up at the airport, so we weren't seated together. We were off on our big South American adventure and our excitement was hard to contain. We agreed to adjourn to the aisle for drinks mid-flight. As we got to the gate, I surveyed the scene and promptly locked my eyes on two nuns. I was at that point ninety-nine percent sure that they would be sitting next to me. I just had that knowing. Sure enough, we boarded and me and my two nuns were cosily seated together in row twenty-five.

The little old nuns were keeping a beady eye on me. They totally busted me trying to keep my Kindle on to finish my book during take-off, firing me disdainful stares, so I quietly put it away. Thankfully they started napping shortly after but awoke during the dinner service, when I requested numerous refills of wine, smiling into the nuns' penetrating eyes. Potentially, the nuns may have been raising eyebrows in my direction due to the wafts of smoke that seemed to keep floating our way, but I'd quit smoking some time ago. After dinner I met Ange by the galley for a much needed catch-up drink away from the eagle eyes of the convent.

We got on the whiskeys with the assistance of a very helpful and handsome steward who refilled us with pleasure every time he came past. After much flirty banter, Gonzalez returned from business class with an entire bottle of eighteen-year-old Chivas Regal. A definite upgrade. He poured us a fresh one, himself a gin and tonic, and we toasted to a great flight. The female hostesses came through and were not impressed at this makeshift party, but we pretended not to notice and kept Gonzalez' gin undercover until they left.

Minutes later, Gonzalez, who was now on his third gin, invited us to the cockpit for a cigarette.

"What?" we said as we looked at each other with genuinely shocked faces.

"Oh yes, the captain smokes, a lot, so we can smoke with him during the flight," he said in a thick Spanish accent like it was no big deal. How very retro. That's what the nuns and I had been smelling.

Ange and I politely declined but were genuinely devastated not to have been able to say we smoked a fag with the captain in the cockpit en route to Peru. Later Gonzalez came by and gave us a business-class toilet bag each, and asked for my number so that we could hang out in Lima the following night. A booze upgrade, business-class accoutrements and a date, and we were only halfway to Lima. This trip was looking to be an absolute pearler. And so, it began, not entirely in a particularly spiritual fashion, but with the boozy gusto that seemed to be the ironic norm whenever I attempted a legit spiritual journey.

My plan of four to five months' travel around South America before settling down in Buenos Aires to drink fabulous wine with hot Argentine men, eat steak, perfect my Spanish and write was completely blown out. Before I knew it, I had chewed up my allocated travel time and only made it from Lima to Colombia. I could blame this on budget overland travel, but really I was having far too much fun to be on a schedule. Schedules were made for the 'real world', and I'd left that and the dreaded 'nine to five' far behind me. We hadn't even ventured to south of Peru, Bolivia or Argentina yet, figuring we needed at least three more months. It seemed excessive to even contemplate continuing further, but I was no stranger to most forms of excess, and this was certainly the tamer of the bunch. More importantly, the festivities of Manfest 2014, otherwise known as the Football World Cup Brazil, were part of my fantasy agenda for the trip.

Although we'd had a tonne of fun and hair-raising adventures (that shall be saved for another book), so far my expectations for any kind of transformational experiences had been barely met.

Machu Picchu, although beautiful and more challenging than I thought to hike the Inca Trail, certainly didn't do it energetically for me. The Colca Canyon trek was a hair better but perhaps that was the giant condors flying above us, which gave it an air of mystery at least. Same goes for the beautiful Lost City jungle trek in Colombia and its ancient ruins. Other sites like Lake Titicaca, an interesting vortex in Bolivia, and the Island of the Sun in the centre were the closest I got to sacred energies, but yet again, I wasn't blown away. I found this oddly curious given the reputation for this area of the world and its powerful sacred sites, but I had noticed a lot of spiritual tourism that felt inauthentic. I continued my general attitude, which was to let fate take its course, and if I was meant to somehow meet a legit shaman and head to the jungle for plant medicine then I would. Similarly, we decided to leave the World Cup up to destiny. If we managed to get tickets in the ballot, then we would go. It was once in a lifetime, after all.

So, albeit late, I applied for a string of matches in round two of the World Cup ballot ranging from the most boring qualifying games to various final matches. My tardiness was reflected by most games being already marked 'oversubscribed'. When the ballot was drawn, I did manage to get something from the half a dozen games for which I had applied. The one and only match I drew was the third versus fourth place final in Brasilia. As it happened, Brasilia was the closest city from which to travel to Abadiânia and John of God. I immediately knew I was meant to go there.

They say that you are 'called' to John of God and his Casa de Dom Inácio de Loyala, the spiritual healing centre in central Brazil; and that once it comes into your consciousness, the Universe conspires to get you there. Once I spent time there, I heard remarkable stories of amazing synchronicities bringing people to this place, and realised I was no exception. I thought it could be an interesting experience to add to my repertoire given I was around these parts. Oprah herself had been after all. How could it not be, when you were visiting a medium and psychic surgeon who worked with prominent saints, doctors and nurses no longer in physical form to perform miraculous healings?

The next day I booked a ticket in my makeshift 'Portengol,' a hybrid of Portuguese and Spanish, and after farewelling Ange, got myself on a bus. I kept my eyes peeled en route and thankfully spotted a giant 'Abadiânia' sign in the middle of the highway about an hour and a half in. I got off, grabbed my backpack and followed a few others down a side road, hoping I was heading in the right direction and somewhere a little prettier. So far it looked very wild west. Dusty, red clay, earth streets, a few run-down old crystal and clothing shops, plus a café or two. Nervously thinking I was not quite sure what I had got myself into, I asked directions to my pousada, 'Caminho Encantado,' and set off down a side road. It dawned on me that I had absolutely no idea what I was doing here nor what to expect. I knew at this point that physical healings and miracles happened in this place, but I soon came to find that this was not really what it was about at all. Physical healing is what John of God is famous for, but is only a small element of what goes on in Abadiânia. Really, if you scratch beneath the surface it's a mind-blowing trip to another dimension.

I arrived at my accommodation down the end of a paved road containing various pousadas, private residences and cats. I sat there feeling slightly unsure and out of place while waiting for Ulrika to arrive, who I had been corresponding with regarding a room. A slightly older German woman with flaming flowing hair, tanned skin and bright blue eyes arrived in a floating, colourful outfit accessorised not only with silver Indian hand jewellery but an array of crystal necklaces, charms and a leather pouched belt. Oh yes, I had arrived. At hippy central.

Ulrika was quite surprised to see me. Usually her vague email enquiries never eventuated, but here I was, standing there in the flesh a couple of days after messaging her.

"I like your spontaneous spirit," she said with a raised eyebrow and an interested glint in her eye.

She showed me a few rooms and offered me her 'official Casa appointed guiding' services. As a first-time visitor, it's recommended to visit the Casa de Dom Inácio with a guide due to the slightly complicated protocol and Portuguese proceedings.

Given my post World Cup over-fiesta'd state, I happily handed the reins over to her, accepting her services for the Casa session the next morning. I settled on a simple, bright room with a lovely pyramid ceiling littered with small, starry downlights, and a stunning view of the countryside. Later, after some food from the nightly buffet of fresh salads, rice, beans, pastas, meats and fruit, I accompanied Ulrika to check on one of her clients while she gave me the run-down on what would happen the following day.

JOG was in the Casa every Wednesday, Thursday and Friday. There are two sessions a day, the first at 8am and the second at 2pm. All participants and Casa volunteers wear head-to-toe white clothing, underwear and all. This is so that the energies of different beings of light (or 'Entities', as they are called in Abadiânia) working through JOG can easily see your blueprint of energy for diagnosis. These Entities are the conduit for high vibrational healing using Universal, Source, Creator, God, Divine Energy – or whatever term you resonate with for the unseen energetic forces at work on our planet. João de Deus, as he is known in Brazil, always reminds everyone that "I do not cure anybody. God heals, and in his infinite goodness, permits the Entities to heal and console my brothers. I am merely an instrument in God's divine hands."

Allegedly, JOG doesn't remember anything of what happens during the sessions when the Entities are working through him. He is a medium in full meditation, to the point of trance where his personality self goes elsewhere and steps aside so the spirits can work through him. There are many of similar nature throughout Brazil, where culturally this is somewhat more accepted.

I was taken on a tour of the Casa in the dark, a complex of basic white buildings with painted blue accents comprised of the Main Hall for Casa sessions, various connected Current meditation rooms, crystal bed session rooms, a cafe, a crystal/bookstore and a garden with wooden benches. We passed a small room full of crutches, canes and wheelchairs that had been discarded, no longer needed after successful miraculous healings. It was quite impressive. As we made our way back to the pousada I was told to spend the rest of the evening thinking of three things I wanted to ask the Entity for help with at the session the next morning. Shit, I'd mostly been thinking about beach, booze, boys and the next fascinating destination in my travels over the last eight months through Peru, Ecuador, Colombia, Panama, Bolivia, Argentina and Brazil. I needed to shift gears pronto.

The next day I was so excited I was up with the larks at 5.45am, getting ready for my 7.30am date at the Casa. I met Ulrika and her other clients at the cafe. One was an anorexically thin German girl who couldn't eat because her body rejected everything she tried to put into it. Another two German women had brought their young daughters, one of whom was partially deaf. Lastly, there was an Italian who had lived all over the world and was enthusiastically into his second week of JOG'ing. Aside from the company, I was more interested to note some peculiar sensations in my body, like waves of energy washing through me.

The Casa sessions are organised into groups for 'Primera Vez' or 'First Time' people, who are brand new to JOG, 'Segunda Vez' or 'Second Time', for those who are in the system, and 'Revisão' or 'Revision' for post-op care after a spiritual intervention operation. I got my 'Primera Vez' token and surveyed the scene. There were a fair few hundred people of all shapes, sizes and various states of health. I saw an old man limping around with a cane, a middle-aged woman in a wheelchair with a breathing tube, a young woman with no hair, and a severely disfigured child. There were also many completely healthy-looking normal people. Given I was able-bodied and in pretty good health, I started to feel a little self-conscious about coming to this place out of curiosity when so many people with serious illness, disfigurements and life-threatening diseases came to seek help. We waited a good while outside before following Ulrika, taking a side entrance and squeezing into the middle of the crowd.

Various speakers took the stage, reciting prayers into the microphone, telling of their personal experiences and giving motivational speeches. Some spoke in Portuguese and a few in

English. This happened while João was out the back, getting into trance and incorporating whichever Entity, doctor or saint might come through for the session. I stood there wide-eyed and taking it all in. Despite the Casa being non-denominational, with all faiths and beliefs welcomed, some of the material sounded highly religious. I felt myself prickling immediately and regressing to my thirteen-year-old self who had Christianity shoved down her throat at school. I had a deep knowing even then, that most religious information has been distorted and manipulated far from its original true intention and pure form.

I was bemused, consciously trying not to judge, knowing I needed to remain open. Ultimately, prayer work raises the vibration, no matter the denomination. The energy was getting so strong in the Hall, it was palpable. I could feel the force of it now, it felt far more powerful than what I had felt outside the Hall. Now it hit me in the chest like a wave of hot air, taking my breath away. It felt like going from an air-conditioned office onto the street in New York on a hundred-degree day. I felt quite heady, almost like I could faint. This was followed by a wave of tiredness, and I struggled to keep my eyes open. Others didn't feel anything at all.

Earlier, the translators had worked our three questions into Portuguese to present to JOG. I was a little put on the spot. I really wasn't prepared after spending the last eight months on a carefree career break, frolicking around South America in an attempt to use joy to find my purpose. My instinct was to front up and see what they said was for my highest good, but I was advised that they preferred attendees to take an active role in the work and healing there, so it was better to be specific first off. I had spent so much time travelling and having fun that I really hadn't tuned in to why the hell I was really here or what I wanted out of it. I had just come for the experience more than anything, not considering what I wanted nor needed. I asked for help with hormonal balance and spiritual development.

The Entity who is taking the reins that day, calls the order of the queues depending on the amount of people, the healing issues at hand, the energy level supported by the Current meditation and other factors 'beyond our knowledge'. There is no set order and sometimes they can throw a wild card, throw the rule book protocol out the window and do something entirely different. They run the show and you never quite know what's going to happen.

Before I knew it, Ulrika was herding me towards the queue of flowing, white-clothed people. The monitors of the queue took my 'Primera Vez' token and told me to take my bag, which was strapped cross-body on an angle, and swing it over my shoulder instead. This was so that it did not block the energy. They reminded everyone that crossing arms or legs, sweaters tied around the waist, scarfs wrapped around necks – all blocks the energy flow, so it was vital to keep all bodies as open vessels so the work could be done.

I was ushered into the first 'Current' room in the queue, where about eighty people were sitting on wooden church pews in meditation with their eyes closed. Supposedly the beings of light working at the Casa use people's bodies and their energetic field or light to anchor and amplify the total energy for the work being carried out. This can last for hours and hours, and the Entity keeps working until every single person has been seen. The room was calm, imbued with a sacred, church-like ambience, with music playing quietly in the background. There were a couple of advisors standing at the front of the pews, leading prayers and guided meditations. I recognised a picture of King Solomon on the wall, Jesus and a few other Ascended Masters and Saints I didn't recognise.

This first room is to cleanse everyone who comes through the door before they get to the second room, where João is situated at the far end. I was nervous as I made my way in silence, following the snake of people into the second Current room. To my right and left were more pews and another approximately four hundred people sitting, again with their eyes closed in meditation. Where the pews ended, there were a dozen large, comfy, padded armchairs, six on either side of the room, reserved for mediums or terminally ill people. Six giant crystals, the size of a medium height person, were lined after the last padded seat, leading to the final chair at the back of the room where João was sitting. I tried to peek but couldn't see much through the queue of people, translators and small entourage of helpers. Closer to the front of the queue, I could see another one hundred people meditating in another room to the left. João was up ahead looking like some kind of old royalty, sitting in a big wooden armchair on a small stage, flanked by a man and a woman on either side while people kneeled before him with heads bowed.

Suddenly I was at the front of the queue. João looked aged, and seemed a little peculiar, probably from being in trance and out of his body. My consultation lasted only a few seconds while the translator read my list in Portuguese. João took my hand in his, in the sweet, gentle way of a grandparent, and spoke a couple of short words in Portuguese while scribbling on a white piece of paper and handing it to me. It was translated to me as "two crystal beds and some herbs". I was then quickly moved on through the final Current room into the Blessing room and a church-style bench and asked to close my eyes immediately. The blessing, in Portuguese, lasted a few minutes before I was told to open my eyes and move outside. It was all a bit of a whirlwind and almost a let-down really, compared with my delusions of having the Entity tell me how amazing I was, imparting some wisdom in regard to where I was in my journey, or changing my life in some dramatic way. He barely said five words to me. Slightly deflated, I immediately went to the store to book the crystal beds and with luck got two, back to back starting in ten minutes. Perfect timing.

Each private crystal bed therapy room had a single bed with an apparatus thirty centimetres above the bed containing quartz crystals cut specifically for each chakra and corresponding coloured lights inside. I laid down and cuddled up with a blanket, listening to the soothing music being piped into the speakers in the room. An attendant called back in to put a piece of cloth over my eyes and I sank into a deep relaxation. It's unclear whether I fell asleep or whether I went into some kind of altered state, but when the door opened to denote the end of the session forty minutes later, I came to, feeling like it had been ten minutes. I got up and made my way back to meet Ulrika and the rest of her group feeling incredibly spaced out. When I got there, Ulrika advised me to go and get a bowl of the healing soup that volunteers make in the soup kitchen, apparently also charged with healing energy as per the protocol advised by the Entities. The vegetable noodle soup was lukewarm at best, so I ate some of the veggies and then surreptitiously slid it back into the dishes pile before heading over to the Farmácia to pick up my prescription. Every single person gets the same passiflora (passionflower) herbs, which are then layered energetically with your personal prescription by spirits working with the actual people serving in the Farmácia. The herbs themselves don't do much at all; they are merely a transporter for the energy, taken three times per day, with each meal.

I headed back to the pousada to relax before lunch. I was to go back in front of the Entity in the afternoon session at 2pm, to go in the 'Segunda Vez' queue to be re-evaluated and receive my next step, after completing the first instructions. I'd heard over lunchtime chit chat that the Entity had a handful of standard prescriptions: herbs, crystal beds, a trip to the sacred waterfall, to come back another time, or a spiritual intervention, so now it was even more of a let down to be merely 'stock standard'. A spiritual intervention can be prescribed for physical, spiritual, emotional or energetic issues and is essentially an 'operation'.

This operation is either invisible or physical. The physical operation is generally performed on stage in front of hundreds of people in the Great Hall, and often involves cutting the skin or some kind of surgical procedure. The invisible spiritual intervention is the same work, but done energetically or invisibly; the choice is yours. If you feel you need physical proof, then physical is opted for, but they say there is never a need, aside from in your beliefs. All operations are done under spiritual anaesthesia, with no drugs of any kind. I heard that the methods used are far in advance of any medical knowledge known today, and the Entity will always ask doctors in the crowd to come forward to watch what he is doing up close.

The doctors are amazed and say this is not possible under the current practice of medicine.

You are limitless. You are light. You are love.
You are expansion, peace and joy. You are oneness. You are grace.
You are the vibrations of purest divine
consciousness and Source energy.
You are all you came to be and more.

Elevate your perspective of what is truly possible.
Extend your beliefs out far and wide.
Be prepared to be surprised, charmed and curious,
as to your new sense of being in these new energies.

We reassure you of your path at this time.
Remain in the frequency of joy. Let anything else wash over you,
as you feel the waves of new energies surround you.
Be in the stillness of this place.
And consciously acknowledge all that is available to you,
to bring it forth into your experience.

Under Spiritual Anaesthetic

I was just as nervous the second time around, and as I neared the front of the line, the Entity again took my hand and said something brief in Portuguese.

The translator said, "Come back tomorrow at 8am."

Ulrika, who was standing with me looked slightly confused, but we were already being ushered out to the blessing room. Clearly no questions or clarification here. Following the blessing, once outside Ulrika double-checked with the guy who had done the translation and he reiterated that yes, we were to come back in the morning for the 8am line. It was a little disconcerting that my guide didn't even know what was going on and I was bloody paying her.

Refreshed and ready for the next instalment, I arrived at the Casa cafe the next morning to find Ulrika and the Italian, Mossimo, having a coffee.

"I have some news," Ulrika said with a curious looking smile on her face. "You vill be going for a spiritual intervention this morning..." she said dramatically in her German drawl, "... if you choose to, of course. There vas a mistake yesterday. The voman who stands by João, she has been vorking with him for over tventy years. She came and found me at the pousada last night. She had to tell me that the Entity meant operation at 8am, not the 8am line. The other translator isn't used to vorking there. He didn't know the difference."

"Okaaaayyyyy..." I said slowly. "Change of plan then! No worries!"

"Well, what plan did you have?" asked Mossimo, laughing. "There are no plans here!"

Ulrika updated the group as they arrived one by one, and I

realised I could feel something happening in my body. It felt like waves of energy coming in and filling me up, similar to the day before but much, much stronger.

A short time later, Barbara, or as she preferred to be called, 'Starshine', arrived. She was a very sweet eccentric sixty-ish-year-old woman from Seattle who lived in Australia. Did I actually have to call her 'Starshine' though?! I just couldn't keep a straight face. Aside from the over-the-top, new age connotation, would you seriously choose the name 'Starshine' if you had a lisp?

We made our way back through the crowds and to the side entrance of the hall again. By this point, I was feeling seriously woozy, like, almost-need-to-sit-down woozy. There were no seats left in the tightly packed Great Hall, so I steadied myself against one of the rows of seating, realising I was completely out of it all of a sudden. I was barely able to keep my eyes open, and now a little nauseated. Ulrika advised me that the spirits were preparing me for the spiritual intervention and not to worry.

My line was called, and I steadied myself into the queue with a few deep breaths. We were being funnelled straight through into the blessing room for the proceedings. After being seated, we were asked to close our eyes and put our right hands over our hearts, or over the area that needed the most attention if we had a specific injury. JOG came in, incorporating Dr Augusto this time, and said some words in Portuguese which apparently translated to something along the lines of, "You are being blessed by the spirits of the Casa de Dom Inácio, and with the almighty power of God you are healed."

The attendants then asked for anyone who would prefer a physical operation to raise their hand. I was madly fastening both arms securely at my sides. I had heard stories from Ulrika of her hand having shot up with no intention to do so or put it up herself. Ah, hell no, I didn't want some trance channeller slicing me open on stage in front of hundreds of people. Not in a million years! The night before, I had overheard a girl in my pousada telling someone about her friend who was in line to see the Entity and was given surgery right then and there, with a queue of people behind her. She had one of the 'nose jobs' wherein a sharp, metal, surgical-scissor type object is thrust right up into the depths of the nasal passage and into the brain. Apparently she could feel everything that was happening, without pain. I was learning to 'expect the unexpected' in Abadiânia and that when working with spirit, anything could happen.

My experience of my invisible spiritual intervention felt like pricking, prodding and other strange sensations inside my nose, stomach, lady bits, chest, right bicep and one of my knees. I felt an injection sensation in my arm and lots of pricking in other places. It lasted maybe around fifteen to twenty minutes and I was told they could work on up to nine issues at once. Go the spiritual realms and their efficacy. When I opened my eyes, I was whirring with energy. I realised just how heavily medicated I felt. I knew that they gave you a spiritual anaesthetic, but was not expecting it to feel anything like actual drugs. It felt similar to when I had my wisdom teeth out. I was in a haze, while the world around me was going at a different pace.

I slowly started to gather myself together and move behind the rest of the people towards the door. I was hit by blinding sunlight as I exited, which only heightened my altered state. Ulrika grabbed my arm, took one look at me and said, "Mmm, looks like the vork has been very strong." Crikey, was that good or bad?

I very woozily made my way around the corner on her arm for post-surgery instructions: Take a taxi back to your pousada, no matter how close in distance. Twenty-four hours of bed rest. No reading, writing, email, Facebook, internet. Just sleeping or eyes closed in bed. One should aim for no contact with others, or minimal if it can't be helped. For the next seven days, no heavy lifting, strenuous exercise or sun exposure. Post-op herbs are required from the Farmácia, and while taking them for the next two and a half months, you can't consume any fertilised eggs, spicy food, chilli peppers, black/white pepper or alcohol. If it's your first surgery, then you must abstain from sex, with yourself or others, for forty days. Lastly, we had to write our names, addresses and dates of surgery on a piece of paper for the basket at reception so the Entities knew where we would be for post-op care and for our 'white night' seven nights later, when the spiritual surgeons come to take stitches out and check for any further adjustments.

I was in a complete and utter daze, trying to get into my head the rather large laundry list of things I had to do. They were blabbering on about the order in which to take herbs, at which point I switched off. Does not compute, does not compute. Body like lead, I dragged myself around to complete everything before Ulrika put me in a cab. Raphael was there to greet me at the pousada and helped me mark the meal chart, ensuring I would get delivery to my room for the next twenty-four hours.

When I got home shortly after 9am, I caught myself in the mirror noting my glazed eyes, with pupils as big as saucers. I chuckled to myself. Man, these spiritual drugs were no joke. I fell into bed and a deep slumber, despite sleeping nine hours the night before.

I was smack bang in the middle of a war scene. I was hiding in the trenches and reloading my weapon. There were bodies everywhere, and bombs going off all around. A couple of other guys were with me in the trench, peeking over the top to assess the situation. I was a man. It felt like the 1950s.

I awoke three hours later, dripping in sweat and with a severe case of cotton mouth. I felt like I had been on some marathon drinking binge, passed out on the beach and woken up in the heat of the blazing sun the next morning. The spiritual anaesthetic certainly seemed to have similar effects on the body to a normal chemical one. My lunch was delivered and I picked at it before falling back into bed and into another delirious sleep. At one point I woke up, feeling a wall of heat on top of me, after an array of incredibly vivid and bizarre dreams. I woke again hours later, at 4.30pm, with more ferocious thirst.

I was surprised when I awoke later that afternoon to feel that the anaesthetic had worn off slightly. I could feel dull pain and extreme tenderness inside my entire stomach area, both front and sides. I couldn't lie on my left side altogether, as it was just too painful. I necked more blessed, healing water to deal with my insatiable thirst, but after sleeping so much, I wasn't particularly tired. I lay on my back with my eyes closed for the next couple of hours before dinner was delivered. That night I slept in similar spurts to during the day, 7.30pm to 11.40pm, then again until 4am and again until 6.30am, feeling more adjustments in my body during this time and energies lingering in my room. I had more peculiar dreams that I couldn't quite capture, but which added to the intensity of the experience.

The following day, after fulfilling my prescribed twenty-four hours bed rest, I got up and showered. I gingerly moved around, feeling pain tweaking in both my sides and stomach. I stared at myself in the mirror, wondering what the hell I had got myself into. This was well beyond any visceral energy experience I could have hoped for. After some beautifully ripe, sweet papaya and mango for breakfast, I walked up the dusty earth road to Frutti's cafe and sat there enjoying the morning sun, doing some journaling and watching the world go by. I then went to the Casa to sit in the gardens and do some prayers. I noticed that all the benches had brass plaques and various names in Portuguese; 'Moment Present Om', 'Jesus', 'Compassion', 'Paz'. I sat down and set my intentions with prayer and journaling, then had a nap and some lunch before my first Current session at 1.30pm. I wanted to be in the energies as much as possible, to help the healing from my operation, from which I was feeling significant effects.

Current sessions can be anywhere from two to six hours, and on rare occasion sometimes more, as the session continues until every single person has been seen. When busloads arrive from all over Brazil at the same time, there can be thousands of people to get through. Therefore, people tend to queue up early to get a 'good seat'. I looked around me in the queue and saw people armed with special pillows, meditation seats, eye masks and shawls. I nervously looked down at my trusty water bottle and empty hands and thought, 'Ah well, she'll be right!'

The first Current room is where you sit unless you have been told by the Entity to sit in another room. This room had the advantage of being guided in English, which could be a saving grace through the longer sessions, as they tell you what is going on. You sit with your body open, feet and arms uncrossed, with at least one foot on the floor to connect with the colossal crystal bed that the Casa is built on. The first room is also known as the 'cleansing room', as all of the people in the lines come through this area to be cleansed before going in front of the Entity. The very first front seat, right by the door where people enter, is known as the 'vomit seat' as the energy can be densest there. A rubbish bin is permanently placed there at all times for any sudden urges. I was told the Entities advise people to sit in Current as much as possible during your time at the Casa, as this is where much of the healing work happens. During the Current sessions you get a deep cleansing, and often various emotions come up to be released as the Entities continue their work on you. Some people even receive spiritual interventions while sitting in the Current. I overheard an American guy talking about his "amaaaazing" Current sessions while in the queue.

"Ohmigawwwwwd," he said boastfully. "Last time I was shown the entire story of the Universe starting with the big bang right through to today." Whoever he was talking to had met an apparition of Mother Mary, and someone else was taken on an astral travel journey into other dimensions. All of this sounded pretty phantasmagorical and as I sat there waiting for everyone to be seated and the session to start, I was brimming with excitement and anticipation to see what happened in my first one.

The advisors told us to close our eyes and started saying a few prayers. My enthusiasm lasted all of twenty minutes before I started feeling distracted, agitated, uncomfortable and wondering when it was going to be over. I listened to the prayers and the guidance of the advisors. I did a few deep breaths and small visualisations. I was sitting there with my eyes closed, with not much happening at all. Frustration kicked in. Where was my light-being who was going to come chat to me and give me some life-changing intel? Where was my journey into the beyonds of universal time and space? I sat there feeling every inch of my sore arse while time dripped by as slowly as a triple-filtered coffee percolator. I wondered why I wasn't one of the chosen ones for some kind of other worldly divine experience. I did a pretty crap job of anchoring the light within me, let alone in the Current room, and by the time the session finished, a little after 5pm, they couldn't do the closing prayers quick enough before I was up out my seat, grabbing a shot of blessed water and marching out the door.

I stopped by the prayer triangle in the Main Hall on the way out. There are three wooden prayer triangles in different places in the Casa where you can place healing requests, photos, prayers and letters to the Entities with your wishes and desires for yourself or others. You remove your shoes, take your written request and tuck it into the frame before standing or kneeling in front of the triangle, pressing your forehead into the centre of the wall while you pray. The centre of the triangle was marked and worn from all the heads who went before me. When I put my head against the wall I felt a rush of energy, coming in waves. I'd felt similar weird feelings over the years, not really knowing exactly what they were or meant. The waves of energy washing through me felt quite intense and I stood there until they died down, offering my prayers for the planet, myself, friends and loved ones. The triangle shape is a symbol of a 'portal' to another realm, related in some way to the Pyramids. Putting a request in a triangle is just another way to communicate with the Entities of light at the Casa, and in my short time there I had heard of many instances of these requests coming to fruition. I finished with gratitude and steadied myself before moving away slowly and putting my shoes back on. My footsteps interrupted the silence as the next person moved up to make their requests.

You are right where you need to be.
For there is much energetically happening for you at this time.
Be conscious. Be conscious always with your intention,
every minute of every day.
For this is how you maximise what's on offer to you.

Your light is needed here and now.
This time is upon us. It is time for you to step out.
To not judge and live from the heart.
For your heart knows all the answers for you.

Connect with the heart and work with it. Make it up. Be creative.
The old archaic rules will hold you back.
Yes, structure is good, but you are burning
the old in order to create the new.
So, respect the old but there is far more for you in the unknown.

The cosmic heart is vital for you to tap into.
Familiarise yourself with planetary things
but do not limit yourself to what is down in the books, teachings, texts.
There is far more for you within self
than anywhere else in this world of yours.
You are your best teacher.

Go there. Go deep.
Conjure the ancient knowledge within.
For it is many times stronger and more powerful
than what is available to you outside.

Shit Gets 'Crazy' In Another Dimension

The rest of my week following the intervention was intentionally chilled as I followed the strict post-op care instructions. I coasted around Abadiânia, writing, meeting new people, attending an occasional Current session and settling into the experience. I perused the main street, taking in the small, quaint bookshop and a few other shops bursting with white clothing, charms, dreamcatchers, jewellery and crystals. One afternoon I bumped into Maren and her eleven-year-old daughter Amelie, both German, who were also in Ulrika's group. They were heading back to a crystal store which they had been raving about further down the street, run by another German girl who apparently looked into your eyes and prescribed the correct crystals for you. I tagged along with them, wandering up the dusty red road slowly.

Chimes rang softly as we entered the store, and I saw a young woman wearing glasses, with short, messy, blonde hair. She was bouncing around in a world of her own, looking for something between the many tables laden with artefacts and crystals. She grabbed a crystal from one table and took it to another, flitting between them like a fairy. She suddenly noticed Maren, who had shouted out to her in German, and they embraced and started conversing. She then bounced over to me, right up to my face, wide-eyed, taking in all of me with her gaze.

"Hi, I'm Gerda," she said, giggling in a voice that matched her pixie-like persona. "Let me know if I can help you with anything." And off she went, back to ferreting around for a particular stone.

I asked Gerda what crystals she thought might be helpful to me and she led me over to the doorway, where it was lighter. She looked deeply into my eyes for thirty seconds or so.

"Hmmm." She cocked her head to the side and adjusted the angle of my face. "I've never seen eyes like these. Ever." And then she wandered off to find my stones.

Some minutes later, she plonked me down in a chair off to the side and crouched down, looking at me curiously. "Most people, there is just one stone for them," she said. "Two occasionally for some people… and very rarely, three," she finished as she plonked three stones into my hand. "Sit here, close your eyes and hold the stones to your heart. Feel into them." She closed my hand around the stones and bounced up off her crouched knees to move away.

I closed my eyes and felt into the stones. My head started bouncing. They were quite overwhelming. Certainly strong, I'll give her that. I noticed my ever-busy thoughts had calmed down a little. I looked down at the stones; the first was a larger, oval-shaped, polished stone that was dark and stormy looking, but had flecks of shimmery blue and orange tones. The other two uncut stones were much smaller, but of similar size. One was aqua blue and the other a burnt, orangey-looking hue. They were pretty colours but very raw. I looked down at them stacked in my hand, telling Gerda I wasn't sure, and I didn't like the look of the dull grey stone.

"Do you know what this is?" she asked, holding the stone up to the light. "There are spirits in this stone. This is your stone. It's a very important stone for you. This is labradorite – a mystical stone, not only to protect from other energies but to connect with the higher self. This blue one is aquamarine, for protection and calming the thoughts, and then finally, imperial or gold topaz for unconditional love," she said, wrapping my hands around them. "These are your stones."

I questioned a few different settings but was advised the stones wouldn't work best like that. They needed to be over the heart.

"Take them home tonight and see how you feel." She grabbed the stones to wrap them up for me.

"Okay," I grumbled. "I'll bring them back soon."

During the weekend I met two girls from LA, Melissa and

Susan, after an evening stroll to Sunset Hill. The heavy sun sank behind beautiful, fiery colours, marinating over the endless landscape of rolling hills. Shortly afterwards, we sat at Frutti's café discussing the ins and outs of the Casa experience over green juices and ginger tea.

"If anyone knew what we were doing in this place, they'd think we were certifiable," I said. "Prancing around in white outfits, touching our foreheads into magic-manifesting triangles, sitting eyes closed in meditation for half a day, lying on beds under crystals with flashing, coloured lights and watching some random old guy cut people open or scrape people's eyeballs on stage."

We were all in hysterical fits of laughter. It sounded completely bananas. Yet here we were, rolling with it like it was the most normal thing in the world.

The deeper you get into the Abadiânia experience, it becomes apparent that there is far more to it than meets the eye. This place has such a high vibration that you are not just being worked on when you go to the Casa or when you are in session with John of God. You are being worked on twenty-four-seven by an immense team of beings of light. Whatever you have come here for, the Entities know what your soul needs most to work through in order to bring you back to wholeness. So, everything is orchestrated with divine will in the world around you to clear, heal, and transform you to the next level.

You might meet someone who tells you a story about the exact thing you needed to know to shift something in your consciousness that was holding you back. You may get into an altercation with someone in a store, to show you that your relationship with judgement and compassion needs to be looked at. A stray cat may appear, needing love and attention, to help you open your heart. The Universe is always speaking to us, inside Abadiânia or out, but often in our daily lives we pay little or no attention. When you are in spiritual retreat on top of a crystal vortex and consciously working to heal and release all that is not serving you, the volume is turned up. Things happen so synchronistically and quickly that it's like being in another dimension. I found myself again wondering 'where the hell am I, and what is really going on in this place?'

The last couple of nights, I had awoken at 4.44am to scratching and scraping noises coming from the hall entranceway by the main door or the balcony. It sounded like something was very busy running around and scurrying away. I wanted to get up and see what was making these noises, but every time I woke up, I was too sleepy to rouse properly and didn't have a torch to allow me to investigate. My imagination had made a break for it and I had gone from envisioning giant spiders to goblins to some kind of weird, killer gremlins. I was now a little scared as to what I might find. Who were these 'creatures of the night' and why were they waking me up in the wee hours? I spoke to my Austrian neighbour about them one morning.

"Oh yes," said Engelbert, laughing. "I hear these creatures you speak of. I have no idea what they are." Oh thank God, I thought with some relief. It wasn't just me then.

For the remainder of the week, I went to a couple of the Casa Current sessions to aid in my healing recovery from the 'operation' and also to give back to the cause. The pain subdued a fair bit after the first day, and was almost gone by the third day following the intervention. I was amazed, not only that I had absolutely real and noticeable physical pain and symptoms from this spiritual intervention, but also that I was recovering so quickly. On the seventh night following the intervention, I prepared for my 'white night'. I dressed in white for bed, put a glass of water by my bedside and laid down. As I lay there, I asked the Entities of the Casa to please come and check that everything was okay following my spiritual intervention, to remove my stitches, and to do any other work necessary to help me along. I thanked them very much for being there, and then went to sleep. I woke up a few times during the night but didn't see or feel anything particularly different. I woke early, sent blessings and thanks to the doctor and nurse spirits who attended to me in the night, and then drank the blessed glass of water by my bedside, as instructed.

"You can ask for your soulmate, you know. I asked for mine and I got it," said a voice down below me as I stood outside Frutti's after farewelling my friend. It was a pink-haired woman in a purple, crushed velvet coat sitting at the table outside. I'd seen her floating around. She was very tall and slender, and was from somewhere in northern Europe from what I could tell by her fair skin and blue eyes. She sounded slightly Nordic, although I wasn't sure. She always seemed to be furiously writing, which was no different from now, as she was talking to me yet writing at the same time.

"There are politics at play here, but you need to get in front of João once a day and ask. The more you ask, the more you get," she said definitively. "Wow, you're a really old soul. Really old. And you're powerful too. An academic, very, very smart."

I glossed over the compliments. "Yeah, I've taken a few days to work out what is going on here, and I'm still trying to figure it all out to be honest, but it's bigger and more layered than I ever imagined."

"They need you doing the work," she said. "That's why they brought you here. There's a few of us here, on a different level. They'll bring you together with them too."

She was leaning sharply down against the table, almost like it was keeping her up. "Because of 'interference', the Entities can't go in and heal the world. That's why people like us are important to the process," she whispered.

I was part fascinated by this interesting character, part flattered and part very unsure. There was something slightly unnerving about her that I couldn't quite put my finger on. I mentioned that I had been putting requests in the prayer triangle, like turning the media system on its head so that it is a force of good, and completely rewiring the education system to include all things energetic.

"Ooh that's brilliant," she cooed. "I hadn't thought of that. Most people aren't like you. They wouldn't think of asking outside of their hip problem or whatever."

She had been in Abadiânia for a fair few years. She was very, very sick when she came, and she ran out of money after about a year. She told me she went to JOG and said she was having money troubles and he said he'd take care of it.

After the session a medium came up to her and said, "I've been guided to give you money."

They apparently started giving her a thousand dollars every month, for years. I was gobsmacked. I mean, I generally believe anything is possible, but this was escalating to levels I hadn't even thought of. She said she'd received hundreds of thousands of dollars since that day.

"It's limitless here. How out of the box can you get?" she asked. "João is special you know. He's showed me things."

"Like what?" I said curiously.

"I never bother to tell anyone, as they don't believe me," she said, looking down at her notebook.

"Try me," I said.

And then the floodgates opened as she proceeded to tell me how João had appeared in front of her at times, like he'd teleported there, that he had made things appear instantly in his hands.

"He shows things to people who have been in Abadiânia for a while," she said. "João needs our prayers too," she added. He may be a famous trance healer but appeared far from the picture of health from what I saw. Overweight, sallow skin and thinning greasy hair. He had age-spots everywhere and was hardly a spring chicken.

When I got to the Casa, I was in tears. The conversation seemed to have triggered an ancient remembering of something. A realisation of how powerful I was. Acknowledging that which I knew was in there all along. I spent the afternoon sitting in the garden, meditating and writing, buzzing from the energy of the place.

Suddenly I could hear the guitars and some singing. I saw Ulrika sitting afar, in the lead with her guitar, with a group of people gathered in the soup kitchen area. It was the weekly Casa singing session. They were singing "Amazing Grace". They followed this with "Hallelujah" then "Give Me Joy In My Heart, Keep Me Praising," and finally "I'm Choosing Healing Today." I couldn't help but feel the happy clappy, praise-be-to God vibe was a step too far for me. I set off back towards the pousada for the evening.

That night I awoke in the early hours to the scratching and crawling noises coming from the hallway outside. I sat in my bed, wondering what kind of creature was out there. After a while the noises died down and I drifted back to sleep.

I dreamt I had been on an adventure with my brother Mike and was wanting to sneakily stay at some big old family mansion where we were together. It seemed like an old English mansion, and there was a group of ancient-English-looking, ancestor-type people watching TV in the living room area. They gave me a key, which I was pretending to be nonchalant about. Mike went to sleep in the other room and I was to sleep in the main room, where they had been watching TV. They went to bed and left me in the dark, and I went to switch the lights on but none of them would work. I seemed afraid that it was ghosts who were going to haunt me during the night.

You can see between the realms.
You can see that which is not there.
Harness and nurture this power within you
to provide the confidence you need to move forward.

You are on the path; you have rhythm and cadence to do what you do,
in line with the natural rhythms of this planet.
You are in tune. Do you see? You are in tune
with that which you wish to be.
Acclimate in this place of knowing to become who you are.
Who you already carry, within.
In the depths of your being, it is in there.
Your truth. Your whole truth,
of that which you must share.
For it is not to be told, but to be created by you, as an experience.

Do not wait for anything else.
For what you are looking for is right there in front of your eyes.
Ready for the taking.
The insidious gloom has gone. Do not look back for it.
For you have come so far.

Believe in you and all you do. From this place clarity lies.
Dormant within you. Waiting for the recognition.
Recognition of self, of sovereignty and of service.

The Second Coming Of Crazy

Melissa, Susan and I were catching up again at Frutti's when James walked by. James was one of the Casa volunteers, who was struck by lightning when he was fourteen-years-old. He got his life back through the energy work at the Casa. Susan grabbed him quickly for some advice on a distance session to help her friend in a wheelchair back in LA. James's advice contradicted previous information.

"Oh, James got me all confused," she said.

"Well, he was struck by lightning after all," I said, laughing.

The thing about the Casa was that it was mostly self-directed. There was no one telling you what you should be doing aside from the basic protocol for Casa sessions, and even this differed from one to the next. Sure, the Casa Guides give their direction, which is really just their opinion, and it's really up to you to decode what is going on and how to proceed. Everything, at the beginning, is based on what someone else has heard or seen, and you often hear conflicting information. Not speaking or understanding Portuguese definitely compounds this.

At this stage, I was debating the philosophy on whether to take voluntary surgeries or not. The option for volunteer surgeries had been added only a year ago or so, which was possibly to deal with the ever-growing crowds.

Melissa piped up. "The more surgeries, the better. They can't do everything in one, so you gotta pack 'em in."

The LA girls were cramming in as many surgeries as they could before they left, and were very 'pro volunteer'. I felt that if the Entity wanted me to have surgery, it would be prescribed. Something about volunteering and having as many surgeries as possible just didn't jive with me. Surely your body could only process a certain amount at once. Ulrika had a different perspective altogether, that creating the option for voluntary surgeries was 'trusting us to rely on our intuition more'.

I bumped into the Crushed Velvet Creature on my way back to the pousada, and she walked me down the road with her bike.

"This is the pattern of your doubting mind," she said. "It's taking you out of your gut feel, 'being right' and trusting self. Many scenarios will arise in coming days where you have two battling thoughts or POV's with other people, so you need to remember that 'the content will make you crazy'. It's not about the content, it's about The Doubter," she added. "Remember, your first thought is always right." We arrived at my front door. "The volunteering aspect of JOG has only just opened up and is actually all about cutting down the numbers he has to see multiple times. He can shortcut it from three to one instantly," she said nonchalantly.

I mulled it over as I went to sleep, deciding to stick to my guns and not get carried away with the surgery-go-lucky attitude. What didn't make sense to me though was why the Entities and spiritual doctors couldn't just do as much as was required miraculously without having to go through rounds and rounds of the protocol at all. I assumed this was because, like I learned in kinesiology there are many layers to issues that need to be healed in stages and it's rare to have a miracle all in one.

I slept right through without disturbance until I was awoken at 5.05am. Slowly coming to, I felt a hand on my shoulder, pulling me forwards, and opened my eyes. Gazing right and left, I appeared to be alone. I sat up in bed, trying to work out what was going on. I manoeuvred myself to the bathroom quietly, just in case I was to surprise someone. No one there. I hopped back into bed highly confused, thinking what is going on here? What do I need to be shown?

As if on cue, the creatures of the night started suddenly going crazy in the hallway entrance. I heard something being dragged along and viciously bashed against the wall in a distinctly precise and uneven manner. It was heavy sounding. At least the size of a possum or giant rat. I envisioned blood smeared across the bottom of the walls, guts in the middle of the hallway and bits of fluff floating softly through the air. A gruesome murder scene. I felt ridiculous that here I was, a grown woman in my thirties, cowering in my room. Afraid as to what I might find out in the hallway. Is this why I kept being woken by them every night? To face my fears? I recalled my childhood night terrors, when I imagined all sorts of creatures from alligators to sharks, or a hybrid of the two, living under my bed. My wardrobe, a few metres in front of my bed was their other lair, which meant the carpet in between them and my escape route to the bathroom was a veritable nightly headfuck. It naturally died off with age, but now I was left questioning, was there something hiding in the basement of my subconscious?

The next day was Susan's farewell dinner, so we went down the road to the only other restaurant on the very small strip, the 'pay by weight' place, with a delicious buffet of vegies and salads on offer. By this point, Susan had had a massive falling out with Melissa. So, it was just the two of us for dinner. We saw the Crushed Velvet Creature, who we had now affectionately nicknamed 'Crazy' after both witnessing her slightly odd demeanour and tall tales, enter the restaurant. Susan invited her to join us and Crazy immediately launched into the story of her precursor to Abadiânia.

She claimed she was electrocuted in a beauty procedure and fried to within an inch of her life. "My skin was so sensitive that I had to leave the cities and pollution. I couldn't live in a normal environment, as I would react to everything…"

Susan and I couldn't get a word in edgewise at this point and were nodding along in unison. "So, I abandoned everything I had, and went to live outside. No clothes, nothing. Completely naked in the woods for years." I was trying not to catch Susan's eye. "During one brutal Norwegian winter…" (Okay, here we go). "I thought I was going to die, so I left with the little money I had and went to India. To a guru."

Susan raised her eyebrows across the table at me. "Then what happened?" Susan asked.

"I roamed the world from one high-vibration place to

the next. This is the purest and highest I have found, here in Abadiânia, Brazil. So, I stayed. And that was years ago now."

Wow. We certainly had a live one here.

"So," I asked. "What is your role here then? At all these high vibration places?"

"I'm here to do my work," she said. "I felt like I was being pulled to Abadiânia by a tie around my neck. It was so strong. It was unstoppable."

I suddenly noticed her face contorting to the side, and then downwards. In the dim light of the restaurant I could see her trying to mask it by turning her head and gesturing wildly. She was attempting to keep it under control, or fight it off. One of the two. But I saw it.

Susan, sitting on the same side as Crazy, and focused on her food was none the wiser. "So, are you helping the Entities then?" she asked innocently.

"There is only one," Crazy quickly fired back in a surprisingly ferocious tone. "It's all an act."

The plot thickened. We were then completely blindsided by the sudden onslaught of an extreme twenty-minute João-bashing monologue. "There's a lot of light here, but there is a lot of darkness too. João the man is very fucked up. He drinks and never sleeps. Max one to two hours a week." I noticed her face twitching a few times. Almost as though she had a tick or something.

"A friend of mine stayed with him," she continued, "and he stayed up all night watching bang-bang films."

"So, he watches porn?" I clarified.

"No, bang-bang, shoot-em-up films," she said shooting me with her hand. "Fucking violent, movies all night long. I see him with all these stupid Brazilian girls around town. I mean, they just can't say no to him. You can't say no to João. You know all Brazilian woman are trained to do as the men say? They are culturally fucked into not having their own minds. They all bow down to him. It's fucking disgusting."

She ranted and raved about his sexual proclivities and then more and more serious criminal allegations in between bites. These got wilder and wilder as we got to dessert. None of which I can repeat here, nor which had any kind of proof. "He's mentally torturing me. I'm not really able to leave Abadiânia. He won't let me. They've cut off my money supply. They're trying to break me. I haven't been to the Casa for weeks."

I wondered how much of it was made up in her mind, although oddly, the more outrageous the claims, the more incredibly convincing she became. It dawned on me that when you come to a place like this, a spiritual retreat where people come to heal themselves and their problems, there is always going to be a very broad spectrum of energy and extreme characterisations of people. Looks like we'd found one end of it.

Susan was distractedly checking her phone on the other side of the table, something about a potential new script back in LA. I was on my own, in the vortex of the next level of conversation with Crazy. I thought we'd peaked. Boy, was I wrong.

"Do you know what is really going on here?" she was saying quietly. "I mean, it's incredible. The power of João, is like no other," she said, now perfectly calm, making noticeable throwaway comments in veiled terms.

I was beginning to have a hunch as to where she was going with all this. So, I just called it. "So, you think this is the return of Jesus then?"

Pause. No reaction. Straight faced acknowledgement. "Yes," she said intensely, looking around to see if anyone was listening. "I only told you because you asked. You knew, so you were obviously meant to know. I'm not going to lie to you."

She was looking over at Susan to ensure she couldn't hear and hurried to finish as Susan rejoined the conversation. Wow, this was like going through a secret door in a video game I didn't even know I was playing. I was fascinated by this bizarre character, at the same time as being slightly terrified. It was kind of like watching a car crash.

"Did you notice how the cone of silence came up when we were talking about all that stuff? So, Susan didn't hear anything? They did that," she said later as we walked home.

"Oh really? I didn't notice," I replied, edging towards my door.

"But I really want to know…" I couldn't help myself, "Exactly what are you here to do, then?" I was a sucker for punishment. It was too intriguing not to.

She claimed João asked her to help him. She was going to help him banish his demons. To heal and be a better man. But he wasn't ready yet.

"Okayyy," I mustered slowly.

"Yeah, I joked with his one son in the crystal shop and drew the symbol of the double-flanked cross, which symbolises the second coming of Jesus, and said, 'It's the return of Dr Augusto,' and we laughed about it together. You would have seen them; they sell those crosses all over town."

"Shush, please," came a voice out of the dark. It seemed we were disturbing someone in the neighbouring property.

"Oh, fuck off, you old bitch," Crazy spat, in a sudden aggressive switch of tone which jarred me on impact. Further directing us towards my door, thankfully. "C'mon, Jo," she said. "João couldn't come into this life perfect. He came into this life with these gifts, but he is also a man, with darkness that he needs to work through before he can reach the light. Then he will be so effing powerful! But he can't handle the power right now."

"Shush," we heard again from the shadows, and Crazy's head snapped backwards in an almost *Exorcist* style manoeuvre.

"Alright fucking cunt," she said, turning back towards me, uncomfortably standing there in horror. "He needs to figure it out, just like everyone else," she said, carrying on like nothing happened.

"Right," I said slowly in hushed tones moving further to my door.

"Even though he's torturing me…" she said at full volume, referring to her Mexican stand-off with João over her money supply, "… and I can't leave. I would never want to be anywhere else. Even if I could leave, I would choose to be right here, right now."

I got back to my room, and my head was spinning. The whole situation had left me with a viscerally uncomfortable feeling of unpleasantness. I felt embroiled in something I didn't want to be involved in. Or know. Or have conversations about. Crazy's energy had sent me for a complete loop. I recapped the evening in my head. A giant bonfire of a torching of JOG, because he was in fact Jesus's soul, who wasn't playing ball with banishing his demons and transforming into his divine role, as the return of the Christ? The face twitching and contortion? The wild criminal accusations? Not to mention the cursing at the neighbours. Quite the evening. I had to wonder why I seemed to attract the most extreme of characters. Never a dull moment. It didn't seem to matter where I was, or what I was doing, it was the same. I got myself ready for bed, consciously washing off all the negativity I had just been exposed to. Ick. What the actual fuck? I checked my phone: '11.11pm', and my daily word of the day notification from my SpanishDict app flashed on my screen. It was 'oration' which means 'prayer.' How incredibly synchronistic. I said a small oration as I was going to sleep, to banish any energies not of light and not of love, and to protect me in this mad experience of JOG and all that went with it.

Ground into the truth of who you are to bring the answers to the surface.
For the code you need to crack is you, and no other.
The mountains of the abyss are before you.
As oxymoron as that may seem.

Be not afraid for the tipping point is upon you now,
and your mastery lies there.
Destiny is, and will be yours.

For, in the no time space you are concurrently living out this journey.
In parallel. As always.
Time is of the essence as The Great Time is here.
It is not as has been prophesied.

The hidden knowledge you hear of, is hidden inside you.
The true secrets of humanity, the key of everything
gone before, is encoded within.
To be activated at such time as is biologically affluent.

You are the keeper of the codes.
Keeper of the eternal light. Keeper of one.
You will find your way out of this.
You will know. Because knowing is your asset.

Knowing the divine truth within all.
Knowing the divine truth is you.
For the second coming is you.

Where There's A Lotta Light,
There's A Lotta Dark

"Look," Gerda said the next day at the crystal store, with an air of seriousness I'd not seen before. "There's a lot of light in this place, but where there is light, there is also dark. And there is a lot of darkness here. Be careful. There is lots of demonic possession in Brazil. It's full of it. Focus on yourself and don't get distracted by stuff that's not yours. Everyone is carrying out their movies here, and 'Crazy' is very much in hers."

On one hand, I felt that whatever is in your reality, is what you are focusing on, and therefore where you are 'at' energetically. You have to be a vibrational match on some level to even be having that experience. I certainly didn't worry about dark magic or negative energies despite the warnings. On the other hand, I knew that Gerda was right; I needed to focus on myself. Finding myself on the periphery of the drama between Melissa and Susan, and then in the thick of it with Crazy over the last few days, had pulled me off my path. Diverted me away from the whole point of this place, which was about going inward for the answers. Finding the truth of who I really was. Why were these kinds of characters in my reality? Was it to highlight how 'together' I am? Or to remind me not to get woven into other people's drama? Or a reflection of the drama within me? I needed release from the drama. That much I knew.

The sacred waterfall is another part of the healing protocol, a fifteen-minute walk from the Casa. While waiting for the taxi containing the rest of the group, who could not walk there post-operation, I noted the sign containing 'the rules'.

'You must have express permission from the Entity. Never go alone. Men & Women go separately. No photos, videos or equipment. No talking. No Nudity. No incense, candles, crystals or flowers. Do not leave anything behind. Say a prayer of invocation entering. And a prayer of gratitude leaving. Permittance during Casa opening times only.'

With the complete group at the entrance in the carpark, we joined hands and said a prayer before making our way down the path in silence. We slotted in next to others waiting in silence for their turn on the concrete steps near the entrance gate. A group came out and two men stood up to go next, so Ulrika quietly asked if Engelbert and Francois could join them. About ten minutes later they returned, and us five girls got ready to go down. Another two girls joined us, barrelling ahead to get in the water while we went slower to do Ulrika's more ceremonial proceedings.

A few seconds into the walk to the waterfall you get to the first bridge which symbolises the 'past'. You walk over this while thinking of all the things in the past you want to leave behind, being careful not to look back at any point. Then you come to a set of benches where you disrobe into swimsuits and leave your belongings, before making your way down to the second bridge in bikini and towel. At the second bridge, you are in the 'present' and with each step you repeat the mantra 'Be. Here. Now.' There was a short queue before the final bridge leading to the slippery rocks of the waterfall itself. This bridge is for focus on future intentions. I wanted a creative job out of the 'nine to five', to live my inner truth and highest good more fully, and to find my soulmate. I felt quite overwhelmed trying to remember all the steps I had to do, and by the final bridge was rather flustered. I suddenly found it hard to bring things to mind, but I had faith that all the things I had been thinking of, and working with during my time here, would be in my energy field and therefore automatically included.

After the final bridge, I stepped off into the rocks under the rather piddly and unimpressive waterfall. I splashed my arms and legs, the water bracing but energising. I couldn't quite remember what I was supposed to be thinking about, and quite frankly the water was far too icy to allow any fluidity of thought other than 'holy bejesus, it's cold!' I dipped my head in and instantly felt lots of emotion, notably after stepping into my future. I was fighting back the tears under the waterfall. I dunked in three times to wet my whole body before carefully walking around the slippery rocks and back over the bridge past the next in line. We exited and I walked back up to the Casa by foot alone, making my way back to my pousada, deep in thought as to why my future was bringing up so much emotion for me.

The Casa commemorated the anniversary of Dom Inácio's ascension on thirty-first July. He lived five hundred years prior from 1491–1556 and took the path following Jesus, giving away all his possessions and retiring to a cave for many years to write his 'Forty Spiritual Exercises', which are still used to this day. This is one of the biggest weeks at the Casa all year, with busloads of people rolling into town from all over Brazil. I was up early and debating whether I should get in line in front of the Entity, or go to Current. I was planning to join the line to see the Entity, mainly because Wednesday morning Current is notoriously long, and the thought of five times the number of people here to celebrate Dom Inácio in the mix made me immediately think 'seven-hour Current'. Entity Line it is then! As I was showering, I started to feel a distinct wavering. Current? Really? Yes, go to Current. As I got dressed, my thoughts started, Jo, Current is a terrible idea. You've just skulled almost one and a half litres of water this morning and you only have a small apple for breakfast. You'll need to pee like crazy AND you'll be starving in Current. No, no, far better to go in the line, I reasoned, even if you don't have an official guide this week. Just think of those crowds…

And so, I talked myself out of Current and found myself outside the Casa. It was an absolute white-out, teeming with people everywhere. More like a frenzy than a sacred or holy experience. I slipped in the side door of the Main Hall to get more of a gauge as to what was going on. Inside it was even more chaotic, with people rushing to get to the line while Heather, one of the main speakers and monitors, was saying, "Be thankful for this great blessing."

I then saw Ulrika, who said that *all* of the second-time line was going through for an operation. Great, I thought. Crowd management with mandatory operations for the entire group.

"Those having the operation, so all of those in the second timeline must not, I repeat, must not come back to the Casa until Friday," said Heather over the loudspeaker.

What the actual? That was even more than the standard twenty-four hours, and meant I missed the entire Dom Ignacio week altogether, pretty much. I felt royally hoodwinked by the entire thing, while simultaneously being completely and utterly annoyed at myself for letting my mind talk me out of going to Current instead. I wouldn't even be in this situation if I had trusted my gut. So, there I was, ushered through into the Intervention room with gritted teeth and already feeling the effects of the spiritual anaesthetic kicking in. Once seated, I kept my eyes closed for all of two minutes, with barely enough time for a quick blessing from JOG before being told to open my eyes.

I felt like they were still working on me and I was feeling quite out of it, so I attended to the post-op bits before hopping a cab home. I felt whacked out after this operation, but not as much as my first.

Shortly after getting home, I heard Engelbert answer the door for his lunch delivery and, surprisingly, call out to me that Raphael had mine too, given I never marked the chart and had decided to fast. We took our meals and adjourned to the terrace to eat. I sat at the long wooden table while Engelbert faced away from me towards the neighbours.

"Do you think it's okay that we do this?" he said after a few moments turning towards me.

"Well, I don't think the Entities would have put us together unless they wanted us to chat," I said.

"Well yes, I guess you are right," he giggled, turning around.

After eating and feeding the stray cats a few leftover scraps, we popped back into our rooms with a, "See you at dinner!" We soon found out that by feeding the cats we created a monster. They howled and yowled incessantly outside our rooms. I heard Engelbert get up and chase them away, which lasted all of about five minutes before they were back and making even more of a racket. I decided to take matters into my own hands and grabbed an old water bottle from beside my bed. I quietly let myself onto the balcony and then launched at the cats, spraying them with water.

I could hear Engelbert laughing. "Ooh, what will Raphael think when he sees you behaving like a mad thing on the terrace?" he shrieked in his perfectly camp Swiss accent.

I went back to bed and broke the rules by writing in my journal. I also naughtily checked my email and a couple of things online, although only to figure out where in my body they were operating, based on the intense pain I was now starting to feel in my lower stomach and especially up the entire left side of my torso as the anaesthetic started to wear off. I struggled, lying around for hours without being able to sleep. I just couldn't relax.

At exactly 5.55pm, the cats were yowling outside. Urgh. When dinner arrived a few minutes later, Engelbert and I both opened our separate doors, received our plates and then a few seconds later reconvened on the terrace to eat.

"I think I can probably sit next to you now, right?" Engelbert said with a wink as he plopped down next to me on the picnic table.

"Of couuuurse," I said dramatically, causing fits of laughter. "Ooh, don't make me laugh," I gasped, clutching my side. "It's too painful." It was very, very tender, in exactly the same spot as the first operation. "Clearly they didn't properly fix it the first-time round," I joked. "That or I've got some serious problem going on there."

The next morning, Engelbert and I made our way to the Casa. Engelbert was walking slower and slower, one belaboured step after the other. "Well, we have just had suuuurgery, remember!" he stated dramatically. "We simply can't hurry. One step at a time," he said with his lilting, flamboyant Swiss accent rising an octave at the end of every sentence.

I was again trying not to laugh, as my side was so painful. Slowly but surely we got to the Casa, which was heaving with people. It was too much, so we went home to relax at the pousada instead. With strong sessions, the Entities can change the rules, which is why they had said to come back Friday, Ulrika advised. Whether this was crowd management, politics or the truth, I wanted to be as respectful as possible. I was upset to be missing out on the Dom Inácio days but trusted that everything was as it should be.

On Friday I was awake at 5.15am after a terrible night's sleep, tossing and turning and drenched in sweat. I had also been dripping in sweat the afternoon before. There were yellow ribbons around the posts outside and flowers everywhere as decorations for the Dom Inácio day. I sat at the back of the first Current room again, and soon it was chock-a-block full. I closed my eyes and settled in. Once it started, we were told João was incorporating the energy of Dom Inácio on the main stage, and I could certainly feel it. It was the most peaceful, loving, yet deeply enriching energy flowing into my experience. It was made all the sweeter when a chocolate was popped into my hand during the meditation as a present from Dom Inácio. It was even more surprising when we were told we were receiving a special blessing from the Dom and to open our eyes. The Current had been a delightful two hours long after Dom Inácio pushed every single person through for a blessing, disregarding all lines, operations or protocol. It was two hours of the most gorgeous, pure energy I have ever felt. I was really getting the hang of this now. What a treat. Everyone was then told that the next session would start at 1pm, instead of 2pm. Expect the unexpected, as they say. I left the Great Hall and went into the gardens, completely blissed out. We received some blessed grape juice, bread, a Dom Inácio tea towel and a leaflet with his prayers and other notes in Portuguese as a gift.

I breezed into the afternoon Current session on a high and ready for the next round of elevating energy work. No sooner had we started meditating when I heard, "Fuck! Shit! Cunt!" blurt loudly from a man sitting behind me. Wondering whether I misheard, I ignored it and continued centering. Then, just as I was dropping down deeply, "Balls balls bitch fuck cunt balls!"

pierced the serenity at a billion decibels, making me jump out of my seat in fright. I could not contain my laughter. I was sitting in front of a guy who clearly had Tourette syndrome. Naturally. After the third and final burst of expletives, I heard him leave and the next couple of hours continued uninterrupted. The last three hours, however, were a challenge as it dragged on. Suffice to say, that when it finally ended I was very grateful. And completely exhausted. As I left, I plucked a few grapes from the beautiful decorations for the occasion and ate them for an extra zap as I made my way through the room. Ironically, the blessed grapes were quite sour. After a shot of blessed water, we managed to get a group photo with an exhausted João in the garden afterwards. As the sun was setting, I made my way back to my pousada in somewhat of a daze.

We bring you these messages at this time for the benefit of remembrance.
Remembrance of your true divine self.
Remembrance of the being of love and light that you truly are.
Moving closer, back to your divine blueprint in your everyday life.

Welcome your remembrance at this time.
Reach for it. Ask for it. Be with it.
For you have much to remember.
For who you truly are is of utmost importance.

Your alignment in your physical world relies on it.
Too often you are dragged down into your 3D reality.
Detachment from this reality is key.
For your remembrance of your ultimate truth depends on it.

This is your birthright.
Your true self will help you navigate these new energies.
For these new energies are you.
They will seem familiar. And you will know them.
A deep knowing that is from your heart. Where the truth resides.
For you and for all.

Stay in your heart. Access your truth. Be who you are.

Annie Says Abracadabra

I decided to skip the 9am Sunday singing and service in the Casa. I gave it a shot, really only because it was supposed to raise your vibration, but it was far too evangelical for me. Why did everything 'high vibration' have to be so stereotypically eye-roll saintly? Who's to say it's not another form of mass conditioning? And isn't high vibration versus low vibration a judgement anyway? I really fancied, or craved even, a walk and some alone time as I marinated on these wonderings.

The sun was already pretty strong when I left around 8.30am, but I set off in my flip-flops down the dusty, red-clay road. It was a gorgeous walk, with gentle hills rolling on either side, and the sounds of birds chattering away. The road was lined with eucalyptus trees along the dry and dusty landscape; I might have been in the Australian outback. I saw some large birds, around the size of flamingos, come out of the scrub and cross the road. They looked similar to an emu in colour but were much smaller. There were termite hills everywhere, dotting the landscape all around, like an acne-ridden teenager. It was a harsh landscape, nice, but super-dry and almost desolate in appearance.

By 9.30am, the sun was beating down with force, but I was content to wander along. My left shoulder and neck were painful. I had woken up with this a couple of days earlier, which I had noticed over the years usually indicated that I was not listening to my guidance and not moving forward. I was passed by a young boy on a horse who seemed to be having trouble keeping the horse in line. He offered to let me ride, but I politely declined after seeing it bucking and clearly unhappy with him sitting on it. Let alone my chequered horse history. Once I was on my own again and heading back, I was surprised to see a wild cat run across my path and into the bushes below. I was amazed to see so many wild animals in my backyard. I bumped into some friends on the way back who took me to a secret waterfall, where I was given a cleansing foot massage and a dip, a welcome reprieve from the intense sun.

Before some crystal beds, I felt a sleepiness that I had noticed often came over me when the Entities came in to work on me. My energy sensitivity had really reached new heights over the last two months in this place. As I waited outside, I thought about my intentions for the session. I wanted to see what was blocking me, if anything, from progressing swiftly on this healing journey, and if I could move through it. I zoned out before noticing different thoughts coming into my awareness and then dissipating. At the end, I noticed that Annie came up, and I felt pain in the centre of my chest, my heart chakra, and it came to me that my teenage years with Annie had given me a broken heart.

Most of those years Annie appeared to want to be in spirit, formless, without any of the ego or material-world stuff. I found it difficult to grow up with someone who felt to me like she often didn't want to be here, in her marriage, in our house, in her body, on the planet. It always seemed to me that she wanted to be somewhere else. Although it may have only been a phase for her and there were plenty of positives to balance it out somewhat, I guessed that, being a sensitive child this had affected me more than I thought. I always wondered why my heart felt closed, and such walls built around it. I had suspected this as one factor weighing into my unfulfilled relationship history. I truly wanted to be open, but I knew there was old, thick stuff caked around the outside. Parts of my childhood and teenage years were too painful to deal with when I was younger, not just due to Annie, but her and Devo and a fairly volatile environment fuelled by polar opposite points of view, strong personalities and a love of excess. So I guess I built walls to protect me.

My right ear had suddenly started bothering me. The thought came up to put holy water in my ears to help. I did this before my shower, and then felt extremely woozy. My eyes were droopy and I was heady and sleepy all of a sudden, like when the spiritual anaesthetic was coming on. I finished my shower, feeling so out of it I had to lie down. I was reading bits of *Cosmic Healing* by Barbara Brodsky, that I had found in the local bookstore to better understand energy healing. There were tears of recognition of all the energy methods, and truth from spirit that I had forgotten. Deep knowings inside me confirmed by way of the text. I just cried and allowed the processing to happen.

I sat outside, reading in the sun, with much of the material resonating deeply with me. I noted how slowly the papaya was growing on the tree next to the balcony. So much love and energy had gone into it from the sun over months to form this beautifully big, delicious, orange beauty. The natural divine intelligence that flows through all things, all around us was simply awe inspiring. I checked social media and saw the 'death' card as the 'card of the day' I subscribed to indicating new beginnings, and the death of something inside. I shed more tears, realising that I was back in a very similar place I had been before. It felt like I was at the same juncture I had reached years ago in New York and then again in London. I was being asked if I was ready to more fully embrace a life of consciousness and spirit, yet again. The last few dark nights of the soul I hadn't been ready, which had probably been caused by my discordance within. I didn't think I had the courage, nor the tools or consciousness. This time I felt courageous, and willing to trust, wholly and completely wherever this was taking me. I felt that I would have to let go of my personality traits, the reasons I thought I was valued in the world, in order to do this.

I was ready this time, and excited. What could be more exciting than a new adventure, headed blindly into the unlimited Universe with no idea of what would eventuate? Beats the 'nine to five' any day, if you ask me. The same issue of fear of losing my identity, that I had experienced in my late twenties in New York, and later in London, was coming up to be released. Clearly, I hadn't quite surrendered to it the first time.

Chris, my other neighbour, came out on the balcony and caught me having a moment. He had a medium build, bright blue eyes, salt-and-pepper, close-shaven hair and a little stubble around the cheeks and chin. For some reason he reminded me of an elf, mainly due to slightly elvish-looking ears which always made me giggle. Chris was a lovely, but intense, American guy. He was an ex-addict, of *everything*; heroin, crack, cocaine, weed, you name it, he'd done it. Not just dabbling, serious addiction. Now sober, he had even quit sugar nine years prior. No sugar substitutes for him, only a bit of fruit here and there.

"I went through the same thing last year, ya know," he said sympathetically. "Giving up my identity, shedding my skin... except I was forty-nine. You are only thirty-six, so at least you are ahead of the game," he laughed.

I felt like I was being pushed, literally. Not only this, but I had been feeling very woozy and unsteady the last two days. My ears were out of balance and in a fair bit of pain. I was ruminating over all of this and what these physical manifestations in my body meant metaphysically, as I waited in the Casa lines. I tuned in and out of what was happening and had been planning to go into the second time line, but as I mulled it over, I wondered if perhaps I should go in the volunteer operation line. As I stood there, I was experiencing a heightened reaction of incredible heat filling my body. I felt unsteady on my feet, like some huge energy was overtaking me.

I was confused, so I asked for a clear sign of what I should do. The heat continued increasing until I was so hot that I had severe sweats as I heard the last call for the volunteer operation line. I felt like I might fall over, so I steadied myself on a pew and sat down. The opportunity passed. I cried. I cried for the immense feeling of failure that had overcome me, for the decision I felt like I should make but was too scared to make as I was relying on something outside of myself to guide me. I realised this was patterned behaviour around the need to be right. Make the right decision. Say the right thing. There was fear there and mistrust of the self. The emotion passed and I rationalised to myself that if, when I was in the revision line as planned, JOG said 'surgery', then I would know for next time. It suddenly came to me. Was the heat and sweating I experienced periodically linked to a failure to listen to and follow my intuition?

I volunteered for my third surgery the next day after beating myself up good and proper, I didn't feel much anaesthetic, and overall felt surprisingly 'on to it' when leaving the Casa. I jumped in a taxi nonetheless and headed home for a sleep. Following lunch, I found it quite difficult to get back into slumber. The tenderness in my stomach and my left side was back; the right side was also affected this time, and equally as sensitive. I felt quite headachy again, chalking it up to possible third eye opening. My ears were still sore from the infection. It turned out that everyone was sent through for operations that morning, so even if I had decided differently, I would have been operated on either way; there was no getting around it.

Since I was having these very visceral energy experiences and enjoying my development at the Casa, I decided to stay on longer before heading to Buenos Aires. I wanted to spend the next months going inward so I rented an apartment at the edge of town overlooking the earthy red landscape. I knew deep down that I needed to get in touch with myself and listen to the subtle voices of my heart. I needed to trust my feelings and inner nudges, and the symbols I saw in the world, as I knew these were all tied up in my intuitive guidance package. I wanted at the end of this to be able to unequivocally hear and understand my guidance and soul's wisdom, so that I was in touch one hundred percent with the light within. This time was my gift to myself.

I spent my days meditating, writing, connecting and listening to spiritual podcasts and radio shows when I wasn't at the Casa. However, I came to feel that the information available from the spiritual community was always filtered through someone, their mindset and beliefs, and therefore just like organised religion, was not as pure as it could be. I was slowly becoming aware that the spiritual community wasn't the answer, and may even be holding me back. I started a channelling course to find my own answers to the endless questions I had about this reality and my place in it. I wanted confident access to my own truth.

We build our beliefs, structures and rules from all of the data we process, which governs our day-to-day, only to find out that it is outdated down the track. I was sick of going to other people who supposedly had more access to spiritual information about our soul's journey than me. I wanted to be able to get access to everything I needed myself. The new channelling practice had me up from 5am-7am every morning, doing automatic writing and attempting to bring through wisdom from guides, beings, and philosophers who had passed on. I had varying degrees of success. My morning writings followed a very specific process, and although I was writing a lot, none of it felt like profound channelling of wisdom, more like a stream-of-consciousness emptying of my mind, never quite getting to the good stuff. I was also getting frustrated with the teacher who was based in the US, whose ego and mood became more prominent as we went along and began to dictate things more than I liked. She seemed unable to help me troubleshoot for better results. Yet another sign pointing me back to myself.

I did a guided meditation, during which I suddenly saw a tall being from another galaxy. This being had a wide forehead, and a more angular face than that of a human. It was a little bit Star-Trek-looking, for lack of a better reference. The being sent some balls of light into my stomach and head. I asked about the overheating I was experiencing and learned that the root cause was shock. I couldn't quite understand what was required to clear it from the body, but this was progress, nevertheless.

I caught up on Skype with the whanau in New Zealand.

"I have a new addiction," said Annie.

"You don't need any more addictions," I said bluntly.

"But this one is a by-product of the Danish hospital diet," she said enthusiastically. "I've upgraded the coffee to three espressos that Devo buys me from the cafe up the road every day. Devo has lost four kilograms, and I have lost three-and-a-half, and well, I feel great," she finished.

Then, in a major plot twist, she told me she had decided to come to Abadiânia, or 'Abracadabra' as she called it. Not only was she coming to visit, but she was coming for two months, December and January, so that she could get away from the deep loathing of her worst time of the year, Christmas.

"I just want to be with you," she said.

Was she dying?! Did she have some fatal disease? Or had the real Annie been abducted by aliens? This was major. She was my most challenging relationship and now she was coming to live with me, in my small, one-bedroom apartment in the middle of the Brazilian outback, for two months. Entities wtf?! There was no doubt we had some healing work to do.

I was doing anything I could to help accelerate my spiritual progress. On a physical level, I had been continuing my major detox, hoping that it would also help with the flow of information and spirit in my life, as all the yogis and old-school spiritual masters had done in the past. I had been a gluten-free vegan for three months, and coughing up vile phlegm for the duration. My energy levels weren't great, and I was experiencing some immune system issues and slight hay-fever-like symptoms on and off. This may have been coming up for physical healing and recalibration which was great, but it did not seem to be having the heightened effect I was expecting, so it wasn't dialling up any divine guidance or connection I was craving.

I did notice other messages from the Universe, like the caterpillar that had decided to cocoon itself on my curtain; a great omen of transformation, yes, but it wasn't meeting my expectations for clear booming guidance from someone or something other than myself. I did intentional releasing work to remove anything that might be holding me back. Past-life contracts or vows, fears, whatever came into my consciousness, I stuck it in the triangle and asked for help.

It was now the rainy season, which brought with it a different set of challenges. There were tropical downpours and unpredictable weather patterns. I was even hit by a flying-ant storm one evening, with thousands of wriggling and writhing flying-ants hurling themselves against my walls and doors. Many getting inside through the cracks in the building. They were attracted to the light so I switched to working by candlelight and turned on the outside light as a decoy. I put sprigs of fresh mint at my windows to deter any wandering creepy crawlies, but it was a full-scale insect assault and not for the faint-hearted.

As I navigated the emotional ups and downs of energy work, I tried not to hibernate too much, so volunteered to peel vegetables for the Casa healing soup each week. There, I met a Swedish lady who told me all about her work with the Violet Flame, a gift that Ascended Master Saint Germain had brought to the earth, which had the power to burn away any kind of discordant energy. "Perhaps we should send the Violet Flame immediately to Ed, the older American organiser of the volunteering, so he stops yelling at people," I said, laughing.

I also met a French woman who was overcome with tears as she told me her first JOG story; she had asked the Entities to show her how the energy healing of the Casa works. They told her to sit in the Entities Current section, and in her meditation, she was transported to a place where she experienced the fullness of divine love like she'd never felt before. She sobbed for hours and hours in the Current, but woke up with no memory of sitting there and crying. She told me that at other times, the Entity had asked her back to JOG's office after Current, where they did some healing work not only for her personally, but also through her for her dad. She seemed to have endless stories of amazing experiences, which gave me hope that if she could have this, then I could too.

Devo wasn't doing very well on the home front, with debilitating back pain amongst other things, so I printed a photo of him and took it to the Entity one morning. He gave me a strange look but I received the blessing, went to the Farmácia to get the script for his pills and then had the healing soup and sent energy to Devo from it. I then took another of his photos, put it in the King Solomon triangle, and meditated on his health and healing energies once again. I had a particular affinity with King Solomon; it was one of my favourite places and energies at the Casa.

I was experimenting with a range of energy practices, including programming my dreams and walks to receive information from the divine. One day on my usual walk past the local horses grazing alongside the road, I was skipping to get back in touch with my inner child when I saw one of the horses glare at me, and stamp its foot. I didn't think much of it until another horse started snorting and stamping both feet also looking in my direction. It was slightly unnerving, so I slowed to a walk. "I was only skipping," I said, watching the second horse run towards the first as if to join forces. In all the weeks of walking by these horses, this had never happened, but it was bringing up discomfort within me. I felt very self-conscious all of a sudden, so I waited until I was further up the hill before continuing my skipping once again. The weather suddenly turned, and it started to pour with rain as I reached the top of the hill. Just over the rise, I raised my hands to the heavens feeling the rain pelt against my face when I heard a thundering noise behind me. Getting louder and louder, I turned back to see five horses in an arrow formation taking up the entire breadth of the road and galloping at speed directly towards me through the pouring rain. With my adrenalin pumping and not knowing what to do, I leapt up by a tree on the side of the dirt road just in time for the horses to storm through. As I peeked out from behind the ridiculously thin tree of protection, I saw the centre horse snorting and neighing furiously towards me as the group passed by. Almost as if to laugh or rub it in. Then it hit me. Was this a test? Was I supposed to stand my ground against five angry galloping horses to finally put my fear to bed? Damn it, I had just missed my grand opportunity to face my fear once and for all. I leapt back down to the road. "Wait, come back! I get it! I'm ready now!" I yelled, to the horses who were now far away on the next hill over and calmly grazing as if nothing happened. Horses 2. Jo 0.

I often felt waves of gratitude for this gift of taking time out to go inward, experiment and explore other realms of this crazy earthly adventure. This was a wondrous life, and it was exciting to see how it unfolded each day. Life was constantly showing me what I needed to see in order to change and transform. I felt a strong commitment to my personal evolution. I was getting more and more comfortable with letting the societal norms drop away and stepping into a completely different way of being and living. I felt incredibly supported by all the energies at work in this beautiful place. I knew the key for me was to be impeccable with my thoughts, words and actions. My mind was one of my biggest challenges.

Every time I went to the Current sessions, I had a different experience. Sometimes I would have deep emotional release; other times, many different thought forms would come into my consciousness. I was told that the Entities control the music, based on what needs to happen in each session. Sometimes a certain song would come on four or five times a session, when I was going through something deep. Whether easy or difficult, the Current was always effective for energy work, healing and meditation. Not just on a personal level but on a collective level too. I often sat directly in front of a picture of a man in a turban, with piercing deep blue eyes. He was obviously of high spiritual calibre to be pictured and hung on the walls in the Current room. I asked the monitor about him one day, but they didn't know who he was.

I found the discarded head of a caterpillar in the kitchen, and another half-finished cocoon in the making on the couch. I now had at least three cocoons in my apartment, and the one from a month ago still hadn't hatched. Was it the season for them, or what? Every morning, when I got up at 5am to do my channelled writing and morning pages I had to deal with huge spiders who were hanging out on the living room floor. I'd attempt to catch them and release them outside. Spiders were one of my least favourite things and I was aware of a little fear there. However, they were also a strong symbol of creativity, of weaving the web of life and were equated to the numerological number eight, the symbol of infinity, making them a powerful energy to work with. This place had a knack of bringing your fears to the surface to be dealt with, and removing giant brown spiders from my apartment every day was yet another one of them.

In my continuing spiritual study, I had found a site in New Zealand that worked with the Ascended Masters closely, and had Ascended Master portals on their property in Auckland. The six billion people on the planet were apparently divided into eight rays, each under an over-lighting Master which they were able to ascertain for you free of charge.

I excitedly sent in my picture and started wondering which of the amazing Ascended Masters I might be aligned with, Jesus, Mary Magdalene, Mother Mary, Saint Germain and Buddha, to name a handful. My guess was Mary Magdalene, with whom I had a strong affinity, but when a response came back I was told it was El Morya.

When I looked into El Morya, it seemed to blow my more romantic vision of working with an evolved being. Apparently he was a stern master who was very precise and meticulous as he represented God's will and power. This encapsulated the leadership energies of courage, forthrightness, dependability, faith, power, self-reliance and initiative. In other incarnations it's been said he was King Arthur, Malchior one of the three wise men and Thomas Becket to name a few.

A stern master. Yikes. Was that the reason I always felt the need to keep myself in line? I wondered if perhaps the picture of the master in the Current room, to which I was so connected was El Morya. They certainly looked similar.

Weeks later, I overheard a guy sitting behind me in Current say that the painting of the man I always sat opposite was in fact a depiction of El Morya, who was a reincarnation of King Solomon and a Sufi. I was grateful to have received the answer from the Universe knowing my affinity to this picture and the King Solomon Triangle. It all now made perfect sense. I had been naturally attracted to that with which I was working. It was a profound confirmation.

I dutifully went to Current twice a day on the three Casa days each week. I had a particularly stand-out experience when Saint Francis Xavier came through JOG in the Current one morning, and the energy was so strong that it was like the calibre of the Dom Inácio celebration week. The frequency was so beautiful that the tears started immediately and continued for the entire two-and-a-half hour Current session. It felt like I had come home to God, the Source of all that is, Nature, Universal Intelligence or whatever you want to call it. Waves of unconditional love showered over me, and poured through my being. The monitors in the Current room told us St. Francis was on stage and animatedly talking to the audience while taking out a tumour from a man's spine. The man was smiling happily, under nothing but spiritual anaesthetic as he was sliced open in front of hundreds of people.

Apparently, St. Francis worked with Dom Inácio very closely, acting as his right-hand man and working with his whole phalange of angels, which was why the energy was of such high-calibre. I was sitting alongside three men, sobbing throughout. I could feel that I was clearing some family stuff that wasn't even mine. I was told you could clear up to three generations, forward and back, doing this energy work at the Casa.

I had picked some beautiful, magenta, bougainvillea flowers, which I was wearing in my hair during Current. I felt someone touching these flowers twice during the session, although there was no one sitting behind or next to me.

After bawling my eyes out as I prepared lunch afterwards, I went back to the afternoon Current to continue the processing, half expecting it to be a long and painful six hours, as it often was, only to be surprised with a two-hour session of more beautiful energy. It wasn't as strong as in the morning but was the perfect finish as I continued shedding tears and experiencing the deep healing. I just kept crying and crying; even when I thought there was nothing more to come, I cried some more. I knew I didn't need to know what it was, I just needed to do what my body needed and let it out. It was a huge emotional release.

The waves of energy are upon us.
Soft waves moving through every fibre of your being.
Softening, relaxing you into a state of open receptiveness
for the light and love that is flooding the planet.
You may feel the cells of your body expanding with the light codes,
you may feel slightly pulled and stretched here and there.
Allow, allow, allow.
For all expansion is of benefit at this time.

Stretch yourself beyond what you thought possible.
Stretch yourself into the depths of the unknown,
into the abyss of galactic energies,
of Universes within Universes, of worlds within worlds.
The energies of your true nature.

For that is what you truly are and what you
came to be here on this planet.
Your role in the wider multiverse is anchored here.
Yet its repercussions are profoundly felt throughout all time and space.
Remain in the lightness of being and unlimited potential of
who you are to maximize this expansion at this time.

Getting In Touch With My Animal Side

I was sitting on my bed, well after dusk, when a butterfly came flying into the room. I had adjusted the curtain in the lounge, not realising that yet another chrysalis was up there, which must have caused an early exit. I tried to calm it down, speaking softly until it climbed onto my ankle and just sat there, chilling and collecting itself. It was the sweetest thing. After some time of letting it sit there, I had to continue working on my writing, so I let the butterfly hang on the end of my bed. I put a dish of water next to it in case it was thirsty after being bundled up in a cocoon for over a month. Another reminder that good things take time.

It rested there for hours. Meanwhile, the crazy flying-ant swarms started up again and a new, prehistoric-looking, alien-like creature which lived in my fridge came out to hunt them. He caught them in his claws and crunched them down in one mouthful. It was quite something to witness. The kitchen was full of the ugly wriggling ants, so I turned on the outside light as a decoy to lure them out of the house. They routinely managed to get through every teeny crevice in the apartment building, which was clearly lacking in decent workmanship.

Finally, moments after I turned off the light to go to sleep, the butterfly started flying around my bedroom. I turned the light back on and got it to climb on my finger so I could walk it outside into the dark. I shook my finger gently, and it took off into the night. I rushed back inside to avoid the flying ant storm. This particular butterfly had a very different energy from the first one that had finally hatched a week ago I noticed; there seemed to be more of an innocence and purity to it. It was a magical end to the night, but as I went to put down my head for a second time, I heard banging music reverberating through the walls. The flying-ant swarm was now pelting the bathroom window like heavy rain, so there was no way I was going outside to figure out where the music was coming from. The noise of the flying ants and music went on all night.

The little sleep I did get was plagued with intense dreams, and I woke up feeling off centre. My dream-self felt very different from the conscious person I was in real life. I knew that dreams were often metaphorical and symbolic, as opposed to being a literal representation of anything. These felt to me like processing-dreams, dreams where I was working through old behaviour patterns or stuff from my subconscious. It was heavy and I wished for something more light-hearted.

As if on cue, a couple of nights later I had a dream about an earring with an ancient Egyptian female head on it, which left me wondering about the significance. I had never been to Egypt but had been using Isis Oracle cards, which had been gifted to me by a Swedish friend at the Casa. Believing I had possibly had a previous incarnation in Egypt, I had since been asking to bring forth my Ancient Egyptian knowledge and memories. So, something was happening, even if I couldn't decipher it yet. Years later when I finally did go to Egypt I visited the remote area of Armana which was where Akhenaten, a significant figure in consciousness and spiritual revolution to uphold only one God, Aten or light, had reigned. When I visited the tombs, a man asked me if I recognised him from three thousand years ago. I had a significant connection to that energy, that era, and specifically Akhenaten's royal priest's tomb where I was overcome with emotion. Later I was told I was that very priest in a past life, which made sense of the depth of the affinity I was experiencing. Driving away from the tombs and back into town I saw the same woman's head I had seen in my dream on the earrings, on a giant sign on a roundabout. It was Akhenaten's wife Nefertiti.

A few nights later, I had a dream wherein I was dressed in white and belonged to some spiritual group. In one of the rooms, I saw some fresh root-ginger manifest itself live; to my amazement it was growing before my very eyes. Similar to how marigolds apparently miraculously multiply when they were in the devotional presence of Indian gurus. I then dreamt of a black panther with green eyes who was in a house with Annie and me, and I was moving into different rooms to escape it as it stalked around.

I met a European shaman called Mia, who worked with medicine wheels and sweat lodges around Europe. She told me she left her husband because the Entities told her to end the relationship. She did so amicably and he stayed in Brazil with their kids while she travelled around, doing her work. She said that after she did what the Entities said, a whole host of doors opened up to her; various chiefs wanted to come and see the work she was doing with Siberian traditional energy work. They were amazed, and called her 'grandmother', a prestigious title from the elders. I told her about seeing a wild cat on my walk, and about my dream of the panther with the green eyes, and she said it was all about the feminine, recalling personal power and wisdom. She told me to print a picture of it, and to carry it around and continue working with it to see what messages it may have for me.

Doing the Current work for months, I started to become more sensitive to the various different energies, and would often be able to pick which Entity was coming through before we were told by the monitors. Out of the regular Entities, I noticed Dr Oswald Cruz was not my favourite energy, since I often found his lengthy Currents hard work and not very enjoyable. Dr Augusto was very direct and had terrible musical taste. My favourite was Dr Jose Valdavino; the energy was always so beautiful and gentle. On one particular occasion, I felt like I was a big ball of light beaming into the Current room. The energy was so light and joyful that I felt expansive and in grace throughout.

On my walk later that evening in the Brazilian outback, I saw a woodpecker with a flaming red mohawk in a tree. He was going to different sections and tapping to see what was there, then moving on to the next spot and tapping again. 'Keep chipping away,' was the message I got. It was vital to take in the voice of innocence as it appeared throughout the day to me, to take that as the word of the divine and keep experiencing every moment in the fullness of what was being offered to me.

I was now practising more self-love than ever before, gifting myself this trip and time out, eating beautiful, vibrant, live foods. I was sober, meditating, doing breathing exercises or Kundalini yoga, intentions and spiritual work, not to mention sitting in a crystal vortex, working with nature, drinking blessed water and doing various types of healing every day. Considering how much I was following the traditional rules of spirituality and enlightenment, my results seemed lacklustre.

However, I did notice that the more I put out questions in some way, and the more I relaxed into it and got myself out of the way, the more I seemed to receive answers. Either through my thoughts in Current, by overhearing conversations, or via dreams and symbols in my reality. I woke up almost daily with the lyrics of a song playing in my head. I now understood that the guidance wasn't straightforward in the detail or way I was expecting. I knew I needed to practise patience, and that things would reveal themselves when I was ready and in the divine timing that was perfect for me.

The mainly raw vegan diet which was supposed to be energy boosting wasn't having the desired effect, and I was pretty tired and sick much of the time. My lady-times grew worse and worse, with bloating, cramps and emotionally draining PMS. I had consistent nausea and low energy; I was dragging myself around, feeling weak and sore in my body. I had sweaty sleeps, which I assumed could all be detox effects, healing and energy recalibration. I persisted, hoping that the supplements and protein powder that Annie was bringing over might help. Little did I know that I was chronically anaemic which is why for all the 'good' I was doing, I was feeling physically unwell.

The panther with the piercing green eyes visited me in my dreams again. I was in a state of irrational fear in the dream and asked Annie to lock it outside, despite it just plodding around gently and calmly.

It was around this time that I discovered a nouveau-wave spiritual teacher Matt Kahn who had a completely different approach to any other I had heard. He threw out a lot of the old spiritual teachings or brought them through with a completely different perspective, blowing out the limitations of the old thinking with hilarious delivery. It was revolutionary, yet easy and practical, and resonated deeply. Particularly as he addressed a lot of the same spiritual principles that Annie latched onto for years, but which had never sat right with me. I forwarded them on to her with slight trepidation, wondering how she would react but she was surprisingly receptive, which was good news considering she was coming to Abadiânia in a week.

I had struggled with my creative projects, battling procrastination, my mind and my health. I was filled with doubt about how to approach things and lacked real creative drive and inspiration. This was unsurprising, since I was often on a rollercoaster-ride of emotions in the process of healing at the Casa, which had brought up various aspects of self to look at in the process. I attuned to the energies of famous writers like Thoth, Archangel Gabriel, Hunter S. Thompson and Plato to bolster my energy and help me figure out how to do it. I hadn't progressed to where I wanted to be and was constantly beating myself up about it, which was in turn blocking me further, although I didn't realise it at the time.

I had a strong sense that my own heart would lead me to where I needed to go and started focusing more on opening my heart on a deep level, and rediscovering feelings which I now realised I had numbed for years. My mind was still in my way and I struggled with keeping it in line, despite all the meditation and spiritual practices each day. I wanted to connect my heart with my mind, so I had a consistent, heart-centred view. I put my request out to the Universe and waited for answers.

Sure enough, I soon started experiencing pain and tightness in the heart area in the front of my chest. My reality was also throwing up a whole host of high-school-related insecurities around some girls I had met. I found it fascinating how circumstances in this place were orchestrated to bring up anything within that needed attention, to be loved and healed within us. I consistently asked for energetic support from guides, angels, masters and beings of light to work through it. I'd always heard that they couldn't interfere unless asked, due to the law of free will, so I was constantly asking for all the help I could get.

After a morning Current session one day, I felt terribly upset. I was feeling so down and awful that I just sat in the garden outside the Current room, where I overheard a man saying that there was lots of availability for crystal beds because there were no crowds at the Casa whilst João was away in America. I immediately went to the Casa bookshop and booked two sessions starting in five minutes. I raced over and settled into the bed, then floods of tears came, and I balled my eyes out for some time. After the emotion poured out, I calmed down and nodded off, waking up with a hungry tummy sometime later. The girl soon came to knock at the door, signalling the finish. As I went outside, I felt a huge improvement in how I was feeling. I also noticed that it was midday. I'd paid for forty minutes, but ended up being in there for seventy-five, through some miracle. I was so thankful that I had noticed the guidance, acted on it and experienced fruitful results. Perhaps I was making progress after all.

It is I who is here to speak with you at this time.
The black panther of divine potential.
And you are ready. This time you are ready.
For you hold your ground in a way as to solidify the strength of your spirit.
And that commands respect.
For like me, one has to respect the world they live in.
Respect the tools available to them. And respect all life
for what it has to bring you, show you, tell you.

With the black panther comes wisdom. The wisdom of the divine.
The wisdom of new worlds available to you to traverse right now.
Right here. Drifting between dimensions.
The dreamer has come to navigate reality.
For this is what the new world is like.

You the dreamer.
Navigating your reality as you weave,
a dream of fantastical and magical outcomes.
The opening up of the higher dimensions is now being accessed by all.

Stand strong in your power. Stand strong in your truth.
Stand strong in the wisdom of the black cats.

A Clip 'Round The Ears From All Angles

It was days before Annie was due to arrive, and JOG was visiting Australia, which caused a flurry of media activity about João and the Casa, not all positive. This was hardly surprising, since, when you spent months at the Casa, you quickly realised it was rife with rumours and gossip about all sorts. I took it all with a grain of salt, as nothing in my experience had confirmed anything, and the energies aside from that couldn't be denied in my mind.

I received a lengthy note from Annie:

Jo, why do you think so many questions about spirituality/healing/abuse/violence are being raised in our lifetime? Because they must be addressed! For the survival of our species, it is no longer a question of food, it is a question of what level do you think on? What era are you stuck in? It is not just the external manifestation of global warming or economic upturn or down, or being obedient to the current belief systems. It is about taking the bull by the horns, evolving consciously forward, appreciating the hell and madness we are currently enduring and realising that all states of physical difficulty may be just due to stagnation in the CONSCIOUSNESS of a large proportion of HUMANITY, not through any individual fault, but due to a collective faulty wiring (belief system) that has outworn itself!

We are all being rewired for sure, but the people who do the repairs are still operating old-school style! The how and the why and what we do to repair our worn-out system, well, as many plumbers or electricians or builders are out there in the collective, there are as many ways to solve the problem in the old-school way of thinking! What we need is the collective of plumbers, the collective of electricians, etc., to name only x 2 for ALL to Come together as ONE HEART!

Nothing is more frustrating than living for millennia, actually believing that someone else is more powerful than you! (I am talking about the big picture, not personal here). That somehow this 'unknown authority ' has control over you. That we have been beholden to the priests of old (myself excluded this lifetime!) and decided that they hold exclusive power to tell you who GOD is. What ultimately gave those original powerholders the right to form governments/businesses/corporations that exist today as the ultimate symbols of power over the masses, so that they (us) could not move forward?! That is why we are doing our work – for them that got caught in the net!

WE KNOW THAT THIS WHOLE CAUGHT-IN-THE-NET THING HAS ACTUALLY CAUSED THE MAYHEM AND MADNESS – THE CANCER, THE AUTISM, THE DISEASE STATES, VIOLENCE AND ABUSE, DRUG ADDICTION AND SO ON... And these journalists go on to say that we are all about trickery?

Jo ...Hello? They have been duped like all the rest of us! I want someone to confront the media with just WHO IS DUPING WHO? MUCHO LOVE FOR ALL THAT YOU DO... watch and see... XXXA.

In typical Annie style, I woke up to another dramatic crescendo of contradictory emails, just before she was leaving to fly to Brazil. It was 'Panic Annie' in full scale, and doing somewhat of a one-eighty on everything she had just said.

Jo – OK... We just watched 60 Mins current events TV show! Dreadful! UTTERLY DREADFUL! Maybe, THANK YOU FOR EXPOSING THE MADNESS & INSANITY! Yes! I get that! It is probably all TV claptrap and misinterpretation...about time JOURNALISTS were brought to account! But a lot of it is, or may be, true...some folks utterly believe in this stuff, the healing thing... I am not so concerned as I KNOW it is all about healing the MIND… not the body, FIRST… but this timing is not quite right… or IS IT…?? I am coming to this place ONLY because YOU are there! XA.

The next message escalated:

FUCK!!! My friends are texting me – horrified! What the fuck am I coming to? LET ME SAY ONE THING! I am not into all this BULLSHIT of wearing white, or following someone else's idea of RULES ----- Because Jo… I AM HERE TO WORK IT OUT MYSELF! I am not into listening to the Entities either… because they are just the same as us… working it all out as we go along this amazing journey! AS Above… So Below! I am a REBEL! ALWAYS have been, always will be! If there is ONE THING I want to do… it is to be with YOU… no fucking JoG shit …

xA.

And finally:

Look… I get it… people are DESPERATE for a way out of insanity… for a way out of their misery, ignorance, and belief in an outside God! To come save them and all that! I get also that you are way beyond these people seeking what they seek… that you are someone with her head coming into her heart… in a sincere way, as I have always been… Do you understand my concern AND LOVE in this………?

It is so difficult to talk via an email… and express what I need to say! I am one who is for the way of the HEART! Of combining the HEAD with the HEART! Taking any kind of human concoction… medical or herbal… is not my scene. I want freedom from the belief that either is better than the other… Because THAT IS THE TRAP!!!!!!!!! I want to anchor the LIGHT onto this planet! And that has to be FREE of either good or bad/right or wrong…

It has to be something we have NEVER thought of

before… and when we ASK for it… it will appear! BOOM! I AWAIT your response?! XXXA.

Dear Lord, help me. It was very typical of Annie's reactive ways though, so I never responded and just let it go. Although, it was not the first time I had heard such rumours in my time at the Casa. João the man was a human just like the rest of us and still had many human foibles, from what I had heard, from Crazy and the local grapevine.

I had mixed feelings though, which made me question myself. Should I be supporting someone like this, if these allegations were true, in my act of being here? Where there is smoke there is generally fire. Was the energy really as pure and amazing as I had felt? How could the Entities of such pure, divine energy be using a channel that was acting in this way? Or did these experiences have a higher perspective over and above what we could see throughout human perspective? Were they simply part of the lessons certain people went through in order for them to develop as a soul, which was neither good nor bad if looked at through the eyes of the perfection of God and not duality? Was this something they signed up for before they came for their own evolution?

My doubt and worrying mind kicked into overdrive. I had never personally had an indication of anything untoward; it was more through the rumour mill that I had heard stories. It felt like yet another iteration of what we had seen in the past, with gurus in India taking advantage of their devotees, and stories of many spiritual mediums and sex cults because of the high sexual energy they brought through. This kind of thing was nothing new. The energy was still beautiful and healing to me, and I didn't have any personal evidence, so I therefore did not have the right nor inclination to judge.

I decided this was another iteration of my reality, serving me something to make me question myself and my feelings based on what others said. Oh my God, did I get it wrong? Maybe I didn't need to agree or disagree with anything. Maybe there was no 'answer', but my logical mind kept trying to find something to resolve this within me. Perhaps in these instances, I was not to be knocked out of my power or let the doubt derail me. In the next Current session, I kept hearing, 'Trust self' and 'Faith.'

Before I knew it, Annie had arrived, and after a fairly gruelling journey, we were finally ensconced in my apartment in Abadiânia. She came in rather combative straight off the mark, already making comments about us having a potential argument and her adamant views on the Casa, before experiencing anything at all. There was definitely an adjustment period as I tried to stay in my high frequency vibe and not react. Lead by example, Jo, I told myself. Everything is perfect in every moment. I am exactly where I need to be. Everything that happens in my reality is an opportunity to understand myself more, to see and express more love, no matter what the situation. I asked my angels and guides to help me master this.

I took Annie on a tour of the Casa the next day, including the various rooms and meditation spaces. She seemed to turn her nose up mostly, so I just went ahead and did my meditations and prayers, including a request for some serious help with Annie. The tour of the main road and the few cafes, restaurants and shops was over pretty quick, and we went home for lunch, chatting the afternoon away.

We decided to go out to dinner to Alquimia, almost stepping on a small black and white snake slithering on the path in front of us en route. A local guy was trying to kill it.

"How pathetic. Who does he think he is?" Annie said sharply.

I instantly found myself irking at her name-calling, but quickly pulled myself up on it. It was only day one, after all. The way home was equally as interesting when we bumped into a giant bullfrog. The insects were already starting to drive her a bit mad and we were yet to experience any flying-ant swarms or giant spiders, let alone the alien creature living in my fridge. The fridge was now on its last legs, and was soon to be replaced, so I had been furiously telepathically communicating with the alien creature of whom I was now quite fond, to go to the garden, otherwise he'd end up in the city at the repair place. Another day, another weird animal encounter. It was par for the course with me. Yet after enquiring with Casa friends, this experience seemed to be personal to me only. No one else was having any kind of animal messengers cross their path daily, let alone the menagerie of experiences I had. It was another dimension to understanding my personal energy signature, my deep connection to nature and how my unique world of guidance worked for me.

Saturday was overcast, which was a nice change as we wandered up to the market on the desolate road past heavily laden mango trees. Annie's eyes widened at the cowboys on horses, and the rather run-down and supremely rustic state of affairs. There were live chickens jumping around in cages, a makeshift butchery full of meat covered in flies, drunk cowboys passed out at tables to blaring Sertanejo music and stands upon stands of unidentifiable exotic fruits and vegetables. I filled my bags with vegies to stock up for the week before heading into one of the tents for an água de coco and a pastel de queijo.

We hit the supermarket on the way home by which time, the sun was out, and it was blazing hot. Annie needed a few rest stops and a ciggie break en route. I made a simple lunch of guacamole, hummus and crudités, and as I pottered around the kitchen a huge electrical storm came through. We battened down the hatches as the wind and rain pelted against the doors, thunder growled in the distance and lightning danced over the landscape out front. We even had a power cut, but thankfully Annie found the whole thing rather exciting. By some miracle, she had also decided to change her tune about the Casa and was now keen to experience it. I was amazed. I had asked for help, and by George had I got it.

My initial jarring and frustration at Annie's demeanour soon melted into compassion as I was reminded of the tough times she had endured with Devo over the years. I realised she had morphed and changed to survive herself and to navigate the fact that she was one of the first on the consciousness crusade. A time when there was no support, no real clarity as to what was going on and general disdain from the closed minds of the time. I slowly remembered to ignore her overreactions and just let her do and say what she wanted. She was ever the slow Capricorn goat, requiring patience and understanding.

The storms seemed to be keeping away the bugs which was handy. Annie had some crystal beds the following day, which she surprisingly liked despite protesting at having to lie down for forty minutes, and she enjoyed the cake and coffee at Cafe Matreya afterwards and their stray cat sanctuary.

I started some private coaching sessions for my channelling class, to see if that would propel my practice into something more effective and satisfying. The session reinvigorated me, but the following day my practice was more frustrating than ever. I tried the visualisations, the meditations, doing it exactly as I was told, doing it freestyle, intuitively, asking for the volume to be turned up; you name it, I tried it. I was finding it hard to maintain motivation and consistent practice when I wasn't getting results. It felt like my head was fighting my divine destiny.

Monday rolled around, and it was Annie's first day at the Casa. There were loads of people, so it was quite hectic; a bad start, as she hated crowds. When she finally got in front of the Entity, he gave her a prescription for herbs and said she needed to come back two more times. When she realised that didn't mean tomorrow or the next day, she was immediately annoyed.

"There was nothing in there," she said. "No soul at all. It gave me the creeps."

Well, he was a trance channel medium, which means the person steps aside completely and into trance while channelling, so it was hardly surprising to me. She rejected the healing soup afterwards, barely touching it, so we went to the Farmácia to get the prescription of Passiflora.

"Fifty reals is a lot of money," Annie complained. Meanwhile she had given away thirty reals without blinking an eye to the stray cats the day before. Go figure.

"The whole thing is a waste of time," Annie said to me later that evening. "That JOG was dead in the eyes. I was not inspired at all," she added scathingly.

Since when were you supposed to be inspired? I thought, but

held back any comment. It was like seeing an energetic doctor, and he'd said more to her than I'd ever got.

A huge fart noise interrupted the stilted conversation. "It was probably that awful soup at the Casa making my stomach turn," she said. "Hmph."

From our conversations so far, Annie seemed to be in a funk. She was not bothered with anything much in life at all. I found it quite sad. I wasn't quite sure why she had come in the first place as she seemed against the entire experience from the beginning. Now she was here, and it wasn't meeting whatever expectations she did have, I was bearing the brunt of it.

I was determined not to get emotionally involved in her issues. I gave myself regular pep talks to cope. She was up and down like a yo-yo. First, she was reactive, then calmed down, then changed her mind. The bi-polar patterns from my youth came flooding back. I renewed my commitment to myself in living this life of energy and spirit as I saw it, despite her perceptions, remarks or judgements trying to throw me off. Perhaps that was the challenge after all.

By the next day there was, unsurprisingly a complete turnaround, and Annie was contemplating surgery for her eyes and bladder and all sorts. She asked about where I went to Current, in the first room, which I mentioned was the 'Cleansing Room'.

"Well, that's what they *told* you," she said sceptically, as if it may not be true.

Well, I certainly used Saint Germain and the Violet Flame, plus white light meditating there, I retorted in my head so as not to ignite an argument. I had no experiences to denote anything dodgy or bad. We were two very different people though; I was naturally very curious, open, accepting and willing to try new things, whereas Annie was cautious, questioning and generally distrustful.

I bumped into a new acquaintance, Alex at the Casa gardens, where he offered Annie and me some acerola, a cherry-like fruit containing incredibly high amounts of vitamin C. He was a mellow, Brazilian guy a few years younger than me with a friendly smile. He offered to take me to the river sometime.

I was planning on going to the afternoon Current session, but felt obliged to stay with Annie and not abandon her while she was settling in. Later, I found out that Paul Simon had played "The Sound of Silence" and "Blackbird" in the Current room live and there was unbelievable energy. Damn. Every time I didn't follow my intuition in regard to going to Current, something happened to cause massive regret, or to give me a virtual clip around the ears. And Annie would have definitely given Current a go, had she known. I grew up listening to Paul Simon in our house. I think we were both gutted to have missed out.

As the days ticked on it got easier and Annie and I fell into a rhythm of spending time at the Casa, watching the Magical Egypt series, blessing our food and drink, pulling Isis Oracle cards and listening to all sorts of spiritual radio shows, alongside some sacred ceremony. We were like a couple of witches, playing with energy and spirit and having the best time.

"It's a feast for the soul," Annie said.

The healing continued in a multitude of ways while at the Casa, and I was hyper-aware of everything that was happening in my reality, plus the different sensations and emotions in my body. It wasn't long before a small barney with Annie, brought up a lot of old feelings about the ongoing challenge I faced with her. I seemed to get triggered by, and find fault with, her reactiveness and bullheadedness. Our communication often went pear-shaped.

"Nothing I say is serious," she would say, or blame our misunderstandings on her dyslexia and communication challenges. This was difficult for someone who was an expert communicator and took what people said at face value. How else could we understand one another? The discomfort it was bringing up made me question how I was going to get around this as I couldn't go the next seven weeks feeling like this on a daily basis. I needed to figure out how to be less affected by her behaviour. Story of my life.

The following day in the Current, I suddenly felt the same sensations as when I had been operated on previously. It became so acute that I had to excuse myself and go home. I slept for four-and-a-half hours. One of the monitors told me the following day, after the Current session, that one of the Entities was fuming and upset because people weren't doing what they were supposed to do. This made absolutely no sense to me at all. If these were evolved light beings surely they would not throw their weight around and get angry in tantrum-like behaviour? Surely, they were unconditional love twenty-four-seven? I had heard previously that they took on human traits in order to get through to us because we only responded to this kind of human behaviour, but surely there was a loving way to deliver this, rather than this incongruent energy? These kinds of things, plus all the heavy protocol and rules, did make me question the goings-on at the Casa, although I knew it was likely in order to process the thousands of people who came through the doors every day. As much as I acknowledged that certain things didn't sit right with me, I knew that I was in the midst of a very important healing process that was taking me to the next level.

Annie suddenly flip-flopped again in a provocative announcement at dinner that she would not be doing any operations nor attending the Casa, and that there were no Entities or 'they'. Ironically this had echoes of Crazy. It was all frequency she said, and didn't feel right to her. What if they were using our bodies for something sinister? I thought this was fear-based thinking, which I did not subscribe to. She dropped bombs as far as the eye could see from her tangled mind. Was this a test of my faith and self-doubt again? Possibly. Although I was getting rattled less and less with each daily change of tune and outburst, I hadn't quite mastered it yet.

I had questions about a lot of things too. All I knew was that all of that was outside myself, and therefore, wasn't it all a distraction and a red herring? What I felt inside was pure divine energy, sometimes so beautiful and so highly elevated that it brought me to tears. While in Abadiânia, I was experiencing a dimensional reality that pushed me towards myself and increased the pace of things being brought up in reality, things that I needed to deal with, change, heal or evolve.

I felt that if you believed that something could do you

harm, then it would. If not, then it wouldn't. You had to be in vibrational resonance essentially to be a match to any experience. That's how energy works. And if you focused on it, well it could easily manifest it in your reality. There was enough evidence of how beliefs affected reality and the principles of quantum physics to prove that the consciousness had an effect on matter. There were energies to take advantage of here, to accelerate growth, or consciousness evolution, no matter the wrapping. It didn't stop me from wondering about the truth of this place though, given all the controversy.

Meanwhile, I preferred to work with faith as the key, which was my natural inclination anyway. More and more, I was coming to the conclusion that I just needed to follow my own guidance, whatever popped up in complete faith that it was as the Universal Intelligence intended, with the knowledge that we were that. If we listened and acted with the understanding that we were Source, it would accelerate us, and we would be more of our infinite self. This was what I felt intuitively.

I was switching around the order of things I was doing before my channelling practice, to get more flow and bring the unmistakable guidance from my higher self that I was craving in order to step things up a notch. There were connecting exercises and breathwork, various light activations, the use of a blue candle, and Kundalini yoga. I was certainly feeling the influx of different kinds of energy into my body when doing it, although I was still having trouble deciphering any meaning or relevance for me. My channelling teacher had said that we receive confirmation in the physical world of what we bring through in our channelling, so I was also looking out for that and mulling over the relevance of all the animal messengers that had crossed my path.

A spectacular black and white patterned butterfly visited me at the same point on my walk each day. Okay, Guides, I said in my head. I love butterflies, and I totally get that I am in a period of transformation, but you gotta give me something more. As it flew away my eyes were drawn to the other side of the fence post where it landed.

As I drew closer, it fluttered away towards the bush and behind it, about twenty metres away, I thought I saw the behind of a donkey as my eyes focused, trying to make it out. Then it moved and I realised it was not a donkey at all. I was looking at a giant anteater sitting there, staring back at me. The long, grey nose set against the dark, hairy body, and its beautiful, grey, black and white markings, had completely confused my eyes. It was huge, maybe the size of a small bear. I was awestruck. It started to move, "Mi amore, don't go!" I yelled out, as I tried to scale the fence and head closer for a better look. However, it was already aiming for the cover of the bush and soon out of sight. Later, I found out that the anteater symbolises searching for something that was always at hand's reach. It was about being in touch with my inner senses, and sometimes what I needed was to close my eyes and go deeper into my own soul. This direct correlation to my own conclusions of the answer being myself was a deep supportive reflection.

I bumped into the crystal lady, Gerda, and told her about my animal experiences of the butterflies, spiders, wildcat, puma, alien creature on my fridge and the giant anteater. She insinuated that I was hallucinating.

"People who have spent too much time in this place sometimes go crazy, you know," she said.

What if everything was perfect?
What if there was true perfection, of the way that you think?
What if there was nothing to be, change or do?
What if it was there all along yet you have been
fighting it? Ignoring it. Frightened of it.
For it changes your world. It throws you into a space where few live.
Yet this is the place to be.

Know dear heart, that in the strength of this conviction lies truth.
That it was you all along. That your deepest thoughts, feelings,
knowings are your superpower.
If you dared tell anyone.

When you allow yourself to know, the tears
of truth fall down your cheeks.
When you allow yourself to step forward in truth,
you bring what you already know
from deep within.

When you can finally be this truth, you expand a lifetime
and integrate a solar system.
For that is the power of your sovereign self.
The true power of you.

No Really, It's All About Intention

"Dom Inácio's work says to always trust the very first thing that comes to you, because the negativity and mental mind always come in after that," said American Jennifer who had become my sacred waterfall buddy. I had come into the awareness that I had been creating expectations for myself based on others experience, and not giving enough credence to the nature of my unique divine blueprint. We had a multitude of senses and therefore information could come to us in many ways, whether through waking up with a song in my head, overhearing a conversation, seeing an animal symbol, or simply having a thought pop up. They all added up to energetic messages from my vibrational GPS system, my Universe, and it was about being aware enough to take note and decipher what it all meant. Above all, I knew I needed to just let go of my expectations, beliefs and comparisons and let the journey happen. I only realised later how much my own impatience and judgements were holding me back. This was causing further discordance in my own energy field, and therefore keeping clarity and my super-conscious abilities even further away.

I was regularly calling forth anything I needed to release from my past so I could make space to bring in the new. I wanted to live a soul-led life moving forward, aligned with Source and my true divine nature, and that was what I was going to do. I had an 'aha' moment when I ascertained I had belief systems running that 'all amazing spiritual experiences happen to other people and not me'. Although I was becoming more conscious of my different beliefs and how they were limiting me, I wasn't sure what I needed to do to completely clear them. I wanted to experience the most expanded version of myself right now. What was I missing or how was I holding myself back? As I set about clearing this I was aware of different feelings and reactions from old patterns being triggered within me, as my reality brought these to the surface via emails from Devo, interactions with Annie and others at the Casa. I looked at what was arising in myself with conscious awareness, and loved and accepted all of it within me as best I could.

Annie was the biggest one for me. I couldn't say much without her getting upset and perceiving that I was either telling her off, telling her what to do or something else that she could rail against. For someone who refused to entertain anything about herself from the past, she seemed to be constantly throwing our past relationship back in my face. I was walking on eggshells, and could never really express what I wanted for fear of her reactive response. I was guilty only of wanting her to have a good time here in Abadiânia, and hopefully experience some positive changes. I was originally excited to share this experience with her, and now it felt like the entire thing was a complete backfire. Being present and steadfast in my knowing and feeling of what was good for me, rather than being thrown out of my centre by strong characters, was good learning. I realised I was people-pleasing again, trying to keep everything on an even keel to the detriment of myself and ultimately looking for some sort of approval. This was old programming learned in childhood that I needed to clear. I was fascinated by how many pennies would drop when I became heart-centred in this place.

One day Annie got mad at me for pointing out that past experiences with healing issues and their success or lack thereof, were not relevant, nor was there any use for comparison.

"Isn't that just ego and resistance?" I said. "You are completely different from how you were then, and the energy has changed for us in the now. Energy always changes, so you can't compare."

When I got back from Current, she was clearly pissed off, so I suggested a trip to the waterfall to cleanse and lighten things up. I was surprised that she agreed, but we got ready and set off.

I started telling her about the protocol and the way to go about the experience, but as soon as she saw 'the rules' on the sign at the entrance, she was irate.

"I hate rules," she spat. "It is not my thing, and it's so old school. Hmph."

I didn't say a thing. If she wanted to put herself in the box of a 'rebel who hates rules', riling up and getting angry every time she was presented with them, then so be it. She stormed back towards the town, deciding she didn't want to do it. I didn't want her to miss out on what was on offer here, and with this behaviour, did not feel like she was working with the light or doing anything to improve things for herself, and said as much. I could see how she was trapped within her own limitations.

"How dare you tell me I am not working with the light, just because it's not in the way YOU do, and by your rules?!" she screamed. "How dare you!"

She was shaking in anger, and crying. She was right. It was completely short-sighted and unfair of me and was symptomatic of my judging her behaviour. It just felt so clear to me that she seemed stuck in her self-created rut. There were her stomach issues with energy lodged around her solar plexus, no creative inspiration, a lack of interest in food, and all sorts of aches and pains, not to mention her reacting and lashing out all over the place due to the wounding she was carrying. It was incredibly hard for me to navigate, so I immediately reverted to rescuer mode, trying to people-please and make her as comfortable as I could. What I really needed to do was ignore everything, be supportive and let her have the experience of her choice. Easier said than done.

After a heated argument, she agreed only to accompany me, given one could not go alone due to health and safety, so it was not a wasted trip. Thank goodness we were the only ones there. As I was getting changed, I offered to take her down to the waterfall and hold her hand if she wanted. She started disrobing, but was in tears, saying she was petrified of the bush and places like this. She was shaking, so I put my arm around her and said I'd be happy to go slow and do it with her if she wanted to 'feel the fear and do it anyway', and if not, that was absolutely fine as well. She decided to come.

We slowly descended down the path, over the bridge and to the rocks on the other side. I went first, doing my prayers and holding my intentions under the water. Then, I supported Annie into the waterfall. She was shaking and crying, and looked like she was about to fall over given her instability from her bad leg, standing half in and half out. When the water hit her head, she let out a loud, extremely guttural, wailing cry from the depths of her being. It was like nothing I'd ever heard before, and more like a wounded animal than a human. I just stood there in silence, steadying her with one arm. She went in a little more, and I suggested putting her heart chakra into the stream of water, and then the solar plexus on her belly, to help move any stuck energy.

We finished up, soundlessly putting our clothes on and making our way back out to the earthy, red road in the setting sun. Walking home, we saw monkeys playing in the trees and two cute little birds joyfully jumping up and down on branches at each other like a couple of cartoon characters. I thought it had gone well in the end. Annie was completely silent.

When we got home, the thunderous mood returned. "I didn't feel inspired or good from the experience," she said curtly. "I should have said no when I meant no, and I am very angry at myself for not doing so," she said. "I've learned a HUGE lesson."

"Well, what was your intention…" I started asking.

"If I hear you say 'intention' one more fucking time I am going to scream," she yelled. "Intention this, intention that. I am SO over it!" she said, slamming her book closed.

Anything I tried to say to explain or placate her was fuel on the fire. "I don't need a postscript," she screamed, shaking like a volcano ready to blow.

It was an awkward night, and she went to bed, unusually, at 9pm. "I hope I feel better in the morning," she said curtly, before closing the bedroom door.

It was certainly a lesson to focus on me and nothing else, although I didn't feel the same intense turmoil that I used to feel from these attacking outbursts. At least I had stayed somewhat cool during the entire thing. I grieved the fact that I would never have the relationship with her that I had hoped for. I just had to let it go and accept it, and her for what it was.

I did lots of praying, energy clearing and transmuting with the Violet Flame in the Current the following day. I knew I needed to have complete acceptance, and therefore unconditional love for these exterior personas that she threw around to play out her wounds and shield herself from her own truth. Next time I would be more conscious in the moment and not let her energy dominate me. After Current, I took home some of the pão de queijo she liked, and found her sitting outside, still in a very fragile state. She said she had been getting dizzy again all morning. I was compassionately gentle with her and made her a juice before hopping in my bikini to sit outside. I looked up to see a giant rainbow ring around the sun, and quickly grabbed my camera to snap pictures.

"I've seen this once before in Auckland," said Annie.

I had only seen it in a photo that was on the walls of the Casa. Of course, when I went online there was a very boring, scientific explanation of this 'halo', but the metaphysical meaning from the elders of America and Tibet was that it was a symbol from God that all of creation was coming back into balance and harmony for peace on earth. It was a symbol of transformation. Later that afternoon, Annie said some beautiful butterflies had surrounded her during the day and that she had been contemplating some things. She started talking about the waterfall and a past traumatic experience at one, admitting it was all ego and that it was a very deep release of grief for her. She was feeling much lighter and brighter this afternoon and was even inspired to write about it. My prayers had worked. Thank God.

Days later, I came home from Current to a very excited Annie. She had been listening to a spiritual radio show all afternoon, interviewing various teachers, and had written copious notes. "It was all about INTENTION," she said animatedly. I could not believe my ears.

"I thought if you heard the word 'intention' again, you were going to scream?" I said, laughing and ribbing her since she was in such a good mood. She giggled to herself.

So, the moral of the story seemed to be that when Annie's ego reared its ugly reactionary head, I should take absolutely no notice of it. Either way, that was not the experience I really wanted to have with her. It certainly wasn't enjoyable for me. However, there must be a reason why I needed to experience it for something within myself.

I went for a run in the rain and saw two wild boars run directly across the road in front of me and into the bush on the other side. Wild boar symbolised confrontation, courage and truth, but could also be about procrastination and avoidance. Both felt relevant.

Feel the energies swaying through your being
as the seaweed sways on the ocean floor.
Feel your beingness change form in the flow.
The loosening up of your human is needed to be felt,
to allow more of our energy in.

Be like the seaweed and flow with the tide.
Be ever changing as the ocean floor.
Allow the ripple effects to be felt through you.
Not to take on others energy as your own
but feel them move through you,
as you embody the connectedness of all things.

Enter Stage Left Soulmate

I heard that the spirit of John the Baptist had come through on Christmas morning in our Current session, and was offering spiritual baptisms for anyone who wanted them that afternoon at the sacred waterfall. Despite having been baptised when I was a child, I thought this was a brilliant opportunity. Getting baptised, by the spirit of John the Baptist, on Christmas Day, at a sacred waterfall – who wouldn't want to experience that?! Unsurprisingly, Annie immediately poo-poo'd the entire thing. "Urgh, why would you bother? Utter rubbish," she said.

Every man and their dog wanted in on it. Two men from the Casa staff were at the waterfall doing the sacred baptisms and channelling the energy, with a queue right back up to the waiting area. As we waited, we were dripping in sweat from the searing hot day and I started feeling an influx of energy coming into my body which was incredibly strong. I felt utterly walloped by it, but kept drinking my blessed water and moving with the line. I had never felt such strong energy at the waterfall before in all of my dozens of trips there.

Before I knew it, it was my turn, and I squatted down while the man cupped his hands with the sacred water and washed it over my head while reciting prayers in Portuguese. I held in my energy field that I wanted to remember my light always and get my human ego stuff out of the way, as I was being baptised with the pure light and love of this high caliber energy. As he finished, he slid his water-filled hands down my face, and I gave him a hug. Jennifer and I walked back past the hordes of people waiting, and out onto the road, where we were met with the most intensely beautiful sky I had seen while in Abadiânia. There were a few fluffy, marshmallow clouds juxtaposed against the intense cobalt blue and the world around me now looked juicier and more gorgeous than ever.

Our Christmas meal was utterly divine, a gourmet vegetarian feast Annie and I created together and we savoured every bite before Skyping Devo back in New Zealand. I could not resist riling him up about my celebrity saint baptism. He quite quickly changed the subject and said how he thought it was more than enough time in this place, and the sooner we were out of there, the better.

I bumped into Alex in the Great Hall the next day, who greeted me with a big hug and invited me for soup. He'd been taken by a local woman, Flavia, to a spot right next to my apartment late one night, where they had seen three big spaceships and lots of activity in the sky until 4am. I was amazed. I'd have to try and stay up later than 10pm to see them for myself! We organised for him to take me to the river that afternoon following Current, and I spent the entire session after our flirtatious chat imagining passionate South American sex and a fairy-tale love affair rather than meditation. It had certainly been a while. We finally made it to the river the following week, and spent a delightfully refreshing afternoon away from the heat. He was going through a rough time, having lost his relationship, job and money all at once and having to move in with his parents. He was trying to get back on his feet and essentially starting from scratch. The following day, Alex sent a lovely note saying that it had been the happiest day for him since he could remember, and thanking me for being a part of it.

It may have been the nine months of solitude, but suddenly all I could think about was him. I pulled an Isis Oracle card, which warned of the 'Brother of Darkness'. I glossed over it and continued to befriend him.

On New Year's Eve, I went to Current with Alex where I had the most joy-filled experience, and we both felt the energy very strongly throughout. On our way to the waterfall afterwards a huge storm had blown in, à la Wizard of Oz, with wind, rain, thunder and lightning. The rain was torrential by the time we got there, and we had an almighty cleansing as we went in separately with our intentions. By the time we walked out of the waterfall, oddly the sun was out. I walked home to get changed before heading back to the Casa with Annie in tow for the New Year celebrations. The Casa was decorated with streamers, fruit and flowers. Alex and his friend Ze Pequeno arrived, and we enjoyed some non-alcoholic wine, lucky lentil soup and fruit to celebrate and bring good fortune for the New Year. Later at an after-party we kissed before he walked me home under moonlit skies.

Alex and I spent most of New Year's Day in bed. I dropped in to see him in the morning and one hundred percent seduced him, throwing my promise not to control or manipulate things out the window. Alex was supposed to be in the 2pm line to see the Entity but never made it. It felt fun to be naughty and wag Current like a couple of wayward youths. We rang in the New Year with a shag-fest, eating fruit in bed and only rising in the early evening when I took him to visit my favourite secret, local waterfall. We found a pitanga tree on the way, which was full of small yellow, orange and red pitanga berries that were utterly delicious.

The next ten days was a haze of trips and little Casa work with my new-found romance. We went to Anapolis for a business meeting for Ze Pequeno with Annie, then did a weekend trip to Alta Paraiso with just me and the guys. We went hiking, swimming and jumping off huge, twelve-metre rocks. All this time spent with Alex, of course, had the wheels turning in my mind as to what was happening and what it all meant. As much as I was trying to just 'be in the moment' with it, I couldn't help but over-analyse and question everything.

At Frutti's I bumped into Crazy, who hadn't talked to me for weeks. "He's your soulmate, you know. He's the male version of you," she said. I wasn't so sure he was the male version of me at all. In fact, we were more opposite than anything.

It wasn't the most credible comment, given this was the woman who thought we were all here for the second coming of Jesus Christ who was JOG in person, so I took it with a grain of salt. Although interestingly, years later some of Crazy's ramblings came to fruition. The accusations about JOG appeared to have foundation given he was arrested and convicted in Brazil in 2019, although this conviction was apparently going to be appealed. It made me wonder what else she was right about from her mountains of mind-boggling accusations.

I was aware I was ignoring some tiny alarm bells that had been going off in my feels around Alex, but part of me was nervous and felt maybe I shouldn't doubt or judge things before I'd given them a chance. I decided to just trust, let it happen and all would be revealed. My mind chatter, as ever, was my constant nemesis but I decided to give it up to spirit to answer.

In the meantime, Annie was suddenly lashing out at me again, and we ended up in a huge argument. Turns out she was having problems with teeth and gums in her mouth, which was one of her most feared things and she was terribly upset about Devo, who was struggling at home. He had emailed to say that his debilitating back problem, for which he had been on heavy painkillers for a year, was much worse and he could barely move. He was trying to get the house ready for sale, so she was feeling guilty for not being there. She cried the entire day. I took Devo's photo in the line to see the Entity the next day, to ask for help and trusted that it would be given. I also took his picture with me to Current, and worked on sending him the healing energy myself. Annie was outside in the Casa garden, meditating during the Current session with a picture of Devo tucked into her chest.

"Well, he always was a boob man," she joked.

Alex extended his time at the Casa instead of going back to Sao Paolo before his sister's wedding, and despite my doubts, I looked at changing my flight to spend more time with him. We were having a lovely time together, and it seemed silly to cut it off before we gave it a chance. A few weeks wasn't long enough to figure anything out.

We spent his last night in one of the fancy, hexagonal bush huts, where Paul Simon had recently stayed, and I captured some kind of orb energy in a photo above the bed. I emailed it off for an energy reading without any details and was told it was a divine 'Angel of Love.' Of course, I took this as a sign, desperate for confirmation of things for my doubting mind. The part of me that was pitted against my romantically fantastical mind that desperately wanted, and believed, in a fairy tale ending. Alex left a couple of days later for the wedding in Ecuador.

In Alex's wake, I felt my own guilt trip take hold for slacking off with my intentions, projects and practices. As I reflected, I realised that, despite months of rigorous vegan, high-vibration, clean food, yoga, breathing, light-work activations, meditation, prayer, waterfall cleansings, visualisations, mantras, channelling classes, automatic writing and no alcohol, I really hadn't felt the acceleration to my spiritual gifts or connection that I expected. I was doing all the right things, but it definitely wasn't game-changing. I was concluding that all of it was 'old spiritual paradigm' and outdated, so not necessarily truth. For me at least anyway.

Supposedly, the general theory in the spiritual community was that we needed to be 'high vibration' to evolve spiritually. It dawned on me that 'high vibration' seemed to be yet another red herring in the spiritual path, which limited us into thinking we needed to do certain things in order to become and evolve. Yet another belief system imposing rules and limitations. So much of what was deemed 'high vibration' seemed puritanical, happy-clappy, religious even. Yet it was just something else created by the spiritual community that had judgement at the heart of it. If we were now judging our behaviour or things around us as high vibration versus low vibration then we may as well be back to where we started, as we were essentially in the vibration of judgement ourselves.

I decided from now on to celebrate everything that happened in my world or came across my path as the divine being that I knew deep down I was. If we are the Universe. If we are Source energy and contain this divine intelligence in all things. If we are energy in form. Then everything we do, say, think or feel is the divine. By acting otherwise we were in fact denying the divine, creating more incongruency within us, ultimately.

Although I was feeling lighter than ever and certainly more connected and on path, I still felt like it wasn't enough. I don't know what I was expecting, but I wanted 'turn your life inside out' change and transformation, a connection to spirit that was so clear and undeniable there was no doubt. To be thunderously clear about my purpose for being on this planet at this time. Although I had experienced more than ever, I was over being patient and questioned why I wasn't experiencing more.

So, I decided to take a different tack. I started claiming my divine birthright. Claiming it and owning it, to foster the remembrance of who I truly was. To cement my vibration that I was my own answer and open all my gifts I came with. I was affirming in every moment that I was spirit in matter. 'I am divine. I am God. I am love. I am peace. I am wisdom. I am compassion. I am beauty. I am grace. I am truth.' These became my new mantras.

Annie and I finished her holiday on a high with two weeks in a tiny town two hours from Recife on the Coral Coast. Overlanding through the depths of poor communities in north-east Brazil was eye-opening. However, the coast was a shift in gears with lots to explore in new surrounds, great swimming and some wonderful food and wine at various lodges. It was like luxury compared to the wild west of Abadiânia. It was a wonderful end to her Brazilian adventure. I had tried to change my flight to Buenos Aires, and extend it for more time in Brazil to be with Alex, but there was no availability. Cancelling it and booking a whole new flight was the only option to get around it so it looked like Alex would have to come to Brasilia before I flew out, which would only give us twelve hours together. It felt like I was being blocked at every turn, which was making me wonder if all of the positive 'signs' I had been experiencing regarding my 'soulmate' were accurate after all. Alex said not to worry and that it was all part of the process.

"I'd travel further than fourteen hours on two buses to Brasilia to see you, even if it was only for twelve hours," he said.

My heart melted. Was he my soulmate or did I just want a partner full stop, since I'd been on my own so long? What did our souls have to teach each other? The only way I was going to find out was to continue on further, so we made plans for him to meet me back in Auckland in a few months, which was the only way to get around our current visa limitations.

It is I, yes you, who is here to change things.
Each individual in their own time and space.
But yes, as you suspect many practices and teachings of past get in your way.
For the conditioning is long and strong.
But its hold on you is getting less as you are
stepping forward into a greater truth.
A greater you. If only one were to credit themselves.

It is wise to be true to that which you say and do.
For there is alignment in that.
The channellings of the heart flood to you now.
For your heart is the key technology as we step into this new era.
The heart is you and you are the heart.
Source technology is available through you.
It is in your DNA. In the things you say.
Yet you consciously do not know it. Yet.

A Shaman Named Hugo

I had never heard of Capilla del Monte. This was not the plan at all. The plan at this point was to rent an apartment in Buenos Aires, further my Spanish and write my book for a few months. However, when I arrived severe nausea set in. It was clear to me that I had undergone massive energy shifts and my body was struggling to adapt to the different vibration outside that white-wearing world of Abadiânia. No matter what I did in Buenos Aires I seemed to get worse, and I could feel a lot of dark, dense energy. I was sure it would pass but when I found myself dry-retching on the street ten days later I had to admit that Buenos Aires was not the place for me in that moment. With the energy integration being so severely debilitating I followed my instincts, and fled to the mountains.

Capilla del Monte is a tiny town two hours north of Cordoba at the north-eastern edge of the Sierra Mountain range in Argentina. The small town of just over eleven thousand inhabitants is set against the backdrop of Cerro Uritorco. This mountain is famed not only for being the highest mountain in the Sierras Chicas but also for the alleged sightings of UFOs and ETs.

As soon as I got out of Buenos Aires I felt better, and the nausea mysteriously disappeared. I negotiated a good price for six weeks in a small one-bedroom cabana on the outskirts of town overlooking some small lakes, with the grand presence of Cerro Uritorco at the back. I walked into town past shop after shop with alien masks, dolls, spaceships and every other bit of alternative ET paraphernalia you could imagine. I felt dull by comparison stocking up at the health store, fruit and veg shop and supermarket for my aggressive vegan, no grain detox to continue my cleansing regime. I was determined to encourage more of the energy that had started to make itself clear to me in Abadiânia and focus on my writing, which was the purpose of the whole trip in the first place.

I busied myself for the next couple of weeks not only with cracking into my writing, but with daily walks with my three adopted stray dogs, a strict detox diet regime, energy activations and meditation. I blasted myself with light language frequencies to clear karma, release habits and anything holding me back from moving forward and connecting to my soul self. I often caught the sight of Cerro Uritorco out my kitchen window. On some nights the mountain had a mysterious glow around it, almost like it was being lit up by a full moon when we were nowhere near it in the moon cycle.

I was perfectly happy in seclusion, relaxing and enjoying the countryside on my own. When I finally ventured back into town on more of a leisure trip my local dogs flanked me at each side for the walk. This caused an absolute furore when the large fluffy white alpha male went into the territory of other neighbourhood dogs, starting a huge fight. Much worse was my other very meek, but oh so sweet brindled dog, who got her arse handed to her by the local dog mafia. This was rather hard to watch and particularly jarring to my two weeks of peaceful detox, so I snuck over the highway and into town leaving them behind.

"Oh my God, so much to tell," said Candace over a coffee in the town centre. I had met Candace months ago in the north of Peru, a tiny pocket rocket from Panama who grew up in the United States.

"This place is crazy, isn't it?!" she continued. "I'm staying at this really cool hostel where the owner is a hip-hop artist, but you'd never know by looking at him, till the sun goes down that is!" she said, laughing. "They were playing a song called "My girl from Mars" when I arrived. I was the only sober one amongst a bunch of kids getting wasted and blasting the owner's alien/spiritual/political hip-hop! Absolutely bananas!" she said.

"Oh wow," I exclaimed.

"Yeah. I was drinking tea and the owner was hammered so I gravitated to the only person over twenty-two, the random toothless old man rocking his head and tapping his foot to the blaring hip-hop. He hadn't said a word all night, but once he got started, woo-boy! He's been living here for thirty years and seen twenty-plus UFOs, at least one up close and personal, like a kilometre away through the forest. He said it was blinding." Candace looked at me wide-eyed.

"Oh my, I love all this local knowledge," I said, waiting for more.

"This town is like a magnet for all types; spiritual, natural, scientific, religious and curious. And supposedly the idea behind all of it is that they are trying to prepare themselves to be evolved enough for the aliens to make contact! To come and rescue us and take us into that higher vibrational realm. The people want to be energetically open and spiritually sensitive enough to receive their messages because apparently, some people receive their transmissions all the time. In fact, supposedly just last week they met with the President of Chile! The aliens that is. Hmm, no one knows the content or outcome of that meeting though," she said.

"Holy shit!" I exclaimed. "Well, it all sounds pretty out there. We are certainly in the thick of it. Some more than others…" I said, laughing at her.

"Oh yeah, you laugh now," she said "But the name of the alien city is Erks Orion. Also, the name of the beautiful creature's band. That drunken, Latin Muslim, temple residencia-owning, artist activist rapper, haha. What an ironic piece of work he is. Last night, he got started on a rant about how the US government is going to ruin all of our chances to be saved by the aliens, or really, I should say, the more highly evolved humanoids who supposedly deposited our DNA on this planet with the asteroid that destroyed the dinosaurs and have been helping our race along ever since. Because apparently when the aliens come the gun-happy Yankees are going to shoot them out of the sky without warning! He said he's been trying to send the message to the USA to not kill the aliens when they come. And boy was he serious. He laid into me all night for being American and kept asking why we have to kill everything we don't understand. He went on and on about how all we care about are the military and war… pretty tough night for me actually."

We planned to catch up for an adventure the following day and went our separate ways. "Stay safe out there, girl!" I said, grinning as I waved goodbye.

Candace and I headed out for a day hike the following day to Los Torrones, catching a local taxi to the start point just outside of town in the Punilla Valley. The landscape was breathtaking. It was a valley of giants with massive phallic-looking sandstone sculptures towering above and wild condors swooping down over our heads between the rock towers. Our Spanish speaking guide told us they were one hundred and eighty million years old and added geological, botanical and historical facts about the place as we progressed on the two-hour long walk through the valley. At 1400m above sea level our guide pointed out fascinating springs, and ancient geology within the rocks as we trekked up the valley to the top. This particular location is known as the place where the indigenous Comechingon people, and later Angel Cristo Acoglanis would invoke ETs and develop special abilities to help and cure people from several diseases. It was an awe-inspiring trek amongst some incredibly special and unique natural formations. After farewelling our lovely guide, we waited a short time before our taxi driver arrived to take us back. He was a friendly Middle Eastern looking chap in his forties. He was looking back at us in the rear vision mirror, sizing us up as we drove slowly out of town.

"I am an ET. My home is Sirius," he said. "I have a lot of friends who talk to the ETs here. In two years, an asteroid will hit Lake Titicaca to crack open and release the beings that are trapped within." He continued. "You are preparing your body for the new world," he said, looking at me intensely. "You are starting to look like how the evolved humans will be, two to three metres tall, and strong," gesturing to my solid shoulders and build. "You are also an ET."

"Oh yes," I said. "I know, I am allegedly from Mintaka," I said casually, recalling information from an Akashic record reading I had done in London years ago.

The driver beamed at me and then immediately pulled the taxi over and grabbed my right hand. He flipped it over, feeling the various lines on my palm. "You will live for one hundred years," he said. I bloody hope not, I was thinking, I don't particularly fancy being decrepit and rickety. "And you are at the beginning of a nine-year cycle of great change," he said, nodding enthusiastically before abruptly turning back around and continuing our taxi ride.

"Given you quit your job in London to travel Latin America to write transformational travel adventures, he is kind of right," Candace laughed.

For the remainder of the trip, he continued rabbiting on about the upcoming World War III, where missiles and nukes will rain down on us and melt the ice from the North Pole, swallowing huge chunks of the earth. England and Japan would be wiped out, then much of North America and all of Central America would be gone. Afterwards, an asteroid will hit to release all of the people within, whom aren't extra-terrestrials at all, but merely survivors of ancient races of evolved humans from the continent that existed in the Atlantic but submerged into the depths of the great rift when it cracked open. I assumed he was referring to Atlantis, so the Atlanteans and probably the Lemurians who were apparently these beings living in Erks Orion, the alien city, under Cerro Uritorco. Mt. Shasta apparently also had beings in the mountain, as did the Elqui Valley in northern Chile and another valley in Uruguay. Candace was wide-eyed the entire journey, not quite sure what to believe and what all of this meant. I was familiar with Atlantis and Lemuria as ancient advanced civilisations but hadn't thought those beings were hidden inside our earth. This town was turning out to be way more interesting than I imagined.

The following day we took the bus to San Marcos, the town of honey. It was my birthday, so we indulged in a yummy lunch and a cheeky beer at the Piano Bar, breaking my six-month detox for a moment of pleasure with a travelling buddy. After lunch, we set off to hike back through the Sierras to Capilla del Monte. It was 22km which we guessed might take around four-and-a-half hours. Candace had done some digging on this

Erks Orion city the taxi driver had mentioned where apparently people exist in multiple dimensions.

"They oscillate between ours, being the third dimension, and the fourth and fifth dimensions which are only accessible to them because they have evolved to a point where they can sense that stuff," she said. "Sometimes, one of them might be the person walking along right beside you on the street and you wouldn't know it. Isn't that some seriously cool shit? From what I understand, the planet is ascending along with us as collective beings towards a higher dimension, hence all the planetary flux of recent decades. Human consciousness is tapped into the collective mind more than any other time in history!" She said.

"Man, I just love this stuff. So fascinating!" I replied.

Three hours and many conversations later, parched with no water left we discovered we were only halfway, with around two hours of sunlight left in the day. Scanning the thick dense shrubbery in the valley below, we saw a farmhouse in the distance so decided to make our way there to see if we could rouse anyone to call us a taxi. As we arrived at the house we were greeted by a giant leaping brindled male dog, and a slightly less fearsome tan smaller dog. Shortly after an elderly man came into view, beckoning us in through a rickety white picket fence. Candace explained our botched hike in Spanish, which was miles better than mine, while I nodded along and smiled, surveying the scene.

We walked across patchy lawn past three makeshift trestle tables made out of stacked terracotta building blocks with weathered corrugated iron lying across the top. Each was filled with crystals and rocks. Soon we were standing before a rough stone pathway framed by a ramshackle archway through the middle of a complex of small brick buildings off to the left, right and straight ahead. They were separated by a garden bed of purple iris flowers and greenery planted along the centre. I could see an outdoor area with a brick fireplace, chimney and firewood on the left, next to a dome shaped stone oven of some sort and a big beige seventies refrigerator. Everything was very dusty and rustic looking. He introduced himself as Hugo and ushered us into the small brick building on the left signed *Musee*. We waited quietly as he went off to get some water and glasses from the main house. The entire left white brick wall was covered in dozens of photos, pictures and memorabilia. I could see people in ceremony, pictures of Jesus, Saints and ancient Indians plus all sorts of photos with lights. Red beams streaming down the centre, orb shaped lights, or blinding white lights pierced many normal photos. There was an 'Erks' sign at the top by a black and white drawing of an old man. Wherever had we found ourselves?

The rest of the room contained tables and cabinets containing different crystals, stone-crafted mortars and pestles and baskets of fossils that were for sale. As it turned out, Hugo was an eighty-three-year-old shaman who had built this farm on ancient native burial land which was millions of years old. After some water, he motioned for us to head to the left and up the hill to experience his meditation space, while he called us a taxi and made tea. A few minutes' walk later, we came upon a tree with the sign 'Circule en Silencio' and white rocks marking the path up through the thick gorse-like brush continuing up the incline. We continued along the path around to the left and then up for another few minutes before we came out onto a big, wide expanse with three-hundred-and-sixty-degree views of the surrounding countryside. This was the 'Mandalas Lugar de Oración'. There were seven giant mandalas made out of quartz stones before us. There was a giant star, a large triangle, a heart, a circle, an infinity sign and a cross with a small circle above it, all mapped out in chunks of quartz on the dusty earth. Candace and I spent some time meditating inside some of the different shaped mandalas as the sun went down, casting beautiful golden light on us, the dogs and the sparkling crystal mandalas.

On the way back down, I took a fork in the path in the other direction to some old tombs, 'Tumba de la princessa y sacerdotes aborigenes'. This was the cemetery of the indigenous tribes that Hugo had mentioned, with various burial places marked in stone on the site. There were a couple of stone seats for quiet contemplation. The place had an eerie feel at dusk, punctuated by the sounds of the dogs crashing around in the bush in the distance. I kept walking away from the farmhouse, interrupting some grazing cattle and came across a throne made from a huge circular stone, with a naturally formed and curved smooth indentation for the seat. The sign on the tree said 'Sillon de Pedra. Ceremonias' which was obviously where Hugo the shaman did some of his work. I was enchanted with the place, wondering what went on here over time, from the original indigenous people right through to the current shaman. I did a small meditation in the chair, with my palms facing upwards on my thighs to open up to the energies. After the big dog came and muzzled at me a few minutes in, I headed back to join Candace and Hugo in the Musee room.

Candace was sipping on tea and nodding along, while Hugo was chatting away in Spanish. I could pick up various words here and there, but really needed Candace's translation to get the full gist of what he was saying in his thick Argentine accent. It seemed like we were going to be seeing him again the next day. In the taxi, Candace excitedly told me that Hugo was in frequent contact with the aliens whose ships crossed over his place every Monday, Tuesday and Thursday. "He also takes people to visit Erks Orion!" she exclaimed. "Never mind that it's in another dimension..."

"I wonder how he does that?" I pondered.

"I don't really know what he does," she said. "Aligns your chakras with ancient crystals and then I guess we do some ceremony or meditation. I don't know. I couldn't get specifics out of him, but we are going tomorrow, yup. To visit the alien city. Mmm-hmmm. Haha... so cool."

The energies are streaming in from far and wide.
Intend and accept, and be open to this light.
For the upgrades and knowledge to be remembered in this now moment.

All is well and as it should be.
There is nothing else that you must 'do'.
The energies are working beautifully to all who are aligned at this time,
to the capacity suitable for them.

Just be.
Be in the love and oneness
of Gaia, the Universe and multiverses at this time.
For these are the most expansive energies available to you now
and this is what you are here to do.

For the light and oneness of all.
Each contributing their light, in their own unique way.
Which need not be of 'spiritual' means.
For the simple pure joy of laughter is also a way to align.
And each being will align, as is comfortable for them at this time.

Show Me The Aliens!

"Omg!! Que freaky, girl!" I heard from Candace the next day in a message. "I was LITERALLY just opening messenger to contact u when your message popped up! Oooh… what a sixth sense u have. Spoke to the shaman this morning and it was for tomorrow after all. Anyway, given I'm travelling tomorrow, he said that we could meet up this afternoon @3pm to go to a "special" friend's house to do a meditation and chakras over tea. Dunnoooo… I'm really confused by this whole process! Jahaha… but anyway, I told him we'd be there, if that works for you. Also, the girls here at the hostel are keen on ovni hunting tonight so let's defo book a taxi. Although it's so cloudy now there might be nothing to see. When I was looking through my photos last night, the place the taxi driver mentioned to us at Los Torrones is the place that shaman had on the wall too! So crazy."

That afternoon at the meeting point I was waiting a fair while with no sign of Candace nor Hugo. About twenty minutes later, I started to walk further down the road when I saw a white ute pull up on the side of the road. I got close enough to make out Hugo in the front seat. He was smartly dressed in a red and white candy-striped shirt under a brown suede waist jacket, finished off with a French silk patterned kerchief tied around his neck. His hair was brushed backwards down over his collar and his short grey moustache was freshly trimmed. I greeted him and he motioned at the back door for me to jump in. "¿Dónde está mi amiga?" I asked in my basic Spanish as there was still no sign of Candace. After a while we took off again and he drove through town. I spotted her yellow jacket and backpack heading in the wrong direction, looking at a map. I yelled out to her and she ran over and jumped in, with lots of, "Lo sientos," apologising in Spanish that she had gotten lost.

We sat in the back seat, not knowing where we were going, nor what to expect. Hugo drove to the local bakery and picked up some biscuits, then drove through the back of dusty suburban streets before pulling up outside a small house with black gates. A tall man saw us pull up and came out to greet us. His name was Ariel and he spoke English and Spanish so that helped a little. We were invited inside and offered tea. Ariel was a UFO specialist and proceeded to show us many pictures he had taken of the ships on his computer. There was no mistaking what they were. Generally dark disc-shaped things flying through the sky. He had his own show on the internet and was regularly featured on radio shows. He talked about doing a deal with a TV station to buy his content for a show, and be featured on it as an expert. I took it all in with interest. I'd never been much into aliens and spaceships. I mean, I just felt they were out there and that all would be revealed when the time was right. I certainly wasn't fixated on conspiracy theories and UFO sightings and I did not feel like they were a threat. Just other beings sharing the Universe we live in. Going down the rabbit hole with it all felt like a distraction from the real work, which I viewed as holding and expanding your own light, in whatever creative way you see fit. As long as it carried the vibration of joy, you couldn't really go wrong.

Hugo was talking about seven high vibrational hot spots across the globe, similar to here in Capilla del Monte. There were apparently two more in South America, one in Lake Titicaca, the other in Machu Picchu, one at Mt. Shasta in the USA, one in Mexico, one in Russia and the last one in the Pyrenees between France and Spain. Interestingly, I realised I had been to four of these places already. After tea Hugo started doing some chakra alignments. Candace went first and I watched as Hugo unwrapped three different crystals from a wrapped leather pouch. He used different crystals on various areas of the body, mainly on the back for me. The entire process took all of five to ten minutes per person and when he finished he invited us to go and visit the Erks the following week. He also extended an invite for us to go and stay at his ranch 'Posta del Silencio'. Candace was unfortunately on the move the following day, but the invitation was extended to me and he apparently also wanted to teach me some healing techniques. We were in the middle of thanking him when there was a knock at the door. One of Ariel's friends arrived for an excursion up to the ridge for a mandala meditation and invited us to join. We looked at each other with a 'yeah why not!' kind of face, said our goodbyes to Hugo and off we went.

After a twenty-minute walk up through the back roads to a ridge opposite Uritorco, we came to a small platform with a mandala made from the quartz rocks from the mountain opposite. The mandala was rather small in comparison to the grand symbols up at Hugo's place, but Ariel had prepped us to expect as much. The four of us stood in a circle around the mandala. Ariel asked us to close our eyes and take a few deep breaths. He then talked us through a series of guided meditations where we circled around connecting with Pachamama and the beings above. Then we did some mantra chanting. Ariel explained that 'Ma' is the first sound humans make and therefore a sacred sound. We chanted a series of 'Mmmmmmmmmmmmaaaaaaaaaaaaaas' for some minutes, before singing our names towards the mountain. It was hard to keep a straight face when one was casually singing an introduction to a mountain. As Uritorco is full of quartz crystal, the crystal technology could store the sound and then recognise us when we went to visit the Erks the following week.

We wandered back down the mountain road as dusk fell chatting about their experiences in Capilla. It was almost dark when we neared Ariel's house and I looked up towards the mountain and saw a distinct light moving in front of it. There was no flight path running in front of the mountain and I wondered what it was. Ariel yelled out, "Navi, Navi." The light slowed down for a second or two directly in front of us and then sped off to the right. "Congratulations, you just saw your first Navi," he said, high-fiving us.

Devastatingly, Candace had to leave the following day for her next destination, despite me trying to convince her to switch her plans and come to the shaman farm with me. Alas, we said a fond farewell and my wing woman and translator was no more. Hugo had said he would call my accommodation to tee up my stay with him, however after a few days I hadn't heard a peep. I was a little hesitant, mainly due to my very basic Spanish, and being one-on-one with an eighty-three-year-old for days. However, never one to say no to adventure, I eventually got my reception to call him and was told he would pick me up the following day. Sure enough, he arrived to pick me up in the afternoon and we went to the local market to get supplies. He bought some vegetables and fruits and went into the bakery to buy sandwiches. He was rather flummoxed that I was a) vegetariano and b) sin glutem. I attempted to explain my detox to which he nodded along, but he didn't seem to understand why I couldn't eat meat or bread or cheese.

We sat at the end of his long table, covered with a plastic plaid tablecloth. Above the stone wall by the fireplace were five images of various saints; Jesus, Mother Mary, one who looked like Mother Theresa, and another man with an angelic baby. We sat down to a meal of salad, with potatoes and chicken for Hugo. He said a prayer before the meal and then started talking away in Spanish. He was speaking incredibly slowly to allow me to follow, however, some of his vocabulary was above my capabilities and so I got slightly lost. Luckily I took some recordings, knowing I didn't want to miss any detail. He asked if I'd been to Mendoza and Malargüe as this was where great tunnels begin that extend through the Andes mountains to Cusco, Caja Marca and then finish in Mount Albán in Mexico. These are subterranean ET ship lanes he told me.

"The tunnel is about ten metres wide by ten metres tall. So, a round spaceship, shaped like a disc, six metres in diameter can travel perfectly through the tunnel. When you enter into the metaphysical knowledge… Russia is very important. Very important. It's very interesting, the metaphysical knowledge that inside are subterranean tunnels… Inside! You don't know, you don't know... Beneath this is another city! It has a capacity of twenty thousand people! Underneath, Underneath! We don't know what this is... We can't imagine it?! That's why, you, with this knowledge that you are with joy, with willingness, with love of travel and learning... and the more you know, the more you cultivate, the more you learn. Because you travelled here... something brought you here... physically here. Well... then... that is part of your awakening, the assistance that you're receiving from the light beings. When I speak of the light beings, I'm speaking of the Central Galactic Celestial Government of God. Where no religion exists, only the light. There is no religion," he said.

"Yes, yes... I don't believe in religion," I said.

"And I belong to the White Brotherhood and you are going on that path. We do not belong in any religion of the earth. We belong to the Celestial Government of God. Simple. But many people, you see, fight for rights... How do they live free? They live in love; they live with knowledge of another subject... because you... you don't have any more envy. You don't want other people's things anymore. No. You are free. And so full of love that you don't want anything of others. You have received what you need to receive. And with that you have roamed the earth. You are not going to need for anything. They are always going to give you enough, so that you can travel, you can live well and you will continue incorporating the knowledge that you need to write. That is the thing... your preparation. Your spiritual preparation. Your physical preparation. And knowledge."

The phone started ringing and cut us off. I did my best to understand and ask questions, although it was a stretch. My basic Spanish meant I was unfamiliar with all of the terminology for the spiritual world aside from 'energia' and 'Jesus Cristo'. I certainly didn't know how to ask about the healing techniques he had said he would teach me, although I had mostly forgotten about that. I had just gone there without expectation, but very much hoping for a spacecraft visit while I was there. From what I vaguely understood he said I had some blockage in my heart, which had been worked on and cleared and that he was looking for someone to train and hand over to. I could make out that various people had obviously come and trained with him and then left without completion to have families and so forth. Which was disappointing to him as he had no one to hand over his knowledge to. Was he asking me to take the baton from him? It was only after the fact that I found out he was talking about my link to the Great White Brotherhood, which is the council of Ascended Masters, that El Morya was very much a part of. A link to my journey in Brazil at the Casa.

He brought out some dessert of poached pears, which I graciously accepted. If only I had a translator, it would have made things so much better. I helped to clear up the dinner dishes, taking in his rustic kitchen and old school ingredients. I wondered how he survived out here all on his own at his age. While I was doing the dishes, Hugo picked up his guitar and started playing and singing. We sat around drinking his famous herb tea made with dried herbs and dried orange peel, which was apparently exceptionally good for your body and digestion. We retired early, me to a small antique bed that was far too short for me in the stone-walled guest room where I tried to make myself comfortable. It was a bit musty and cold and I went to sleep in all my clothes, hoping to be woken in the night by some rustling denoting an ovni visiting Hugo.

Ye has come at this time of great awakening and shift for a reason, yes.
You are the reason for all things. You. It is you.
Worry not about others and only about that which
satisfies your soul. For others will follow.
A unique perspective is a gift you see. Know this is your gift.
Without unique perspective things would remain the same.
And this is not why you are here.
You are here for greater things and more.
Ground these energies into your being.
Ground in the ways of the ancients as there
is much here for you to remember.

Life-Changing Spiritual Experiences Foiled Again

The following day I awoke to the sounds of Hugo listening to his wireless in the next room. I went to meditate at sunrise inside the mandalas on the hill. The two dogs followed me as I briskly made my way there, shaking off the morning chill. I laid my flax mat in the triangle mandala and zipped up my jacket to keep me warm before lying back to relax and appreciate the serenity and energy of the place. A few minutes in, I felt something flop against my right leg. I opened my eyes ever so slowly to see the smaller of the two dogs happily cosying up to my leg in the beautiful white light of the morning. I closed my eyes again and breathed deeply, dropping into meditation. Connecting with the energy of the stars, bringing it down into my body and then down into the core of the earth, up to the heavens again and back down into the crystal core. Suddenly, I felt a hairy mass jump on to me, jolting my eyes open. The big dog left giant dusty paw prints on my leggings before dropping down to my left and rolling onto his back. He shifted left and then right, repetitively back scratching as his tail bashed at my head. I gave him a pat and closed my eyes again to get back into the silence.

Moments later, the big dog was biting at my hands wanting to play. I sat up and pushed him away gently, which had the opposite effect. Now he was getting overexcited, shown by a giant bright pink lipstick poking out of his nether regions. I ignored it and sat up instead closing my eyes again to get back into meditation. No sooner had I closed my eyes than my shoulder was locked into a tight embrace from his front paws as he thrusted away, vigorously dry humping me. He had a strong grip being such a mighty big dog and I struggled to get free.

Yet again, any attempt of spiritual practice had turned into a comedy of errors. The Universe, with ever the sense of humour.

I gave up and strolled back to the house for a shower, with Hugo pottering around in his pyjamas and slippers asking me if I wanted some cafe de mañana. He had various cereals laid out with yoghurt, and of course a lot of toast, so I made myself a detox friendly fruit salad while he looked on slightly bemused, enjoying his carb laden breakfast.

For the rest of the morning, I went walking around the property, spending time in the sacred sites amongst the cattle and horses. After lunch, a group of eight Argentine visitors showed up, which made me feel a little better that Candace and I weren't the only ones to barge in on the old shaman without notice. Hugo brought them into the Musee and started his spiel.

"So, I think the planet will evolve, and assimilate. It will take a long time, but it will happen. The world evolves in small steps. There is no way the world will devolve. There is no cosmic force to reverse things and to balance and harmonise us. How many demons need to disappear for us to liberate the planet? For every hundred, seventy are demons. How can we convert them? We are just a few. So, in all the world people are working," said Hugo.

One of the Argentine visitors interrupted, "But does the spiritual hierarchy help us?"

"They will always help us, but they will only give the information for the ones who are seeking the ones who are open... we always get what we need. What is right for them is not necessarily what is right for us. We need to show that we are fighting for it, and then it will be given for us. There are some good people, yes. Around the world there are good people and that's what we need to focus on. There are a lot of places in contact with ETs. The region where King Arthur was, where the fountain of Arthur energy was in England, there is an old castle that nobody touches because it's hermetic. They are not from the same religion, they won't tell you anything, because the hermetic is sealed. And that is right for them. The ones that are open to it receive the energy. The one that looks for it will find it. The one who seeks, finds. You see Jesus was only two thousand years ago. Everything that you ask, gets given to you," he said.

He passed around photos of the light beings and answered many questions. Then he took us into another small stone room for a ceremony.

There was a giant cross made out of brick in the middle of the stone wall, adorned in various pictures, crystals and amulets. Just to the left underneath was a table containing many curious objects. An open wooden box contained four different pointed crystals, an amethyst, a smoky quartz, a clear quartz and another I wasn't familiar with. There was a glass vase half full of water, a large condor feather, two dishes of small pebble-like crystals and a red picture frame with 'La Gran Invocation' in Spanish. The room was filled with various forms of ramshackle seating arranged in a circle. Below a small triangle-shaped ledge in the wall containing a picture of a light being, a bottle of holy water, a crystal, another photo and some kind of amulet hanging over both sides of the ledge. He began with a talk.

"The planet, talking honestly, is not okay. If you see the context of the galaxy the planet is not doing well. And that's it. The brothers from Sirius, they are helping us. There are thirty percent of them who are kind of on-call to help us in case of emergency. They are looking after us, but they are not that active. There is a revolution coming. And Jesus is actively interceding, with the Sirians, on behalf of us, and with Buddha to help with this. Buddha came six thousand years before Christ, and that was programmed to happen for thousands of years before that. Buddha first, Jesus second. They just don't arrive like the holy light; it was programmed to be. They came and they caught up under the pink moon of May under the star sign of Taurus in the Himalayas. Between 2001-2007 there were three meetings between Buddha and Jesus. I don't know what's happening in the meetings, but they are gestating something for the planet. Forming groups, praying, helping each other. That's what we do now in the meantime. We work for the light. And for the love. In service. Certainly, we will receive something.

We need to be ready to act when it is necessary. There is something coming from the kingdom of God. It will come to work on the earth relationships. Then the Solar Angels and the Great White Brotherhood will work less on the earth. When the revolution happens, they will be withdrawn from the planet and go back to their place of origin. There will be someone who will be the interim region leader for the planet. This leader will be in the city of Maya. He will guide the life on the planet, because we won't be thinking only about ourselves, as living beings. We will be thinking about life as a whole on the planet, like the birds who sing. It will be a time that is not about the individual, but about the whole. Every living being on the planet will be balanced. It's like we are all going to feel and be connected to all life. What would be of us, if we couldn't feel something when a bird sings? We are not going to think about us. We are going to think about the birds and the flowers because every part of life has a right. All the living beings on earth have the right, because they have all been created by God. That's the same reason that we want life ourselves. We need to care for all our homes and all our families as a whole, as a community. So that's why we have to take action.

Even our country. You see, South America is like a country itself. There was one modern president, who wanted to unify the continent and make the United States of South America. And you know who that was, Lula de Silva. We will be one country, because in the cosmic programme, South America is the continent of the future. With all our different kinds of people, a new kind of people will emerge. We have the most amazing variety of crystals, plants and animals. That is why this continent has been selected by the reign of God as the continent of the future. And that's why we have the importance of praying. The praying for example for this girl who is going to write her book," Hugo said, motioning to me.

"This girl who is going to go back to her place to write her book, about the essence of this meeting, about the moments that she spends here in this epicentre of energy in Capilla del Monte. All of you are here for a reason. All of you are here for something positive, because you have been guided here, and you have the ability to be here right now. Thank you all for being here. Something will be from this meeting. This is happening for a reason. And you have to say thank you to the highest celestial father and all the light beings and for all the people who keep praying for me to keep going and doing this service for God and the celestial beings."

Hugo sat in a seat in front of a giant frosted glass crystal bowl. We all joined hands and began La Gran Invocation, a prayer that came through Alice Bailey in 1945 and has since been translated into eighty languages and used all over the world.

The Great Invocation

From the point of Light within the Mind of God.
Let light stream forth into the minds of men.
Let Light descend on Earth.

From the point of Love within the Heart of God.
Let love stream forth into the hearts of men.
May Christ return to Earth.

From the centre where the Will of God is known.
Let purpose guide the little wills of men –
the purpose which the Masters know and serve.

From the centre which we call the race of men.
Let the Plan of Love and Light work out.
And may it seal the door where evil dwells.

Let Light and Love and Power restore the Plan on Earth.

Hugo used his wooden baton to tap the side of the big crystal bowl four times and it rang out. Then holding the stick inside he encircled it, stretching the sound and increasing the intensity for a few minutes before stopping to let the sound dissipate. A deep harmonic sound was being emitted from the bowl. You could feel the vibrational energy around the circle. Hugo then gave gratitude and blessings, for us, our friends, our communities, the entire world. Although I couldn't understand every word, I let the sounds and words wash over me and into my heart like a flood of light. Then we each said what we were grateful for as it went around the circle, repeating, "Gracias Señor," after each person.

"With the right hand touch your heart and incorporate Jesus from this ceremony. And with your left hand, bring in your connection to all hearts. This house was a house of a Comechingon," he said, referring to the structure we were sitting in and the ancient tribe of native Indians from this place.

"With the energy of a thousand years ago, these stones here carry a lot of energy." He said, motioning for us to touch it. "I made this cross to cement these energies here, to make it last. I blended it into the wall, because they are all local rocks, containing ancient spiritual energy. So, it will last another thousand years. It was ruins, that were abandoned five hundred years ago and once I got here, and I was randomly walking, I felt all the energy from the Comechingon as there used to be a big house here. A house of very strong energy. It's a very special place. This is a place of initiation, and healing. That's why I am very thankful that you have come to see this place. And I wish for you to remember to come back. All people who meet me, I have the intention to activate as much as possible in service of God. In service of humanity and the planet, because that used to be taught by the ancients. That, and we have to look after the planet, and preserve it. We shouldn't be mutilating plants and animals and fish. If we respect everything, life keeps existing and we are going to make our Father so much happier. So that's why I put you in charge. You are in charge of praying for those things so the Father can hear. The more he hears the better. Because the technology made men damage the nature, the climate and all the things being created in the planet. All the deprivation is being done to the planet by taking more than what we need. That's why I thank you for being here. Send out a prayer to revert the planet into a beautiful planet, because if you think about it, it is beautiful, and that's why we have to thank God for being in this sacred place. And I hope that God follows you, and that this place has been positive for you, as it was positive for the Comechingon people."

I had been buzzing with energy the entire ceremony, and although my Spanish was awful, it wasn't needed to feel the full impact of this special gathering.

I stayed another night with the shaman hoping for a visit to the Erks and some ET action, however, it didn't seem to be on the agenda. My Spanish wasn't good enough to understand what was going on and why that wasn't the case. In typical Argentine fashion, shaman or no shaman, he feasted on crackers, bread, cake, cookies, meat and wine. Vino, from a carton and with every meal. He ate a lot of packaged goods, but he seemed to be doing just fine at eighty years plus after all. He was living proof that the old paradigm rules of puritanical spiritual lives were rubbish. He was an amazing shaman, healer and communed with ETs and higher beings. No meat or wine stopping him, a man after my own heart. He turned on the TV in the background and showed me how he charged his remote control on a giant quartz crystal. Apparently, he never needed to replace the batteries. Priceless.

"Two girls came last week so that they could stay," he said, launching into after dinner discussion. "I would have to work to teach them, to help them grow. NO!" he said, shaking his head. "On the other hand, you came with some kind of preparation, you have an intuition for what is true. I saw how you came here without knowing anything, however, you're progressing well. You went to meditate, and I've seen your interest and where you have received all of this physical energy that you have incorporated here. So, I don't want to say don't meet a man, but be sure this man does not erase your mind, your spirit, everything that you have. Someone that doesn't take you out of your path, and the beauty that you have. Some men, they are only interested in connections through sex, those types. And that poor girl who was trying to work for the light, she gets lost. So, I am a little frustrated and demotivated by so many I teach, I keep going... but nothing happens. When you enter into the understanding of the metaphysical you will have fear. You have to prepare yourself, go out into the night, walking in the night and do not have fear. Many women come here for metaphysical knowledge. They stay like you. And sometimes I ask, 'Why don't you go and look up at the sky?' What?! You want me to accompany you? No. They will not see anything. You have to be brave enough to walk in the dark without knowing what is there, and find the information yourself," he said, serving us another cup of digestive tea.

"What I feel in you, is that you continue to train and prepare for a work of light, of love, and hopefully there will be very many like you. Many people, whether male or female, continuing working for the life of the planet. This work of mine needs to be the feminine and the masculine. It has to be complementing energy. If not, when I travel, I search for the feminine identity to help me. You see? We are human beings, and we all have spirit incorporated within… In the physical, that's one thing, and the spiritual that's another. So, men and women need to check their compatibility. They need to live in harmony. To communicate telepathically so that there is no need to tell lies, or say weird things… all would have to be of light! My love, so then… there is no possible way to live badly, it forces us to live well. This is nothing spectacular, because all light is love. Therefore, you go now! Go now, and communicate with me every now and then, how you are doing, via Ariel, and me to you via Ariel."

"Yes, I will thank you, Gracias Señor," I said.

Had I been able to understand the finer points of the translation at the time of the conversation I would have seen Hugo the shaman was pushing me out to experience these beings, these things for myself without him. My reality was morphing and changing to push me into myself once again.

I thought about Alex and how in some ways we balanced each other out. I'd been receiving a series of adorable messages from him since we parted. We were very different and although I wasn't sure where our romance was going I couldn't wait to be reunited with him in New Zealand.

It matters not the content. The surface of it. What is of impact is the feeling.
The feeling of a forgotten society who knew the value of light.
The value of light in all things.
From the king of kings down to the smallest ant.
The light that pervades all.
The light of life.

For when one understands this light, this light that runs through all,
then one understands the value of life.
This purity of light is in your gut. It is in the palm of your hands.
It runs through you like blood runs through your veins.
And in understanding this light, one understands truth.
One understands the truth of this path. The truth of this pain.
Which is that there is no pain. As there is no separation.
There never was and there never will be.

For the light is all-powerful.
The light trumps all.
The light that is long forgotten will reign once again.

A Heartbreaking Premonition

Peaking with fever and the bone-aching pain of the dreaded dengue, I made the gruelling twenty-four-hour flight home to New Zealand. I would not recommend this to any human. Devo and Annie took one look at my delirious self and organised an emergency appointment at the doctor that afternoon. I was flat on my back for the next ten days in our family home in Herne Bay while Devo was recovering from his hip replacement with Nurse Annie at a one-level apartment in town. Many weeks later after a raft of homeopathic injections and a session in a hyperbaric decompression chamber to ensure my body rid itself of the disease, I was finally back to my normal self. Dengue was notorious for playing havoc with its sufferers' health years after being infected if not dealt with properly. You could also die pretty quickly, the second time around.

By the time Alex arrived a couple of months later I was completely recovered and we had been having stupidly cute Skype video calls daily. He had met the family, seen the house and was counting down the hours to see me.

I drove to the airport at the crack of dawn to be there for his 6.30am arrival. Turns out I needn't have bothered. After two-and-a-half hours of waiting, Devo called to say Immigration had been on the phone about visa issues and that he should be through soon. I waited another hour before he finally showed up. It was an awkward hello. He looked like a possum caught in the headlights.

"I need a fucking drink," he said, looking at me with semi-delirious eyes.

Once outside, he grabbed me. "Come here," he said, and

pulled me in. "I haven't even kissed you yet!" It didn't feel natural; it felt weird, but I chalked it up to distance and time.

It was a stunning, late-summer morning by the time we got home, and I popped the perfectly chilled champagne. We sat outside and watched the sun on the water as I caught up on the drama of his interactions with New Zealand immigration who had finally let him in on a very limited visitor's visa. Somehow I hadn't quite grasped the extent of his visa issues, which seemed to have been created from a series of innocent mistakes when he applied to move to New Zealand a few years prior, after his visa in Sydney ran out. He appeared to be more naive and less capable than I remembered. I kept the champagne flowing in a desperate attempt to get back to the headspace we had left in Brazil.

It took at least two bottles to get into bed, and we must have finished three before we ventured upstairs to see Annie and Devo in the late afternoon. We agreed to cook an early dinner at home, so Alex and I decided to take a sobering swim in the rather autumnal ocean. The champagne sure helped; I managed to get in easily and swam around surprisingly happily while my body turned progressively more numb with each second. The Brazilian wasn't quite so enthusiastic and jumped out after a quick dip.

At dinner I busied myself preparing a lovely spread of barbecued lamb and salad. This was the first time I'd brought any semblance of a boyfriend home in twenty years, the last being one of Devo's colleagues and business partner almost ten years my senior when I was eighteen. Enough said.

It was all flowing rather smoothly, and the tension finally started leaving my body, care of the steady flow of delicious New Zealand red through my glass. Devo was attentive and gleeful, nursing a red wine on his expansive chest as he engaged Alex in conversation, clearly assessing the situation, or rather, him.

We ate dinner outside despite the chill in the air. The all-day drinking had at this point entirely opened my honesty box, usually hidden away beneath layers of the familial and politically correct. The conversation took a serious turn, off the back of my new-found perspective from spiritual retreat. While Alex and Annie were smoking cigarettes together, I mustered the courage to say a few words I'd been wanting to say for a long while to Devo.

"I love you to death, Devo, but you need to change some things about the way you behave and interact in the world. Otherwise it is detrimental to your health," I said. "Being so negative with your words, about yourself and towards other people isn't healthy. Getting frustrated and flying off the handle when you don't get your way is putting you and your body in a constant state of stress. These are the kinds of things that cause cancer." Alcohol-fuelled tears fell down my cheeks. I was seriously concerned, and had been for some time. "If you don't change some things in how you engage with life and operate in the world, with regard to your thoughts, feelings and actions, you are lowering your vibration and leaving yourself vulnerable. It isn't right to constantly be in the frame of mind that people are out to get you. To constantly be on the attack or the defence. To worry so much about what you say or do being the 'right' thing all the time in the eyes of others. You should only ever do what you really want to do in your heart. Not for the posturing or pretences. Since I've been home, it's been constant. This is nothing new, but it's really time to change some things now. With all these back and hip issues and all this pain, this is all caused by you. Your feelings, emotions, stress. I'm terribly worried about you."

There, I had said it. It had been a long time coming. He sat opposite me in his wingback chair, face scrunched up, like a kid who didn't like what he was served for dinner, but was forced to eat it anyway.

When I was around it all the time, I found Devo's egotistical, self-entitled behaviour entertaining, and even endearing. Anyone who knew him would agree. He did it with such panache, drama and style that it was a core part of what we loved. He was an amazing, generous and kind-hearted man in so many ways, and incredibly successful. He never took 'no' for an answer. A true larger-than-life personality, he could just as easily act like a spoiled child as a legend, especially when he didn't get his way, which generally happened multiple times a day. The older he got the less patience he had before he would throw his toys out of the cot. The more time I spent living away from New Zealand, the more I found it jarring every time I came home for a visit. He took it on board quietly, before Annie and Alex interrupted us.

The next morning, I woke up with a giant hangover and slightly remorseful about my drunken, crying D&M with Devo. I quickly squashed the feeling with a lot of sex, followed by chilli scrambled eggs and a decent coffee at a favourite café up the road.

Three days later, Devo was diagnosed with advanced pancreatic cancer and given twelve weeks to live. He delivered the news, trying to put on a brave face, his quavering voice giving it away. "You knew," he said to me, shaking his head. "You knew. You must be psychic or something. You bloody knew…"

It was essentially a death sentence. I was, oddly enough, incredibly calm. I attributed my emotional even keel to the months of work I had done at John of God. Had I been the person I was when leaving London, I would have had an entirely different reaction. From the GP to the pancreatic specialist to the Canopy Cancer Care doctor, the prognosis was as grim as could be. Chemo might give an extra few weeks, if that, but it came at the cost of constantly feeling sick. I steered the conversation with the cancer doctor to highlight cases when the same diagnosis had been turned around, or beaten. I was in miracle 'full glass' force. The doctor admitted that there were in fact a few such cases. I had made my point and left it there. Devo opted not to do chemo, given it may mean his last weeks were spent feeling even rougher than he already did.

After the initial shock had worn off, the house became a revolving door for a highly alcohol-fuelled living wake. There was a different knee jerk reaction every other day. One minute I was taking Devo to Brazil and John of God, where Alex was going to be his translator and guide. The next, we were running off to the USA to see some specialist. Of course, the doctors told him that he could not travel far so he let them put the kibosh on all of that.

During any kind of cancer experience, you are inevitably inundated with well-meaning friends and acquaintances sending you the latest miracle cure. The vast amount of information is overwhelming. Devo consulted with a smart, wellness-professional friend Cliff, who was basically another son, to separate the snake oil from the statistically viable options. He opted for intravenous vitamin C, a ketogenic diet and a fledgling pilot programme of natural cancer treatment such as GcMaf immunity enhancement and Mistletoe. The latter two were provided through a barely legal clinic in constant danger of being shut down by authorities. It also cost a small fortune but was backed by molecular biologist studies and anthroposophical doctor recommendations. Then there was the medicinal cannabis oil, which was so strong it had people holding on to the walls for dear life on their way out the door after Devo had tricked them into trying a tiny amount. He was still in firm grip of his naughty nature, despite circumstances.

I sat in the lounge next to Devo, watching his pained face as he tried to fight back tears. I'd done this many times but it never got any easier. He would shake his head as if to fend it off and stuff the emotion back down again.

"Do you think I can really do this?" he asked me.

And, just like that, I knew he wasn't going to make it. "Of course you can Devo," I said gently. "You can do anything you put your mind to, but you are going to have to do the inner work too. It's not just about relying on these natural treatments to work miracles. Your entire thought process and mentality needs to change." My heart broke into a trillion pieces.

Alcohol and tears flowed at all hours of the day, with various people calling around to join in the thin veil of positivity and commiseration. Annie, naturally being as dramatic as Devo, was self-medicating heavily. Alex was also joining Annie for booze and cigarettes on the regular and stumbling drunk to bed most nights.

I knew I needed to stay sober in order to keep on an even keel. The old me would have indulged in an alcohol binge, given the crisis situation, but deep inside I knew that was not how

I needed to handle this. Someone needed to keep it together. I was running or doing yoga every day and joining in the ketogenic diet, whilst trying to sort out Alex's visa issues, lend a hand with Devo's appointments, work my part-time job and keep an eye on everyone and everything else as my world was turning upside down. Little red flags of memories popped up in my mind from the time Alex and I had spent together since we met. He had been at JOG not just because his life had fallen apart, but because of alcohol. He had mentioned it, but I hadn't really realised the extent of the issue while sober in spiritual retreat as I was blinded by the romantic idea of our synchronistically blessed, potential soulmate relationship. Hints of it came after I was already diving in, yet I doubted myself, knowing alcohol was a major trigger for me growing up in an environment tainted by the negative side effects of it. His dreamy easy-going personality was fine when we were travelling, but in the real world now, with the challenge of a lifetime I found it frustrating. He wasn't capable of managing himself, let alone supporting me.

Unsurprisingly, under so much pressure, our relationship became strained. I needed someone who was going to step up, not contribute more of a burden. Thankfully, he needed to be shipped out of the country to Australia while we applied for a partnership visa, to allow him to work and take the responsibility off me. After Alex left it was pretty much radio silence for six weeks. He was so busy trying to make things work in Sydney that I was not top of mind. The glaring issues thrown up by events, plus the distance and lack of communication made it an obvious confirmation for me that it was over. When his Partnership visa finally came through, I broke up with him. I realised he was not aligned with the person I wanted to be. I felt bad that he had come all the way out here for me and it hadn't worked out, but by this point I realised that meeting someone in spiritual retreat was kind of like meeting someone in rehab. It was an ill-fated idea.

*We understand your frustration at this time. And we are very respectful
of giving you the space required to find solutions to the problems you face.
For it is how we face the problems in life
that provide the biggest opportunity to be more in our light.*

*And you are right it is not a case of 'lessons'.
This idea that you are learning 'lessons' detracts
from the power that you are.
The sovereign being, with all the light you encompass
and the truth of who you came to be.*

*For this is the truth. The truth of all that is.
Which is not to say that there should not be any
incongruous feelings or ways of being,
just note how these affect your energy body.
As if you stand forthright within your divine self and your light,
the essence of who you are is on show, and strength
is gained from this act within itself.*

*It is powerful to see the changes in the handling
of the problems faced by you.
We are with you at this time to support and guide you.
To let you know you are loved.
For the light you are, is beyond all else.
For it is who you truly are that you seek , and therein lies the beauty.*

May As Well Add Murderer To My Repertoire

With the looming death sentence being an open license to booze for one and all, it wasn't long before it became a toxic household. I was having flashbacks to my teenage years, which were equally, if not more, volatile. Devo would make excuses, saying there was a lot to cope with between all the appointments and the special diet, but I was less sympathetic. It was far from a healing environment and seemed to be far more focused on other people's priorities and not Devo's.

I went upstairs to his bedroom one day while he was napping and crawled into bed beside him. He looked so frail and ill that I just lay there silently crying, overwhelmed with painful emotion. I missed him already. The old Devo. The Devo I knew. Not this shadow of his former self.

"It's okay, Jo," he said opening one eye towards me. "Everything's going to be okay." But I knew he was lying.

He held my hand and squeezed it as we lay there looking out the bedroom window at the constantly changing whitecaps hurtling down the harbour.

One day Annie said to me that Devo smelled the same as the dying patients from her nursing days. A week or so later, he suddenly told me that he was going to move to the hospice, "… to give Annie a break."

"A break? You know if you go in there, Devo, you're not coming out. It's a one-way ticket in those places."

"Rubbish," he said, brushing me off.

I was furious. Looking back later, I could see that the experience was triggering all sorts of old trauma from my childhood, with Annie as the star of the show. We were not getting on at all. This time, however, I was old enough to do something about it and stand up for myself. I was energetically sound and sober enough to hold my ground despite the hostile atmosphere. I spent most of the months while Devo was sick trying to navigate my way around the politics of personalities in the house. When someone is dying, you don't expect other people to start losing the plot. But they do, and the results are wild. That probably threw me the most, out of everything. I held my tongue as much as I could, but there were times when I just couldn't hold it anymore, let alone allow situations to continue that didn't have Devo's best interest at heart.

Annie wanted the funeral to be what she was comfortable with, a tiny family affair with her favourite spiritual music and far away from any church. In some twisted way, I understood, but I wasn't prepared to have some measly service that did nothing to celebrate the life of this amazing man who had touched the hearts and lives of so many. By this point, things had become so ludicrous that I could only laugh.

As Devo got sicker, he started taking the path of least resistance more often through the family flare-ups, but we managed to steer the plans back to a proper affair so that the hundreds of people who he helped, or who knew, respected and worked with him would have the chance to say goodbye.

Watching someone slowly die, day by day, is one of the most heart-wrenching things to endure. The conscious part of me was excited that he was going on a new adventure, an adventure of the non-physical. That he had chosen this experience and this exit for reasons of a higher perspective unbeknownst to me. That it was in fact happening for me and not to me. I knew that even when he was gone, he wouldn't really be completely 'gone'. Everything is energy; we are made of energy and therefore it's just the body that we move on from. Yet my human self was dealing with grief and loss, knowing that he was no longer going to be on the planet in the physical with me.

It was awful to watch him in pain, to see him lose his quick wit and strong mind to the morphine, and degenerate before our eyes. The morphine seemed to have him fixated on all sorts of unusual things that were really just not that important.

I ran a circuit around Westhaven Marina and up College Hill, stopping in at the hospice almost every day. We'd talk about his to do list and I'd make phone calls for him or check emails. Or I'd help him shower and eat. Devo was thinner and less on to it every time I saw him. He hated that the drugs were taking away the sharpness of his mind. Devo was clearly dying, and we were just waiting for him to let go.

We broke him out of the hospice one day in between pain meds and took him down to one of his favourite restaurants for lunch. Despite being famous for his long lunches, he could barely walk, eat or drink but held court, nonetheless, regaling the table with stories and quipping jokes with the waiters. Back at the hospice later that afternoon, I heard him on the phone to a friend, saying, "When I get out of here mate, we need to do that project..."

Yet I knew it was ending.

As the weeks went on, I decided to employ more energy techniques to support him on his journey. We were well beyond a miracle cure at this point. I had listened to a radio interview of Jean Slatter, who had written a book called *Hiring The Heavens*. The premise of the book was that you could actually hire a committee of spirit beings to help you with whatever you needed, be it selling a house, getting a new job or whatever problem you were trying to solve. Apparently as I had heard before, due to universal law of free will, non-physical beings could not interfere on your behalf without your permission; you had to invite them in.

So, I created the 'Devo Transition Committee'. Yes, I hired a team of spirits essentially to help Devo die. I hired a Spiritual Transition Guide to manage the entire team, a Spiritual Physical Specialist to help him detach and let go of his body, an Emotional Specialist to release any fears around dying, a Logistics Manager to show him where to go when he crossed over so he didn't get lost, a Welcome Team to make him feel at ease on the other side, a Soul Connector to put him more deeply in touch with his soul self and a few others to round out the team like the Spiritual Mixologist to make him a decent G&T when he arrived. I did a small ceremony to officiate the committee and state their mission:

To help Devo transition into the other side quickly and easily, without pain or fear. May he easily and swiftly leave his body behind and go where he needs to be. May this team please help all involved in his transition here with masses of love, light and grief support.

While I was at it, I created an 'Annie Management Committee.' I needed a LOT of specialists for that one! As soon as I did it I noticed an immediate difference in her demeanour towards me, and behaviour which was miraculous.

Only a few days later, I was with close friends and family gathered around his hospice bed, I was telling Devo it was okay to let go, that he was going on a big adventure, of which I was very jealous and that it was going to be bloody amazing. It was probably better than this earthly existence anyway, and he had better come to me in spirit so I had some evidence, since he was the first of us to go.

We were all emotionally exhausted after six months of living through this. We had a barbecue at my brother Mike's house that night, where I finally laid into the wine and let go. When my brother dropped me back home to Devo and Annie's it was after midnight and I stumbled down the bottom of the garden to my pad to crash out. Not long later at 3am that morning, there was a knock on the door of the boatshed where I was staying. I opened the stable door in a dehydrated daze to see Mike, who said that Devo had passed. He and I went to the hospice together to see Devo one last time and say our final goodbyes.

One night the week after he died I was lying in bed and the entire boatshed was filled with the smell of cigar smoke. I was confused looking for an open window to shut out the smoky neighbours, before I ascertained all the windows and doors were in fact shut. It took me a few more moments to realise it was Devo, famous for his indulgence in the finest cigars on any given occasion. It wasn't the last time I was visited with the scent of cigars, and I'm sure there will be many more.

It would be two years before I finally told Annie about the 'Devo Transition Committee' and that days later, he was gone.

"What!" she shrieked dramatically. "You killed my husband?!"

Peace, peace, peace. Calm yourself into the deep space of peace.
For there is much friction at this time. On many
levels, some far beyond your comprehension.

Feel in the flow and go with what needs to be done, needs to be
said, needs to be brought to the surface to cleanse and release.
Bring peace upon you for this is not the time for war.

Let it go, let it go. let it go. No longer worry about others.
For they have their own journeys. It does not serve you, nor another.
What is a priority and the utmost importance is your own journey.
What will be will be. Leave that to the divine.

We ask you to participate in frequencies of the new consciousness.
For this is who you are now.
There is no need to resort to the old in these times.
For that is not who you came to be.
You no longer carry this energy, and it is jarring to engage in it.
You bear the cross, which is not yours to bear.

Be in your heart. Speak your truth. And know that this is enough.

The time is not now to be shaken out of your beingness.
Be vigilant now, with your words, thoughts, actions.
Be vigilant with your truth.
And guard it with your life.

The Sexual Flexitarian

I'd been fucking the pain away for some months while Devo was dying, with a strapping young twenty-seven-year-old American after we bonded over his story of his brother's leukaemia illness on a date. He had excellent banter, was pretty easy on the eye and was apparently an ex-Paratrooper. The sex was intoxicating, but he was hard to pin down which made me suspicious, although I wasn't particularly bothered in the haze of pain and grief. So when I found out he had a girlfriend but was "in an open relationship" I wasn't fazed. Although slightly perturbed that he hadn't been honest with me in the beginning when I asked outright. Why wouldn't you be if it was all out in the open as he said? I woke up to a text the next day following the Paratrooper's confession, which had been sent in the wee hours. "Sorry I became that guy. If you happen to want lots of orgasms and stuff. Come join. She really loves girls…"

Now this was a very different spin on this whole escapade. My sexual appetite was raging, like an unsatisfied lioness who had gotten the leftovers of yesterday's kill. The threesome carrot had been dangled and the more I thought about it, the more I wanted it. I had never been particularly into girls, but if she was going to have her way with me, I wasn't going to stop her. That, combined with having amazing sex with him at the same time, seemed like I'd be winning all around really. Kind of like winning the pleasure island lottery.

However, as time went on he was becoming more and more elusive and unreliable. I had finally gotten to a point at thirty-eight where I simply was not going to allow myself to be treated as less than I deserved, let alone fourth on a priority list. I wrote him off in my head, letting the sex go and not pursuing him or the illicit fantasy any longer. He soon faded into the distance.

Three months later, I received a text in the wee hours of the morning. "You likely hate me. I am likely drunk. Can we have great sex again???" Always good to keep them wanting more. However, he had very much missed the boat. By that point, I was sharing my bed with a girl.

Through a strange sequence of events, Gostosa and I ended up shopping for a man to have a threesome with one night. She was a beautifully vivacious Brazilian who was almost Amazonian-looking with her tall, fit and lean body. She was a little tomboyish but there was great beauty hidden behind the façade. She had a killer smile and beautiful big doe brown eyes framed with long dark lashes. After I met her through my brother, I had been randomly bumping into her around town for months, and this particular time she was my saviour. We were tucked away in the corner at a party where I was lamenting about my unfulfilled threesome fantasies with the Paratrooper, while trying to avoid the drunken guy at a party who had eagerly recognised me from Tinder.

Somehow late in the evening we escaped to a bar where she was suddenly eyeing up potential talent. This intention was never discussed, it just seemed to manifest itself over the course of the evening. Despite the fun of man-shopping, after a few potentials went nowhere, we called it quits after the bars shut. We weren't going to settle for anything less than the best.

At the scene of a last stop at my place for a quiet nightcap on the way home, she planted one on me.

"Ummm, wh, wh, wh, what are you doing? I'm not sure this is a good idea," I said, stammering as I back-pedalled out of the situation. "I don't want to ruin our friendship," I added hastily, in hindsight also hilariously, since we were more acquaintances than friends.

She ignored this and continued to kiss me before I blurted out, "I've never done this before!"

"What?" She looked at me, genuinely shocked and confused.

"With all the things we were talkin' about, I just assumed..." she said in her beautifully rhythmic accent.

"Nope. Never been with a girl before."

"Okaaaayyyyy," she said slowly, her deep brown eyes widening.

"I'll make us another drink, shall I?" I said, trying to alleviate the awkwardness. We had another couple of drinks, and talked and made out some more. That first night was quite awkward and weird for both of us, but there was no doubt we got on like a house on fire. I had certainly wondered why she kept appearing in my life for months. There seemed to be something undeniable drawing us together like a magnet.

We continued hanging out on the hunt for a guy to fulfil my threesome dreams. It was basically any guy's fantasy, a hot thirty-one-year-old Brazilian and a thirty-nine-year-old Kiwi who was in the best shape of her life, thanks to my militant exercise regime during the grief of the last nine months. There was plenty of opportunity to show-pony around, pashing in public and garnering lots of attention from all avenues in our pursuit of a man for a threesome. We even joined 3nder, which most people pronounced 'Thrinder' and/or referred to it as the 'Tinder for Threesomes', which eventually ended up in a legal battle. However, we had our champagne and oysters profile pic uploaded and we were good to go.

On a few occasions we were all teed up and ready for action with a potential contender when Brazilian Girl put the kibosh on it. After a few sets of blue balls, I soon began to realise that Brazilian Girl didn't really want a man involved at all. What she really wanted was me.

I was still freshly grieving, and Brazilian Girl provided beautiful, nurturing energy for me in the year after Devo died. We were tender and soft, and cared about each other deeply. I felt supported and safe enough to heal without any of the pressures of men. In addition, she had overflowing, bubbly energy and was fantastically up for anything. Every week we were on some new adventure, whether it be hiking, spiritual travel, surfing, camping, meditating, clubbing or just chilling out and cooking an incredible meal. The fun included a series of big nights out over the course of many months; we were partying with unashamed abandon. The partying certainly helped with my inhibitions and experimentation, but I seemed to be more attracted to her contagious passionate personality, than her sexually. Don't get me wrong, she was a super sexy young Brazilian woman with a great rack of envy-igniting thirty-year-old boobs, but I'd just never had any kind of physical attraction to females before. For me it ticked almost all the boxes; I was loved and adored the way I truly wanted to be, I was supported emotionally, and I was able to share my spiritual life and deepest thoughts honestly and completely. When she was Yin, I was Yang, and vice versa. It was an amazing partnership. We ebbed and flowed and had the most incredible time together, growing, shifting, releasing, changing, expanding on a multitude of adventures.

It took some time to get used to this different way of doing and being, but it was fun to experiment, nonetheless and our connection was undeniable. My mind, however, was having a hard time with this new reality: the reality of being in a same-sex relationship. It is all well and good being a supporter of the LBGT community, having a myriad of gay friends and being a regular at the gay pride festivals, but when I found myself in a relationship with someone on my own team it was a whole different experience. As the months flew by, I had periodic freak-outs as I navigated my fears and doubts, judgement of myself and judgement from others.

It took me forever to tell anyone. Mainly because I wasn't sure myself. Not long after I told my brother he made a joke in his usual insanely brutal style for a crowd, "Well Jo's full name is actually Joanna Lesley Anne Walden," he said. "Or should we say Joanna Les-bi-an Walden!" Everyone roared with laughter. I was always slightly paranoid that everyone thought I was gay given all my friends were married with kids years ago, so it stung. "Still no man?" they'd ask every time I came back to New Zealand for a visit. And my favourite, "You better get a move on my girl if you want to have kids." Yes, because finding a man and pumping out kids was living the dream. Obviously.

A whole host of young, hot celebs like Kristen Stewart, Cara

Delevingne and Miley Cyrus had recently been all over the media as coming out bi or pansexual, but although I was massively on trend, it was hard for me to fathom and comprehend this experience in myself. I struggled internally with it all, but I knew I had to experience it on a soul level to allow me to see parts of myself that were living in fear. I always saw life as an incredible, divine reality that fed us experiences with people, places and things to show us where we needed to do the work, and this had not changed. The work itself was to uncover our programming and limited beliefs, to completely transform and awaken ourselves to our own magnificence.

This was a big one for me, bringing up a lot of material to work through in the realm of growth and healing of my intimate relationships. The issue was, no matter what I did, I was still feeling the same feelings of doubt. I didn't have the natural sexual urges I had towards previous lovers yet everything else worked so well. We experimented with everything; vibrators, strap-ons, body parts, dress up, porn. The Brazilian Girl was incredibly proficient down there, showering me with teasing kisses, touch and love.

As time went on I got more used to it and I was at least able to come, mostly. It just happened to help when I thought of being banged relentlessly by a giant cock. This was the most amazing relationship I had ever had, yet it had a distinct piece missing for me and therefore I was plagued with confusion. Grief can also kill your libido, and I wasn't feeling hugely attracted to guys either to be fair. This only clouded things further.

The funny thing was, it felt acutely amplified in my crazy over-thinking mind because I wasn't actually technically gay. However, society loves their labels. It was like a double whammy being judged for being gay when I wasn't actually gay, which no one could understand given I'd been in a relationship with a girl for a year. I get that this was a lot for people to get their head around, that I didn't fit into their little box, but I was sexually fluid, having fun and experimenting. In my heart of hearts, I knew there was a soul contract going on here. I was attracted to her soul, to work through my shadow and experience a soul expansion together, not the fact that she was a woman. I was, in fact, learning to see beyond gender.

Although I could see the bigger picture of it all from a soul level, I oscillated between being liberated enough to go with it, and just not being able to go there at all. Girl sex for me was like endless foreplay, never quite sealing the deal, never quite one hundred percent satisfying and never quite floating my boat. It didn't matter how amazing the loving was. It just didn't make me tick.

Your definition of love is small and clouded in the human experience.
But love cannot be defined.
For it is expansion, it is joy, it is the wild oneness of peace.
It comes to you in many forms, unbounded and without constriction.
But perception is limiting the bounds of this love.
So, an adjustment of perception and consciousness is required.

Be open, take advantage of the limitless opportunities available to you.
Beyond what the mind knows and can hold.
For the container of the mind is too small for
the vast perception of the heart.
The technology of the heart, just now being discovered,
has far more to know and available to you through the heart.

Explore your heart. Play in the heart.
Leave the mind at home and adventure out
into the vast expansiveness in joy.
The excitement the heart brings is the key.
For it is here that your ability to manifest your
greatest desires is aligned. In truth.
Of oneness and the truth of all that is.

The heart, the heart, the heart.
Don't define your heart based on your linear mind. Feel into it.
Feel into the greatness, the expansion, the limitlessness.
For the heart is never-ending. Through all space and time.
The heart lives on. It is an energy not a muscle.
It is where to live from. It is where no conflict lies.
It is the space of freedom. The freedom you wish to find.

The Punani Says No

One weekend I took Brazilian Girl up to Kawau Island, my old childhood holiday house. I cooked us both a lovely dinner of crispy duck legs with a mushroom and red wine sauce, served over celeriac mash with some sautéed Jerusalem artichoke. We toasted the meal, my first cooking duck, her favourite, with a bottle of 2000 Brunello di Montalcino picked from Devo's cellar. The duck was a sumptuous success and feeling the effects of too much wine I enjoyed the sparks and flames of the open fire lying on the couch as Brazilian Girl fussed around it, making sure it was giving out enough heat to keep me warm. She came back and joined me as we lay cuddled together on the couch. We always fit so well together, which I found surprising as I never envisioned feeling so content wrapped in the arms of a woman. I always thought I would miss the gigantic arms of a man's embrace, making me feel safe and small.

She was talking about how happy she was with me. How she felt so fulfilled. How she had never felt like this before. How I was her everything. "I want to talk to you about my dream," she said. "But let's talk about it tomorrow."

My tears plummeted down onto her sweater in a small downpour, like a waterfall after the rain. The tears were coming quicker than I could raise my hand to my eye to wipe them away from view. My nose was filling with snot and I got up quickly, hiding my face, to compose myself in the bathroom.

"What is going on?" she asked.

"No, it's not the time. I don't want to discuss things after drinking so much." I said, grabbing more wine, but as I lay there the dam was broken and I couldn't stop the tears.

"Come on. This is not fair. Just tell me," she pleaded, her

face holding back the horror of what she was about to hear. I had to be honest and I had to speak my truth. No matter how much I knew I was going to hurt her.

"There is just something missing… " I started. "I love you, deeply, and we have such a great relationship, an amazing time together always, but nothing has changed from the same problem I always had. I struggle with this sexually," I said.

"What am I even doing here?" she yelled half screaming, half crying.

I knew we had a choice in this moment, to deal with it in a conscious expansive way, or go into the drama. It was awful but I had to love myself enough to want to try and find the full package. A relationship that satisfied me on all levels.

I sobbed, as she cradled me in her arms. "Every time you want me, and you rip my clothes off and I don't feel that back. It hurts me, and it hurts you." I said, choking. "You deserve to be loved fully, and completely by someone. We both do."

I felt horrific. I was a little drunk. Very emotional. And sick to my stomach full of duck.

"I want to feel desired. It's clear you don't desire me. I just thought that love was enough. You proved me wrong, I'm sorry," she said, her gorgeous little face forlornly looking down at her fidgeting hands.

"I've had a recurring dream for months. And in every dream, you go off fucking these guys," she said quietly. "And then finally this morning, I dreamt that you didn't go off with the guys. You wanted me. You finally desired me, and it felt so good. I can't believe I had that dream and now you are breaking up with me," she said. "I've never felt insecure with anyone the way I do with you," she said between snot and tears.

"Well that's because I never gave you anything to feel secure about," I said, very aware of my own shortcomings in the situation. "C'mon, it's time for bed," I said, making a move from the couch towards the fire grate to secure it for the night.

We cried ourselves to sleep and I awoke a few hours later to her sobbing quietly in the dark. "I don't know what to do. I don't know where to be. My whole life is a mess. I felt safe and secure with you, despite everything. Now… I have nothing," she said, hyperventilating with deep grief.

Why does honouring yourself and doing the right thing have to be so painful? How is that right, true or just in this world? I thought.

She asked me questions. Had I ever felt aroused by her? Was there any time when it was good? I'd debated this in my head for months. I'd questioned myself continuously.

Could it be that I was scared of the societal ramifications of being in a long term same sex relationship? Or was I blocking myself sexually because of fear? Was sex really more important to me than having someone I could trust, rely on, have fun with, love me wholly and completely, warts and all? Someone who loved me in a way I had never been loved before? Did sex even matter if we are all ascending into higher dimensions? Could it be that this was a karmic lesson of unconditional love and trust?

She asked me if she could have done anything better? Anything different to satisfy me?

"It's not you. You are perfect. I could not have asked for a better partner in this journey. I think it may be the same case for any girl as I've never been naturally attracted to women," I said as I sat up suddenly to take some deep breaths. The nausea was overwhelming. I ran to the bathroom and dry retched, but nothing came out.

Back in bed she said, "I feel like the nice guy who finishes last," crying again. "You let me be who I am," she said. "I am fully comfortable around you, to be myself. I can say absolutely anything to you and I've never felt that way before. That's why I wanted to spend every minute with you. To take you everywhere. I'd drive seven hours down to Mahia for you. I'd fly across the country for you. I'd go anywhere for you. Just to be with you."

The tears continued to fall in our embrace, and we drifted back to sleep for a few more hours. We finally got up and washed each other gently in the shower. A soft kiss here. A small joke there. She wrapped the towel around me drying me all over. "You must get all the folds," she said. "My mother always said that."

"Are you saying I'm fat?" I exclaimed.

And with cheeky eyes she gave my crotch a dramatic rub. "It's your punani's fault," she said definitively. "If it weren't for that we wouldn't have a problem," she said.

"It's true," I replied. "I can't change what my sexual urges are though. My punani has a mind of its own."

"Well… I'm going to ask the Lemurians and Pleiadians and all the beings of light and love to fix your punani!" she said with a melancholy laugh. "To do some alterations."

I mustered a soft giggle trying not to cry again. I had to hand it to her, she was an amazing lateral problem solver that's for sure. Always trying to find a way around things. She never took no for an answer.

Back in the bedroom, before I could even grab my clothes off the floor, she had thrown me on the bed and was kissing me from my neck down to my feet. Hundreds of tiny little kisses. Kisses everywhere. She hovered over my nether region and looked at me under fluttering lashes before diving in. She was putting her heart and soul into it. She always did. She was always determined to give me pleasure. I honestly wished I could have that natural urge within me, for her, in the way that she did for me, but the chemistry just wasn't there.

"What about you?" I asked, as she would often do herself at the same time given my feelings. I just couldn't bring myself to touch her one more time.

We walked down the hill through the ferns en route to The Cathedral, a sacred grove of puriri trees.

As we walked holding hands, breathing in the sun and surveying the mudflats at low tide, the seagulls squawked away the silence as the swoosh of a wood pigeon's wings flew by into a puriri tree for the last of the summer berries. We talked of fond memories. "Remember when I asked you to be my girlfriend at Danielle's fortieth birthday?" she said. "I was really happy that day. And then the next day you freaked out."

"Yeah," I said. "I remember."

Heading into the bush a giant wallaby bounced across the path in the distance and I could hear his heavy thumps as he thundered away. "I know I have truly enjoyed and valued every moment I have had with you," said Brazilian Girl. "And I am truly thankful for that," she said, looking at me with those adoring eyes. She squeezed my hand again and looked back to the track. My eyes were filled with liquid heartbreak.

Ten minutes later we got to The Cathedral. The early afternoon sun was streaming through the trees throwing dappled light to pattern the bed of leaves upon which we walked. There were some green plastic chairs and an old table, so we grabbed a chair each wiping off the few raindrops and dead leaves.

Sitting to meditate, I was just finding the stillness when Brazilian Girl leapt out of her chair trying to escape a curious bush fly. Her irrational fear of insects still cracked me up given she was from the insect capital of the world. She never would have survived with my animal menagerie in Abadiânia. I heard the crunching of leaves as she moved into the distance to reposition herself. The interruption totally threw me off, so after some visualisation and general distractedness I peeked a look to see her sitting cross-legged in meditation at the base of a big puriri tree, the roots holding her there in their embrace. I could see right through to the beauty and peace of her soul. My tears joined the trickle of water I could hear from the stream next to us.

I moved carefully across the leaves trying to disturb the peace as little as possible and parked up next to her at the base of the tree. I tried to mediate again but was overwhelmed by emotion and spinning thoughts. I silently asked the nature for healing, for the plants, devas and elementals to please help move some of this grief and pain through me, and her. To help transmute it into the light from which it came. I asked for a thousand angels to surround us both in their healing embrace.

I heard some light rustling next to me and opened my eyes. Brazilian Girl was looking down at the base of a scallop shell she held in her hands. She dug her hands through the dead leaves and into the earth in front of her, placing the shell inside and then covering it over with debris. I knew she was burying her sadness. Burying the pain of the last couple of days. And I started to cry again.

She leapt up and made her way towards the huge ancient tree at the back of the Cathedral. She was standing down at its base, the roots taller than her up to the small cliff where the tree was positioned. Magical roots intertwined from great heights, almost creature-like coming out of the earth. She had her hand against one of the roots, eyes closed, as I looked on from the ridge above.

"C'mon – let's walk down the river?" she asked.

I climbed down in amongst the dead branches, leaves and ferns. She was bounding ahead, and I struggled to keep up, unable to see through my teary eyes magnifying everything into an unfocused blur. She waited for me at the next turn in the stream as we got to another maze of roots.

I sobbed, "I think we should ask The Cathedral to take all of our sadness and wash it away."

"I've already done that," she said, quietly.

When the stream turned to mud, we leapt back up the bank and out via the traditional track, arm in arm.

"Let's go to the pier?" she said as we reached the turn-off and hung a left over the bridge and down the concrete path to the wharf. The wharf had aged so much from what I remembered. It was rickety and in need of some TLC. I couldn't spot any stingrays as the tide was too far out.

I took a seat to enjoy the view and Brazilian Girl joined me, placing her cellphone on my knee, smiling at me as she stepped forward a few steps to the edge of the wood and then before I knew it, she was diving off, fully clothed. I jumped up and ran to the edge of the wharf.

"Oh my God, what are you doing? Isn't it freezing?" I said.

"Yup," she said grinning. "It certainly is."

"Well I hope you are asking Yemanja (the goddess of the sea) to cleanse you while you are in there!"

"Yup already did that," she said submerging herself again.

"That's why I love you," I said. "You crazy Brazilian you."

Go softly.
For it is in the softness of your tread that can offer the greatest healing.
Notice this does not make logical sense however be assured this is in truth.

Softly, softly.
The energy of the mother's love.
The divine feminine in her purest form.
Basking in her glow.
Softly, softly as she goes.

We are here for you. With the great love of eons of time.
That has existed forever in the ether.
Waiting for you to awaken to this joy.
For the joy for you, is the joy of love, and is the joy of all.

We are thankful for you bringing your particular
love vibration to the earth.
To the galaxy, and the multiverse.
For all have the responsibility of their own love vibration.
The vibration of which the New Earth is built.
The old earth will not disappear. It will transform into something new.
A new energy, vibration, consciousness and
dimensional reality that serves all.

Let the darkness fade away and honour the light in all ways.
For you are light. And light is love and love is God.

Shapeshifters And Stargates

Off the back of the heart-wrenching break-up, I wanted to get away. I was researching information about sacred sites in New Zealand to explore, visit and attune to when I came across a woman I had never heard of before. This was rare for teeny tiny New Zealand, where we joke that we have zero degrees of separation. Soluntra had a hokey website that looked like a unicorn had vomited a rainbow on the screen. It was hard to read, and looked more like cosmic soup than anything; there was a lot of complex information and visuals.

She talked about all sorts of different suns, stargates, serpent wisdom, dragon lore, mandalas, DNA activation and the diamond light matrix. Every article I read sounded like a new crazy, cosmic adventure undertaking light work for the planet towards unity, consciousness and the New Earth. Despite the unpalatable design, I resonated with the energy behind it. I saw she was doing a star line journey to Lake Taupō, a New Zealand stargate in ten days for the upcoming winter solstice. 'The stargate you are, inner and outer, are one' the website said. I had no idea what this meant, but found myself emailing her to ask if there were any spots available. She responded right away that she could fit me in, and so I booked in on the spot, set to leave in six days. I was sent a bunch of info about gear and food requirements for the trip and the accommodation. For such a crazy, cosmic bird, she was certainly all over the detail, no airy-fairy business at all there.

Despite the emotional rollercoaster from the break-up, I was surprisingly on an even keel from the crystalline activations and empowered truth channelling course I had been completing for the last six weeks. I felt comfort in what I was doing and was keen to continue processing and expanding my energy.

The night before I was to head off to Taupō, I noticed I was extremely headachy going to sleep, to the point where I was scrunching up my face in pain under the covers. I thought this very unusual, as I was well hydrated and had been having a healthy week with no wine the last few days in preparation for the solstice energy work. I finally dropped off to sleep despite the pain and found myself in the midst of a dream where I was a crystal crime fighter. It was the style of the 1970s TV show *Monkey Magic*, with me flying all over the cosmos and doing battles with a small bag of crystals against an ancient Chinese man who looked exactly like Mr Miyagi from *The Karate Kid*. Every time I thought I had won; he came back with a vengeance and there was another battle. There was no blood and guts however; it almost felt like training.

The dream culminated in a final battle wherein I eventually triumphed by remembering to use five specific pink crystal stones; my rose quartz buddha, bright pink agate, mauve heart-shaped ametrine, magenta fluorite and a pink amethyst. They were very important stones for me in this dream. After the battle was finished, I had to hide and keep the crystals safe and out of sight, and ensure they were not damaged, such was their grand importance in a wider cosmic plan. Then I woke up.

As I was driving down to Taupō and contemplating the meaning of this vivid dream, a memory of reference of one of my guides being a wise old Chinese man came flooding back into my consciousness. Then I suddenly realised the same man had actually appeared in my dreams twice in the last few months; the first time, showing me shapeshifting as he melded in and out of a pile of luggage on my front porch, and then in another, teleporting. All of them were some kind of teaching dream. Of course, he was my guide! Finally, I had proper radio contact!

I arrived at the Tokaanu Lodge down the southern end of Lake Taupō at dusk as the temperature plummeted. It was certainly a fair few degrees colder than Auckland. No one seemed to be around, so I just checked into my alpine style self-contained unit which I was sharing with an unknown quantity from the group. I felt a slight uneasiness at the prospect of this group journey and what it might bring.

While I was waiting for my lucky-dip roommate to arrive, I shuffled my Oracle of Illumination deck to draw cards for the journey ahead, when a card flew out and onto the floor. It was the Olive Gateway card of Co-operation. It spoke of how my resonance was designed to awaken others, and how there was the possibility to heal issues of vulnerability as I worked in partnership with fellow seekers. Emotional adjustments would take place as I surrendered to the Goddess. It was amazingly fitting, considering my internal dialogue. What if I needed an escape route?

My roommate was Deidre, a skinny, fifty-six-year-old woman with a thick and twangy Australian accent. She had a wide smile, a thick nose, and a hint of native Australian culture in a way; she was hardened and weathered, like the landscape she was from in outback Victoria. This was her first time working with Soluntra in person. Neither of us knew what to expect, or really what we were doing, so I felt better knowing that I wasn't the only one.

That night we had to do a meditation to connect and get all our chakras spinning before we went to sleep, and set our intention to go on a soul travel to Meads Wall, where we would be physically working the next day. I had never done soul travel before, but apparently it was relatively easy. You don't usually remember anything consciously and Soluntra would come and pick us all up to make sure we didn't get lost and went to the right place. The following morning, I had no recollection of any soul travel, as I had spent most of the night, oddly wide awake.

We met the rest of the ten people at Soluntra's unit the next morning, where she handed out a pack of information and mandalas for the work we were to do over the next five days. We stood in a circle holding hands to align, ground and connect the group, through a meditation using all of the available suns – from the sun within our hearts, right up through all of the galactic suns up to Source energy, and down to the inner sun within the earth. We were a conduit for the energy, up to source and down into the earth. I never knew there were so many suns, but I went with it, following the meditation as we linked up around the circle. Apparently, the ancient civilisation of Atlantis had messed up the earth's connection to the stars with their advanced technology, so this whole mission was about reopening the connection to bring the star lines in through the stargate in Lake Taupō on the solstice.

In order to do this, our physical bodies would act as a conduit between heaven and earth. The itinerary was daily activations and clearings with sound and light at various sacred sites that were energy portals or contained a certain energetic resonance to prepare us for this work. We would be healing, transfiguring and upgrading not only our physical bodies, but our emotional, mental, spiritual and light bodies in order to hold more light and embody more higher dimensional consciousness. The intricacies of all this was like Soluntra was talking Swahili. I had no idea what she was on about, but it sounded like a cool adventure, and I was always up for an adventure that was for sure.

Soluntra spoke about dark forces such as the terrorists, reptilians and illuminati losing their grip on the fabric of our reality, which is why things were getting worse on the planet before it would get better. She said that when we were in unity consciousness we wouldn't hold on to any of this anymore; it would go right through us. Old paradigm thinking was being discarded. It didn't escape me that this was also what Hugo the shaman in Argentina was talking about, albeit in different lingo.

"Gurus used to tell people, 'you are not your body,' to keep people controlled and trapped via old paradigm thinking. But you are your body and it is light," she said. "We are only trapped in the third dimension (or 3D, meaning a perception of reality or a state of consciousness) by fear. As soon as you clear that, it ceases to exist."

We did various clearings, looking at whatever came into our awareness when working on a particular area, as this was what needed to be addressed. It didn't matter if we couldn't identify it, but if we could, we were not to judge it, but to drill more into it via questioning, to bring it deeper into our conscious awareness for release. At one point, I felt like I was being strangled. I felt more and more constriction to my throat as the exercise went on. It came to me that I was being strangled for speaking my voice as the light of God in some other life or dimensional reality I had existed in. Whatever it was, was still in my energy field viscerally so I breathed into it, with love, acceptance, honour and thanks, breathing until it dissipated.

We then worked with twenty-three mandalas for the activation of the chakra system and our light body. Each mandala had sound codes with it, which we sang three times with our eyes closed after breathing the mandala into each chakra.

"Your life and body are the best barometers of where you are at," Soluntra said. "We take on imprints of information to be of service when we incarnate into the physical, to clear or transmute for the group soul or the collective." My body was buzzing after all of the breathing, singing, visualising and activating.

After lunch I volunteered to drive up Ruapehu mountain to our first sacred site, Meads Wall. Two other girls joined Deidre and I to carpool up the mountain. One was a bubbly young Chinese-Australian girl who lived in Sydney, called Diana. The other was Shivani, who lived in Auckland and was of African heritage but looked more of Indian descent. She had one slightly mysterious eye which sometimes appeared closed or more open, which made sense in an ironic way once I realised she was some kind of 'seer'.

It was rainy by the time we left to drive up Mount Ruapehu, a sacred mountain not only to the Māori but anyone who is energetically aware. It broke to a few rays of sun halfway up and I wondered if the Elemental beings were going to hold off the weather for us, as we had so humbly requested. When we got up the mountain there was snow everywhere and the learners Happy Valley ski field was open, with many enjoying the first early snow of the season.

The rain started through the mist as we passed the cafe and ski lifts out the back, through the snow towards Meads Wall.

There was a rock climber scaling the wall right by where we were sitting to perform our work. I bet he'll find this 'interesting' I thought, wondering what other people would think of us chanting and meditating and singing.

It became clear that the water element was necessary for our work there, as the rain was relentless for the duration. It made sense though, considering we were working with water codes and light templates, which were being anchored in this place. I was huddled under my umbrella, as I didn't have any waterproof pants. I had unsurprisingly prepared poorly given the trip was so last minute. I felt the intense cold through my rain jacket, without proper warm gear underneath and no gloves. We were there for a couple of hours and it became abundantly apparent that this was not the wisest choice of attire in the blustery freezing conditions.

We were activating at this particular site called Meads Wall because of its energetic nature as a hyper-dimensional doorway. This wasn't because it had been in the *Lord of the Rings* films I'll have you know, but because of its energetic significance as a portal to access different dimensions simultaneously, which assisted in the energetic work we were to perform. We connected and grounded, used our coloured mandalas and singing of the toning sounds, working with different forms of our light bodies to prepare for our journey through the doorway. We worked with vibrational essences that Soluntra specifically created from the wall at the Equinox two years previously. These were absorbed into our energy bodies to help clear out any trapped patterns and programmes affecting our lives via our cellular memory so we could be clear for this sacred mission.

Then we finally moved, in meditation, through the doorway to meet with the Council of Light, a collective group of higher energy beings who oversee various planetary assignments. They were there to discuss what was about to occur at the solstice. I was usually not able to 'see' beings clairvoyantly, so I connected through my imagination. I sang myself an operatic entrance into the meeting and went on a magical journey that was so clear I was astounded. I also asked for help with my writing and mission on this planet.

I came to, abruptly when my umbrella slid to the side. Deep in meditation and my other-worldly journey, I had forgotten I was holding it up the entire time. I steadied myself and then went back into the meditation, but it was difficult with the umbrella. I opened one eye, looking around me at all the snow and our group perched on the rocks in the pouring rain, clutching mandalas. I had to laugh. The places I find myself in, honestly!

I was thankful when the meditation finished. My hands were burning with the cold after having to hold the umbrella up for hours on end. I poured some tea from my thermos and then readied myself to leave as we climbed up through the rocks to the top of the wall. The wall was a huge, solid piece of rock that went way down into the ravine below at an elevation of above 1100m. The true scale of it could only be seen from this angle at the top. Apparently, a few of the group had seen the rock climber shapeshifting as he was climbing the wall while we were doing our activations. What? A real live shapeshifter and I had missed it! What were the chances? I was gutted, especially considering my shapeshifting dream months ago.

The second day we headed off to Lake Taupō, first stopping to energetically greet the lake, great vortex and stargate. In 2008 NASA scientists discovered that every eight minutes a network of magnetic portals on the earth connect with the sun. Energy portals of this kind were spoken about in ancient texts, often found at sacred sites, which were in fact stargates and linked up to the cosmos through these doorways.

I had been woken up to someone calling my name, during the night, which reminded me of the last time this strangely happened when I was at John of God. I asked Soluntra for any insight.

"Well, it's pretty high frequency at John of God, isn't it?" she said. "And the work we are doing is very high frequency too. The old spiritual paradigm would have called this a 'guide', but perhaps it was some aspect of you that was trying to get your attention." I was certainly feeling all the energy work already and I was excited to see what was to come.

We went to a spot further north on the lake in preparation for the next stage of our work. We started off with a connecting mudra, a movement using the entire body to anchor our kundalini energies. We were made aware of our role of guardians of the earth, and then sang songlines of light through the planet to where energy needed to be repaired, in the grids. We did a meditation using the crown chakra as a lotus flower, and mandalas for help clearing karmic gunk through the grids. This would clear the way for the star line energies to come through the stargate during the solstice.

We picked a role out of the hat to prepare what we needed to individually do for the finale solstice mission in two days. There was Co-ordinator Of The Cycles, the Holographic Harmoniser, the Oracle/Seer, the Code Keeper, the Cosmologist, the Crystal Guardian, the Cosmic Messenger, the Light Energy Technologist, the Multiverse Bridger, the Elemental Systems Co-ordinator and the Ray Balancer. I pulled Cosmic Messenger, which seemed appropriate. It dawned on me that I needed to tell Victoria, who was the Crystal Guardian, about my crystal crime fighting dream and the power of the pink stones.

"The stargate is not like a normal multi-dimensional doorway. It is a state of being. You are the stargate, the union of form and non–form, which is within us all as the conduit between heaven and earth," said Soluntra.

As we sat by the lake she then guided us into this state of non-form while in form, in our body, through breath awareness. We went out into the vastness of the Universe, and then into the stillness and centre within. The stargate of the lake, and us as the Earth stargate, were all integrated as one.

The next stop was Craters of the Moon, a walk-through geothermal activity; where there was also another portal of an 'Inner Earth Doorway,' which was important for connection with the Elementals and for their part of the solstice mission. There were massive craters with steaming mud dotted around the site. I was amazed at some of the ferns and bracken which could survive in amongst the heat, simply incredible, enduring plants. An absolute miracle.

We sat on the wooden-planked walkway for a meditation and it was nice to feel the warmth seep from the ground into my boots. Upon connecting with the Elementals in meditation, they showed me the image of a single open eye. I asked what this meant, and I suddenly got that 'they were keeping an eye on things.' So, they literally gave me the picture of 'an eye.' I had to laugh.

We walked around to a second vortex in the park. This crater was covered with thick spurting steam, loudly whooshing as we overlooked it from the platform above. I saw Soluntra grabbing her camera and pointing it at the rock face that was the outer border for the edge of the crater.

"I have to capture this roaring dragon," she said.

I glanced over to my right and saw the rock face at the bottom shaped exactly like a dragon's head, with a beautiful slanted eye defined from the rock. It was facing upwards and I could see the mouth was blowing a constant stream of steam. I tried to capture it on video but the mist flooded in and I missed my opportunity. I was amazed. Had I just seen a dragon? My very first dragon?

That night, I dreamt I was going out surfing and it was very rough. Some guy helped me as I started struggling in the huge waves. He took me right down under the water to the bottom of the ocean, where it was safer. A gigantic wave came and crashed down with such thundering force that I felt it vibrate heavily all through me, almost crushing me. He showed me some special V-shaped ridged rocks way down at the bottom, V-shaped symbols that weren't just a part of nature, but something more. These V shapes were causing this unexpected alchemy, which was why there was such a big crash in that particular spot. Then, after the big wave, I rushed into the shore, timing it right to race out on to the sand as the water sucked me back in with force as the next wave came. I made it out okay.

The light symbols that you see are the portal to the new world.
The new life you dream of and the experiences
you wish to bring through.
The self-imposed limitation is the only barrier to these experiences.
For consciousness plays a huge part in this, and your
consciousness is one with your reality. And therefore,
your reality is the provider of your experiences.

Knowing is your origins. This is your strength.
The strength of knowing the fortitude of the light
above all else and through all things.
For we have been through times of darkness as have you.
Which is of divine perfection and the harmonious
balance called for by the universal law.

Relax and flow. Remove the barriers of the mind and you will know.
We are one with you. As is this knowing.
Think of this from the inside out and you will side step the mind.
Because we lie deep within, as a facet of your divine being,
a true facet of the diamond you are.

Connected By Water

The next part of the mission the following day was to Lake Rotopounamu, another sacred site and small crater lake just south of Lake Taupō. Here we would be working with the element of water and my significant dream about water the night before was interestingly aligned. My dreams had seemed to become far more prophetic and linked to what I was doing in my physical world of late, which I noted with great interest.

The vortex of this sacred lake was the spinner wheel for the earth's chakra system that would send the star line's energy through the earth's grids, vortex and chakra points. Learning about the energetic role of different parts of our planet was fascinating to me. Just like the role of all of the elements that make up our physical body, and their energetic significance that I learned about in kinesiology and eastern medicine, there is more than meets the eye to that tree or lake or hill that might be in front of you. The earth has chakras or energy centres just like we do in our bodies which is why there is more energy aligned with these places.

Interestingly Soluntra said that the crown chakra of the earth, currently in Mount Kailash in Tibet was moving as the earth evolved, and was now anchored in Mount Titiroa, right here in the South Island of New Zealand. People would still make pilgrimages to Mount Kailash for years to come and it may take three hundred years for the energy and awareness to completely switch entirely to this new location, but I was enthralled with this information. I had heard various prophecies over the years about New Zealand being the place of 'first light', which would be the first country to 'wake up' due to its significant energies anchored here from previous ancient advanced civilisations of Lemuria. All of this of course was out of the bounds of our current understanding of science and history.

The lake was a twenty minute walk through gorgeous native bush of mānuka, nīkau palms, ponga tree ferns and giant tōtara and rimu trees. Everything glistened from the morning dew as the sun beamed through. I could hear the fantails chirping away, and another bird I didn't recognise singing up in the trees. As we were walking the track, I noticed an older Māori man hobbling along the path. He was very thin, shaking a lot and walking in bare feet. I felt emotion welling up from my heart as I passed him, saying "Good Morning," on the way through. He looked like an amazing being, on some kind of pilgrimage and I silently asked for the angels to be with him and help him on his way.

We stopped at the first beach we came to at the southern end of the lake. As we energetically greeted the lake and took photos in the beautiful morning light, I noticed the old Māori man arrive, drop his backpack and walk straight into the water. He stood there a few metres out, his rolled-up tracksuit pants getting wet on the ends from the lake, and I could hear him chanting beautiful Māori karakia, or prayers. A surge of emotion welled up from my chest again and my eyes filled with tears.

Soluntra finally arrived and we got up to do a sequence of connecting mudra, while trying to give the man his space. I let the tears fall, trying to keep it as quiet as I could, but knowing that I needed to let this emotion out, to fully expand into the heart opening that was on offer to me in this moment. I had trouble breathing after a while; my nose was blocked with snot, making the upside-down mudra a challenge.

We sat down under the trees, this time working with mandalas and sound codes to integrate our multi-dimensional selves, bringing in awareness and transmuting any blocks throughout different dimensions of reality we exist in as energy beings. I couldn't stop stealing glances at the old man. He was now holding crystals while in the water, and singing haunting Māori karakia to the lake, steadying himself on a small branch. I could see his body shaking severely, every ounce of him committed to this mission, despite his physical limitations.

Some minutes later the man came over and addressed our group. "I don't mean to disturb or interrupt," he said slowly, methodically, peacefully. "I know what you are doing here. You may have seen me doing my ceremony over there in the water. I am also doing this work. I am working with a team to support the crystalline grid."

Visibly shaking, he grasped at a thin branch, rebalancing himself as he struggled to stay upright. "I just wanted to tell you that I am here to anchor the energies and codes into the grid for the solstice tomorrow. I will come back tomorrow. And I may camp here. Well, I'm not sure, but I will be here for the solstice doing this work. There are others too. There is a group at Lake Titicaca in Bolivia. I'm not too sure exactly what they are doing, but I know they are there."

By this point there was no break between the tears, rolling down my cheeks like the endless waves of the ocean.

"Yes, there are lots of us doing this work now," Soluntra said. "Thank you so much for sharing with us, and everything that you are doing."

"Yes, I heard last there were four billion angelic beings who have come to help with this work on the earth. Well, I don't wish to interrupt, but I just wanted to say…" he said, as he turned slowly towards his ceremony spot and shakily made his way towards his backpack, where he lay down on a silver emergency blanket.

Wow. Just wow. I felt a huge heart-opening taking place in the centre of my chest, appreciating the amazing synchronicity of this man being here at the exact day and time that we were, the Universe conspiring to have us do our work here together, and amplify it, powerfully, in unity to prepare for the solstice.

We continued our work, this time working with some different light codes that Soluntra had channelled through in 2012 at Mt Shasta. Water connects everything on the earth, and all is connected energetically, so we were reprogramming our bodies (being seventy percent water), through light codes imbued into our water. We took a sip.

"We are bringing in new light codes through the water of our body, which is connected to all bodies of water on the planet, cleansing all toxins and impurities, harmonising, replenishing and rejuvenating each molecule. Through us, all water on the planet will be ready to receive the star lines. We are one heart, one earth, one cell. All One."

I got super headachy after the second code, my body reacting to the release. I drank a lot more water to clear it, and after a snack we packed up, moving toward our next spot around the lake. I said a heartfelt goodbye as I passed the man, "It was amazing to work with you," I said, holding my hands in prayer position with my head bowed towards him. He looked up, bringing his hands to prayer position in gratitude as we left.

We found another sunny spot to keep us warm for our next stop on the lake, where Soluntra guided us in working with plant essences.

"I've been making essences since the early 1980s," she said. "In nature, is everything we need. Now, we don't have to ingest it physically, we can receive it with love from the plant vibrationally instead. It's far too hard in 3D with all those little physical bottles, cleaning them and sending them, oh gosh, I did away with those years ago. I send everything vibrationally now."

I was amazed, yet it rang true. Of course, we didn't need to create or consume things physically. Everything in our reality is ultimately comprised of energy and vibration. It made complete sense to me.

I chose a jagged-edged leaf to work with. We connected with our hearts, tuning into the plants.

"Just become aware of which chakra, or it may be multiple chakras where you are receiving love from this plant. Or you can tune into what area of your physical body you may have felt this plant essence go, somewhere in need of balancing. Or where in your emotional body this essence is going, for any old stuck emotions. Where in your mental bodies does this plant transmute any old programmes, patterns and belief systems? And in your spiritual body, does this plant assist with anything to do with our experience here to awaken more fully our divinity?"

I scanned through each field that made up the entirety of my being as we went, getting information that this was for my mental and emotional bodies. I also understood that this plant was helping me to be less sensitive to others' energy and criticism, to have a thicker skin for my mission and book, to speak out about my conscious awareness through my holistic experiences and understanding. That made sense now that I thought about it, due to its jagged-looking shape. I also ascertained that it was to help with my hormones and ovaries.

We then asked how many times a day, and for how long this plant vibration needed to be delivered for us. Mine was for four weeks, five times per day. In that moment I also received the insight about my blocked creativity. When I was young I chose business over my natural inclination towards my creative and intuitive self, which had totally blocked these areas for me when I shut them off to myself. However, this could be strengthened easily; all I needed to do was follow the inspiration.

"Mt Pihanga to our right is not so much a mountain of crystal, but a mountain of consciousness of beings of the Earth and Stars. It is a meeting place and receives and transfers light through the Earth chakras and grids," said Soluntra.

She then guided us through an energetic doorway into the mountain where there was a gathering of many beings from many light councils, each with their own connection to the earth. What did I need to do for this solstice? The council put a magenta stone into my heart chakra. I needed to stay in the heart. They also put windscreen wipers on my third eye to keep it as clear as possible. Then I was given some symbols/codes from what looked like high priests, who made way behind them, for Isis. As the session came to a close it came to my awareness that I needed to drink tonnes of water this afternoon and tonight as a big flush was required to get rid of old cells, old programming and the old me.

We finished the afternoon by working on bringing in our diamond light body through guided meditation, mandala and singing song codes. I could feel the abundance of light pouring in, tingling as it rushed through my body. I could see the light flickering like sparkling diamonds behind my closed eyes. We had done all the energetic preparation work and we were now ready for the solstice.

Your will is done.
That is the power of the stargate you find yourself in at this time.
A surging forth of dimensional energies is flooding to your planet,
through you, anchoring the light at the capacity you are able.

Align with these energies, breathe them in and through you.
Intend for your expansion into oneness of all that is.
Peel back the layers, open yourself up to the
goodness from the galactics at this time.

The Greater Central Sun has many gifts to bestow on you, of divine
Source energy from above. And we, as the very aspects of you in
other dimensions, ask you to recognise us, claim us, own this within
yourselves to elevate you into other timelines of most benefit to you
in this now moment.

Be still and feel the power of this moment. Be still and feel the power of
your heart as you connect to the cosmic heart and the heart of our mother.
Through all hearts combined we step forward
into new territory. A new age.
And it starts within yourself.
For the self is the all that is.

'X' Marks The Solstice Spot

Wednesday dawned and the rain held off again as we left for the Tokaanu wharf at 6.45am. We lined up along the slippery old wharf, faced towards the east for the sunrise. I was thankful for the extensive cloud cover, which meant it was above freezing temperature. I could see a few black swans and smaller birds coming to life out of the darkness as it turned to light. We did some breathing, meditation and intentions to clear out anything not loved within the self as we stood waiting for the first rays of the sun.

At 7.24am the distant sky was tinged with orange, some minutes later concentrating to more of a scorched yellow at the very bottom of the horizon. We greeted the sun as it came up, feeling at one with everything as the rays came down into our hearts, through us into the earth and flowed out to all creation. It didn't last long, and the grey clouds prevailed, preventing a more striking start to the day.

Soluntra started singing, "We are one with the infinite sun, for ever, and ever, and ever."

The group joined in, as did I, but I couldn't help but feel a bit trite doing it. It was enough for me to be in the energy and appreciate the first rays without having to get all evangelical on it. For the love of God, couldn't the spiritual songs get a makeover please! As the colour spread to the tips of the sky, the many swans were now gliding across the silvery lake in morning light, crying out their morning greetings to each other. We meditated on our roles for the solstice again in the beautiful stillness, as the last of the pink-orange colour reflected out onto the water. Then it was back to the lodge and out of the cold for breakfast, and to pack our bags for the day out on the lake on a boat.

Soluntra had been told by spirit that morning that beings from the star Sirius had placed an energetic diamond at Motutaiko Island at the December 2012 solstice, especially for us to receive now, which would allow us to energetically hold the star lines through us. After a half an hour boat ride we reached the island, Captain Ed circled around it while we reconnected with our diamond light body, again using the meditation, mandalas and sound codes on the top deck.

I felt a lot of energy coming in as I absorbed it through my heart, and it dissolved. I welled up as Soluntra told us that this was not only preparation for the star lines, but also a special and personal gift for our own journey, which would unfold however it was meant to for each individual. I felt the immense love of these beings as we connected with the Sirians.

Our next stop was an 'x' that Soluntra drew on a tourist map, also channelled through that morning. Captain Ed did not seem phased by this rather haphazard positioning at all, and promptly got out his navigational map, looking at both maps side by side to work out the exact position based on the surrounding landmarks. Soluntra had total trust that he would find the right place, and left him to it, heading back up to the top deck for the half hour journey there. Shortly after we arrived at X-marks-the-spot we did our usual connecting and centering when we heard Linda, the cabin crew, calling out from the deck below, "I can see bubbles coming up down here. Ed, come and look at these bubbles!"

The sun was out and we could see the snow-covered Mount Ruapehu in the distance. We closed our eyes to begin the connecting meditation again in epicentre of the stargate. From all our prep work, our energetic bodies were aligned; we had changed our molecular structure at Meads Wall, integrated our multi-dimensional selves, and were one with the cosmic water. We finally leveled up to a new expansive state of being, as we consciously worked with ourselves as a stargate, a conduit, a portal, ready for the star lines to come through. We connected in oneness with the Sirian beings and all the star tribes and councils that were with us for the event, aware of our roles, mine as the Cosmic Messenger.

During our ceremony I was speaking light language in my mind and sending it around the multiverse via the spinner wheel at Lake Rotopounamu. I worked with the pink Buddha and pink crystals from my dream, energetically placing them in the vortex and working with their energy. The sun got brighter as the star lines came in, a sharp burst of energy, through us, through the earth grids, out through the spinner wheel and into the heart of Gaia. I felt a sudden sharp pain in my chest area, full of tension and pressure. I massaged it, trying to break up the discomfort as we sat there in the sun on the top deck, absorbing the energy and experience quietly.

Afterwards Captain Ed told me that he wasn't expecting to be able to anchor there, but when he aligned it with his navigation map, it corresponded to a volcanic peak beneath the surface, which was why there were bubbles coming up. Soluntra had no idea what was at this spot, only that we needed to be there, and seeing the energy flowing and coming up from that place, it was now clear why. I was impressed.

I felt a strong headache come on after a bite of lunch. I downed a litre of water quickly to try and flush it out as we cruised to our final stop on the lake to view the Ngātoroirangi, another sacred site. The boat pulled into Mine Bay, a small bay just west of Taupō town on the northern end of the lake. As we pulled in closer, I could make out a stunning Māori carving of a huge face around fifteen metres high, etched into the rock wall.

I then realised that there were more intricate carvings to my left and right in the rocks around the wall. I saw the water dragon or famous taniwha, a Māori chief, a mermaid, the wind, tiki and many kinds of Māori symbols and mythology. All of the sculptures representing tīpuna (ancestors) and kaitiaki (guardians). Ngātoroirangi himself was a great and powerful high priest with the mana (authority) to carry the most powerful deities. The artwork detailed his face with beautiful spirals and curved lines, all of which were symbolic of his various spiritual connections. I had never seen the carvings before, only accessible by boat, and the sacred beauty and messages were truly something to behold.

After a closing ceremony at our original position on the shore of the lake halfway home, we dashed back to the southern end of the lake and our motel in time to cook our dinner to take to Soluntra's unit for the last group gathering and wrap up of the journey. I'd experienced significant shifts and aha moments, new knowledge and techniques which I felt were helping me step further into alignment of what I was here to bring through to the planet in my writing. That night, worn out after a big day, I dreamt that I was heading off on three more important activation missions with my crystals for the solstice, although I could not recall with whom. When I woke up the next morning, I knew I had continued my work via soul travel in my light body during the night.

In culmination of all the energy work on the journey, I had some deep knowings and awareness come in. I knew that I would never find my super-conscious abilities, the ultimate truth of who I was as a part of this greater consciousness, the divine intelligence that pervades all things and expanded reality we live in; if I kept looking, viewing or perceiving ultimate intel outside of myself. Anything to do with old paradigm spiritual thinking, of working with spirit guides that are separate from ourselves or viewing other energy beings as being more powerful in the spiritual hierarchy than us, was ultimately a belief system holding us back from our full potential. I had frustratingly never been able to have significant success with experiences of this first hand in a way that made me believe it was true, and that I was communicating with intelligent energies outside of myself. I knew there must be a reason for it; it just wasn't the reason I thought. I wasn't broken or blocked or doing it wrong. I didn't need to be fixed as I had been led to believe. The gift was looking me straight in the eye and I couldn't even see it.

I now understood that the pineal gland (third eye) wasn't necessarily about seeing fairies or beings. It was about seeing through the illusion of this 3D reality. About seeing into the real layers of existence. About seeing differently from our visual eye and the reality in front of us. In the past, intuitives were seeing, labelling and channelling these beings based on their current state of consciousness and understanding. I realised my natural in-built technology had inherent understanding of the new paradigm, where none of this old belief system was necessary. That's why I never had any success with it. A deep resonance with everything as part of my own being was ingrained within me, as the level of consciousness and understanding I came into this life with. It was not supposed to be like everyone else. It was making far more sense now that I realised there even was an old paradigm and a new paradigm, but of course it seemed logical given we are in a constant state of evolution and change. It was the new consciousness, the new ways that I deeply understood with a level of knowing that could bypass my logical mind. The new energies of this change in consciousness the world was going through are what some term the New Earth and where we are evolving to. Living not just as physical beings, but as the energy beings we truly are, anchoring this consciousness into the physical. Being light in form.

Opening up to universal wisdom in whatever form
will remove the outdated need of the personality self
to identify it with a certain being or character.
For each is working within the frame of their divine blueprint,
and therefore whatever comes through is
purposeful to their energy signature.

The way your body is treated affects you in every moment of every day,
food is energy, coded with information.
Opening up to the most expansive form of divine wisdom and truth
from the Universal intelligence will ensure
the purest essence of you in every moment.

You are never outside of this access.
If you act on it, and own it, and are responsibly conscious in every moment
in your interactions, you will remain the open channel.

Know that you are channelling divine wisdom
in every moment and be that.
For that is which you came here to be. And
that is how you will effect change.
Be conscious, remind yourself often, and act with integrity.
The expansive knowledge of the Universe
and beyond is at your fingertips.
No special practices are needed,
if you embody this knowing and this idea in your now moment.

Raw Food Reroute

After the workshop, I'd originally planned to stay in Taupō for another night or two on my own, to integrate, process and stay in the energy. However, the Universe had other ideas. My roommate Deidre and I were shown the *Serpent of Light* book by Drunvalo Malcheizedek at the local raw food café, where we stopped off on the way to find another sacred lake in the area before dropping her off at the bus station. The book talked about a sacred site, which was supposedly the most powerful site in Aotearoa. It was about an hour in the opposite direction from where we were planning on going, and required obtaining permission to go on the land.

"This is the place the other cafe owner, Alexandra, was telling me about yesterday!" Deidre said, looking at me with eyes lit up. "We have to go, right?"

"I guess so…" I replied.

I was a little unsure. I had been quite keen to go to Lake Tarawera, which was apparently a Lemurian Moon Temple, on a mission to find a sacred waterfall across the lake that contained dragon eggs and amazing rocks. Was I really being led here, or was it more to do with Deidre? Phil, the café owner, took us into the office to show us on Google Earth. It could be difficult to find if you didn't know where you were going.

Phil mentioned that Brett, from whom they usually got permission to visit, was away travelling, but to try and find someone else to ask. If not, just go anyway. It all sounded a bit complicated. No more complicated than trying to find a boat to get across Lake Tarawera to find dragon eggs at a sacred waterfall though, I surmised.

I took a few photos of the relevant pages of the book for

reference. Skim-reading the first couple of pages, I saw that the Sirian star beings had buried a crystal in this place. Interesting, given we had just been working with the diamond they had placed in the island on the lake in 2012. Deidre had also had the Sirian Council of Light come into her dream the day before which only added to the synchronicities. I edged towards the door after saying goodbye. Deidre would be in here gas-bagging all day if I let her. We hopped in the car and headed out of town in the direction of Te Kuiti. Off to the Temple of the Four Winds we went.

The weather was atrocious as we made our way on the highway winding through a gorge along the Waikato River. It pelted rain for the entire forty minute journey, which we drove mostly in silence. When we turned off onto state highway thirty, the stormy weather continued, although it became patchier as we progressed.

Not far along the highway, I was looking around at the funny green mounds and various rock formations in the landscape, and it felt like I'd been here before. I was aware that the landscape was very different to the norm around here. It reminded me more of English landscape but with an other-worldly feel about it. I could feel the centre of my chest flaring up again with the dull pain I had been feeling there on and off since the solstice journey.

"I can feel it," Deidre said, interrupting my thoughts. "I can really feel it."

As we cruised down the drive, we saw a rainbow appear in the distance over the rolling farm hills.

"Stop," said Deidre, jumping out to take a picture.

"Wow, what an amazing sign," I said. "We are clearly meant to be here." I could feel the excitement pumping in my chest.

We turned into the farm complex Phil had shown us on the map and continued on to the first house, where I knocked a few times, then a few more while the rain sprinkled on my head. No one home. I looked around at the farming areas full of equipment; no sign of anyone there either. We pulled into the driveway behind a black car we'd seen on the move, as a rather rough-looking, massive Māori fella came out to greet the lady who had just arrived. I introduced myself with slight trepidation and asked about permission to visit the site. They directed me along the top road to Ian the farm manager, who lived in the next house, eight hundred metres away.

The farm was a complex maze of muddy roads leading to different houses and parts of the land. We followed the top road as directed and managed to get to the house. We ran up to the ranch slider in the rain, greeted by a couple of cute but stinky dogs. After a couple of minutes, a man opened the door.

"Hi, I'm Jo, are you Ian?" I asked.

"Yes," he said, looking highly uncomfortable and assessing me with a narrowed gaze.

Realising he may have thought I was from the authorities, I quickly followed up that we were looking for someone to give us permission to visit the temple and sacred site on the land. He relaxed and said that was fine and asked what kind of vehicle we were driving. I pointed out my silver Mitsubishi and then asked for directions, telling him we had no idea where to go. He directed us back down, past the previous house we had enquired at, to the farm gate which had a sign on it.

"Go through the gate and then in an hour or so you might get there," he said, looking at my shocked face in the rain. "Nah, you'll be there in about five minutes," he added cheekily.

"Phew! Thank God for that!" I said. "Thank you so much!" as we waved goodbye.

It was pouring with rain as we headed through the gate onto the grass path, huddled under my umbrella. After a few minutes we rounded the corner past some cows and pigs to see a couple of barn-like structures and a small hill in the near distance. It didn't look like much at all. We walked down the hill and to the left towards the red, carved marae-style entrance. There was a grave site to the left, just inside.

Before entering, we took a moment to say a prayer, ask permission to enter from the ancestors and ask all of the beautiful beings of divine love, light and pure source energy to be with us on our journey. We thanked all of the beautiful synchronicities and signs for leading us to this place, and asked that we receive all activations, light codes and energetic alignments available to us in this moment as we gave our respects and light to the energies.

We sat quietly, connecting with our own Source energy and the earth, meditating and taking in the vibration of the place. I felt waves coming in. They were soft and gentle, yet powerful at the same time. We took shelter in a stunning, circular building made out of gorgeous native wood that was hidden from view behind the dilapidated barn structures from out front. Inside we could see shining brass finishings in the larger room, which was a beautiful seven-sided temple space. Its crisp, fresh and clean scent of our native rimu wood was so inviting. There was a central beam holding up the highest point of the ceiling, with beams for each panel splaying out like a star from the centre.

We sat ourselves down on the church-pew-type seating and fell into meditation. I could feel the same waves of energy I had felt outside, but much stronger now without the elements as a distraction. We meditated for about twenty minutes or so, until the cold set into our bones from our wet clothes, so we slowly moved around to take in the energy we had just received, plus a snack and drink of water. We locked up and then headed back over the stile and through the paddock in silence in the rain. I was feeling truly grateful for such beautiful, energy experience being shared with me. It seemed to round off the week perfectly.

Back in Taupō I dropped Deidre off, saying a heartfelt goodbye. She felt like an angel in disguise behind that tough Aussie outback exterior. I then set off to find a place to stay for the night, when Brazilian Girl called me mid-search. She was in a state, in tears on the phone, not coping without me and not coping in general really. She was questioning her future and if there was anything left for her here in New Zealand at all. I felt for her, I'd been there before looking to change jobs or countries to distract me from what was really going on deep inside. Despite promising myself a weekend alone to integrate, I had too much compassion and love to leave her by herself when she was swimming in a sea of doubt, loneliness and feeling utterly lost. I knew how awful it was, so I told her to come down to Taupō if she liked and chill for the weekend. I booked an intuitive massage from a card I picked up at the raw food store to help integrate all the energies I'd been experiencing over the last week, while I waited for Brazilian Girl to drive down. As the masseuse Louise was working on me, she explained that she had learned intuitive massage from her grandfather and that she had been using it ever since. She was working on my upper back when she asked if she could speak freely.

"Of course!" I said. "Please do."

"Well, you have what I call 'angel buds' here, that I can feel in your back. It means that you have had at least one, but in your case many incarnations as an angelic, and in the angelic realm. You have Archangel Raphael *all* over you," she said. "You have his emerald green everywhere. And Raphael is the joker you know. He's the dunce, the comedian and always having fun, but when it's time to get down to business, he's the most amazing healer there is. You are like him, you can have fun and joke but when you need to get down to what's important, you do. And Archangel Gabriel is very much with you, but you need to call on Archangel Michael more."

"Michael is, well, such an everyman's angel," I said. "I don't usually bother him, as I'm sure he has loads to deal with."

"Well, he's the warrior side of you, and if you bring in more of his energy he will help with any criticism on this path you are following," she said.

I made a mental note as it confirmed the messages I had received from the plant a few days before at the lake. Raphael was the healing, Gabriel was the communication and Michael was the warrior side. All representative of the different energies available within me if I called them forward.

"What is your connection to druids?" she then said.

"Druids?" I asked. "Gosh, don't they just hang out at Stonehenge dressed in capes?"

"No," she said. "I can see you as a druidess in another lifetime. You were very well regarded and used to service many towns. Show me what you have," she added. I was confused. "Oh, you are holding a handful of hawthorn berries. They are amazing for heart health and for the immune system. You had an enemy though. You are wearing a green cloak, as is common in druidism, but yours is different. It's so blended with the colours of the forest and plants that it actually acts as a camouflage. It's like you were invisible. Look into the druids. Get in touch with your druid self and see what comes."

Wow. I certainly wasn't expecting to hear any of this coming for a simple massage. And all of it so aligned with what I had been feeling and experiencing. She went on to tell me that I didn't need to carry someone else's burden. Which could have been Brazilian Girl, or Annie or Devo. The pain I felt in my heart chakra was where my ribcage had literally cracked open when Devo died, and it was finally melding back together when it got ripped open again by more heartbreak. Given the pain I was feeling in the centre of my chest, it was certainly on point, and I could connect with the essence of the hawthorn berries to heal.

The energy is changing. Yes, in rapid leaps and bounds.
We feel the sense of rebellion within you coming alive.
To kick off the old and leave it behind.
It's almost as if every day you are living in a new realm.
One of more light and love and opportunity.

Feel the lightness of this time, for it is a time
of which you have been waiting for.
A time which ushers in a new age. A new way of being and doing.
For you are learning a new way to live.

This new energy demands that of you. Everything is different.
See it with new eyes. Hear it with new ears. And feel it with joy.
The changes are visceral to those of you who know.
Those tuned in to this enhanced perspective. For those awake and not asleep.

Be how you wish to be in this moment of infinite possibilities.
For this is where you reside now.
Your true nature is in alignment with these new energies.
For this is the technology.
The technology of the New Earth.

Death Drop Deception

When I got back to Auckland, I realised I was pretty much tripping balls. It was like I had a new body, or was looking out of this body with new eyes. Things looked different. I felt physically different. I noticed rainbows jumping out of windows, cars and my surroundings. I experienced lots of nausea again and knew I had to change my diet to a lighter form of nutrition to keep it at bay. It lasted for almost two weeks straight.

In the wake of the solstice trip and energy work, I had some very vivid and significant dreams. In the first I was on an energetic mission in some kind of hotel-like space on a different planet. I was in a group with a bunch of non-physical beings and we all had a role to play. They gave me a code to work with, which looked like a bunch of V-shapes. I took the code into my heart. I was then given a device that had earphones so I could hear messages and transmissions from these beings, which I thought was odd until I remembered I was a 'Cosmic Messenger', and the V shapes were the same as in the underwater dream I had on the solstice journey.

In a second dream I was sitting with two large beings standing next to me. I was saying, "What about this particular spiritual practice?"

"No, it's not about that," they would say.

"But what about this other one…?" I said again.

One of the beings said, "No, it's not about any of that. It was always about the heart, it is only about the heart, and it will only ever be about the heart. It's all about heart technology."

The other being nodded, "There is nothing as effective or important as the heart. The key is, and always has been, the heart."

I had no idea what heart technology meant, but I shared it

with everyone I could to see if I could discover exactly what it was and how I could use it. I discovered the Institute of Heart Math, which did a huge amount of research into the heart, its capacity of being five thousand times stronger than the brain mind, and its ability to know what was going to happen seconds before something eventuated, which denoted its powerful intuitive capabilities. I discovered that most people think that intuition comes from the third eye, when in fact it comes from the heart centre. The third eye focuses information, but intuitive intelligence comes from the heart and centre of our being. All the information I was receiving was bang on the money.

In the third significant dream, I was told by some beings to meditate on a pyramid with an eye in it for twenty minutes per day. This symbol is known as the 'all seeing eye', but when I looked it up, I was thrown by the fact that it was potentially related to the illuminati, or the 'dark side' and therefore disregarded it instead of doing my homework. It was only sometime later when I came across a site that said the 'all seeing eye' was the symbol of the Mintakans. The Mintakans who had been referenced in my Akashic Record reading many years ago in London. I felt chills as the light bulb went on. They had the ability to perceive with one mind and draw their energies together into the collective unconscious or group mind in order to see as one. I was being called to see through the one mind of this consciousness.

I continued investigating more of what was energetically available to me in New Zealand, taking advantage of the fact that I had ended up, by default, permanently living here now for the first time in sixteen years. I couldn't help but feel I had been drawn back here for a reason, and I was going to find out what it was. As we attempted to navigate a conscious break-up, Brazilian Girl accompanied me on many exploratory trips. We were as close as ever, but truth be told although we weren't having sleepovers, we spent far too much time together and were still reliant on each other. Essentially we were in a co-dependent relationship.

I would dissect the vast confusion of my feelings and the

energetic layers of the situation with friends, wondering if I was, in fact, scared or blocked? Delving into why I wasn't sexually attracted to this amazing woman who might be my soulmate. I missed the closeness. I missed the cuddles. I missed her. What if I was making a grave mistake?

"But it's because you're not a real lesbian Jo!" my friend Georgie said. "You went from Brazilian boyfriend to Brazilian girlfriend with a polyamorous Paratrooper in the mix, not to mention the death of your iconic father and you moved countries. No wonder you are confused. If you need cuddles, get a cat." Oh, the irony of replacing one pussy for another.

Despite these workshopping sessions with friends, my feelings were so all over the place that I couldn't ascertain what was right for me. My doubts continued to plague me that I might have done the wrong thing. I had no trust in myself, so six months later Brazilian Girl and I had gotten back together to give it another shot. I couldn't live with myself if I didn't truly try to unpick what was going on within me. She may be right. I could be blocked. There were so many different factors weighing in to my current situation that I was willing to look at all possibilities. I signed up for three months of quantum light coaching with a woman named Jessica Alstrom who I had been following in the USA. With her incredible super-conscious abilities, if there was anyone who was going to help me see the layers of this issue, and what was really going on, then I thought it was her. However, in our first session she basically blew any unpicking out of the water. There was nothing to unpick she said. We came together for a reason, but not the reason we thought.

Being settled in New Zealand was giving me the space to dive deep into not only myself, but what was happening in the bigger picture. More and more I was coming to the understanding that this planetary consciousness shift and all the new energies that went with it were concentrated in the southern hemisphere. I could certainly feel the distinct difference, having experienced both. Some of the older sacred sites throughout Europe just didn't feel like there was much energy there for me at all. The patriarchy-dominated northern hemisphere was collapsing under the pressure of the rebalancing that was taking place, seen in a myriad of dramatic current events across the globe. When I heard Soluntra talk about the Crown Chakra of the New Earth being at Mount Titiroa down the bottom of the South Island months before, I knew I had to go there to check it out myself.

The night before I was leaving for Invercargill to stay with my friend Damian I was awoken in the middle of the night. I was feeling bothered as I lay awake next to Brazilian Girl after few hours' sleep, until I heard a morepork singing outside. Morepork, or ruru as it is called in Māori, is a native New Zealand owl known for intuition, spirit and wisdom. I felt the visit from this spirit animal was reminding me to listen to my own wisdom, although at the time I thought it was about my pending mission the next day.

The next morning, I flew to Southland, excited for what lay ahead. We headed off on the two-hour drive from Wairio to Te Anau. There was snow on the mountain, so we needed to be rugged up. For some reason, my brand new cosy winter coat was missing. I had almost given up, seated in the car in Damian's spare Swanndri when it popped into my consciousness exactly where it was, in the wardrobe where Damian had put it unbeknownst to me. Since we were running late, Damian was hoofing it on the gas. He suddenly launched into all sorts of sensitive information about his childhood, current anger about family frustration and how hard it was being a progressive gay man living in the deep south. It kept going and going. "I don't know why I'm telling you all this," he said.

It seemed a significant purging was taking place before the sacred mission to the pure, divine energies of Mount Titiroa and the Crown Chakra of the New Earth. Better out than in, I say. By the time we arrived, it felt like a change of energy was happening, and we left the past behind.

Damian and I made it to the helicopter departure pad at 10.05am, not too bad, considering the curveball of jacket-gate. I noticed twinges in my heart chakra area immediately. In the frenzy, I had completely forgotten to grab the roses I wanted to take up to gift to the mountain. Damn it. I would have to offer some plain quartz crystals instead that I carried to gift different places of the earth. I decided it was the thought and act of offering that really counted.

We met the pilot and got weighed, ourselves and our gear. Yup, I'd definitely put on a few pounds. Time for a fitness tweak. I should probably be climbing the mountain on foot instead of choppering up there. Then again, I swore no more mountains after Kili almost killed me. As I came back from the bathroom, I heard Damian asking the pilot whether he'd ever experienced a 'death drop'. I had no idea what a death drop was, but it didn't sound like a positive question to be starting the trip with. We got a safety briefing before getting in the chopper, strapping in and putting on our headphones.

Damian sat in the back with a trainee student, and I sat in front with the pilot and the amazing open front window through which I could see everything. We lifted off the ground, teetering ever so slightly as we got lift-off. It had been a while since I had been in a chopper, and my stomach was fluttering with nervous excitement. Soon we were way above the office and winging our way over the beautiful New Zealand landscape. We flew over stunning Lake Te Anau and tonnes of silvery native beech forest. Lake Manapouri and its beautiful islands were sparkling to my right. The sky was azure blue with the white and cream capped mountain up ahead.

"There's a little bit of snow," said the pilot, nodding towards the range up ahead, "but that's just the normal colour of the mountain."

"That's because it's full of crystal!" I said, unable to hide the grin on my face.

To the right, we could see down a beautiful valley to some other small lakes. As we flew closer, the trees stopped and the mountain became rocky. There were rocky jewels littered between the tan and brown terrain, with bits of snow in some places. We flew over a ridge which revealed more velvet folds and rocks as we followed a valley up and over another rocky ridge littered with snow. The pilot then did a slow, rotating, three-hundred-and-sixty-degree turn for us, climbing higher and higher, and finally looking back over Lake Manapouri in the background.

I was staggered at this stunning beauty. It was absolutely magical. I stopped filming and, as I placed my phone in my lap, was suddenly thrust downwards, the safety belt holding me in place as we headed straight for the crevice of the mountain at speed. I lost my guts rollercoaster-style, and then felt my stomach in my mouth as the pilot pulled up, narrowly missing the ground.

"I waited for you to stop filming to do that," he said, laughing. "Otherwise it'll end up on social media and I'll get in trouble with the missus!"

"That was awesome!" Damian and I cried in unison.

My heart was still pounding out of my chest as the chopper hugged the carpet of black and white rocks and snow. We suddenly came up over a smaller ridge which revealed an alpine lake glistening turquoise and deep blue. We curved around to land on the flat area next to the lake.

The pilot rushed out and opened the door for me. I was so dazed with the ridiculous beauty that I got out onto the snow and burnt yellow grass still wearing the earphones plugged inside. The pilot passed our bags from the lower compartment, plus a handheld UHF radio, and we scurried, crouched down, towards the lake and out of the whipping winds from the blades. The chopper took off and as the wind slowly left with it, we were alone on top of this great energetic being. We made our way a few steps over to the small pebble beach by the lake. The colours were even more magnificent at ground level. Our excitement was bursting at the seams. It was as though we had landed in another world.

The silence was peppered with the delicate sound of trickling water from the alpine lake down the hill from where we had flown up. To our right were rough, jagged peaks of black and white, leading up to what the pilot told us was the true peak of Mount Titiroa. On the other side of the lake was another peak, but this one was yellow-brown with rounded, smooth, amazing stone formations. Standing there looking at the remarkable difference between the different sides of the mountain with the stunning azure blue alpine lake in between, I suddenly got it. I realised what I was looking at was the soft divine feminine on one side, and the more rugged divine masculine on the other. That's why this was the Crown Chakra of the New Earth. It was the perfect balance of masculine and feminine in one place. I looked over and saw the faces of the ancestors in many of the stones looking down on us. The hairs stood up on my arms. It certainly felt like we were not alone.

After many minutes of wondrous awe, we started to think about where to begin. I did an opening ceremony, first cleansing us with Palo Santo, a selenite wand and Tibetan bells. I called in energetic support to help us experience and integrate the new paradigm energies that were available to us here, new ways of being and doing, coming from oneness, connection and harmony. We sat in meditation on the beach as I guided us through a connecting meditation and visualisation.

I was feeling strong energies coming into my field. I took some deep breaths, taking it all in, and humbly requesting permission from the guardians of the space to share in their wisdom, love, light and new consciousness energies. I'd soul-travelled there while I slept a few times during the previous week in preparation.

After we finished the meditation, we sat in silence before stripping off naked and heading into the alpine lake for a skinny-dip. The freezing water numbed the lower part of my legs as I waded out some way along the shallow beach area to the deep, icy-blue drop. I held my breath and just went for it, diving in, immediately frozen and clambering back out but tingly and invigorated all over. Now, that was the proper way to finish an energy cleanse.

I rushed back through the knee-deep water, still in shock from the cold. Damian went in for a second dunk. Although the water temperature was arctic, the sun was warm on my skin and there was not a breath of wind. Despite the sun, it was still a little chilly after the icy plunge, so I towelled off at a relaxed pace and put my clothes back on slowly, still taking it all in. Damian was, by this point, wandering around with his wanger bouncing around, like some nude space tourist looking at various alpine plant specimens from another world.

We started to climb toward what the pilot had motioned was the 'official peak' of Mount Titiroa, which logically seemed the 'right' way. It was extremely rocky, with black, sharp, jagged edges breaking through the snow. We stopped at some interesting large stones and did a hongi introduction, requesting permission to access the top site. These were some large stones sticking out of the ground, similar to the Avebury standing stones. I noticed that on two in particular, three large, round holes went deep into the stone. I had seen smaller holes exactly the same on some stones on Waiheke Island, at a sacred site and stargate where I went on a vision quest months before. I had found it just as unusual then as I did now. I had the strong sense again that we were being watched and were most certainly not alone.

As we slowly made our way up the steep rocky incline, I had a nagging feeling that I couldn't get rid of. I kept glancing over to the other side and the more rounded stones and triangle-shaped rock formation on the other peak that had first caught my eye. I'd read on one account that it took one-and-a-half hours to climb up one peak, but was not sure which, so with a three-hour turn-around I wasn't sure we'd have time for both.

I looked down over the landscape littered with all these amazing giant stones. I stopped in my tracks. "Damian, I'm getting the vibe that I need to go to the other side. We're only likely going to have time for one, so I think I need to turn around and go up there."

"I think we can probably do both," Damian replied, "but whatever you think, doll. You do what you need to do."

We turned around and headed down, communing with some amazing stones along the way. As we got to the flat area in between the two sides, there were some striking stones. Large ones standing together in a tunnel-like formation were most certainly, by the feel of the energies, some kind of cosmic gateway. We stopped and did the hongi greeting here, conscious of what we were stepping into as we went through. The energy felt subtly different to the senses. We took our time integrating and feeling into the energies of the various stones and admiring the spectacular view out over the valley and down towards Lake Manapouri far away.

We continued walking past different stones and over others, looking at amazing specimens of alpine flowers and plants along the way. It really was another world up here. Standing at the base of a pile of sizable stones building to a cone-shaped point, I realised it had looked deceptively small from the other side. Now, here at the base, it looked steep and challenging.

We climbed over stone after stone; my bright pink thermals underneath my matte-black, faux-leather pants were pulling, making it difficult to stretch to a full stride while leaping the rocks. I had my big, wintery coat tied around my waist by this point, getting a bit of a sweat on as we made our way up in the blazing sunshine. We leapt higher and higher, the stones getting bigger and more difficult to navigate over, through and around. It was requiring some serious climbing skills, and after scuffing the knee of my pants, I was cursing wearing them; they were now ruined. Who could have known it was going to be so hot? It was perfect weather.

Damian was up ahead, leaping from stone to stone like a nimble monkey. I was significantly slower, taking my time. Damian could ascertain from his front-foot position the best way up, and a few times pointed me around a different way. After a good hour and fifteen minutes, we were almost at the top. My stomach was unsettled, and my knees weakened whenever I caught sight downwards. Finally, thirty minutes later Damian pulled himself up between two giant stones, with quite a struggle to reach the very top.

"This top stone is vibrating when I touch it!" he yelled down.

I contemplated trying to pull myself up and then lost my stomach again as I looked down over the valley and a few tufts of white cloud below. We were pretty bloody high. I lay down on the giant stone and breathed deeply. I was a stone away, and close enough I reasoned, despite a small pang that I was missing out. The vortex energy was strong, touching the top rock or not, and I lay there, drinking in the sun and assimilating all the energies.

Sometime later it came to me that I needed to sing to the stones. I'd been singing to stones when my inspiration told me to for months now, so although it was bananas, it was nothing new. I just thought that if I was a stone being, I'd love it if someone serenaded me while I was sitting stationary for millennia.

This time however, as I started, I got an image of myself toning in the sarcophagus of the Great Pyramid, which is known to reset your energy field. I needed to sing and tone while lying on this great stone ancestor to align myself with the resonance of this being. I needed to feel my body vibrating with the stone. I started humming and singing softly. It wasn't loud enough to get my body vibrating, so I yelled out to Damian that that's what we needed to do. I started singing louder and louder, until I could feel my chest reverberating with the stone. I sang scales hitting low notes and high, covering all bases and feeling which notes were most resonant. I could feel my chest and heart opening. I sang and toned and imbued my love and thanks into the stones until it felt complete. We made our way down the other side, carefully descending and lowering ourselves off the amazing stones.

I suddenly received the message that the stone beings play an important role for me. That my honouring, love and care of these beings was my heart and that my song reverberates deep within their being. My song of love and joy. My song of faith and trust in the unseen, and of depth where there appears to be none. The stone beings had much to teach me. 'Based on the truth of nature, you cannot go wrong,' I was told.

There were some interesting stones above the hill by the lake, which were also calling. My boots were crunching over tonnes of sparkly cream and white crystals which were flecked with black or dark green. It was a mixture of granite and quartz, and what looked like different kinds of tourmaline. It covered the mountain top. No wonder the energies were so pure and palpable up here.

Further down, on flatter ground yet still high above the lake, we came across stones that were very square in shape and stacked together. There were about eight of them, with four being absolutely rectangular and almost like giant bricks. They looked very, very similar to the stones from the mystical Kaimanawa Wall, giant stones that were potentially square cut by whatever technology they had in a different age, which had slowly rounded and weathered over thousands of years. There was something very 'Stonehenge' about them. With their position at the base of the vortex peak, overlooking the distant Lake Manapouri, the alleged Galactic Crossover Point, and the Titiroa peak and alpine lake to our left, this felt like the positioning of an old temple. I got shivers. I saw a flash of giant stone structures in all their glory, in another time, an ancient Lemurian time, a time of understanding and reverence for the power sites of the earth.

We sat on some of the stones and did a guided meditation to bring light into our field, chanting with a mandala saved on my phone. We felt light and buzzy afterwards, investigating some more stones close by, overlooking the other side of the mountain. Despite the entire mountaintop being covered in patches of snow, it was still incredibly warm in the sun and I was perspiring in all my layers. I stripped down to my singlet, somewhat gobsmacked but feeling utterly divinely blessed by the temperate weather we were being gifted with to enjoy the full entirety of energies, dimensional doorways and vortexes of the mountain.

I was lost in thought as I embraced stone being after stone being, feeling the different energies and lying around this amazing playground, just being. We decided to radio the helicopter base and ask to be picked up as late as possible. We didn't want to leave.

This day is one of relaxation and play.
Creative expansion is set for opportunity, as the inspiration hits take hold.
For the key is in grasping these moments, milking these frequencies
for the balancing of your own energies.

When we stifle our own natural impulses, we block
ourselves off from the magic within,
from the magic inherent in us as an energy being.
Our capabilities are masked, yet they don't need to be.

Follow the inner compass.
Follow the feelings, ideas, impulses, creativity
and flow where it goes in the moment.
It will get you there. It will ground you and support you into your being.
Into parts of the wholeness of self, which you do not recognise or remember.
But they are there waiting for you to wake up to the wholeness of self.

There is nothing broken. Nothing to be fixed.
Some unlearning and deconditioning, yes,
and uncovering of your deepest essence,
but there is nowhere to go but inward.
Into the depths of self to retrieve that which is buried in there.
Deep down within your being, waiting for the safety to bring it through.

Freestyling Down The Mountain

It was after 2pm when I was suddenly ravenous. We had left the soup flask down at the beach, so made our way down, crunching over the crystal stones, the reflection blinding us as we walked. We came down from the other side of the lake onto the brown grasses, spiky plants and tiny flowers interspersed with melting snow. I wanted to investigate some interesting stones that were positioned right on the lake. Interestingly, from this side you could see the stone was broken into three distinct pieces. One wondered exactly how a stone might break like this.

Back sitting on the beach, we pulled out our cheese rolls and poured two cups of homemade tomato soup care of Diane, Damian's mother. Despite it being quite warm, the soup was simple and tasty, and the cheese rolls were the perfect accompaniment.

Leaving our bags, we wandered around the lake to investigate the other side, seeing down into a valley, and another lake, which was white and entirely frozen. Here we were swimming with nude abandon up top when fifty metres down, the water was frozen solid. The water from the lake was trickling from the edge, right down a stony stream to the bottom. We sat down again, taking it all in. We crouched down next to the stream, slurping up the cold, alpine water directly into our mouths as we hung our heads over the side, watching out so as not to get stabbed by the spiky plants living alongside.

We then walked over and up towards some large rocks a third of the way up the side of the official mountain peak, where we had yet to explore. It was already 3pm and the helicopter could arrive any time now, so we weren't going to have time to climb the other side. This side of the mountain was completely shaded in the afternoon. It was harder than anticipated. Over halfway there, we were traipsing knee deep through drifts of snow.

It was a bit of a treacherous roulette, given we couldn't see where we were stepping or what was hidden underneath. Suddenly, I was surprised to be knee deep in snow with my boot stuck, falling on my hands and knees to crawl and pull my leg and boot out.

The top of the snow was now iced over, which meant we had to stomp through it. This was trickier than it looked, and I started to feel a nervous twinge eating at me. We were almost to our giant rock destination when we started to sink even deeper. There wasn't much higher ground to work with, and the waist-high wading was becoming even more taxing.

Clouds started streaming over the peak and down towards the lake. I shivered with the cold and zipped up my neck in my jacket. The weather had changed dramatically in seconds. Suddenly we were descending into thick fog as clouds and mist streamed in from every angle.

"Damian, I think we should radio the base. If the chopper can't land due to the weather, we'll be stranded up here all night. They did say that we should radio if the weather started setting in."

"Oh yes, you're right," said Damian, taking out the two-way radio. "Although I think we'd be fine if we got stuck here for the night."

"Um, let's not go there," I said.

"Manapouri Helicopter services, come in, please… Er, over?" he said hesitantly into the receiver.

"Roger that, Manapouri Helicopter services here," said a female voice.

"Oh hi, it's Damian and Jo. Um, it looks like it's getting pretty foggy up here, so you might want to come and get us sometime soon… er, over," he said.

"We're about twenty minutes away," we heard back. "Over."

Oh, thank God. We decided to start making our way back down. It was going to take some time, considering all the ice and snow.

"Well, we'd just cosy up together. With all our gear, we'd totally be warm enough," Damian said, rabbiting on. "We could huddle under a rock. We could totally survive the night."

"In sub-zero temperatures?" I said, unconvinced. "Ah sure, but anyway, we definitely do not want to be stranded here all night. Yes, we might be fine, but no, I don't want to test out your theory, thanks."

"Well, Diane packed us loads of snacks you know, so we totally won't starve," he said.

Not my idea of fun, nor that much fun to think about really. I couldn't even imagine what the night-time temperature was up the mountain, but I'd hazard a guess at fifteen below zero. Not to mention wind-chill factor.

We were traversing more icy snow and it was pretty tough going. "Are you alright?" he yelled back before I heard, "Fuck this," and saw Damian dive face first onto his tummy and slide down the hill on the ice, picking up a substantial amount of velocity before vigorously trying to turn himself around, narrowly missing some sharp stones jutting out about twenty-five metres downhill.

Now, that was a genius idea. However, I wasn't about to ruin my lovely new coat, nor my face, so I climbed out of the snow and went feet first instead, sliding down the ice rollercoaster. I felt the exhilarating joy of a five-year-old combined with the boring, practical fear of a forty-year-old as I went faster and faster, realising I had absolutely no control to steer myself away from the jagged rocks peeking out from the surface of the snow. As long as I could keep my boots out in front of me to break my fall, I'd be okay, I said to myself. I started edging right towards a large rock when I saw Damian brace himself to potentially try and break right and grab me before I hit the rock. I leaned left, just managing to manoeuvre myself enough to avoid the crash.

Damian grabbed me as I got to the lower plateau. "Are you alright?" he said.

"Yeah, fine," I said, trying to act cool. The adrenaline was pumping, my heart was pounding, and I was a little shaky on the feet. "I think we should go this way." I pointed left where there were more rocks to climb on breaking through the snow.

It was a steep passage down, with some serious hazards. No more arse-sledding. And I didn't really fancy any more trudging knee-deep through the wet either. Without the warm rays, the temperature had plummeted. It was rapidly growing foggier and more mysterious. Well, okay, maybe a little scary. I noted tinges of fear welling up inside me on this side of the mountain, the more masculine side. My inner divine masculine obviously needed some work. Duly noted.

I made my way carefully, but with determined speed, down the rocks and snow. There was no sign of the helicopter as we reached the bottom twenty minutes later, only a whole lot more cloud rushing in from all angles. The cloud was so fast-moving that it was mesmerising. I could see different-coloured halos around the sun through the cloud pouring down from the top of the Titiroa Peak. The entire feeling of the site had changed, and I realised how incredibly lucky we were to have had such a perfect day to really experience the beauty of the energies here in all their glory. Thank you, beautiful Mount Titiroa!

We did a closing ceremony to honour the mountain and all its energies, doorways, vortexes and beings. I was devastated to have forgotten the roses for an offering, instead throwing some quartz crystals that I had been charging in various ceremonies and full moons and global sacred sites into the lake with my prayers of thanks. I imagined the most beautiful flowers I could think of and sent a vibrational offering of beauty, with all the love from my heart. I was overwhelmed with gratitude for the experience and everything I absorbed and remembered into my being. I felt alive, vibrant and full of love for this magical place. Mother Nature and the weather angels had shined upon us with great enthusiasm for the entire day. I didn't realise just how rare this was until the following weeks when I read that the Fiordland area had rain and poor weather for the majority of the year and experiencing clear weather up Mount Titiroa was nothing short of a miracle.

Ten minutes later the chopper arrived. The pilot's 'missus'

was also on board this time, so there was no chance of any flying acrobatic shenanigans on our return. The trip back was just as beautiful. The lake was shimmering in the distance, clouds hugging the mountains as the afternoon sun became more golden in its glow. I was absolutely buzzing with the beauty of it all. I finished off my time in the South by staying at Lake Manapouri for a few days, to experience the lake, which was apparently a galactic crossover point. I saw some beings shapeshifting in the clouds at dusk. An ET, a joker face and an anonymous mask with messages of hidden things being exposed. Although the May weather was already wintry, I did nature walks and cleansing skinny-dips in the freezing lake to completely absorb and integrate the energies from the trip up the mountain. I was still very much processing, but it felt like tapping into those energies was helping me anchor into my purest infinite self, the truth of who I really was.

Lightness.
Lightness of the breeze through your hair. Lightness of being in all ways.
Lightness in attitude, thoughts, actions and emotions.
The lightness is there, ready to caress you, if you open up to it.

The subtleness of this light can be missed easily.
If you look too hard, it will not be found.
However, the lightness is there for you in all moments.
In the now, always it will be.

The silence holds the lightness.
The light in the space in-between.
Carry this lightness with you always in these times.
For it is the age-old remedy for all.
Light is medicine. Light is life. Light is joy.
And light is your destiny.

Light, light, light.
In all forms available to you.
For that, is the beauty of light.

The Tipping Point

Although I was working while Devo was dying and the year afterward, there came a time when my job, which I thought was going to be a great transition out of traditional agency life, wasn't what I thought it was going to be at all. The company was a little haphazard and unreliable, and my role ended prematurely. They transferred me to a part-time commission sales role instead, which was not what I wanted to do at all but it kept me afloat while I sourced new opportunities. My next contract, which I thought also had great potential, fell through a month into the job when the creative director had a falling out with the client. Sitting in an interview and pretending to be enthused about the traditional agency world, my stomach churned. I just knew there was no energy left in that old world for me. It felt like I was being nudged in another direction. I decided to trust myself and my intuition. I quit the corporate world to focus on my writing and work on a business idea involving strategic planning for the soul, and getting people into alignment and flow through energy consciousness.

I gave myself freedom from the rat race to trust in a bigger plan. To allow myself the time to fully develop my energetic gifts, deprogramme myself from 'doing' to 'being' and expand my consciousness via light activation and practices. Although things were opening up, and I certainly felt more connected and expanded, I still didn't feel like I had cracked open the treasure chest that I knew was within me. I was still on the hunt to find the truth of who I really was. To experience my most magnificent self and bring all my super-conscious abilities back online, something I had felt buried in the depths of me since I was a child.

I had dreams and ambitions of a career in the world of

consciousness and energy, which I had started to pursue with my business development. Although I had incredibly successful initial results, I wasn't cracking it in the way I wanted, and thought I could improve. I started looking further into the principles of our reality based on quantum physics, which other scientists and teachers such as Gregg Braden, Dr Joe Dispenza and Dr Bruce Lipton were also working with. I was halfway through my three-month mentorship with my Quantum Light Coach Jessica, which mostly confirmed my own deep knowing and intuitions about what was going on with me. How my internal world was reflected in my relationships and circumstances, and pointed to how my relationship with myself was what was really holding me back.

I always had an acute natural awareness of the deeper layers of how I was interacting with my reality. That my whole reality had been set up for self-realisation, expansion and finding unity within. I believed that the quantum field of intelligence, or the Universe, or Nature or Source or God or whatever you like to call it brings us exactly what we need in each moment to bring us into greater alignment with our full expression of self, and our divine plan. "Everything happens to pressurise the diamond buried inside," said my coach.

I had an inherent knowing that everything was constructed by all aspects of my multi layered being – my mental, emotional, physical and spiritual bodies, my soul and my consciousness to give me the right challenges, tools, skills, belief systems, programming and gifts to propel me into wholeness, break down the masks and align me with my true self. Who my parents and brother and friends were, my physical make-up, where I was born, accidents, traumas, blessings and challenges. All of it served a purpose. It was about seeing beyond the narrative of what was playing out in front of me and looking to the metaphor of the true meaning behind it.

My patterns with men echoed the emotional unavailability of Devo. Annie's temperamental spiritual ego had me fearful of stepping into my own truth of spiritual wisdom. My relationship with Brazilian Girl had created so much doubt and confusion within me that I questioned whether I even knew what was right for me in the first place. Now my fundamental safety net of my father and his giant shadow didn't exist. My consciousness was bringing me situations and experiences for the very wounds I needed to heal, for the fears I needed to overcome and the patterns I needed to break, in the process of waking myself up out of unconsciousness. Of getting beneath the exterior layers of dross underneath to what was there all along, my beautiful, magnificent, true divine self.

Quantum physics told me that everything around us, is a projection of us. That every person who I was connected with reflected my consciousness in some way, and if I was finding it a displeasing experience or reacting to them in any respect, that reflection was a trigger, or a marker for me to change something in my own energy and state of being. Other times, when witnessing this in others, the best thing we can do is hold the space for them when they are in it. It was my responsibility to understand these cues, and course correct to bring me back to our most natural state of being, which was love. However, in the past I'd fallen into the trap of self-judgement and beating myself up when I recognised these things. If I remembered I was a spiritual being having a physical experience, it took the emotion out of it. If I detached and merely viewed these events in life as a directional guidepost, then I would have been able to process it correctly. Sometimes despite awareness in the moment, it was easier said than done.

My lifelong tendency towards self-criticism and self-judgement had been creating a war within me, which was essentially blocking me from everything I wanted. These opposing forces were creating separation within myself. Layer in my regular wrestling matches with doubt and self-trust and I had myself a completely disempowered state of being. Care of, yours truly. Jess, my coach explained, "When you doubt yourself, you don't trust yourself and then the Universe doesn't trust you, because the Universe is a reflection of how you see yourself." So, by not trusting myself, I was continuing to manifest experiences that were here to support me in finding that trust within myself again. Which would continue until such time as that happened.

I knew that Brazilian Girl was playing her role to help me in many valuable ways, but the most important was to trigger me to repair the serious doubt and mistrust within me. She wanted us to move in together, officially, and start building our future as a couple. Despite how in love with her soul I was and all that she offered me, I couldn't deny that I might be making sacrifices or settling if I chose to continue being with her. I couldn't commit.

The night when I broke up with her for the second, and final time, it had been marinating in my brain for too long and I just blurted it out in bed, like an over-brewed vinegary kombucha. It was a horrific delivery and she started throwing up in the bathroom, which continued on for hours. I awoke to see the changing colour of the dawn through condensation clouded windows and incredibly sore eyes. I looked to my right, she looked so sweet, innocent and kind. Like a child. The emotion came like a tidal wave washing over me. I struggled for air through each body-shaking sob. After a few minutes, I could see the slits of her swollen baby bird eyes opening. She pulled me close, keeping her eyes closed, stroking my hair. My body shook less and less with every stroke.

"I thought this was my fairy-tale," she said croakily. "That you were my princess. And I wanted to marry you so we could have a big party and I could tell everyone how much I loved you."

It struck me like a knife. I felt pain in the centre of my chest. And my heart broke a little bit more as her dreams shattered through her beautiful Kiwizilian poetry, that she never knew she had.

Oh God, why does she have to say the most perfect things all the time. I'd never felt this loved before. I'd never had someone so devoted to me. Who accepted all of me. For who I really was, and not just my 'Jo the party girl' self. It was all I ever wanted, and here I was saying no to it. Turning that love away.

I looked up at her, tears streaming, "I'm so sorry," I sobbed. "I never meant to hurt you. I wish it could have been different. I truly do."

"It's not your fault," she said softly. "I'm the one that didn't take no for an answer."

We laid around continuing our talks. "You have taught me so much," she said during a hiatus in the tears. "I've grown so much over this couple of years with you and I am so grateful. I didn't even want a relationship. Then we started hanging out and I realised it was different with you. That there was something more there. That a relationship didn't have to be bad. That it can be full of all these good things. And I'm so glad for that."

I told her I felt the same. That she taught me how I deserved to be loved. That I never knew I could be loved like that, because I didn't think it was possible. She had truly loved me, truly madly, deeply. She had been patient and accepted all of me, the good, the bad and the ugly as I struggled through it all.

"Yes, I did. That was really hard for me too sometimes. But I just accepted. And I truly loved you for all of you," she said.

"And I did the same for you," I finished. "I'm still here for you," I said softly as I stroked her hair. "I'll always be here for you no matter what." More grief. More tears.

"I just don't want to become another one of your stories," she said, looking at me with pained eyes.

"Darling, you are certainly not another story. I mean Hot Bartender, yes, Alex, yes, the Paratrooper yes, but not you. We're going to be friends for life. You're too important to me not to."

"Maybe it's just not the right time for you," she said. "Maybe at another time you will open up and maybe this will be right."

"Maybe," I said. "I may be wrong about this whole thing," I said welling up again. "But I have to find out," I said quietly.

We lay there in silence, holding on to each other, not wanting to let go.

"I'm so thankful for this experience," she said, stroking my head. "Every single minute of it. I learned that I am beautiful with you. I had heard that before, but I truly believed it, for the first time, with you. And I thank you for that." She looked at me with a sad smile. "We were such a hot couple," she said. "The hottest girls in town."

"Yes, we were," I said. "And we still will be, just in a different way."

I could hear her stomach growling from under the duvet.

"Do you want me to make you some breakfast?" I asked, voice wavering.

"Yes, I'm starving. I want your chilli scrambled eggs please."

I cuddled into her side. "I just don't want to leave this space with you," I said, swallowing my tears. She started crying. We both knew that when we left that bed it would be the last time we'd be lying naked together, skin against skin.

The break-up opened the floodgates of a tsunami of emotion that had been locked up within me. The grief of my beloved Devo, and all of the heartbreak I had ever experienced seemed to flood out all at once. The depth of my grief was beyond anything I had ever felt or imagined. It was a thousand times worse than when Devo died. It felt like someone had taken over my body and it was no longer in my control. Nothing helped move it through any quicker, or relieved the pain. I tried all the tools and techniques I knew, yet nothing scratched the surface nor provided an ounce of relief. All I could do was sit at the bottom of the pit in the discomfort of myself, and my naked vulnerability of my wildly raging emotions.

Emotions cloud reason. You can't see it when you're in it. Without emotional stability to bolster me, my old nemesis of self-doubt smelled blood. It reared its ugly head again, in some kind of echo effect, a test to see if I was really sure of myself. Was I wrong? Was I just sexually blocked? Maybe I had lost the best thing that ever happened to me? I needed to be one thousand percent sure of myself, so I consulted a therapist to help. In one small exercise he proved to me that my natural inclination sexually was strongly towards men, which deep down I knew and wasn't really the question but was good to have confirmed by 'official' means.

After some further discussion he said, "Are you seriously asking what I think you are asking?" trying to hide his incredulousness. "You know the church have been trying to do the reverse of this for centuries right?"

Yes, I was asking him whether it was possible to make me gay. Reverse conversion therapy I guess. "Well I've really heard it all now," he said.

In that moment I knew that if I was having to rewire myself completely for love, then maybe that particular love wasn't in fact meant for me after all.

*The zero point in which you find yourself is
the reason for the discomfort.
Fear not, all is aligned and ready for you at this time.
There is nothing you need to be, nor do, for you already are,
all that you came to be and more.*

*There is much good here for you.
And this process is one of relaxing and letting go of everything
that is now outside of your vibration.
For there is expansion, and joy in that.*

*For it is you who carry the spark of the divine like no other.
It is you who know the answers to that which you seek.
What is seeking you, is you.
And it is pertinent to understand this aspect
as you move into your next phase.*

*Trust is required in order to grow.
Following your inner knowing above all else.
Your inner knowing is strong and powerful, if you don't discredit it.
Own the multi-dimensional being that you are. All aspects of yourself.
For you can block them off no longer. There is great work to do.*

*Incredible expansion is available to you at this
time and we are here with you.
Supporting you. Guiding you. We are you.
Ready for you to make the leap.
The leap into the unknown.*

Dragons And Liquid Love Lakes
And Light Language, Oh My

When I saw the dragon in the clouds flying over the lake on the drive down, I knew I was in for something special. Lord knows I needed it as I was recovering from months of unexplainable illness. I couldn't work out what was going on with my system until I discovered an activated crystal grid I had made hidden under my bed, which was obviously quite potent as my body had been in cleansing mode ever since.

"Well, you wanted serious upgrading of your frequency, and boy did you get it," my coach said laughing. "Only you would make yourself sick with a crystal grid under your bed. Honestly." At least I knew it worked!

I was on a mission to find a terracotta-coloured house somewhere in Tokaanu that allegedly housed the human guardians of the sacred mountain and lake. They might be doing something interesting for the Winter solstice I was told, when I enquired at the raw food café, which had led me to some interesting adventures a few years before. I drove alongside beautiful Lake Taupō as the late afternoon sun changed the hue of the cloud palette as I was contemplating my intentions for this solstice mission.

"I intend to fully experience and know my own wisdom and the truth of who I really am," I said out loud to no one but myself, "to physically feel this in my body, like really feel it in the depths of me, so that there is no doubt," I finished. "Oh, and I intend to figure out the ending of my book so that I can complete this project and birth it into the world," I added.

Then I saw the dragon. It stayed perfectly formed in the clouds for the entire twenty-minute duration of the remainder of the drive as I kept stealing glances at it from behind the wheel and trying to take a photo without causing an accident.

After unabashedly pulling into the stranger's drive I was greeted by a tall man in his sixties with blonde-grey hair flopping about his head as he welcomed me with kind eyes and a wide smile. Lingering in the background was a woman of similar age who felt slightly less relaxed and a tiny bit apprehensive. I ploughed on introducing myself and was invited inside for tea by Raeul. After some polite chit-chat, I found that Raeul was an amazing cellist and Annwyn was also writing a book, which was being channelled through, and both worked with energy and spirit. In fact, spirit had sent them to this particular location and house. For what, was yet to unfold and be revealed.

My dreamy visions of joining in a sacred solstice ceremony and communing with beings of light were however dashed, when after a cup of fresh lemon verbena tea Annwyn apologised for not inviting me to their private ceremony. They showed me to their mineral hot tub where it was to be happening, which was also an energy vortex at the edge of their native New Zealand garden. Annwyn had just got back from a divine mission to Egypt and Greece and needed space to integrate.

"Oh, my goodness, do not apologise," I said, despite being slightly crestfallen.

"Let me take your number and we'll let you know if we end up going to the lake tomorrow," she said.

When my alarm went off at 3.10am I wasn't sure whether to go. It was a chilly five degrees, which I could certainly feel despite the hot pink thermal pants I'd worn to bed. I lay there for a good twenty minutes umming and aahing, but something propelled me to go. I threw on some clothes and ran out the door driving five minutes down the road before realising I didn't have any supplies, no torch, food or water. Hot tea would be better though. Did I have time? I needed to be at the lake at 3.54am which was a nine-minute drive and ten-minute hike away and it was already 3.20am. Fuck it. I spun a U-turn and barrelled back to my cabin quickly boiling the kettle and filling my drink bottle which thankfully held hot or cold, as of course I hadn't thought through preparations enough to bring a thermos. Or a proper torch I realised, as I was heading out for a hike in the middle of nowhere in the middle of the night with merely my iPhone.

By the time I got to the huge tōtara tree guardians at the entrance by the gate, I did a quick hongi, asking permission to enter the sacred land and co-create with the energies. All I heard was, "Hurry up you're going to be late!" I went careering in a half-run, half-walk, mad dash up the bush path with my tiny iPhone torch highlighting the roots and stones as my chest burned in the now three-degree temperature. My coughing became uncontrollable, and it was already 3.47am. The hike was longer and steeper than I remembered. Not to mention particularly dark and spooky being all alone in the bush, in the wee hours of the night. My shortness of breath and incessant coughing from the remnants of my chest infection was making it tricky to go at full speed. Damn me and my super-powered crystal grid cock up. At the pertinent time of 3.54am I was still on the bush track and possibly just over halfway there. I stood still for a second contemplating doing some kind of ceremony right then and there, before deciding, that given time was just a construct and everything was quantum that it didn't matter and to just keep going and make it back to the sacred Lake Rotopounamu.

I arrived eight minutes late to a wonderfully clear night full of stars and a three-quarters full moon above the lake. The landscape on either side was reflected in the perfectly still water. I bent down greeting the deva energies of the lake and introducing myself energetically three times with a personal mudra, saying, "I am Joanna of Light." I bowed to the lake before taking some of her water and anointing it to my chakra points.

Despite being a few degrees, the lake felt warm and I seriously contemplated a swim. The only thing holding me back was my logical mind with thoughts of my lingering chest infection and lack of towel. I wasn't sure what the solstice energies would bring but I offered my services to be a conduit for whatever was needed. As I stood there in meditation I felt my heart ache, which it often did when activated. After some time of prayers and energy work an intuitive global healing came through which was orchestrated from the heart of the galaxy to the heart of the lake, through my heart, to the hearts of all on the planet. As the healing meditation came to a close, I opened my eyes and saw a shooting star leap in celebration in the distance.

The following morning, I went back to the sacred lake for the two-hour hike around the outside, which I did in an anti-clockwise direction and continued to commune with the energies. I was meditating on the beach at the far side and gearing myself up for the midday influx of solstice light in a couple of hours, when Annwyn and Raeul appeared. After telling them of my solstice experience earlier in the morning Raeul said, "Rotopounamu is the lake of the second emerald stone, green being symbolic of the heart and linking to Glastonbury Tor in the UK. The lake is filled with liquid love so it's no surprise about your global heart healing."

"Oh, my goodness that makes total sense," I said, amazed. "I also saw a dragon in the clouds on my way down yesterday."

"That's because it is a dragon lake," said Raeul calmly.

"It's funny, after all my adventures around the world to all these different sacred sites and the most potent energy I feel is right here in New Zealand," I said. "I've come to the understanding that this is because as the earth shifts and changes in her own evolution, all the ley lines and energy vortexes shift with it. New Zealand seems to be aligned with the new consciousness energies and where we are evolving to, and that's what my being is most resonant with."

"Yes, that's exactly right," said Annwyn. "New Zealand is the place of first light on the planet. And not for no good reason. This is the place that not only gets the light of the sun first in the world on any given day, but the light is first returning here from what was lost during the ancient advanced civilisations. Consciousness is waking up here first, despite how dense it appears in our country and its people. And this particular spot here in this area, this is where the light was last to disappear during the last Golden Age, during Lemurian times. So, it has returned here first, and we are helping to protect and guide this through, with our energy and consciousness work." That night the black panther with the green eyes visited me in my dreams again for the third time. It stalked up behind me and I could feel the hot air from its breath in my ear as the hairs raised on my arms when it sniffed me. First right then left, I could feel its whiskers brush my neck while I sat there. Although I felt an initial rising fear, it dissipated quickly as I held my ground and sat there calmly before it sauntered away.

The following morning, I was invited for coffee at Annwyn and Raeul's beautiful sacred property before I drove back to Auckland. "This place is the sacred headwaters for Lake Taupō, which comes from the Whanganui River," said Annwyn. So here we are right in between Lake Rotopounamu, Mount Ruapehu and Lake Taupō which makes this a beautiful vortex of energies which is why it's so special."

I sat between Annwyn and Raeul and suddenly my deepest thoughts started pouring out of me.

"You know I've been on this journey, searching for all these years trying to figure out the truth of this reality and who I really was in it. I've come to realise that if you are constantly searching, you are always in the energy of searching. So, it's perpetuating a loop that will in fact never resolve itself. I've been on all these adventures all around the world and followed my passions for travel, adventure, and energy, worked with various spiritual teachers and practices and I never got the answers I wanted because I was looking outside of myself. I gave everything and everyone authority over me, and truly did not value nor trust myself and my own wisdom. So the net result, was that my soul and my Universe was just constantly forcing me into myself," I said, taking a breath.

"It didn't matter what teaching or mentor or class or practice I was undertaking, if it was someone else's modality or material, even if it was an ancient practice that was ten thousand years old, it generally didn't give me the results I desired. To experience my true divine self and the pure expansive potential of my soul, unhindered, in human form. I didn't seem to be able to have the experiences of archangels or ascended masters or different energies and beings that I was chasing. I was always in awe of others with these gifts and I felt there was something wrong with me, that I must not have the abilities at all, or be a blocked lowly human with lessons to learn and karma to absolve in order to have access to my super-conscious gifts. Such says the old spiritual paradigm. But now I know that's not true. That's just another form of programming, of looking outside of the self, which is in actual fact disempowering to our sovereignty, by the mere act of doing so," I said.

"Yes, because you came in so grounded, with a level of consciousness that was in actual fact more aligned with your true divine essence as the God self. Angels and Masters are projected aspects of ourselves, which we need when we are at a certain level of consciousness, but we are moving into a time when this is no longer needed. It's not about reconstituting self, but coming from the God or divine self," said Annwyn, in between channelled bits of light language.

"That is exactly the conclusion I have come to!" I said. "We're not broken. We came in with everything we need, and it's already inside us. It's just buried beneath the layers of programming, conditioning and limitation, waiting for us to come into unity within, to understand ourselves as super-conscious beings, claim it for ourselves and operate as such. I don't believe we're here learning lessons or balancing enough karma so that we achieve this. We already are this. It's a deprogramming and uncovering and remembering more than anything. Yet I just feel there is so much rubbish in the spiritual community to lead people down the garden path," I continued.

"Yes," said Annwyn, who was starting to channel. "It's a spiritual jungle out there. And I can see you've been wading through it. Almost like sifting through the spiritual dogma," she said.

"Yes. I didn't realise at first that the spiritual community is equally as full of as many mistruths, old paradigm thinking and misinformation as any one of the structures we live within normal 3D life," I said. "At first it's all love and light, positive thinking and peace, love and mung beans, then it's full of spiritual hierarchy, before finally it gets so overcomplicated with modalities and activations that it becomes overwhelming. And almost all of it directs you outside of the self, or gives power to someone else in some way, shape or form. That's not real. Well it's not been true for me in my experience anyway," I said. "I can understand that it's all well intentioned, and perhaps that some of these concepts are perfect to meet people where their consciousness is at the time, so the idea of spirit guides and angels and seeking energetic support and help outside the self has served its purpose based on the level of consciousness of humanity, but I feel we are well and truly moving past that now. Everything must change if we want to bust out of the old. Even the ancient mystical eastern religions and philosophies were created and have been handed down through human filters and differing times of levels of consciousness that we have evolved from now."

"Absolutely. And there are people peddling this and that and making money by getting people to think they need something outside of themselves. When they have everything they need right here," said Annwyn, pointing to her heart.

I relayed my dream about heart technology being the most important thing we could use. I knew the multidimensional abilities of the heart were the key, although I had found in my experience that when the emotional body or the nervous system was out of balance, as mine was in London, the heart shuts down, which disconnected me from my connection to all things, greater awareness and understanding.

"I feel like there is still so much misunderstanding about consciousness and energy. I see many examples of well-meaning lightworkers who are inadvertently adding fuel to the fire because they don't actually understand energy 101 and how to use consciousness. Like when people use 'protection', it comes from fear based perception which actually opens you up to that very energy you are trying to protect from. Or when people protest about saving the whales or mistreated animals, or write posts that Mother Earth is angry and dying. They don't realise they are aligning with that energy, and taking on that frequency, purely by the act of them buying into that level of consciousness. Then the action of directing people's emotions to these issues is actually feeding more energy to that level of consciousness, which is contributing to the problem, not helping. As Einstein said, and quoted by Annie, 'You can never solve the problem at the level it was created'. If we really, truly understood consciousness and how we can use a higher perspective to hold something in the vibration of the divine to rebalance and realign energy, we'd be so much better off."

"Yes, it's about discernment," said Raeul, "and taking responsibility for the self and how we use our consciousness."

"Similarly, I now suspect that the old model of working with different aspects of self like Ego, Inner Child and Higher Self is in fact energetically keeping us further away from unity within. We have the inbuilt ego or personality self for good reason, we just need to understand it and manage it correctly while being led by our true divine self. The ego isn't the enemy here. Neither is the mind. It's part of our divine make-up and serves a distinct purpose. I don't believe we have to bring the higher self into the body either. It's already in us! Our divine self, our God spark, our true self or whatever you want to call it. It is us! We have never operated without it, yet we are led to believe otherwise by various teachings and the distractions of the modern world."

"Yes, it's so important not to get distracted by the spiritual jungle or trapped by spiritual facilitators," said Annwyn. "You are extremely grounded. Spirituality isn't all airy-fairy up and out there," she said, pointing skyward. "Real spirituality is at ground level with the highest consciousness. And that's what you are bringing through."

I felt the hairs on my arms raise as chills went around my body. "Well funnily enough, my original title for this book was 'Show Me The Fucking Fairies'," I said. "It's a metaphor, for this honest enquiry into the world of philosophy and spirituality. An edgy, humourous search for truth. I've moved through various phases and teachings along the way, and spectacularly messed up at times but all of it served a purpose. So if I could shortcut anyone else's journey with my understanding and experience, or inspire a different level of consciousness, or even just a laugh then it would be an honour to be of service in that way," I said, smiling.

Two-and-a-half hours had passed in what felt like no time and I felt more crystallised and confident in my knowing and gifts than ever before. I hadn't found my purpose because it didn't exist yet. I was here to hold a level of consciousness that didn't match up to what else was already out there, and for good reason. I had shared some of my controversial innermost thoughts about spirituality and consciousness that I had been holding back in fear. Fear that I was wrong. Fear that others were more qualified. Fear that I would upset the apple-cart. Fear of owning my inner truth, given how persecuted Annie had been for doing similar. Yet all the conclusions I had reached from my years of personal experience were confirmed and validated in the discussion. It was exactly what I needed in the moment to propel me forward and another proof point for the self-trust I was making a point of rebuilding within myself.

As I drove home I realised that Annwyn and Raeul had been holding space for me in a vibration that was allowing me to really acknowledge and feel my true divine knowing that was there all along. It was the same deep truth of the higher perspective of my divine self, that pervaded my awareness during 9/11 in New York. I could physically feel the deep knowing of who I truly was in my body. It was an amazing reflection to receive in my reality. I smiled as I realised that my intentions for the weekend had come to fruition perfectly. I now felt more confident in my truth than ever, even though it didn't match a lot of the spiritual material out there. I knew deep in my heart what I was here to do.

Listen. Listen to the deep yearnings of the Universe
through which you are connected in the heart.
You can hear the truth and wisdom. It is there for the taking.
For the purpose of good.

The heart is the supreme voice to be heard above all others.
Not in hierarchy, but in an energetic manner.
The wisdom of the heart has much to offer.
Like the path of the rose it stems from the
place of pure unconditional love.
The heart has much to teach you. There may be other
energetic teachers who cross your path, yet none are
more powerful than that of your own heart.

The multi-dimensional nature of this vehicle is mostly
unknown to you. Yet you have the key.
The heart is not only here to teach you ways
of being, but the supernatural too.
Exactly what you have been searching for.

By dropping down into this cavernous space of the heart, and zero point,
this is the first step into the beauty of the unknown.
The heart is the supreme intelligence of all.
When you come pure of heart you have access
to all that is meant for you.
Delve deep. Go in. Spend time in this place
with the familiarity and comfort of your lounge room.
This place is there for you and only you.

Opening The Door To The New Humanity

Manifestation is a bunch of arse. The guru is dead. Your ego is your amigo. Our mind is a divine instrument. And we are all masters.

What if all we knew about consciousness was wrong? What if the earth wasn't a school, there were no lessons to learn and we were perfect just as we are? What if believing in a higher power outside of yourself actually disempowered your own energy field? And everything you had ever been taught was just keeping you from the power of your divinity? What if changing your perception could change the world? What if, what if, what if?

If you think this is the part where I become miraculously perfect, find my fairy-tale ending and have all the answers then you didn't get to know me very well in this book at all. I have learned a tonne, had some incredible consciousness shifts and my love for adventure continues. These days I've just got stories about levitating in crystal caves and ripping my shorts off while leaping barbed wire fences into sacred sites, versus going on a bender. Despite thinking my levelling up meant leaving my personality and naughty brand far behind me, I have been shown otherwise. Following a nerve-wracking initiation in the sarcophagus of the Great Pyramid, I was having a massage to integrate the energies afterwards when the Egyptian massage lady suddenly flicked my nipples, massaged far too close to my clitoris and tried to go down on me! All while whispering creepily, "Oooh you sooo beautifuuuul." Ironically just as I had well and truly realised my foray into lesbianism was a complete failure. I seriously wondered what the hell the Universe was playing at but I had to laugh. Same stories, different setting.

Having to lose the personality was yet another outdated perspective after all.

Over the course of my twenty-plus years of investigation into all things energy, spirit, healing and consciousness, I've gone from looking outside of myself to supposed 'higher authorities' (physical and non-physical) for the answers, to a complete one-eighty, trusting my inner wisdom, over and above all else. No matter if it was a highly regarded ancient spiritual practice, or a new spiritual teacher with millions of followers.

I spent years in London unconsciously programming myself further from where I wanted to be. I was unknowingly disempowering myself energetically in many ways. Not listening to self and my own wisdom was a key blockade to my development. What did I really know about anything? I thought. Surely there was something wrong with me? As I wasn't a success by society's standards, or the spiritual community or my own expectations. I viewed others as more expert than myself by default, not giving myself the respect, love and attention I deserved. All of our cells and subconscious mind are always listening, accepting, processing and adapting to everything we tell them, whether it be true or not.

Although I always had the awareness that life was happening for me, not to me, I kept meeting the same challenges in order to wake myself up further. It was an energetic reorganisation of my inner being. At that time I wasn't speaking my truth or living it, and I was mostly hiding away in the spiritual closet. I was scared to really embody what was buried under my masks. And those separate identities of self I was operating from, slowed the pace of my natural in-built powers of alignment and creation, which was why things never felt like they were coming together for me.

I learned the hard way that taking ourselves to task for past occurrences only dismantles our frequency of self. My inner critic, judge and police kept me locked in a boxing ring, which lowered my vibration and drowned out my inner divine intelligence. However, I was aware that even catching ourselves in judgement, is a form of judgement itself and therefore cements that pattern of judgement within us. All I needed to do was accept myself no matter what, and consciously manage my emotional body to neutrally observe everything that was going on in my reality. By being conscious in the present moment, we can course correct with ease and grace.

I came to realise that personal empowerment is about taking radical responsibility for the self and owning our sovereignty. By claiming, knowing and trusting the powerful energy beings that we are. When we start seeing beyond what we see in front of us in the physical, to the energetic layers beyond, then we can start to achieve the impossible and what we have only dreamed of. When we don't trust, we deny ourselves potential, and the full experience of what could be.

By the time I got to John of God I was thoroughly sick of myself and acutely aware of how my words, thoughts, feelings and actions were affecting my field. The power of the word is sacred for a reason. I was finally experiencing more visceral energy experiences again, which brought me back to myself, in my connection to the Source energy that I am. I was starting to figure out that not all information in the spiritual community was helpful, and that I needed to use discernment to cut through the bullshit, not be distracted by the spiritual jungle, and always have an active role with one's consciousness.

When we view the higher perspective in all things, we understand that we live in a vibrational Universe, where there are no mistakes, no 'good' or 'bad', 'right' or 'wrong'. Everything is there for vibrational reorganisation and is born of consciousness. We inherently know that the divine intelligence that pervades all things is never off-track, despite how we may judge our experience. Or get in the way. The totality of our experience is always bringing us back into alignment with our Source energy and our most magnificent true self. Everything is orchestrated to bring us back to our centre. And transmute more fear, directing us back to love. Energy doesn't lie.

This planet and everything on it is in a constant state of evolution. Nothing stands still for a second. It is a constantly changing reality, which matches the level of our consciousness in each moment. Inside is unmanifest. Outside is the holographic world, which we co-create with the divine intelligence of the Universe. In order to change our outside world, we must adjust the belief systems and energy within ourselves. Our body is an indicator of what is going on beneath the surface, and our subconscious speaks to us to give us clues in the seconds before the mind kicks in, if we let it. Everything is fluid and ever evolving, and will continue to be as long as we live. Our truth, funnily enough changes with it, as we are one with this ever-evolving Universe.

In my experience, the real answers we are looking for aren't found in books, places or teachers. They are not found in the past or in any teaching or practise that is already in existence. Sure, these may help us briefly, at a particular point in time depending on where our consciousness is at, but ultimately they are not our answer. Which begs the question, why then are we holding on to that which has gone before like it's the Holy Grail? The 'truth' we so desperately cling to makes us unavailable to hear anything new.

After chasing truth around the world for years I no longer believe there is one absolute truth, or one answer. Truth evolves, as with everything, which may be a contradiction but it's still truth. We are all energetic beings with an individual divine blueprint, therefore there is no one-size-fits-all solution to anything. The more we can acknowledge our uniqueness as the gift, and step up to own the power of our individuality and creativity, the more power we will have. We are our answer, and we are here to help shift the consciousness of the planet by being who we really are. Not what the world has told us to be.

We have moved past the old paradigm of hierarchical standing in spirituality. We don't need teachers, guides and gurus any longer. We are all made of the same light, divine, God, Source energy. We all have our own divine expertise, embodied by no other. We are already masters, with our own special form of genius, if we would only recognise this in ourselves.

You are your own shaman, your own healer, your own answer. You know yourself better than anyone. The more we embody our deepest knowing and make ourselves the ultimate authority, the stronger our connection to the divine intelligence within. By claiming, owning and embodying one's true sovereign self you hold and align to your highest vibrational essence, as it perforates your physical being even deeper, opening you up to that which has not gone before. You live your divine essence.

We have been gifted with incredible energetic differentiation and technology in the body to support us in this experience. Despite gurus telling us for centuries 'the body is merely a human vehicle' and 'you are not your body', I believe our body is incredibly important as a barometer of our emotions and thoughts, and is uniquely connected to our super-conscious gifts. The whole point in my eyes is to be in the body, to be light in form, to bring heaven to earth during this time of great change and evolution on the planet. Literally everything we need to solve any form of discordance within, is available to us in every moment via the technology we came in with. We may not have come with a user manual, but we did come with a fully operational working model.

It's easy to fall into the trap of endless healing on our personal transformation journey, trying to get to a point where we are 'fixed'. Quantum physics tells us that where our attention goes our energy flows. In the words of Dr Bruce H Lipton, PhD "... thoughts, whether negative or positive, determine our biology." In peer reviewed studies he has proved that genes respond to life. It only runs in the family if you believe it does.

What if there was nothing wrong, there was nothing to heal and nowhere to get to? What if beliefs and perception were the only things holding you back? Isn't it time to use our consciousness to embrace our wholeness instead of focusing energy on all the ways in which we perceive, or have been told we are 'broken'? What if that health problem is merely a tool to help you shift your consciousness and realign you back to love? What if a simple perspective shift was all that was required to break the healing loop we might be stuck in? How 'bout if we could shift illness and pain by reprogramming the body from a higher perspective? Imagine if seeing and trusting ourselves as the master that we really are, was the most powerful thing you could do for yourself?

Our emotions are intelligent technology that shows us where we are at vibrationally in each moment. As soon as I started working with a technique to balance my emotional field and what my body was showing me in the present moment, it plugged the energetic gaps and put me on more of an even keel. When our emotions are in balance our nervous system is relaxed, more of our heart can open. When we are more in tune with our heart, we honour the light in ourselves and those around us. And we have more access to our multidimensional state of being.

Despite all the work I had done on myself with this therapy and that, I came to realise in more recent years that as much as I was tuned in, actively doing work on myself, healing, searching and incredibly aware, I was unconsciously in avoidance of myself. There were parts of myself I was embarrassed by, disowned, or didn't want to see. So, my experience in my reality were circumstances and people being orchestrated to help me find the parts of myself I had buried the deepest, that I didn't want to face, to burn through all of the layers down to the depths of who I truly was. We are where we are because of who we have been. Bringing awareness to these buried places of myself started to give me freedom. I had to make peace and detach from the old to bring in the new.

Circumstances and people that come across our path give us opportunities to rise out of our own limitations. Anything that happens in our field of perception has resonance within us somewhere for a purpose. Nothing exists in our lives that doesn't have significance for us. You simply can't experience something you are not a vibrational match to on some level and our feelings are a barometer to understand our frequency as it happens. This means radical responsibility, without judgement, from a neutral position for the totality of our life experience and adjusting ourselves in the moment. Putting it in to practice however can feel ambitious depending on our awareness, programming and emotional state.

Annie, as challenging as she has been for me, was playing her part perfectly. As did Devo and everyone else. Without any of it I would not be who I am today. Annie was courageous, she was well ahead of her time and living with her through her experience showed me not only how I could do it differently, but the three stages of truth. First, it's ridiculed, second, it's violently opposed and third, it's proven as self-evident. Paradigm shifters are always going to get some flack, and we shouldn't be afraid to upset the apple cart. She did her best with what she had at the time, and a lot of what she said is now common knowledge in the spiritual field. Most importantly though she really drilled into me to rise up, question everything, challenge what I believe and find my own answers. For that I am eternally grateful.

Despite spending years searching, I have made peace with the fact that the future and my purpose, wasn't to be found. It was everything I already was. I wasn't broken, or blocked or lacking in special abilities or learning lessons to become whole, and I didn't need to become something else. I just had to know and trust the structure I came in with, instead of looking outside of myself.

If you don't detach, your Universe will ultimately do it for you. We are meant to live in a world without deep attachments that keep us stuck. After my world truly fell apart with a series of events involving Devo, Annie, Mike and Brazilian Girl in New Zealand, I worked through the fog of yet another dark night to reclaim the parts of myself I had lost or given away. I was forced into myself in more ways than ever and despite it bringing me to my knees, I came out the other side stronger, and with more wisdom than ever before. I slowly started to rebuild, this time with radical responsibility for everything that was going on in my reality, without judgement and in unfailing love and support of myself.

I started course correcting my energy, with conscious awareness in each moment of every day. I followed my inspiration, channelled my inner wisdom and stopped looking for any kind of exterior guidance or signs. By this point I had learned that 'signs' weren't going to tell me if someone was my soulmate, or what decision I should make. My coach Jessica taught me that this is because the Universe is a reflection of us. This time, the thing I did most differently that was the game-changer was I decided to fall madly in love with myself. To love and accept myself for exactly who I was. To trust myself like never before. To apperceive that I knew the way. To support myself no matter what. To truly acknowledge the divine within me. To have faith in the unknown. To become my own soul's mate.

All of my adventures from the Camino to London to South America and beyond, everything had consistently pushed me into myself. I never found what I was looking for because I was looking in the wrong places, with incorrect expectations. Expectations equal constriction. However, it was all divinely perfect. The Camino set me free, giving me the confidence to make my own way, London gave me the opportunity to work through my programming and self-limitations that were holding me back, Kilimanjaro showed me I could conquer the impossible and to just keep putting one foot in front of the other no matter what, Brazil taught me how to open my heart and New Zealand helped me remember who I truly was.

The ultimate truth, our connection to something greater than ourselves, to nature, to the divine intelligence, to our genius – is found within. It might be covered in self-created beliefs, limited by programming, or hidden under trauma, but it's still there. No one else heals you. You heal you when you are in your true potential. All you need to do is step into it.

We are not what we have been told. I have always felt like an old soul. I've had glimpses of this wisdom deep within, an understanding of reality in ways that made no sense to others and felt I've been here many times before. I wasn't remotely surprised on a recent trip to Egypt when I remembered another lifetime in Luxor with the familial sounds of the call to prayer and donkeys on the Nile. I now know that all of the wisdom from all of my incarnations was in there all along, sitting in my vibrational field ready to be accessed. I have experienced this directly, when I got myself out of the way. If there was something I really excelled at on this journey it was getting in my own way!

We are conditioned to hold on to people, places, things and experiences. To bring the past into the present. To understand and take cues from what has gone before. The desire to hold on to that which is changing stems from our need for safety. When we do this we only contribute more energy to the past, as opposed to new potential. Yet we wake up brand new every day, realigned after an automatic reset each night. We are given the opportunity to step away from everything outside the present moment and begin anew. It's a matter of choice. Yet we most often revert to unconscious programming and living a life on autopilot.

We are something bigger, deeper, more important than our day-to-day lives on this planet. We don't have to learn anything or activate anything or train in anything. In fact, doing any of those things can sometimes perpetuate the old systems, outdated programming and the old ways. In all creation, destruction is necessary. It's up to us to build things in a new and different way, to build the future.

Life is the great mystery school. Life is our guru. It shows us vibrationally in every moment where we are at. Even our body guides our way. There is a perfection to life even during the most extreme of weather. It is a balancing aspect of the earth and the self. Trust that which you are and all will become clear. Everything provides the contrast we need to wake up out of the dream. To realise ourselves, and our magnificence, as who and what we truly are.

We are our own wisdom. Our imagination is our superpower. Our heart will show us the way. This consciousness that we have, as our true divine intelligence, has the most potent effect on everything we see. If we would only accept, acknowledge and know it for ourselves. That provides the activation of remembrance. Remembrance of why we are really here. Remembrance of our true self. Remembrance of all our individual energetic and intuitive gifts, our genius, that we have brought with us to this planet right now for a reason. We have faith that everything we face is happening not only for us but for planetary evolution as well, and that there is something playing out beyond our knowing. When we hold space for the options to show up and release control, this wider perspective allows us to receive from the greatest potential.

There is never going to be an ending, or a 'getting it', or finding the answer once and for all in this crazy experience called life. Your relationship with yourself governs every other relationship. We must align our own energy first. Our possibilities are in fact infinite in the quantum field, and at every moment we have a choice. To choose to expand or contract in whatever way we wish. The journey of consciousness isn't complicated. It's simple and straightforward. It's all there: the genius, the mastery just waiting for us to claim it. To remember ourselves in our sovereignty and trust the magnificent powerful light being that we are. This will open the door to advanced consciousness, to the new humanity, and living our greatest potential.

Knowing the illusion of the virtual reality in which you live,
knowing how your energy contributes to your experience, and the whole,
knowing you have the power to change anything at any time,
and step outside the box, of that which you were born and have created.
That is the challenge.
To live in your truth outside of that box, no matter what.
That is mastery.
The only thing in the way, is you.

Afterword

We follow our instincts. Follow our heart. Even when we are doubtful. When we are unsure. We just keep going. And we eventually find that we were on the right track all along. If only we could have not worried, not questioned, not doubted. Just gone with it, putting fears aside and throwing caution to the wind, knowing and trusting that we would never lead ourselves astray.

Then you realise that there is nothing to fear. Nowhere to get to. Nowhere to go. That every dark night is key to your expansion. That everything is taking care of you, in the perfect timing. And you are exactly where you need to be; because of all of the moments that have gone before. Everything is divinely perfect, and orchestrated on every level of this human experience for our highest good. Are you going to experience it with detachment, consciousness and joy, or are you going against the flow?

We co-create with an unknown quantity, the divine intelligence in all things. How we perceive our experience in any given moment is how we connect with, expand or constrict the data available to us vibrationally. The more we tune into the narrow perception of what is happening in the story we see in front of us, the more we program it to contribute that same energy into, not only more of our experience, but the collective energy on the planet. Instead of transmuting and realigning it to the greatest potential with our God consciousness. When we can harness and come into our own as the sovereign beings that we are, we stand in our power. It is our consciousness that continues to facilitate change on the planet.

I am still a work in progress to living my best life, as I am always dreaming outside that which I see in front of me. Not in a restless way, but with a wondrous, magical curiosity of wanting to experience more layers of this beautiful reality that we exist in. More of the unknown; that which I cannot see but feel deep within me. So, I impart wisdom from my experiences, knowing that there is more to come, and that which has gone before, is a mere stepping stone to that which will come to be.

If you want to experience more of your most magnificent, unlimited divine self, shift your reality or join me for transformational travel, you can find me at www.joannawalden.com

Light within me
Light around me
Light beside me
Light is me

Acknowledgements

Immeasurable thanks to my parents Devo and Annie for being well outside the bounds of 'normal' parents, and in doing so, giving me an upbringing that gifted me the opportunity to be who I am today. To Mike, for being the funniest and most inappropriate person I know, always, and keeping it real with his unfailing support and brotherly love. To Mr Puss for almost always allowing me cuddles in my times of need... almost.

To all my friends and whanau who believed in me when others didn't and stuck around during the tough times, and to all of the non-physical cheerleaders who came to the party and contributed their energies, I am so grateful. Love and thanks to my incredible editor Brooke, who propped me up when I needed it, protected my story when I couldn't see it and kept going until it was the best that it could be, because of it. Immense appreciation to Ann to whom I am in debt for being the most amazing mentor, guiding me through and encouraging me to believe in what I wrote and created.

Special thanks to those who helped me with my book at various stages Sylv, Ferg, Jess, Damian, Jackie, Tracey, Angela W, Angela G, Anna S, Lauren K, Megan S, Joanne, Catherine N, Katie B and Claire C. To Penny H for helping me get it out to the world. Russ Flatt for capturing the true me in my photos and Eithne Curran for hair, makeup and creative colab. To my extremely talented designer Lukas for creating my website, for this amazing cover design and making it all look super stylish.

To all those who came across my path and featured in this book, named and unnamed, without you none of this would have come to light, so thank you!

Resources

Soluntra King www.evenstarcreations.com

Annwyn & Raeul www.goldenagementor.co.nz

Jessica Alstrom www.jessicaalstrom.com

Gregg Braden www.greggbraden.com

Bruce H Lipton, PhD www.brucelipton.com

Matt Kahn www.mattkahn.org

Lukas Kelly www.busydesign.com

Joanna Walden www.joannawalden.com

Reviews

I'd very much appreciate it if you could review *The Inside Hustle* on Amazon, or your preferred platform. Reviews are crucial to help spread the word. Please also share on social media and feel free to tag me on Instagram and Facebook @iamjoannawalden with #theinsidehustle and #joannawalden. You can find links on my website. I'd love to hear about your reading experience and your own energy shifts and changes.